RUSSIAN & SOVIET THEATRE

TRADITION & THE AVANT-GARDE

RUSSIAN & SOVIET THEATRE

TRADITION & THE AVANT-GARDE

with 457 illustrations, 64 in colour

Translation from Russian by Roxane Permar

Edited by Dr Lesley Milne

Konstantin Rudnitsky

Thames and Hudson

Title page: Alisa Koonen in Racine's *Phèdre*, directed by Tairov at the Kamerny Theatre, 1922.

Acknowledgments

The publishers gratefully acknowledge Dr Lesley Milne's invaluable contribution in editing the final text, translating the captions, providing the list of further reading, editing the notes and reading proofs, in close association with Dr Konstantin Rudnitsky.

Mrs Alla Burakovskaya in Moscow provided comments on the original draft of the translation and was able to answer the numerous queries which were bound to arise in a work of this magnitude.

Acknowledgments should also be made to Dr Avril Pyman of the University of Durham for her comments and suggestions on the original draft of the translation.

Mr J. M. Walton of the Drama Department, University of Hull, assisted in the compilation of the further reading list and provided much help throughout with technical terms and the translation of various theatrical ideas.

2004002885

Contents

EDITORIAL NOTE
Plays discussed in the text are illustrated in the plate section at the end of each chapter.

Author's Preface

Public and professional interest in the early stages of Soviet theatre when Russian ideas and experiments shook the entire theatrical world, far from diminishing as the years pass, seems actually to be increasing. The focus of that interest, however, varies. Not so long ago, people in Europe, the USA and Japan were studying Stanislavsky, investigating his 'System' and trying to arrive at a deeper understanding of his work at the Moscow Art Theatre. Then they became equally excited about Meyerhold and his 'bio-mechanics', about theatrical Constructivism, about the so-called 'circusization' of the theatre and about Eisenstein's few but remarkable productions. Then they discovered the Russian Futurists' theatre and the extravagant creations of Khlebnikov, Kruchenykh and Mayakovsky. After that it was the turn of Vakhtangov and Mikhail Chekhov. And now many are looking at the work of Alexander Tairov, Alisa Koonen and their Kamerny Theatre, while at the same time there is a resurgence of interest in Stanislavsky and Nemirovich-Danchenko and their complicated but fruitful collaboration and theatrical achievements.

These shifts are due in part to the caprice of fashion which swings from one extreme to the other, at one moment pressing forward with the avant-garde, at the next retreating to the aestheticism and refinement of tradition. In part, however, they are due simply to the accident that new material is constantly being made available by individual scholars working in the archives publishing manifestos, designs, drawings that had previously been known only to a few. Russian aesthetic thought during the initial post-Revolutionary years has astonished both the theoreticians and practitioners of today with its unexpected freshness, vision and undimmed relevance, and once again it is firing the imagination.

Sometimes these ideas have been so compulsive that attempts have been made actually to recreate in every detail the staging and acting style of productions of the late 1910s and early 1920s. On the basis of Malevich's drawings, one of the American universities has recently revived the Futurist opera *Victory over the Sun*, while a 'living copy' of Meyerhold's famous production of *The Magnanimous Cuckold* was produced by a group of enthusiasts at the Guggenheim Museum in New York; there have also been public demonstrations of the forgotten exercises from Meyerhold's 'biomechanics', and so on. To be quite frank I personally have no confidence in such undertakings. This is not only because the authenticity of a 'copy' separated from the original by the space of fifty years is clearly dubious, nor even because the roles which in the past were played by actors of incomparable genius (such as Igor Ilinsky and Maria Babanova in *The Magnanimous Cuckold*) are now performed by diligent and conscientious, but far from brilliant amateurs rendering the 'copy' colourless and tarnished as it tries in vain to convey the emotional wealth of the original. No, the main reason is that any theatrical event which is isolated from the social situation that engendered it, torn from the artistic soil where it was originally rooted and artificially transplanted to another, inevitably loses almost all its energy and beauty.

As distinct from painting, architecture, sculpture, poetry, prose or music, the art of the theatre is always, by its very nature, contemporary and cannot live a full-blooded existence outside its *own* time. The Parthenon or Notre Dame de Paris, the sculptures of Phidias or Michaelangelo, the fugues of Bach or the sonatas of Mozart, the canvases of Bosch, Rembrandt or Van Gogh all have the capacity to give aesthetic pleasure to people of many generations. But if a person from our time, through some miracle, turned up in the crowd of spectators at a medieval mystery play or Shakespeare's Globe Theatre, he would probably be deeply disappointed. Lines which would make all the rest of the crowd laugh or feel excited, angry or horrified would not affect our envoy from the twentieth century. The fool would not amuse him, the villain would not disturb him and the hero would not excite his admiration. He would watch this spectacle, overcoming his boredom with difficulty. He could not yield, even for a minute, to the primitive magic of the performance. Between him and the actors would stand the space of the intervening centuries, like a transparent but impenetrable wall.

Why talk of centuries? Now when we hear gramophone recordings of the voices of great actors from the beginning of our century, their stilted declamation seems comic and forced. When we see the famous theatrical stars of the 1920s, recorded on celluloid film from the era of silent cinematography, their mime, gestures, poses, almost seem like caricature. But that's the way it is, for their time has passed, and those for whom they were great and famous are no longer alive.

There is no chance that what is great in the art of the theatre today will also be great tomorrow. Tomorrow it will become something different.

I am recalling these universally known truths in order to clarify the aim of this book. What I want to do above all is to convey to the reader the atmosphere and spirit of that time with which we are concerned. If this task is even only partially fulfilled, then the reader will understand and feel the meaning, significance and beauty of performances that left the stage long ago – and not only celebrated and legendary performances but unknown and forgotten ones too.

The first years after the Revolution, when the Russian theatre was suddenly confronted by a new social reality and a new, unrecognizably transformed audience, were years of the most interesting exploration, speculation, innovation and experimentation, and also the most intense debate among theatrical directors. It is therefore quite impossible to comprehend the art of each of these directors individually, in isolation from the others. Each of them – Stanislavsky, Meyerhold, Vakhtangov, Tairov, Eisenstein, Mikhail Chekhov – can only be fully understood in relation to the rest, keeping constantly in mind the intensity of their mutual attractions and repulsions, the clash and rapprochement of their ideas, the diversity of their activities and, of course, the general flow of the time that carried them along. The public's tastes and the new society's spiritual needs were not by any means defined immediately. Some directors who were actively setting the tone in the early stages are now less well known. Special attention will thus be devoted to the works of Sergei Radlov, Nikolai Foregger, Alexei Gripich, Nikolai Petrov, Fedor Kaverin, Ilya Sudakov and even the now completely forgotten Igor Terentiev whose work created a furore in the mid 1920s, whose ideas, angrily rejected then, are now being reassessed and successfully put into practice.

The Soviet theatre of the 1920s and 1930s tested the accessibility and effectiveness of the most diverse theatrical forms – from street theatre to studio theatre, from clamorous Futurism with its global pretensions to the quiet intimacy of domestic drama, from the overtly propagandistic to the subtly psychological, from abstract allegory to the most concrete reality of everyday life. At first glance the early history of Soviet theatre is incomprehensibly multifarious, and it is difficult to imagine how the 'performance meetings' of Vladimir Mayakovsky and Vsevolod Meyerhold are compatible with the aestheticism of Alexander Tairov, how Nikolai Foregger's so-called 'music-hallization' or Sergei Eisenstein's 'circusization of theatre' relate to the 'emotional realism' of Mikhail Chekhov, why Strindberg's tragic *Eric XIV* and Gozzi's *Princess Turandot* appear simultaneously in the work of Evgeny Vakhtangov or how the intense drama of Mikhail Bulgakov's *Days of the Turbins* can co-exist with the jubilant gaiety of Beaumarchais' *Le Mariage de Figaro*, produced under Stanislavsky at the Moscow Art Theatre. Nonetheless all these outwardly completely heterogeneous productions were closely linked to each other.

Sometimes these links are particularly evident in productions of the classics, such as Shakespeare or Ostrovsky. Sometimes they are even more obvious in work on contemporary plays, such as those by Mayakovsky and Bulgakov, or by Konstantin Trenev, Vsevolod Ivanov, Boris Lavrenev, Nikolai Erdman and, a little later, Vsevolod Vishnevsky, Nikolai Pogodin, Alexander Afinogenov or Vladimir Kirshon.

The directors, actors and writers of the theatres of different nationalities – the Georgian (Kote Mardzhanishvili, Sandro Akhmeteli, Ushangi Chkheidze, Veriko Andzhaparidze, Akaky Khorava), the Ukrainian (Les Kurbas, Gnat Yura, Amvrosy Buchma, Mikola Kulish), the Azerbaidzhanian, the Jewish – will occupy a special but essential place in the book. This is not for the sake of comprehensive, encyclopaedic coverage but as a means of providing as clear an idea as possible of the basic trends in the theatrical life of the country at that time.

I am well aware that a short study of theatrical explorations during the post-Revolutionary years cannot claim to be either a thorough investigation or an all-encompassing survey. It has other aims: to outline the main lines of development; to show what kinds of impulses inspired the various theatrical forms; to look at the reasons which caused some movements to be extremely popular at first then to die out rapidly, while others gradually gained the sympathy of a wide audience and brought the stage together with the new social reality.

They say that if a book has been interesting to write, then it will be interesting to read. I do not know to what extent this is true. I can only confess that I have found this work fascinating, and I would like to hope that if nothing else it might arouse the reader's curiosity.

1 Pre-Revolutionary Theatrical Explorations

Vyacheslav Ivanov's Ideas on Theatre

Strange and even improbable as it may seem, the question of the theatre of the future – what form it would take and what place it would have in public life – was one which preoccupied the minds of leading thinkers and writers in the period between the two Russian Revolutions of 1905 and 1917. It was the subject of endless discussion and furious debate by people who had momentarily forgotten their usual pursuits, who had either no links at all with the theatre or who had come into contact with the stage only accidentally, peripherally. A typical example is the *Kniga o Novom Teatre* (*Book on the New Theatre*), a publication elegantly designed by Alexander Benois and issued by the publishing house Shipovnik in 1908. Only one of the authors of this large collection of articles was a professional director: Vsevolod Meyerhold. The rest were critics, artists, prose writers and poets, more or less unconnected with theatrical practice. Nonetheless the book stimulated great interest and was followed by two more collections, *Krizis Teatra* (*The Theatre in Crisis*) and *V Sporakh o Teatre* (*In Debate on Theatre*), both of which consisted of articles purely theoretical in character and passionately polemical in tone. It was as if Russia's historical fate depended on solving the problems of the theatre. Even more intense debate was conducted in journals and newspapers. Extensive articles devoted to the art of the stage were written by Valery Bryusov, Alexander Blok, Leonid Andreev, Zinaida Gippius (under the pseudonym Anton Krainy), Vasily Rozanov, Andrei Bely and Vyacheslav Ivanov.

One of the most utopian theatrical ideas of the twentieth century was put forward by Vyacheslav Ivanov, a man completely outside the theatre, an armchair philosopher and a poet seemingly immersed in the past. This idea was never carried out, but it is worth describing briefly because it proved to be tenacious and long-lived. A decade later, under different social conditions, it returned like a boomerang, though in a modernized form quite unlike what it had been before, to seize the imagination of the bold theoreticians in the Proletkult and LEF (the Left Front of the Arts). Some knowledge of Vyacheslav Ivanov's Utopia will enable us to understand what kind of hopes the Russian thinkers and writers placed on the theatre on the eve of the upheavals which transformed Russia and Europe.

For Vyacheslav Ivanov, the theatre – potentially the most powerful of all the arts – was fully capable of replacing religion and the Church for a humanity which had lost its faith. Of course what he had in mind was not the theatre of his own time, vulgarized by bourgeois drama and serving primarily to entertain and amuse the public – such pitiful buffoonery aroused in him only disdain. In his eyes the 'theatre crisis' was indissolubly linked with the crisis of faith. It is no accident that at this same time the Russian materialists

V. Bazarov, Anatoly Lunacharsky and Maxim Gorky were quite seriously trying to unite scientific socialism with religion and imbue it with the character of religious belief, seeking to deify the cosmos and the people. Their 'God-building' opposed the 'God-seeking' of Dmitri Merezhkovsky, Vasily Rozanov, Sergei Bulgakov and other idealists who proposed, on the contrary, to cleanse the Christian faith of ecclesiastical impurity and political bias. Both of these artificial conceptions were from the outset confined to a narrow circle of intelligentsia and doomed to wither in that hothouse atmosphere. Ivanov, however, believed that he had found a kind of panacea through which it would be possible to restore to people their lost faith.

In his view what had to be done first of all was to return the theatre to its ancient prototypes, to the traditions of ancient religious rites, classical tragedy and the medieval mystery play and, on the basis of these traditions, to create a new type of mass performance – a 'collective action'. While he borrowed this term from the Russian Slavophiles of the last century, the structure of the 'collective action' as Ivanov perceived it was undoubtedly inspired by Nietzsche's famous work *The Birth of Tragedy*. For Ivanov, the Nietzschean 'Dionysian quality' imperceptibly and unintentionally acquired the character of a universal brotherhood which was, of course, completely alien to Nietzsche. Such an attempt to combine the incompatible, to relate Nietzsche's philosophy to the Christian moralizing of Lev Tolstoy, is generally typical of Ivanov. Nietzsche's arrogant individualism was turned into theoretical support for a benevolent collectivism; the Nietzschean disgust for religion in general and for Christianity in particular became the stimulus for the creation of new religious ritual. For the 'collective action' was, of course, conceived not so much as a theatrical experience but as a cult – to be performed outside the Church yet in essence Christian.

Ivanov spelled out this idea with absolute clarity, stating that 'theatre has nothing to do with aesthetics'; it serves not beauty but 'the good and the true'. He maintained that the people 'no longer want spectacle and nothing but spectacle, and they are tired of theatrical illusion; it seems, rather, that what they want is action – true action, not the reflection of action.' 'The theme of the potential of the new theatre' from Ivanov's point of view was 'the theme of the coming cultural historical revolution, the focal point of which is the struggle for the stage.'[1]

No one had previously thought the theatre capable of taking on such a vital mission or that the 'struggle for the stage' could have such serious repercussions. For Ivanov the theatre was the lever which would make it possible to implement 'the cultural historical revolution' on a global scale.

In order to realize the 'collective action' Ivanov proposed first to eliminate the box stage and all the footlights and to create a completely open stage similar to the ancient Greek *orchestra*. There should be no division between audience and actors: everyone participates together in a kind of majestic liturgy, combining mystery play and divine worship. Choral singing, group dancing and the crowd's synchronous, euphoric movements will instantaneously unite and bring together all the participants, who will merge together in a kind of inspired unity. S. S. Averintsev, the most recent scholar of Vyacheslav Ivanov's work, notes, and not without a certain irony: 'Evidently this is how Schiller's vision in "Ode to Joy" – "Embrace, o ye millions!" – is supposed to come true.'[2]

A spiritual community is created during the 'collective action' which has an ennobling effect on everyone involved and thus exerts a beneficial influence on the lives of the people. This irrational, elemental cleansing through exaltation will liberate the people from the shackles of bourgeois commercialism, break the chains of rationalism and make them forget the mundane notions of common sense; they will be cured for ever of deception, hypocrisy and cynical calculation and finally all humanity will change for the better – no more, no less.

Every Wednesday philosophers, poets and critics gathered at Vyacheslav Ivanov's flat which was at the very top, on the fifth floor, in the corner rotunda of a banal, but substantial building on the corner of Tavricheskaya and Tverskaya Streets (the building has been preserved intact to this day) and was called, somewhat pompously, 'the tower'. Here poets read their new poems, the most diverse issues were discussed and, of course, there was much thought and speculation as to how the 'collective action' could be brought about more quickly.

To start with, Vyacheslav Ivanov wanted to accommodate the public in premises, like a hall, where the furniture would be scattered about 'by whim and inspiration'. The stage would be concealed behind a curtain which would open suddenly – either from the right or left, changing from day to day. The actors would begin to recite or sing on the stage itself, then descend into the audience, mingling with the crowd, distributing costumes and masks to everyone who wanted them and involving those present in a communal creative improvisation.

As an idea, this appeared attractive but even at that time, in 1908, the poet Andrei Bely warned against the 'hasty popularization' of Vyacheslav Ivanov's views. Speaking ironically, he said: 'Let's suppose we go into the temple-theatre, robe ourselves in white clothes, crown ourselves with bunches of roses, perform a mystery play (its theme is always the same – God-like man wrestles with fate) and then at the appropriate moment we join hands and begin to dance. Imagine yourself, reader, if only for just one minute, in this role. We are the ones who will be spinning round the sacrificial altar – all of us: the fashionable lady, the up-and-coming stockbroker, the worker and the member of the State Council. It is too much to expect that our steps and our gestures will coincide. While the class struggle still exists, these appeals for an aesthetic democratization are strange.'[3]

Bely's scepticism was well-founded. S. S. Averintsev writes, 'after centuries of European rationalist culture it is impossible truly to become a real shaman, a real Scythian or a real Dionysian priest. All that is possible is to play the part according to the measure of your talent.'[4]

The theatre people to whom Vyacheslav Ivanov presented his views understood perfectly well that his Utopia was impossible to realize. The thought of transforming a performance into something like an act of worship did not appeal to them at all. But the idea of merging actors and audience in a combined, improvisational performance appeared somewhat more attractive. Acting, however, had to remain acting.

As to the 'cultural historical revolution', the dream which Ivanov cherished – after the entirely real defeat of the Russian Revolution of 1905, the theatrical world preferred not to look as far ahead as this.

The Theatrical Experiments of the Russian Futurists

The short interval between the Russian Revolution of 1905 and the outbreak of the First World War brought important changes to Russian life and society and to the art of the theatre. Harsh governmental repressions, mass arrests and executions of Revolutionaries, the decline of the liberation movement were all quickly reflected in literature and art. The theatre turned away from politics and consequently lost interest in contemporary drama.

Up to this time every one of Gorky's new plays had been an enormous social event. His premières were anticipated with impatience and greeted with excitement and passion. Now, however, Gorky was writing and publishing play after play, but they were not performed: in 1906 *The Barbarians* and *Enemies* were brought out; in 1908, *The Last Ones*; in 1910, *The Eccentrics* and *Vassa Zheleznova*; in 1913, *The Zykovs*. None of these works aroused the same interest as his earlier plays had done. No one attempted to challenge the censor when performances of *Enemies* or *The Last Ones* were banned. *The Barbarians* and *The Zykovs* were not banned, but even so no prominent theatrical figure thought them worth producing. Subsequently, two or three decades later, their merit became obvious to everyone. The Symbolist plays by Maeterlinck and Hamsun and the allegorical dramas of Leonid Andreev which had at one time strongly interested Stanislavsky, Nemirovich-Danchenko, Meyerhold and Komissarzhevskaya, also quickly went out of fashion. Two productions of dramas by Alexander Blok, two or three productions of Leonid Andreev's plays and one or two productions of Fedor Sologub's plays were virtually the only examples of contemporary drama in the entire decade.

The unfading classics dominated the repertoires. Gogol, Pushkin, Turgenev, Ostrovsky and adaptations of Dostoevsky were staged at the Moscow Art Theatre, Gordon Craig was invited to work on *Hamlet*, attempts were made to stage Molière, and Goldoni was performed. Meyerhold delighted the Petersburg public with magnificent productions of Wagner and Glück on the stage of the Mariinsky Opera and Molière on the Alexandrinsky stage.

But from 1910 onwards an antipathy among Russian theatrical innovators to all 'literature', including the classics – in fact against the written word in general, began to make itself felt. Theories were devised to justify the compulsion to rescue the actor from delivery of text of any kind. Wordless action was attractive because it created the possibility of proving the autonomy and intrinsic value of theatrical art, its complete independence from literature. Practice kept pace with theory. Both the experienced Meyerhold and the still very young Tairov experimented with mime. They each staged the same mime by Artur Schnitzler set to music by Ernst Dohnány – Meyerhold under the title of *Columbine's Scarf*, and Tairov under the title of *The Veil of Pierrette*. And although the productions were in no way alike, they both aroused lively interest in theatrical circles.

At the same time, another group of young poets, notably Velimir Khlebnikov and Vladimir Mayakovsky, were envisaging the possibility of a theatrical spectacle totally without precedent. Hardly had the Russian Futurists declared themselves – scandalously and sensationally – than they immediately tried to seize the stage. In 1913 Mayakovsky sweepingly declared: 'The great break-up which we have begun in all spheres of beauty, in the name of the art of the future – the art of the Futurists – will not stop and indeed cannot stop at the door of the theatre.' The Futurists immediately tried to break this door down, for they believed that 'contemporary theatre only functions as the enslaver of the word and the poet'. ('The uncivilized enslaver', as Mayakovsky put it more precisely.) Authoritative figures such as Stanislavsky or Yermolova were of no significance in the eyes of the Futurists, and they did not give twopence for innovators like Meyerhold. 'Until our arrival,' announced Mayakovsky, 'theatre did not exist as an independent art.' And the poet promised to create without delay the 'new, free art of the actor'.[5]

Futurism, of course, had arisen in Italy and its main theoretician was Filippo Tommaso Marinetti, whose first Futurist Manifesto, published in 1909, contained a complete programme – more negative than positive – for a new movement. Futurism is commonly defined in terms of Italian Futurism, which is why people try to understand the Russian Futurists – Khlebnikov, Mayakovsky, Kruchenykh, the Burliuk brothers and Vasily Kamensky – on the basis of Marinetti's declaration.

In actual fact there was little in common between Russian and Italian Futurism. They were united only in the desire to sever all ties with aesthetic tradition, with the art which had preceded them. And both the Russians and Italians proclaimed 'dynamism', the cult of speed, as the major principle of the art of the future.

Beyond this, basic differences begin to emerge. The Italian Futurists believed that the new art should not be concerned with such insignificant matters as love and they slighted and despised love motifs. But in the poetry of the Russian Futurists, love lyrics preserved the full traditional richness of their power.

The Italians displayed no curiosity whatsoever towards history generally or archaic language. The Russians on the contrary, especially Khlebnikov, delved deeply into antiquity and readily used words from former times attempting with their help to refresh and renew contemporary language.

The gulf between the Italian and Russian Futurists was revealed with utmost clarity as soon as the guns of the First World War began to thunder in Europe. Marinetti and his associates greeted the war with great enthusiasm. Chauvinism and militaristic zeal dominated their art. The Russian Futurists, by contrast, adopted a fiercely anti-war, anti-imperialist stance. The poetry of Mayakovsky loudly and wrathfully proclaimed a curse on war.

Although there were, of course, no far-sighted or calculating politicians among the Futurists, nonetheless the bold anti-war propaganda that they conducted first of all directly contradicted the official, self-congratulatory patriotic propaganda and, secondly, openly supported the Bolshevik slogan 'War against War'.

This most important factor helps explain why several of the Futurists' public appearances evoked such a strong response and why the Bolsheviks treated the Futurists much more sympatheti-

Poster advertising the first Futurist plays at the Luna Park Theatre, 1913.

cally than did the representatives of the other – bourgeois – political parties, especially as they had expressed their disgust for chauvinism, senseless bloodshed and sabre-rattling even before the war had begun, particularly in their theatrical experiments.

The first two Futurist plays were performed from 2 to 4 December 1913 in the Luna Park Theatre on Ofitserskaya Street in Petersburg (the same theatre where, in December 1906, Meyerhold first presented *The Fairground Booth* by Blok). These plays – Mayakovsky's tragedy *Vladimir Mayakovsky* and Mikhail Matyushin's opera *Victory Over the Sun* with a libretto by Alexei Kruchenykh – were, despite all the differences between the talents of their authors, similar in content, united by a deep antipathy to bourgeois mediocrity and the regimented mechanization of civilization.

Similar motifs appear in several of the earlier Futurist plays written by the strange genius Velimir Khlebnikov. In Khlebnikov's poetry prophetic predictions combine with an obscure, almost shaman-like verbal rumble; a universally comprehensible speech with deliberate *zaum* (a 'trans-sense' language); neologisms with archaisms; lines of childlike simplicity with lines the sense of which does not yield a simple decoding. All this astonishing patchwork

Self-portrait by Velimir Khlebnikov.

emerged spontaneously in Khlebnikov's art. Unlike his fellow Futurists, not even excepting Mayakovsky, he was not good at self-advertisement, nor could he consciously organize sensational events (although he often found himself at the very centre of sensational Futurist programmes – on stage or in print). Outwardly the most quiet of the Futurists, he was essentially the boldest among them. Everything that Khlebnikov wrote in dialogue form, and that could possibly be perceived as remotely resembling a play, looked extremely bizarre and theatrically totally unrealizable.

Khlebnikov's play *The Little Devil*, subtitled 'A Petersburg Joke on the Birth of Apollo', was probably written no earlier than 1908 and no later than 1909. Like all Khlebnikov's early work it is heavily dependent on the mature Blok, who was already by then the idol of student youth, holding sway over the hearts, if not the minds, of Russian intellectuals. (This dependence, incidentally, is little studied by literary critics.) The links are revealed in a number of verbal echoes – for example: 'The snow, eternally young, dresses her shoulders, covers her figure with down' from Blok's *The Unknown Woman* (1906) and 'The light blizzard weaves garlands of snow about her body' – from Khlebnikov's *The Little Devil*. They are equally close in some remarkable moments of polemical rejection.

The absurdist devices to which Blok resorts in *The Unknown Woman* only slightly distort reality by suddenly interrupting common, everyday dialogue with bursts of nonsense and inanity. In *The Little Devil* these devices acquire a formative energy: the structure itself becomes chaotic. All logical links between episodes are severed and, in principle, anything at all can happen and anything can be said.

In the action, side by side and on an equal footing with officials, beggars, policemen, old men and women, idlers, hawkers, waiters, and so forth, we encounter animated sphinxes and caryatids. Hercules, fresh from propping up the pediment of the Petersburg palace of Princess Dashkova, puts in an appearance; there are pagan gods and goddesses, Perun and Hera, naked witches, a Crow and a Mammoth, the French Liberté and even a character called A Glass of Beer (who, as indicated in a stage direction, 'takes on the dimensions of the universe').

Many of the Khlebnikov fantasies are mischievously high-spirited. The sphinxes, 'like seals, fling themselves joyously into the water, then dive and swim about'; Hercules' handshake makes everyone groan with pain: the Devil is sentimental and loves 'to visit churches on the day of Tchaikovsky's death'; the French Liberté appears in the beer hall saying 'I dropped in to get warm'.

But sometimes the poet's jokes become malicious. The role of the Russian military man 'with the long moustache' is not humorous but sarcastic, satirizing him as a pompous fool who is 'proud of his straightforwardness' and given to lofty declamation of platitudes.

During the 'first Futurist theatrical productions in the world' in the Luna Park Theatre, Khlebnikov's words were only heard in the prologue to the Matyushin-Kruchenykh opera *Victory Over the Sun*. This prologue is very interesting in its own right, for here Khlebnikov not only tries to create a new (noticeably Slavonicized and archaicized) theatrical vocabulary but he also devises a completely new system for the actors' roles, looking forward to a concept of acting which would draw upon the old traditions of the fairground to create an oracular and prophetic style for the future.

These ideas, concisely expressed in the Khlebnikov prologue, were first put to the test in the tragedy *Vladimir Mayakovsky* and later in *Mystery-Bouffe*. As for the work which had actually followed the Khlebnikov prologue, *Victory Over the Sun*, it did not, alas, live up to Khlebnikov's expectations.

The Matyushin-Kruchenykh opera has undeservedly gained a huge reputation. The text of the libretto is primitive, poor and flat; the action marks time on one spot and Matyushin's music is hardly capable of arousing interest save among the most devout historians. It is the drawings by the artist Kazimir Malevich for the set and, in particular, for the costumes which have brought fame to *Victory Over the Sun*. It is difficult to say to what degree Malevich's ideas were realized in the 1913 performance for the production was very amateurish, had minimal financing and was prepared hurriedly. 'There were two rehearsals in all, and hasty ones at that,' recalled Matyushin. 'It was a long time before Malevich was given the materials for the stage sets.' A year and a half later Malevich himself wrote with resentment that his plans 'had not been successfully realized' due to the ignorance of the production's organizers.[6] Nonetheless, even what was done according to Malevich's designs far surpassed the capabilities of the author of the libretto.

Kruchenykh's libretto is unpolished in both meaning and language, the slackness of thought which can be felt throughout is poorly concealed by a boisterous, excited outpouring of speech. Forms which for all their shocking luridness are rationally constructed (such as The Fat One, who marches out ahead of his own head with 'the head two steps behind') and the numerous hollow attempts at wit do not provoke even a smile.

The poet Benedikt Livshits subsequently recalled that the 'bright spot' of the whole production 'lit up in a quite unexpected place, independent of its musical text (that is from Matyushin's music) and light years away from the libretto'[7] (composed by Kruchenykh). Malevich had daringly applied the principles of Cubism to the extravagant costumes of the characters and, despite all the flaws in their execution, it was these costumes which became the centre of attention.

Malevich scholars argue about whether the sketches for *Victory Over the Sun* should be considered Cubist or should already be ascribed to Suprematism (this term, invented by Malevich, stands for

Pre-Revolutionary Theatrical Explorations

an art without objects) and looking at the sketches for the set designs in particular it is easy to see why. Malevich painted the backdrops utilizing pure geometric forms: his renowned 'black square' appeared for the first time in one of the sketches for this production alongside straight and curved lines, musical notes, signs resembling question marks. There is no concern for top or bottom, no allusion whatsoever to any particular place of action: the very concept of 'place' in his scenery is disregarded. It simply represents a kind of sombrely abstract background for the actors' performance.

The sketches for the costumes are quite another matter. They comprise a series of grotesque, sarcastic portrayals of militarized characters – half robots, half people. There are a great number of these costume designs and far from all of them were executed. The most characteristic are the figures of the 'Strong Men': the faces of some are covered by medieval knights' visors, others' heads are replaced altogether by metal prisms and the bodies are clad in armour plating. Malevich's mechanized parade of devils, as Matyushin explained, was supposed to have foretold the 'end of future wars'.[8]

On the day of the first performance of *Victory Over the Sun*, 'there was terrible, continuous uproar in the auditorium. The spectators were sharply divided into the sympathetic and the indignant.' The bite of the critics, according to Matyushin, 'was toothless, but they could not conceal our success among young people.'[9] This is most likely an exaggeration, for the reviews were mocking or outraged and they did not mention success, even among the young. One newspaper said of the sets and costumes that they undoubtedly 'are original, but hardly comprehensible to the mind of the ordinary mortal'.[10]

The tragedy *Vladimir Mayakovsky* was much more accessible to the audience, and caused much more excitement (both works, the Matyushin-Kruchenykh opera and Mayakovsky's play, were performed twice each). The tragedy's vigorous, fresh text resounded splendidly, delivered from the lips of Mayakovsky himself. His performance in the leading role was so strong that even the critic A. Kugel (who perceived the Futurists' performances as impertinent mockeries of the public) in all sincerity advised the poet to become an actor. He had, said Kugel, a good stage presence, due to his height and his uncommonly beautiful and supple voice; it was time he gave up Futurist ravings and devoted himself to something worthwhile.[11]

In August 1913 Malevich wrote to Matyushin: 'Mayakovsky is producing a drama that will bring great delight. He is solving everything for us brilliantly.'[12] The Futurists acted as a small but ideologically close-knit group. Differences, and they are very considerable, lay only in the scale of their poetic talents.

This is why the poet himself became the focus of attention in the production of the tragedy *Vladimir Mayakovsky*, both as the performer of the leading role, and, above all, as the author of the stirring text. Malevich's prognosis of 'great delight' was not borne out, but the theatrical ideas of the Futurists this time prompted serious reflection by even the seasoned critic P. Yartsev. His article published in the newspaper *Rech* is in fact the only evidence of a contemporary that makes it possible to understand how the tragedy was staged and acted.

Small panels (or 'screens') placed at the back of the stage near a backdrop covered with rough cloth served as scenery. Throughout the prologue and epilogue there glowed a square panel designed by Pavel Filonov, which was 'painted brightly with various objects:

little boats, houses and wooden horses, as if someone had strewn a pile of toys around and children had drawn them.' Yartsev acknowledged that 'it was very cheerful, colourful, warm and merry, reminiscent of Christmas-time. A small flight of steps draped in brown calico stood in front of the footlights. Mayakovsky, making his entrance, ascended these steps as though he were mounting a pedestal.

The panel for the first act was painted by I. Shkolnik to correspond with the poet's line 'the city in a web of streets'. His sketch has been preserved intact and corroborates Yartsev's description of 'a city with roofs, streets and telegraph poles collapsing onto one another'. For the second act Shkolnik painted 'another city of tumbling roofs, streets, walls and street lights' which, according to Yartsev, looked 'pinkish and unpleasant'.

Mayakovsky's descriptions of the characters undoubtedly created problems for the artists. How does one show on stage the Man Without a Head or the Man With Two Kisses, and so forth? Filonov found a simple solution. He presented the poet's fantasy in the form of his own fantastical images, as a series of ingeniously painted cardboard figures which were brought on to the stage by the actors. Unfortunately Filonov's sketches – if there were any – have not been preserved. 'The actors,' wrote Yartsev, 'move, holding in front of them the cut-out cardboard figures which portray what they are playing and, when they speak, they look out from behind these figures. They move slowly, in straight lines, always facing the public (they can not turn because there is no cardboard to the back or side of them). They wear white lab coats and line up along the sides of the panels, a little closer to the rough cloth backdrop.'

Yartsev maintained that Mayakovsky's tragedy emerged on stage as a 'monodrama' in which only the poet himself was 'a real person' and the other dramatis personae were the products of his imagination. The poet remained on stage as he was in real life: with his own face, in his own yellow smock, in his own coat and hat with his own walking stick. The other characters remained abstract.

Two years before the première of his tragedy in December 1911 Mayakovsky had been in Moscow, where he would have been able to see the Craig-Stanislavsky production of *Hamlet*. This had been conceived as a 'monodrama' in which only the Prince of Denmark is a 'real person' and all the other dramatis personae are seen 'through the eyes of Hamlet's soul' and are only 'imagined by him'. It is possible that Craig's concept had to some extent influenced that of Mayakovsky.

However, Yartsev perceived an altogether different idea in Mayakovsky's Futurist production, namely the intention of 'bringing back the actor in his pure form – the fairground buffoon who frankly introduces himself and, while performing, is engaged in obvious interaction with the audience. The Futurist poet addressed the audience in the prologue and the epilogue and gave his commentary on the events taking place on stage; smoking his cigarette, he treated very much as "theatrical devices" the monsters who appeared on stage and said things to him; he did not even look at them but strolled around the stage. He only accorded them a little attention in the second act when they started to bring him their tears. In his first appearance he handed over his coat, hat and stick to one of the ushers and even, after fumbling around in his pocket, gave him a coin for his service.'[13]

As there is very little information about Mayakovsky's acting début, it is worth citing one more forgotten, ironic review.

'Mayakovsky appeared on the stage with head held high and, after having taken up the pose of the self-confident Prutkov, turned to the audience and asked it "to darn the holes in his soul". The packed house met the poet's appeal with a deafening roar of laughter. This hardly disturbed Mayakovsky who proceeded to recite a long monologue about himself in verse.'[14]

In both this sarcastic reaction and Yartsev's serious article, the figure of the poet himself predominates, overshadowing all the remaining characters. The other dramatis personae, as Benedikt Livshits recalled, were 'entirely cardboard'. [15] Another memoirist, Alexander Mgebrov, also confirmed: they all 'filed by, one after the other' and were quite unexpressive – like 'living puppets'.[16]

One puppet, this time a lifeless one, particularly fascinated the audience. At the beginning of the performance 'something stood in the right-hand corner of the stage, covered by a sheet and looking like an enormous knot. As it later turned out,' wrote Yartsev, 'it was a shapeless puppet.' It 'played the part' of a personage designated in the cast-list as 'His Female Acquaintance', with an accompanying note: 'doesn't converse'. When the poet 'tore the sheet away from the puppet with a tragic histrionic gesture' everyone saw a five-metre-high peasant woman which Filonov had made from papier mâché 'with ruddy cheeks and dressed in some kind of rags'.[17] 'Next the poet demanded the all-but public burning of the puppet-woman, who could not love but only kiss. And the monsters proceeded to drag her from the stage.' At the end of the first act, two news-paper vendors ran across the stage crying out 'Figaro! Figaro!' 'It seems,' summarized Yartsev, 'that life goes on, looking after its own interests, not caring for the great emotions and deeds of the poet.'

In the second act the monsters and women brought the poet 'their tears in the form of little canvas bags stuffed with cotton wadding' and 'disgusting little bags shaped like lips swollen from kisses. . . . The poet's suitcase is brought onto the stage, the poet puts the tears and lips into it and says that he will leave the people who have milked him dry.'

Benedikt Livshits wrote that 'in the centre of the production was the author of the play, who had turned his piece into a monodrama. . . . It was an unbroken monologue, divided into separate parts which were just distinguishable from each other by intonational nuances. Only Mayakovsky himself moved about on the stage, dancing and reciting, and revealing no desire to relinquish one effective gesture or to tone down one note of his splendid voice.' The show, concluded Benedikt Livshits, 'abolished the boundary between lyric poetry and drama'.[18]

The new poetry aggressively seized the stage at the very moment when directors were trying to banish words entirely from the theatre.

In this respect particular interest attaches to the technique of delivery, to which Mayakovsky, as both author and director of the production, accorded great importance. One of the amateur actors, a poor student who had been initially attracted by the possibility of earning a wage (the Futurists paid two roubles per rehearsal and five roubles per performance), then later refused to participate in the performance, wrote a letter to the newspaper Den (The Day) in which he complained: this author 'requires words to be separated from each other by a pause three measures long.'[19] While this is probably an exaggeration, there is no doubt that Mayakovsky, as another participant in the show reported, specially worked out 'the declamation of his lines. The secret lay in shifting at the proper time from great melodiousness to a simple, conversational, even slightly trivial tone.'[20]

Among the audience at the Futurists' performances, Mgebrov noted and remembered Khlebnikov, 'concentrated and calm to the point of abnormality', while Benedikt Livshits recalled 'Blok's concentrated expression'. Although the young Pasternak was not at the performances in Luna Park, he later wrote: 'How simple it all was! Art was called tragedy. And so it should be called. The tragedy was called Vladimir Mayakovsky. The title concealed a brilliantly simple discovery: that the poet is not the author, but the subject of lyric poetry, which addresses the world in the first person. The title was not the name of the author, but a description of the content.'[21]

All this is expressively and accurately stated, but considerable further clarification is required. First, comedy went hand in hand with tragedy in Mayakovsky's play. Using his own terminology, it may be said that already at this time 'mystery' and 'bouffe' were closely allied. The poet appeared as hero, prophet, and simul-taneously as fool, buffoon and clown.

The system of powerful metaphors is hyperbolized to globality. Mayakovsky freely employs grandiose generalizations, as if looking down on the entire planet Earth and merrily, even brazenly, endowing the metaphor with shattering, destructive force. When the Old Man With the Cats declares 'things must be cut to pieces', the Man With the Stretched Face immediately counters, 'but perhaps things must be loved?' Mayakovsky deliberately maintains a dual position. On the one hand, 'inanimate objects' are hostile to man and even 'the white teeth of the enraged keyboard' torment the musician's hands. The poet clearly loathes the Ordinary Young Man who 'has invented a machine for chopping meat'. On the other hand, the Man Without An Eye And A Leg predicts the uprising of objects, which come to life, speak and liberate themselves from the power of people.

All these fantasies are confused and chaotic, primarily because the tragic and the comic, the prophetic and the flippant in both the play and in the image of the hero co-exist on equal terms, in grotesque fusion. Moreover it is impossible to anticipate where, when and how the 'bouffe' will supplant the 'mystery' or when the 'mystery' will turn into a 'bouffonade'. It is, however, perfectly clear that from this early, shockingly impudent and intentionally complex work, extends the thread that would subsequently lead Mayakovsky to the simple clarity of the global metaphors in Mystery-Bouffe.

By curious coincidence Marinetti's first theatrical declaration appeared in the same year, in 1913, when the Russian Futurists presented their first productions to the public. Marinetti, however, relied on light entertainment, variety-show amusement, with 'audience participation in the action (sing-along, retorts in response to appeals from the stage)', that is on theatre of small forms, miniatures and sketches, 'fast, light, ironic'[22] and always ready to flirt with its audience. The Russian Futurists on the contrary, revealed from the outset an attraction for majestic, unwieldy forms. Their very jokes in Victory Over the Sun and the tragedy Vladimir Mayakovsky were menacingly dark. Although the talents of the authors of these two plays cannot be compared, in both cases the action on stage was dominated by the presentiment of impending catastrophe and seethed with hatred for 'the fat men' who were hiding in their 'shell-like houses' and surreptitiously preparing to turn mankind into 'red meat'.

The Kamerny Theatre

The Kamerny Theatre of the director Alexander Tairov and the actress Alisa Koonen opened in Moscow with the première of *Sakuntala* by Calidassa on 12 (25) December 1914,[23] soon after the beginning of the First World War. After a short time the critics began to call it a Futurist theatre. 'The Kamerny Theatre,' asserted one Moscow newspaper in 1918, 'knows no limits in its enthusiasm for extreme Futurism.' The well-known critic, Yury Sobolev, expressed himself even more definitely: 'Alexander Tairov stands on the left flank of Moscow directors. He is undoubtedly the most "left"; perhaps in his own field he is even more left than Mayakovsky or Burliuk are in poetry.'[24]

There was some justification for such a judgment, although Tairov had not contemplated Futurism when he embarked on his path. Even before his own theatre opened he had been engaged in a bitter debate on two fronts. He categorically rejected both the 'naturalism' of Stanislavsky and the 'conscious theatricality' of Meyerhold. The Moscow Art Theatre was censured as a 'literary' theatre, one where the art of acting was reduced to the position of 'servant to literature'. Meyerhold's work was condemned as 'graphic', forcing the actor to serve again not his own but another field, painting. At the Art Theatre the actor is in the end only a slave to the writer, and in Meyerhold's theatre only a slave to the artist-designer. Tairov wanted to stop this slavery once and for all. He fought for the theatre's complete independence from the neighbouring muses, who seemed to him like insolent parasites. The stage is not a place for the exhibition of artists' canvases, even talented ones such as Golovin or Sapunov. The stage is not a platform from which the word of Dostoevsky, Tolstoy or Chekhov should resound. The stage is the stage: an arena for the actor's performance.

Such a conception of the theatre inspired Tairov to concentrate on variations of themes from the Commedia dell'Arte. The old Italian comedy of masks was then, after *The Fairground Booth* by Blok and Meyerhold's production of *Columbine's Scarf*, the very latest vogue in Petersburg. The Harlequins and Columbines had settled in the Russian north and made themselves at home. Blok and Meyerhold however, in reviving the Commedia dell'Arte, had of necessity turned towards the grotesque. The dark reality beneath the surface of this light-hearted genre had to be revealed through its cracks, tragedy had to be revealed in comedy, the smirk of emptiness through farce and slapstick and then, through horror and pain, the insolent comic grin.

It was on this point that early in his career Tairov adopted a different position: he did not want to mix the humorous with the terrible, but required a genre of virgin purity where comedy would be comedy and tragedy would remain tragedy. Two of Tairov's early productions – *The Seamy Side of Life* and *The Veil of Pierrette* – demonstrated both these extremes.

Tairov staged *The Seamy Side of Life* by Jacinto Benavente at the Reineke Russian Drama Theatre (on the Admiralty Embankment in Petersburg). He succeeded in attracting the artist Sergei Sudeikin, the composer Mikhail Kuzmin and the ballet master Boris Romanov to work on this production and to unite their talents in a struggle against the moralizing and satire in Benavente's play. The Spanish dramatist had tried to refine the comedy of masks in the style of Beaumarchais, but the young Tairov, shunning satire and didacticism, wanted to return to the spontaneous and unpredictable improvisation of the players. It was not the 'seamy side of life' which

concerned him at all, but, on the contrary, the colourful surface of the everyday and the glitter of festivals. Sudeikin aligned the scenery along the footlights, emphasizing the symmetry by placing to both left and right identical arcades, pergolas, balustrades, burning lights, and so forth. Boris Romanov grouped the dancers with exactly the same symmetry. The critics waxed lyrical over the 'voluptuousness and langour' that emanated from the stage and were enraptured by the curtain, which had been sewn together like a Harlequin's costume from bright yellow, green, red and blue diamond-shaped pieces of fabric, as well as by Kuzmin's 'languorous music'.[25] For the complete success of the production, which had been beautifully organized and well thought-out (although not without its saccharine excesses), Tairov lacked one small detail: actors. The feeble company of the Reineke Theatre, obeying the director and ballet master, had diligently fulfilled their instructions, and almost all of the crowd scenes, dances and mimes had worked well. However, as soon as they came to the dialogues, verbal duels, soliloquies, and so on, the 'enchanting beauty' of the comedy disappeared. The critics did not even name the actors who performed the roles of Sylvia and Leander (the first pair of lovers), Columbine and Harlequin, Pulchinello and Sirena.

Scholars of Tairov's work do not usually mention *The Seamy Side of Life*, probably considering that the director's talent was not yet fully developed in this rather banal, early work. While this is true, something is nonetheless lost by not comparing *The Seamy Side of Life* with *The Veil of Pierrette* which Tairov staged a year later (in 1913 at K. Mardzhanov's Free Theatre in Moscow). For if in *The Seamy Side of Life* Tairov had wanted to present the quintessence of the Commedia dell'Arte, the unadulterated 'harlequinade', then in *The Veil of Pierrette* the motifs of the Commedia dell'Arte were transposed to the register of a chemically pure, unalloyed sense of the tragic. By the time Tairov staged *The Veil of Pierrette* he had more experienced performers, including, most significantly, the actress Alisa Koonen who henceforward occupied the central position in almost all of his productions.

Like Meyerhold, whose production of the same mime by Schnitzler, set to the same music by Dohnány but staged under a different title, *Columbine's Scarf*, had enjoyed enormous success as early as 1910, Tairov also turned to mime in his desire to prove in practice that theatre can succeed without any spoken text, without a single word, for theatre has its own means of expression independent of the verbal. However, as opposed to Meyerhold and even to spite Meyerhold, Tairov, in taking on the same piece, wanted to avoid the buffoonery and mischievousness of the Meyerhold harlequinade, 'to show,' as M. Bonch-Tomashevsky wrote, 'genuine, not puppet-booth tragedy'.[26] In contrast to *Columbine's Scarf* with its grotesque, excited and jerky rhythms, its 'Russian ugly mugs' and its comically excruciating vulgarity, *The Veil of Pierrette* represented an attempt to create a silent 'mystery', a stirring, tragic poem of love.

The debate with Meyerhold was conducted literally on all points. Tairov's mime opened against a cool background of silver columns designed by Anatoly Arapov. The haughty stillness of his scenery and its imposing appearance had nothing in common with the chaotic and dynamic stage designs of Nikolai Sapunov. In Meyerhold's production the main role was undoubtedly that of Pierrot, whereas for Tairov Pierrot's sufferings were of secondary importance. Meyerhold's Harlequin was impertinent and confident

Sketch by Vera Mukhina of the costume for Pierrette (Alisa Koonen) in Schnitzler's *The Veil of Pierrette* directed by Tairov at the Kamerny Theatre, 1916.

to the point of impudence, while in Tairov's production Harlequin (Alexei Chabrov) was doleful and hopelessly in love.

Pierrette (Koonen), who bore no resemblance whatsoever to Meyerhold's saucy Columbine, became the heroine of the production. 'The combination of little girl and martyr' in her was astounding. Koonen enthralled many with her 'impetuous movements, her wide-eyed look of astonishment at the world as she flung her arms open in horror. It seemed that an explosive charge of passion had been laid within this puppet, and with it she had been plunged into the most dark and unreal tragedy where the only alternation was between strokes of fate, but never of her happiness.'[27]

Over two years later Tairov revived *The Veil of Pierrette* at the Kamerny Theatre. This time one of Burdel's students, Vera Mukhina, virtually unknown to anyone (although subsequently a famous sculptor), was invited to help the artist Arapov: she was commissioned to design the costumes. Koonen's Pierrette, in place of a ballgown with its mass of billowing flounces, was startlingly attired in a stiffly starched white costume which angled out geometrically in all directions. The new costume's rigid, broken, sharp-edged forms completely altered the heroine's appearance and dictated different body movements: not the grief of helplessly falling arms, but a proud stance and resolute gesture. Pierrette's striking costume of 1916 looked like a kind of construction that the actress carried on to the stage and can perhaps be perceived as the nearest precursor to the principles of 'constructed costume' elaborated shortly thereafter by Alexandra Exter and later adopted by Alexander Vesnin in *Phèdre*.

Such signs and portents clearly show the wavering path of Tairov's search for a style. He did not immediately find his way but continued to wander and change direction.

The critic Abram Efros wrote that in the first years, from 1914 to 1916, 'Tairov's theatre did not seem exceptional in any way. It was one of many,' and all of them 'were alike, all were set against the old theatres' and 'sought fresh forms and methods'.[28] In the repertoire Shakespeare was staged alongside Labiche, Calderón alongside Wilde and Rostand alongside Claudel. The mixture of artists was just as flagrant: the recent Meyerholdite Sudeikin preceded the inveterate 'naturalist' Simov of the Moscow Art Theatre; the highly experienced stylizer Arapov somehow managed to get on with Exter and Vesnin, who were inclined toward the most resolute form of Cubism. This constellation of titles, names and trends seemed aimless and senseless.

When faced with the typical alternatives of art at the time of the First World War, either plaintive realism or play far removed from grim reality, Tairov manifestly revealed a preference for play. It is precisely this playfulness which made the Tairov theatre one of the many, 'trivially fashionable', as A. Efros expressed it.

Nonetheless, while quickly churning out the 'trivially fashionable' shows — little light-hearted, mischievous things, which brought in takings and provided the newly born theatre with the necessary income — Tairov gradually prepared the company for vital changes. As soon as the Kamerny Theatre had been founded Tairov declared the line of footlights sacred, inviolate. To step over it was strictly forbidden. The stage area, devoted to the power of art, was separate and apart from the audience, whom art could and wished to affect. In this sense Tairov's festive theatricality was in principle different from that of Mardzhanov, Vakhtangov and even Meyerhold.

On the other hand, however, Tairov did not want the kind of relationship with the public that arose at the Art Theatre where the audience was gradually drawn into a stage world made to resemble everyday reality, a recognizable world into which they then mentally transferred themselves from the auditorium to the stage.

Tairov's work existed only on the stage, and there it was everything. Utterly and completely. The proscenium arch rigidly defined its boundaries, its edges. All productions were arranged in the firm belief that beyond the line of the proscenium there is nothing and can be nothing.

The polarized genres, tragedy or comedy, guaranteed a distance from the everyday. The archaic quality of the 'pure' genre (according to Tairov's terminology, either a harlequinade or a mystery) contained the energy of a generalization which recoiled from contemporaneity, and this was precisely what the director required.

The art of the actor was perceived either as serving the sacred will of tragedy or as the joyful play of the performer, but in no way as part of the measured tone of ordinary existence. The Kamerny Theatre was not interested in either the everyday or the psychological side of the individual characters. The strict division of the stylized world of the theatre into tragic 'upper' and comic 'lower' was proposed. Tragic comedy which inclined toward a grotesque combination of the 'upper' and 'lower' held no attraction for Tairov. His entire system was distinguished by its geometrically clear, linear outline.

At first from time to time, and then more often, he would set completely unexpected tasks for himself and the theatre, both from a formal point of view and from that of the repertoire.

Sakuntala was the first production which truly exemplified Tairov's programme. The exotic appearance and the sensational originality of the whole enterprise (an ancient Indian drama appearing for the first time on the Russian stage) prevented critics from appreciating the true value of the form and essence of the production. Pavel Kuznetsov, a highly talented painter working in the theatre for the first time, was the designer. The East, which he knew well, had nothing in common with the India of Calidassa. Kuznetsov's India had more than a tinge of Bukhara, and its sunny radiance seemed to shine on Central Asian sands. Kuznetsov reared up four mighty blue horses to the right and left of the stage, standing in two pairs, like caryatids, on large pedestal-like vases. Between them stretched the flat, almost completely bare stage floor. The monochromatic colour schemes of the changing backdrops – green, rose, blue – emphasized the emptiness of the stage. Only occasionally did stylized saplings appear at intervals, transparent carved outlines against the single colour of the background. The impression created was of a space prepared for dance, for the performance of a ballet.

Until then nothing similar had been seen on the Russian dramatic stage, although in 1910 Alexander Benois had ironically entitled his article about Meyerhold's *Don Juan*, 'The Ballet in Alexandrinka'. That, however, had been an obvious polemical exaggeration, since dancing, or rather, the careless dance-like movements of Don Juan (Yuriev) alone, had not defined the entire structure of Meyerhold's production of the Molière masterpiece. In *Sakuntala*, however, Tairov had given a dance rhythm to everyone, without exception, organizing the performers as well as the whole visual form of the production according to choreographic principles.

In 1921 in 'Zapiski rezhissera' ('Notes of a Director') he confessed, 'ballet productions are the *only* productions in the contemporary theatre in which I can still experience true creative joy and excitement.' He called ballet performers 'the *only* actors in contemporary theatre who understand the significance of the corporeal in our art.' The ballet stage 'is the *only* one in contemporary theatre which has protected itself from dilettantism and remained within the realm of genuine art.'[29]

I have repeated and underlined Tairov's view on the unique significance of ballet as it makes it possible to understand, unerringly, his idea at that time of grafting choreographic means of expression onto the dramatic theatre – the balletic co-ordination of movements, the beauty and purity of pose and gesture. While Tairov had no desire to learn anything from either Stanislavsky or Meyerhold, he was ready to adopt much from Diaghilev's ballet masters – primarily from Mikhail Fokine but also from the dancers Anna Pavlova and Isadora Duncan. Meyerhold could not understand why Tairov tolerated 'balletic devices in his performances.'[30] It seemed to him that this was the negligence of the dilettante. In fact, it had been an entirely conscious and firmly elected position, tested for the first time in *Sakuntala* and subsequently predetermining many of the formal characteristics of Tairov's productions.

The balletic method of organizing space, where the centre of the stage is empty and the entire stage floor is clear, appealed to Tairov for several reasons. First, this method allowed the actors to demonstrate to great effect their physical virtuosity, since at that time (and subsequently) Tairov attached great significance to the 'poetry of the body'. 'The main material of the theatre,' he said, 'is

the actor's body.'[31] Secondly, the aesthetic of the ballet performance assumed the presence of the prima ballerina, and therefore a centripetal score subordinated to the heroine. For Tairov, who always wanted to move one heroine, Alisa Koonen, to the centre, it was natural to try to employ traditional balletic principles in a dramatic production.

In the role of Sakuntala Koonen derived much from Isadora Duncan. Tairov had advised her to study Duncan, saying that in Duncan's dance 'there is a kind of earthly gravitation which seems to make the gesture heavier, creating its volume.'[32] The 'earthly gravitation' in Koonen's style of acting spoke not only sculpturally but – and this is no less important – intonationally. Koonen's Sakuntala, wearing a head-dress resembling a halo and attire similar to a kind of tunic or an Asian robe, curved her body like a liana, bashfully turning her eyes away from Dushianta, yet her voice was demanding and impatient and knew no shame. It was the voice of the flesh.

The 'body painting' used by Tairov in this production had been dictated by his antipathy to the kind of theatrical costumes which concealed the movement of hands, feet and torso. 'Beautiful costumes of the best contemporary artists – full of colours, magnificence and movement in the sketches,' he wrote, 'fade and hang shapelessly when they cover the actor's body, crushing and impeding it.' This is why he advanced the 'principle of nakedness of the body',[33] essentially a purely choreographic one. He proposed 'in place of the theatrical costumes to which the public are accustomed, half-naked bodies of actors painted in various colours, from lemon to peach to black. . . . The actors will face a difficult task – to convey the purity and primal nature of emotion. This is where the naked body must also help.'[34] Koonen, the heroine, was given small buskins and the remaining actresses performed in bare feet, their hips and legs draped while their shoulders and chests were hardly covered.

The success of *Sakuntala* with the public and critics was restrained. Tairov explained that this was because he had been forced to present the production 'in an incomplete form' and because he had 'almost no actors who could grasp and embody . . . the new creative and technical tasks'.[35]

Sakuntala had indeed been produced in a hurry, and the actors, except Koonen, were weak and inexperienced. But, more importantly, the critics had not at first understood, had not divined Tairov's aesthetic position.

The art of the Kamerny Theatre did not aim to touch contemporary life directly. The exoticism of *Sakuntala* had nothing in common with the social reality just outside the theatre building. Affairs at the front were going badly, the Russian army was retreating. The Russian state system had expended its strength, the once-powerful empire was beginning to tremble. A melancholy and depressed mood pervaded Moscow. But art was being created on Tairov's stage which knew no Moscow, of the past or of the present – did not know and did not wish to know. 'We are not advocates of the depiction on stage of the drudgery of tedious, everyday existence,' stated Tairov, 'of emotions of which there are many in life as it is.'[36]

Alisa Koonen, who held complete dominion over this stage, had not been affected by the excitability and unease characteristic of all Russian theatre during this period, from Meyerhold's lavish Alexandrinsky productions to the modest productions at the First MAT Studio. A stranger to the fashionable neuroticism, it seemed as though she were in the wrong epoch, speaking in the scorched language of passion. Her heroines recalled exceptional, uncomplicated characters and 'times simple and rough', as Osip Mandelstam described it. They did not evoke pity, did not need sympathy. They came on stage to perish or conquer. Their wide open eyes were demanding; their gait was womanly, steadfast. Tairov's bowstring was stretched taut and the Koonen role flew straight like an arrow. Koonen's voice, powerful and warm, low and melodious, ideally obedient to the rhythm of the lines, fired and expanded the delivered word. Coming from her lips words gained new significance and weight, they filled with new meaning. Koonen extended the limitations of the text and animated the director's score, imparting a tragic power to Tairov's work.

Alisa Koonen was the first actress who managed to preserve within the integrated structure of the directorial theatre all the rights the old theatrical system had guaranteed the heroine. What Komissarzhevskaya had not succeeded in attaining with Meyerhold nor Duse with Craig, Koonen attained with Tairov: she was able to find great freedom in submission to the director's will.

Tairov made the next decisive step after *Sakuntala* only two years later, staging *Famira Kifared (Thamyras Cythared)* by Innokenty Annensky (1916). This production marked the first time that Alexandra Exter collaborated with Tairov. Efros hailed the production of *Famira* as the 'birth of a new theatricality'.[37] Although this may have been overstated, the desire to move away from the beaten track in *Famira* was certainly felt. What was new here was Tairov's rejection of the very idea of stylization. He staged Annensky's stylized antique tragedy, striving to strip the Symbolist veils from it, to break through to the primal archaic. Annensky had transposed the ancient theme to converge with the Symbolist idea of the absolute power of fate. The poet strictly designated the limit, the threshold beyond which man, even when invested with great talent, had no right to cross: for beyond this threshold ruled not men but the gods.

Without changing anything in the text, Tairov created different emphases: the challenge which the actor Famira threw down in the face of the gods was of greater significance to the director than the retribution that followed. His Famira (Nikolai Tseretelli), both blinded and stripped of his talent, nevertheless remained recalcitrant and unyielding.

As if in juxtaposition to the play's emphasis on fate, Alexandra Exter gave the set a monolithic solidity. 'Cubes and cones,' wrote Efros, 'large, densely coloured, blue and black masses, rose and fell along the steps of the stage' where 'harmony of blocks dominated' and 'the forms and rhythmic arrangement of steps were finely regulated. This was a triumphal parade of Cubism.'[38] Altogether it was the first theatrical victory for Cubism, preceding Massine and Picasso's Parisian *Parade* (1917) by one year and pre-empting Meyerhold and Dmitriev's *The Dawn* (1920) by four years.

Nonetheless the Cubist set for *Famira* did not avoid representation. The abstract form could easily be perceived as a real landscape: the cubes were stacked like rocks, the cones resembled cypresses. Exter broke up the flat stage floor and suggested that Tairov conduct the action on the wide steps of the gently sloping staircase. However, this still did not mean that the set had been turned into a construction and had become, as Tairov expressed it, 'a versatile and obedient keyboard for the actors'.[39] For the three-dimensional set was stationary. Its outlines were dominated by horizontals, recalling the Wagnerian sketches of Adolph Appia.

The set built by Exter and the entire directorial score for *Famira* obeyed the principles underlying the organization of a ballet production. In particular the hero, Famira, related to a picturesque grouping of maenads and satyrs in the same way as the prima ballerina usually relates to the *corps de ballet*. The essentially choreographic resolution of a dramatic production proved to be a bold and completely unexpected innovation in itself.

The costume design preserved several traits of 'Hellenistic local colour' but the tunics, *pepla* and *chlamydes* (crimson red for the maenads) barely covered the actors' naked bodies. Not daring to bare the maenads' breasts, which would have been too risky for that time, Exter and Tairov turned the Bacchanates out with false breasts and even marked them with 'blood-coloured and alluring points of nipples'[40] which embarrassed the prudish critics. Moreover, Tairov employed 'graphic' make-up for the first time in *Famira*: 'Since the actors' bodies were mostly uncovered, they hit on the idea of emphasizing the relief of their muscles with thin lines of shading. This created a striking effect. The drawn lines were not of course visible from the auditorium, but the bodies seemed larger and exceptionally strong.'[41]

The system of lighting used in *Famira* had been recently created by Zaltsman for the E. Jacques-Dalkroze School of Music and Gesture in Hellerau, near Dresden. By placing the electric lights behind a fairly thick cloth, Zaltsman obtained a dispersed 'tonal light'. Summoned to Moscow by Tairov, he used a combination of white and blue lights in *Famira*. In his 'tonal light' Exter's stairs, cubes and cones appeared more monumental, the costumes brighter and the actors' movements more noticeable. The groups of maenads and satyrs particularly benefited under this lighting.

Tairov wanted to give the language of body movement equal status to that of speech, for to him gesture meant no less than text. Four alternating elements shaped the score – mime, dialogue, song and dance. Their inter-relationship had been painstakingly thought out: in the 'voiced ballet' the lightness and ease of the theatrical language was accompanied by a slow heaviness of movement and the deep, guttural singing by the tense excitement of the dance.

After *Famira* Tairov turned to Oscar Wilde's *Salomé*. In making this choice it seemed he was submitting to fashion, for everyone was reading Wilde, enthusing over Wilde and vying with everyone else to quote from Wilde. After *Salomé* had been banned to both Meyerhold and Evreinov in 1908, it was surrounded by an aura of particular secrecy. People were expecting something outrageously sinful, scandalously explicit. According to Koonen, Tairov 'tried to overcome the preciousness of Wilde's speech and the floridness of his style.'[42] The task was far from easy, for the play was performed in Konstantin Balmont's translation which intensified both the preciousness and the floridness. The tone of the production was defined by the sets. 'The actors were supposed to follow Exter and not Wilde,' explained A. Efros. 'She was the aim, he but a pretext.'[43]

By lowering the proscenium arch, extending mighty steps horizontally along the line of footlights and erecting very wide columns, the artist tightly enclosed the space. The columns projected forward, and the steps dictated the actors' movement downward, toward the proscenium. The silvery-black and silvery-blue costumes sparkled against the background of drapery which billowed out intermittently now from the left, now from the right. The movement of the coloured canvases imparted a sensation of fluidity to the scene, illuminated by crimson-red beams of light.

Pre-Revolutionary Theatrical Explorations

Tairov etched his *mise-en-scène* within these strict spatial limitations. The long spears of Herod's warriors, now pointed upwards, now tilted threateningly, complemented his severe sculptural line. Laconicism and purity of movement were prescribed for everyone – the monumental Herod (Ivan Arkadin), the supple Jokanaan (Tseretelli) and the proud Salomé (Koonen).

Koonen interpreted the role in her own way, singing not of the excited sensuality of Salomé but of her indignant spirit. Her Salomé, as distinguished from Sakuntala, was neither slave nor victim of an all-powerful love, but a tragic heroine proudly defending her spiritual freedom. This is why Koonen was accused of being 'somewhat cold and serious'. 'This coldness,' considered Sergei Auslender, 'allows the actress always to be severely sculptural; not one uncertain gesture or movement disturbs the strict outline of the role,' nor prevents her 'fine voice from resounding always with such measure and harmony.'[44]

The measure and harmony were manifested in one way or another, not only in Koonen's performance but in all Tairov's early work, including *Sakuntala, Famira* and *Salomé*, and at times even in spite of affectation or preciousness in the text. Like the Acmeist poets, Mandelstam, Gumilov and Akhmatova, who offered as an alternative to the mistiness of Symbolist imagery the attraction of classical clarity and to the 'melancholy and anguish' of Blok the chiselled tracery of concise verse, Tairov also progressed from imprecision to graphic clarity, from plaintive melancholy to austere tragedy, from the lavish festiveness of light-hearted comedy to the resilience and choreographic purity of the harlequinade. But, of course, he became carried away. The Acmeists cherished a sense of measure. Tairov and Exter, however, were attracted to Cubist extremism – that was how they came to be labelled 'Futurists'. The path to productions executed in a grand style required boldness, and Tairov's experiments were aggressive. His 'leftness', however, for all its shocking audacity, nonetheless contained a thirst for harmony in its innermost depths and embodied an ineradicable aestheticicism.

Stanislavsky and Meyerhold. Two Studios

In comparison with the Futurists' audacious experiments and Tairov's extraordinary productions, everything that Stanislavsky and Meyerhold did in the theatre during the years of the First World War appeared relatively moderate, conventional and respectable. If only very recently had the 'avant-gardist' Meyerhold been regarded as the opposite of the 'archaist' Stanislavsky (after the October Revolution the opposition of these two names became, and would remain for a long time, the *plat du jour* of theatrical debates), in wartime Russia from 1914 to 1917 many considered both directors equally devoted to traditional theatrical forms and equally lacking in dynamism.

The Moscow Art Theatre only presented a total of six premières throughout the war years and Stanislavsky did not personally direct a single production, at best appearing as co-director with either Alexander Benois or Nemirovich-Danchenko. Meyerhold also did not accomplish any notable achievements for a long time. Only two of his productions from the war period, Ostrovsky's *The Storm* (1916) and Lermontov's *Masquerade* (1917), have earned a place in the history of the Russian stage.

However, at this time both Stanislavsky and Meyerhold were leading a double life. They divided themselves between large, prestigious, authoritative theatres and experimental studios where they worked with young actors. In the studios, their similarities ended completely. The First Studio of the Moscow Art Theatre in Moscow, organized by Stanislavsky, and the Studio on Borodinskaya Street in St Petersburg (renamed Petrograd at the very start of the war), created by Meyerhold, were strikingly different. As the theatre historian and theoretician Tatyana Bachelis has said, 'It would seem there could have been no greater contrast in the history of Russian theatre in the last pre-Revolutionary years than the First Studio of the Art Theatre with its *Cricket on the Hearth*, and Meyerhold's Studio on Borodinskaya Street with its cult of Gozzi! Soul and body, ethics and aesthetics, truth and fiction – it was as if everything that always constitutes theatrical unity in the periods of its flowering appeared separately in these two studios, divergent from each other.'[45] So why did this occur?

Stanislavsky and Meyerhold both undoubtedly experienced intense dissatisfaction with the state of the theatrical organizations with which they had long been associated. They both realized that while it was possible to present a more or less significant production on the large stages with experienced and confident actors, it was almost inconceivable to afford oneself the luxury of experimentation. The machinery of a stable theatre is cumbersome, and because it depends on the box office and immediate success it therefore automatically orientates itself toward the best results achieved yesterday or the day before. It is not interested in innovation. In this sense the Moscow Art Theatre, the theatre of Chekhov and Gorky, could hardly be distinguished from the imperial Alexandrinsky Theatre, the theatre of Gogol and Ostrovsky. Exerting enormous efforts to overcome the inertia of the old theatrical machinery and the ambitions of distinguished actors, both directors recalled that as early as 1905 they had created, for the first time in the history of the Russian theatre, a kind of laboratory for theatrical experimentation, the Moscow Studio on Povarskaya Street. Their Studio did not last long then, nor had it been open to the public, but nonetheless it laid the foundation for much of their future explorations.

Several years later, working apart – Stanislavsky in Moscow, Meyerhold in Petersburg – they once again felt the need for some kind of experimental, laboratory work with the young. However, the ideas which fired each of them were completely different. 'I have utterly lost faith in everything that serves the eye and ear on stage,' wrote Stanislavsky to Meyerhold in 1912. 'I only trust feeling, emotions and most of all, nature herself. It is wiser and more subtle than we are, but . . . !!?'[46]

This short letter holds the key to the enigma of the opposition between Stanislavsky's and Meyerhold's studios. The area which Stanislavsky staked out with his punctuation – two exclamation marks and a question mark – remained uniquely attractive to him. For several years he had been trying in vain to test out and actualize the principles of his 'system' within the walls of the MAT. The idea of a 'system', that is a combination of techniques with which it would be possible to mobilize the potential of the actor's creative nature to guarantee him truth of feeling and authenticity of the stage 'experience', first came to Stanislavsky in 1906–07 and remained with him until the end of his life. But the 'system', in its first, original variant, did not arouse any enthusiasm whatsoever among the MAT actors, and they used any excuse to avoid the unaccustomed methods of rehearsal that Stanislavsky was proposing. Then when he did manage to thrust his methods upon them, it became clear that they did not by any means always achieve the desired results.

The joint production of *Hamlet* (1911) with Gordon Craig stunned audiences and critics with its boldness of form, but Stanislavsky was forced to admit bitterly that the actors of the Art Theatre 'had not found the appropriate methods and means of expression for heroic plays, with their elevated style.'[47] Yet he had rehearsed *Hamlet* according to his 'system'!

This bitterness was further intensified by the distressing failure of the Pushkin production staged by Alexander Benois at the MAT in 1915. Benois, a well-known graphic artist, painter and a founder of the influential group of artists 'World of Art', boldly embarked on the path of director with the benevolent assistance of Stanislavsky and Nemirovich, and, naturally, tried to bring the same ideals to the theatre which inspired him in representational art. His great passion, his *idée-fixe*, centred round a love for olden times, for the old way of life, and for old things in particular. He declared that his production of Pushkin's three *Little Tragedies* would appear as a solemn 'trilogy of death'.[48] On stage, however, the action developed with depressing sluggishness. Benois had erected impressive structures on the Art Theatre stage in order to show old Vienna in *Mozart and Salieri*, old Madrid in *The Stone Guest* and old London in *The Feast During the Plague*. The journey to the past of these three European capitals was organized with such exceptionally great thoroughness that the production ended up being extremely cumbersome, heavy and unwieldy. During rehearsals, arguing with each other, Benois, Stanislavsky (who took part in the staging of *The Feast During the Plague* and *Mozart and Salieri*) and Nemirovich (who worked on *The Stone Guest*) 'stretched' Pushkin's little tragedies 'to enormous proportions' – forgetting that they are 'little'.

Pushkin's works 'lost their charm in being transformed to monumentally realistic, even tedious dramas,' wrote Pavel Markov. 'The theatre weighed down the verse, literally converting it to prose in the name of its multiplicity of meanings. Benois' cold and beautiful painting defined the production's style, and the psychological overload of images was in conflict with Pushkin's text.'[49]

A remark of Fedor Sologub's is interesting in this context: 'Pushkin was not only a great writer who portrayed certain heartfelt feelings well in dramatic form, but a poet as well.' The actor of the Art Theatre however 'seems to regard it as a heresy to recite verse as verse – he is convinced that one should not speak poetry line by line, but according to the punctuation. The verse is turned to shreds,' because 'the Art Theatre wants to interpret Pushkin's created legend as a conscientious, everyday portrayal of events and experiences.'[50]

Stanislavsky drew what seems to have been an over-simplified conclusion from the failure of the Pushkin production when he wrote, 'the actor must be able to speak'.[51] Such a belated revelation, which struck him as the MAT was approaching its twentieth anniversary, would have appeared childishly naive if he had not linked the demand for a highly expressive theatrical language with the demand for absolute truth of feeling, sincerity and depth of the actor's experience.

The most distressing thing for Stanislavsky was the simple fact that in the *Hamlet* of 1911 and the 1915 Pushkin production, the MAT actors, himself included, remained very distant from the requirements of the 'system'. Either they declaimed in a stilted manner which made it impossible even to dream of sincerity of feeling, or they played authentically, naturally, even though this ordinary, everyday manner irreconcilably contradicted the tragic poetry of Shakespeare or Pushkin.

In seeking a way out of this impasse, Stanislavsky, with characteristic maximalism, did not even contemplate a return to the everyday 'conversational' play. On the contrary, he was genuinely fascinated by Alexander Blok's belatedly romantic, chivalric drama, *The Rose and the Cross*, composed in beautiful verse, but, as distinguished from Pushkin's little tragedies, extremely tedious from the point of view of its theatrical effectiveness. Work on this production, for which the artist Mstislav Dobuzhinsky was first engaged, to be succeeded later by Ivan Gremislavsky, dragged on for more than three years (from 1916 to 1920) but never got as far as rehearsals. It was undoubtedly stylistically linked to the concept for the staging of Byron's *Cain*, an idea which was realized after the Revolution. Meanwhile, in the Studio Stanislavsky was conducting quite different experiments.

The Studio (which became known as the First, since the Second then the Third Studios soon arose under the auspices of MAT) was necessary above all for his studies with the 'system'. It had been conceived exclusively for experimental and pedagogical purposes. Here Stanislavsky determined to achieve what the principal MAT company obstinately resisted – to conduct a series of consistent, carefully conceived experiments on the application and realization of new methods of working with actors. In the First Studio was a company of unspoilt, talented youth, who were prepared for any difficulties, whose dream was to study and act, but most of all to study acting, which augured well for the success of Stanislavsky's project. He was willingly joined as assistant by Leopold Sulerzhitsky, a staunch supporter of Lev Tolstoy's moral teachings, who believed in the 'system' even more strongly than Stanislavsky himself: if, according to Stanislavsky, the 'system' should and could become an aid in the actor's work on himself and on his part and set him on sure paths toward integrity of feeling, then Sulerzhitsky believed the 'system' was capable of morally elevating all the student actors.

While a wide programme of experimentation was conceived, Stanislavsky had not envisaged it for either the creation of complete productions or for the presentation of these productions to the public. Least of all had Stanislavsky wanted to turn the Studio into a theatre, even a small one. He did not need a theatre, but a creative laboratory. The creation of a kind of nursery for young directors had not entered into his intentions either. But as the young MAT artists who had gathered in the First Studio all yearned for parts, and the temptation to demonstrate successful results of their studies of the 'system', at least to the incorrigible sceptics of the principal company, was very great, the students were not discouraged from presenting, in their free time, on their own initiative and at their own risk, first one production then several others. These productions were directed by the most enterprising and talented of Stanislavsky's and Sulerzhitsky's students.

The process of transforming the 'laboratory' into a theatre happened quickly and soon broke free from the leaders' control. Stanislavsky and Sulerzhitsky only hastily reviewed the students' work. In the end, the results were quite unexpected for never in his life, either before the First Studio or after it, did Stanislavsky prepare so many highly gifted and independent directors. The following all came out of the First Studio: Evgeny Vakhtangov, Richard Boleslavsky, Boris Sushkevich, Alexei Diky, Alexei Popov, Ivan

Bersenev, Serafima Birman, and, last but not least, the great actor Mikhail Chekhov who subsequently became head of the First Studio.

The character of the First Studio's productions (in all their diversity) was to a significant degree pre-determined by the necessary poverty of the furniture and scenery, inevitable under circumstances when performances arise spontaneously, impromptu. The space was so small that it was not even possible to build a simple, crudely knocked-together stage. Stage and footlights were thus relinquished, and the students performed on the floor directly in front of several rows of chairs. The actors could go right up to spectators sitting in the first row. Coarse fabric usually served as scenery against the background of which would be placed some completely authentic details. Pavel Markov described how 'a fireplace or an oven in which a warm fire blazed in accordance with all the laws of realism would appear among the folds of the fabric. Portraits would hang on the swaying cloth "walls", a window covered with hoar frost would stand out. It was important to impart a sense of the room – not the room itself.'[52] Sulerzhitsky explained, 'we do everything by the most primitive means. Our sets are canvases on hooks.'

Such poverty sharply contrasted with production design at that time in the MAT. The First Studio knew no luxury; its designers are unknown. No one wanted 'to serve the ear and eye' here. This was a 'chamber' theatre not only because it presented performances in a large room rather than a large auditorium, but also because life, enclosed in rooms, between four walls, was more often than not the object of its art.

However, the theatrical convention of the 'fourth wall', obligatory in early MAT productions, was not possessed of sacred inviolability for the actors of the First Studio. As has already been said, the actors could go right up to the spectators in the first row. The imaginary line of the fourth wall was crossed at this moment, and the possibility of direct interaction with the public arose. There was no acting on the edge of the proscenium, no special emphasis on the conscious theatricality which Meyerhold loved so much and which carried with extreme acuteness the sense of theatre, but only the most sincere outpouring of innermost feelings to the public.

The theatre's intimacy imparted a special colour to its art. The term 'emotional realism' was soon in use: truth of feeling took on a confessional aspect. The proximity of the public did not even allow the smallest concession to craft, necessitating an absolutely life-like tone, movement and gaze. It turned out to be possible to achieve such naturalness in the studio conditions largely because here the actor was freed from the many demands of outward expression indispensable in a large theatre. It was not necessary to force sound – everyone heard the softest whisper. The necessity for expansiveness of gesture fell away – any, even barely noticeable, impulsive movement was perceived without fail and taken in by the audience. Nowhere before had the language of the eyes attained such eloquence. Every glance became as rich in meaning and distinct as a spoken line.

All these possibilities offered by the small 'chamber' theatre were used differently by the young directors of the First Studio.

Vakhtangov, whose directorial will immediately manifested itself, focused on the poignancy of psychological portrayal, on abrupt and extreme play of contrasts. As the future showed, the path along which he was feeling his way proved to be the most promising. In Vakhtangov's productions of *The Festival of Peace* by Hauptmann

and *The Flood* by Berger, Expressionistic notes sounded for the first time on the Russian stage. They had, it is true, been heard earlier in Leonid Andreev's plays, but the theatre had not been able to reproduce them. It was Vakhtangov who first ventured to implement change, to imbue the whole atmosphere of the action with questioning unease. He heightened the nervousness and excitement of the dialogue, fearing neither a frenzied nor a hysterical tone. His work irritated Stanislavsky who said 'it was some kind of disease, hysteria,' and the actors performed 'neurasthenically'.[53]

It is easy to understand why Stanislavsky, the creator of the Chekhovian 'theatre of moods', regarded Vakhtangov's experiments with hostility and did not appreciate the innovation which subsequently, in the early 1920s, carried Vakhtangov to the Expressionism of *Eric XIV* and *Hadibuk*. Stanislavsky was much happier with the intimacy, cosiness and warmth of Boris Sushkevich's productions. He considered Sushkevich's production of Dickens' *The Cricket on the Hearth* the Studio's 'greatest achievement'. He wrote that in this production, 'perhaps for the first time those deep, sincere notes of super-conscious feeling began to resound, in kind and in extent just as I had imagined them.'[54]

The Cricket on the Hearth, presented for the first time on 24 November 1914, was a significant production in many respects. Played in the spirit of a 'Christmas tale', it was harmonious, naive and tender. '*Cricket*,' wrote Markov, 'essentially . . . marked a protest against war.'[55] In the climate of chauvinistic intoxication during the first months of the war, the production's idyllic atmosphere, the directness and naivety with which it preached humaneness, goodness and faith in mankind, were perceived as an attempt to counter the propaganda of violence, hostility, and all military slogans in general.

Indeed all five productions which the Studio succeeded in putting on during the war years were permeated with this same mood. Tolstoyan ideas determined much in their art and if it is at all possible to speak of a political programme in this theatre then that programme was pacifist.

With regard to artistic form, Vakhtangov and Mikhail Chekhov, both passionate adherents of Stanislavsky's 'system', brought nervousness, morbidity and sharpness to the art of the First Studio. Vakhtangov persistently aimed for grotesque poignancy and ambiguity of forms (on the borderline between the comic and the tragic). Mikhail Chekhov, like no one else, knew how to slide suddenly into the grotesque from the most ordinary, everyday, even intentionally dull realism. Chekhov and Vakhtangov (and, following them, a number of other actors) time and again interrupted the everyday flow of life with unforeseen expressive shifts.

Such shifts did not contradict the general ethical spirit of the art of the First Studio. On the contrary, they intensified the energy of the defence of compassion and goodness that animated all of the small theatre's activities. Nonetheless Sulerzhitsky protested: 'Hysterics aren't necessary. Get rid of them. Don't get carried away by the idea of playing on nerves.' He asked, 'give all the warmth which is in your heart, look into the eyes of each other for support, gently encourage each other to open the soul.'[56] Tenderness, warmth and sincerity were all concentrated in *Cricket* and displayed in unadulterated form. But 'playing on nerves' remained extremely attractive to both Vakhtangov and Chekhov.

In the Studio, conflicts between the elders (Stanislavsky, Sulerzhitsky) and the youngsters (Vakhtangov, Chekhov) transpired and became ever more apparent. 'Relatively quickly,' recalled Alexei Popov, 'in the course of something like two or three years of vertiginous fame, in the Studio were sown the seeds of an ironic attitude to the 'system' and to the ethical foundation of Stanislavsky's teaching.'[57] These conflicts came to full light after the Revolution and finally led to a dramatic split between MAT and the First Studio.

However, still before the Revolution, another extremely vital issue defined itself. Everyone was forced to consider whether an art form which had matured under 'hothouse', 'chamber' conditions could exist on the large stage and stir an audience. Was the First Studio doomed to remain a small theatre for a select few or was it capable of leaving the 'chamber' and addressing itself to a wider public?

In February 1917 Nemirovich wrote to Zinaida Gippius, '*Cricket* has already been played about 175 times and it could perhaps be played another 100. . . .' But if the production were to be transferred to the large stage then 'the impression', he suggested, 'would scarcely be a shadow of what is now achieved in the Studio. And this is not only my opinion, but also that of Stanislavsky.' Nemirovich explained that in the Studio's tiny space, 'the performers do not have to force either their voices or their feelings, and hence preserve sincerity and individuality in their purest form.' Here 'it is possible not to be afraid of revealing the awkwardness of movements'; here 'not one successful detail is lost, and failures are easily covered up.' But all this is possible '*only* in an intimate situation, here, in the Studio, only in intimacy. . . . The Studio's small stage does not at all mean a reduction in requirements, it is simply *another* form of theatre. And the more ideal it is, the more fragile – fragile in both a spiritual sense and in the sense of rupture – is its link with the art of the large theatre, in its present form.'[58]

All of Nemirovich's apprehensions were confirmed as soon as the productions from the First Studio were transferred to the large stage of the Art Theatre after the Revolution. But during the war years the impoverished, small theatre, where there were no more than eight to ten rows of chairs, not only raised its voice against violence, in defence of humanity, but also tried many means of theatrical expression for the first time which, as we will see, were subsequently used with great effect in the art of Vakhtangov and Mikhail Chekhov, where they acquired tremendous power.

Unlike the First MAT Studio, the Studio on Borodinskaya in Petersburg which Meyerhold directed gave almost no public performances and the whole nature of its activities was quite different. For Meyerhold was fascinated by other issues and had different experience behind him. If at that time Stanislavsky refused to believe in 'what serves the eye and ear on stage' then Meyerhold was absorbed first and foremost by the external – visual and aural, sculptural and musical – side of the theatre. His most remarkable productions during the war years, *The Storm* and *Masquerade*, triumphantly completed a cycle in his work executed under the sign of theatrical 'traditionalism'. Meyerhold's conception of traditionalism signified:

—renunciation of the reproduction of a past epoch through realistic everyday detail in the name of the reproduction of the artistic style of that time, of the author, and of the theatre;

—a strong emphasis on the beauty and magnificence of spectacle as counterweight to concern for historical authenticity;

—an inclination for a symmetrical placement of the sets, their frontal emphasis, and likewise for symmetry in the staging;

—renunciation of the illusion of 'realism' in the name of the principle of play, openly declared, realized before the eyes of the spectators and addressed to them;

—a penchant for merging the space on stage with the space of the auditorium. The stage looks out onto the auditorium, the scenery is often made to blend with the architecture of the auditorium and, at times, even the lighting of the stage and auditorium are the same.

It is obvious that all these principles contradicted an art which aspired to create the illusion of real life on stage, a truthful copy of reality, of either the present or the past. It is also obvious that such methods entailed a completely unexpected interpretation of classical plays which, under Meyerhold's direction, were suddenly transformed beyond recognition.

The première of *The Storm* on 9 January 1916 took place in the tense silence of a puzzled and hushed auditorium. The public had reacted without much concern to the changes Meyerhold had previously made in his interpretations of Molière or Calderón. After all no one had been able to state conclusively how Molière or Calderón should look on stage. But how to play Ostrovsky everyone knew, or thought they knew, and of course the audience at the première in the Alexandrinsky Theatre, inveterate theatre-goers all, knew exactly. The challenging, haughty and peaceful elegance of Alexander Golovin's decor shocked them rigid. They were astounded by the theatrical language, which sounded unusually elevated, cold and slight, without the 'juiciness' obligatory for Ostrovsky. There was no 'juiciness'. They were disturbed by Katerina (Roschina-Insarova), nervous and jerky, and, according to the critic Liubov Gurevich, 'all saturated, as it were, by the nervous excitement of life in a capital city'.[59] They were dismayed because they did not see the usual and expected picture of 'the Kingdom of Darkness' on the stage. The critic A. Izmailov asked, 'Is this a room in the home of the Kabanovs in Kalinov, or is it the palace of the Romanov boyars in Moscow with decorated oven tiles and glass gallery? Is this a provincial madwoman or a countess from *The Queen of Spades* dressed in a costume practically dating from the times of dear Catherine?'.[60] Dikoi failed to frighten and Kabanikha did not appear terrifyingly grim. Alexander Kugel was indignant: 'the Kingdom of Darkness' had turned into 'the Kingdom of Fantasy'.[61]

One way or another Meyerhold's *The Storm* caused a sensation. Some critics bitterly inveighed against it (A. Benois was especially irritated), but others, in particular Eduard Stark, praised it enthusiastically. And in a year's time, on the eve of the February Revolution of 1917, Meyerhold's production of *Masquerade* by Lermontov caused an even greater sensation. This production must be described in greater detail as it ran for a very long time, right up to the Second World War, and its influence is still to be felt to the present day.

Masquerade was staged as a 'tragedy within the frame of a carnival'.[62]

First of all, the 'frame' itself. Not for the first time, but more consistently and firmly than ever before, Golovin and Meyerhold unified the stage decoration with the decor of the Alexandrinsky Theatre auditorium. The usual curtain of the Alexandrinsky Theatre was raised for the duration of *Masquerade* so that when the audience entered the auditorium (which had been ornamented in the eighteenth century by the great architect Rossi) they were immediately struck by a gilded, decorated and sculpted proscenium arch which had been erected on the stage. The columns of the arch echoed the columns flanking the boxes in the stalls as if carrying their rhythms from the hall onto the stage, continuing their movement. Rossi had given the architecture of the hall gold ornamentation against a white background while Golovin decorated the architecture of the stage with the mirror reflection of this motif, white ornamentation against gold.

Impending catastrophe became the emotional leitmotif of the production. Meyerhold perceived the imagery in the Lermontov *Masquerade* as 'on the border of delirium and hallucination'. While it would have been possible to evoke such a feeling in a variety of ways, in this case mobility became the most important means of expression for Meyerhold. During the performance Golovin's decor and curtains conducted their own silent and mysterious play, both accompanying the actors' performance and responding to it. The tone of the production was already set by the main front curtain which divided the forestage from the stage: red with black, gathered in lavish festoons, finished in silver with playing cards spread out in a fan shape just beneath its centre, ominous in its heavy blaze. There were five curtains altogether, and their movement in turns divided the play's progress, breaking it up into sections, imparting a new mood to each episode, while simultaneously driving the action on, creating a sense of its progression, with everything accelerating down a slope toward death and madness.

While individual episodes flowed from one to another, each one nevertheless possessed its own inner logic and completeness. When the curtain was lowered, concealing the main part of the stage, the play continued downstage, in the line of the proscenium, or even closer to the public, on the forestage. Then the curtain was raised, revealing a new set and once again the action moved back to the depth of the stage.

The spell-binding succession of noiselessly moving curtains imparted an overall impression of uncertainty and instability to the outlines of the production, a disturbing unease to its opulence, while at the same time allowing the director to present many episodes 'in close-up' by suddenly bringing them forward.

The sequence of planes and rhythms organized by the fluctuation of the *mise-en-scène* was both the law and the meaning of the production's entire form. It imparted a nervous pulsation to its measured, fatal course.

Meyerhold even risked fragmenting whole monologues (this wouldn't surprise anyone now, but at that time it confused both actors and audience). A monologue might be begun on one set, continue on the forestage (the curtain coming down behind the actor's back) then be completed in another set.

The semi-circular forestage was extended to the first row of the stalls over the orchestra pit and was framed on the left and right by two staircases with handrails descending to the orchestra. Here two light-blue vases were raised on marble columns, and there stood two massive sofas. A little further back and likewise symmetrically placed were tall frosted mirrors facing the illuminated auditorium and reflecting a sea of lights. All the furniture on the forestage, with its symmetry and solidity, sharply contrasted with the assymetry of the interiors revealed in the main stage area.

Of the production's ten scenes only two, the second (the masquerade) and the eighth (the ball), filled the entire stage area, from its very back to the edge of the forestage. In the remaining eight scenes where two-hander, three-hander and soliloquy scenes predominated, the interiors were arranged in shallow, relatively small spaces. To compensate for this, in the masquerade and ball scenes Meyerhold's many-figured compositions made an overwhelming impression with their ornate, capricious and nervous dynamics.

One of the critics perceptively called Meyerhold's *Masquerade* an 'opera without music'. It is important to note the director's characteristic methods for the creation of the 'musical' score of the action in the drama. He searched for and found the equivalent in gesture for every fluctuation of emotion. In other words, he gave to each actor in each scene the kind of acting that could if desired be conducted without words, in mime, and still be understood, be 'read' by the audience. The 'blueprint' of the performance set by the director for *Masquerade* dictated firstly the observance of the rhythm of the verse-line, secondly the shifts in the stage area as envisaged in advance and thirdly an obligatory body movement to denote any changes of emotion. And this is still not all. The score to *Masquerade* assumed an obligatory body movement as sign ('full stop') within the limits of each separate emotional movement, a sign which preceded the next movement of emotion. The concrete forms could here be various: throw gloves on piano – 'stop'; lean back in chair – 'stop'. These 'stops' could be more or less apparent to the audience, although this was not the essence; the essence was that the actor had no right to omit a 'stop'. This entire system of 'punctuation marks' obeyed a fixed rhythm governed by the director. The actor's freedom is in subordination to the score. And this is not a paradox, for the whole rhythmic organization of the production not only prompts to the actor the necessary emotion but also creates space for it and gives it free rein. More important is another factor: knowledge of the score brings inner calm to the performer, confidence in himself and in his right to enrich this score with a multitude of nuances accessible only to him, the actor.

Here, in the acting style of the opulent *Masquerade*, was laid the foundation for the future concept of 'biomechanics', which stridently declared itself for the first time after the Revolution in productions outwardly completely dissimilar to *Masquerade* – ascetic, severe and devoid of both the sense of fatality and carnival-like brilliance.

The 'biomechanics' of the early 1920s do, however, have other sources. During rehearsals for *Masquerade* which dragged on for a good five years ('Meyerhold,' wrote Kugel sarcastically, 'built the production like a pharaoh his pyramid')[63] this Meyerholdian idea had been partially tested under entirely different conditions, much more relaxed and easy, in the Studio on Borodinskaya. If the First Studio had been necessary to Stanislavsky for studies on his 'system', then Meyerhold, who was known at the Studio under the pseudonym of Doctor Dapertutto, wanted to foster actors who commanded the long-forgotten and almost completely lost techniques of street, fit-up theatre. He wanted to resurrect and renew the old experience of wandering players, mimes, thespians, *jongleurs*, Russian 'merrymen' and actors of the fairground booth as well as of the Italian Commedia dell'Arte. He contrasted the refined, intellectual and psychological theatre (that is, first and foremost, the Moscow Art) with the crude and cheeky popular theatre; the theatre of half-tones, nuances and 'moods' with the theatre of extremes, prepared not only for tragedy and buffoonery, but even (and this is an important distinction between Meyerhold's and Tairov's programmes) for the grotesque combination of the high with the low, the beautiful with the terrible, and the comic with the heroic.

In turning to the old forms of popular theatre, he had in no way contemplated their careful reconstruction. What was important to him was something else: the revival of old techniques with new aims, the cultivation of an all-powerful actor whose strength and power would lie in the ability at any moment to compel his body to express what it had to express and his voice to convey what it had to convey. The 'feeling' which so troubled Stanislavsky did not interest him at all. Meyerhold did not, on the whole, like this term, preferring to speak of 'excitability'. He was sure that excitability would emerge of its own accord as soon as the precise outward form, in gesture and intonation, was found, assimilated and mastered by the actor. Therefore he taught his students the art of theatrical movement, dance, acrobatics and fencing, but set as almost his main priority their musical ability.

The guidelines for acceptance by the Studio on Borodinskaya declared that every candidate must display:

—a degree of musical ability (instrumentalists have to play, singers have to sing);

—a degree of physical dexterity (gymnastic or acrobatic exercises; excerpts of mime with acrobatic stunts extempore);

—ability to perform a scene without using speech on a theme set on the spot;

—clarity of diction;

—knowledge of the theory of versification and in the fields of painting, sculpture, poetry and dance.

These prerequisites illustrate sufficiently clearly what end results Doctor Dapertutto sought. At lessons in the Studio priority was given to mime variations according to the scenario motifs of the Commedia dell'Arte. The technique of mime was thoroughly elaborated, brought to the point of virtuosity. But all the exercises, as Sergei Bondi, a former Studio pupil and subsequently an eminent philologist, recounted, 'were done to music. I was playing something quite simple from the classics, Boris Alpers [later to become a well-known critic] was acting, better than I was, and we had to move. What was important was that the movements of the actor's body in space should serve as a counterpoint to the music. Meyerhold demanded not a direct or outward correspondence to the musical rhythm, but explorations of more distant movements, inwardly founded through association and contrast.'[64] Another former Studio pupil, subsequently the renowned director Alexei Gripich, confirmed that in this kind of training and improvisation lay the 'embryo of biomechanics' and that in the Studio Meyerhold 'sought the path to the creation of a genuinely popular theatre'.[65]

Meyerhold's theses have been preserved as noted at that time by one of his Studio pupils. The basic points are as follows:

—'In the very essence of theatre there is a complete absence of freedom and a complete freedom of improvisation.'

—'Freedom is in subordination.'

—'More precision, joy and sparkle in movements.'

—'It is necessary to be excited, to know that it is a joke when you go on stage.'

—'Clowning and showing off are prerequisites for the actor. The simplest simplicity must contain an element of showing off.'

—'Art is a juggling act.'[66]

These notes, despite their brevity, give a sufficiently clear idea of where Meyerhold was heading and what he was trying to achieve in his Studio. His pupils mastered the technique of an actor's work under the most primitive theatrical conditions, in close and unconstrained contact with imaginary spectators. They learned to control voice, body and movement in set rhythm and tempo. Ideally Meyerhold would have liked to make them virtuosos: to polish the simplest skills to perfection, to automatism. Nothing sacred, nothing mysterious! The professionalism of agile, skillful actors, always ready for any task the director might set – that is what he sought.

Meyerhold made his students juggle with balls and study acrobatics, yet basic attention was initially devoted to mime: acting without words required maximum expressiveness of the body.

One circumstance which outwardly would have seemed quite immaterial was later to acquire great aesthetic significance in Meyerhold's practice. The artists Yury Bondi and Alexander Rykov, in line with Doctor Dapertutto's requirements, made sketches of everyday workers' clothing and festive, ceremonial costumes for the student actors. These costumes, identical for everyone and for everyone equally comfortable, appeared in the Meyerhold productions of the first post-Revolutionary years, in *Mystery-Bouffe* and *The Magnanimous Cuckold*, although, of course, in an altered form. The main principle, however, of all the actors appearing in identical overalls (*prozodezhda*) and not dressed differently, not wearing costumes 'according to roles', is one which was preserved and predetermined much in the ascetic outward appearance of the sensational Meyerhold productions during the period of 'the denuding of the theatre'.

The Meyerhold Studio very rarely presented its work publicly. Unlike the First Studio of MAT which had been quickly turned into a theatre, small but real, with posters, box office and repertoire, the Studio on Borodinskaya remained an experimental laboratory. It is noteworthy, however, that these experiments to which Alexander Blok reacted with disapproval apparently interested Mayakovsky, who spent time at Borodinskaya Street. The paths of the traditionalist Meyerhold and the Futurist Mayakovsky were manifestly converging.

Several months after the Revolution an article was published in the Bolshevik newspaper *Pravda* in which the author asserted that before the Revolution several masters of the theatre 'were turning to the popular theatres of the preceding epochs with increasing frequency. They saw true theatrical achievements in them and wanted to proceed from them. How otherwise can Meyerhold's longing for the Italian popular theatre of the Commedia dell'Arte be explained? The awareness that our period had completely lost all true principles of theatrical action compelled Meyerhold to turn to the Italian popular comedy in order to find these principles, to take from it everything that is eternal in theatre and transplant it to our soil. The possibility and even inevitability of the change of audience which the Revolution of 25 October has created, in a literal sense has encouraged those who have thirsted for the revival of theatre and seen this revival not in the aristocratization of theatre but, on the contrary, in carrying it out on to the street. That is why Evreinov is now lost somewhere, has vanished, and Meyerhold is working, working with feverish intensity. It goes without saying that there is no longer any need for him to limit his explorations to the area of Italian theatre. He is turning his aspirations directly to the people, who can create their own original theatre, their own principles.'[67]

Meyerhold's fundamental line of development is defined accurately in this article, and its future direction predicted exactly. Six months later Mayakovsky handed to Meyerhold the manuscript of his play *Mystery-Bouffe*.

In the decade before the Revolution (1907–17) the most diverse theatrical ideas and forms contended and clashed. For some the theatre's function was to reconcile man with the force of all-powerful Fate and, following Maeterlinck, they adopted static poses and incantatory tones, likening the theatrical action to the liturgy of the church. The dream of others, like Vyacheslav Ivanov, was that new forms of theatre should actually replace the religious rituals that had become obsolete. Others again took their bearings from the cheerful freedom of the fairground harlequinades, and staged mimes in the spirit of the Italian comedy of masks. Some directors tried to imitate Gordon Craig or Max Reinhardt. Yet others were inspired by antiquity: for example, in 1916 Alexander Tairov's Moscow Kamerny Theatre staged Innokenty Annensky's play *Famira Kifared*, which is based around motifs from ancient Greek mythology. The sets for this production marked the theatrical début of the artist Alexandra Exter.

Sketch by Alexandra Exter of Famira's costume.

'Until our arrival,' Mayakovsky announced, 'theatre did not exist as an independent art.' His tragedy *Vladimir Mayakovsky* was performed in the Luna Park Theatre in Petersburg in 1913, alongside *Victory Over the Sun*, and the two were described as 'the first Futurist theatrical productions in the world'. *Vladimir Mayakovsky* was the more successful, and its author performed brilliantly in the leading role as the only 'real person' in the play surrounded by products of his imagination. Ilya Shkolnik's painted panels portrayed a 'city in a web of streets'; Pavel Filonov designed the cardboard figures which the actors carried on stage to represent the characters they were playing.

Two sketches by Ilya Shkolnik for Act I (*right*) and Act II (*below*) of *Vladimir Mayakovsky*.

Mayakovsky in Kiev, 1913.

Poster by Olga Rozanova advertising
the first Futurist plays, 1913.

Victory Over the Sun

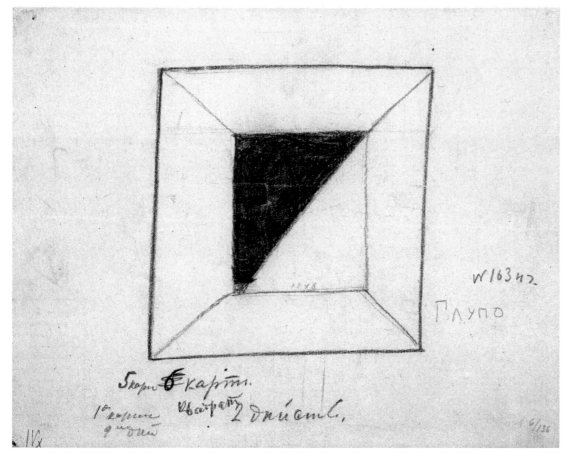

The Russian Futurists stunned the public in 1913 with a production of the opera *Victory Over the Sun* by Alexei Kruchenykh and Mikhail Matyushin. It was a rather confused spectacle, but the sets and costumes by Kazimir Malevich made a strong impression: the militarized figures that he created, half-robots, half-people, inspired deep antipathy to militaristic ideas.

Two sketches by Malevich of sets for *Victory Over the Sun*.

Костюм «Новых»

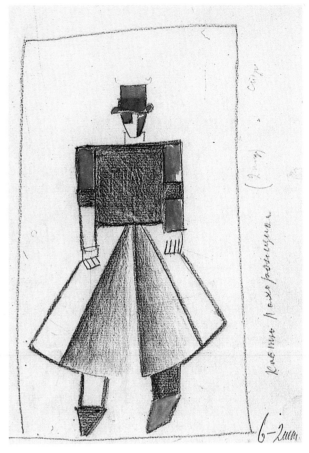

Костюм Многих и одного того же НО зеленый

Костюм трусливых

Four sketches by Malevich of costumes for *Victory Over the Sun*.

Classical designs by Exter

The works of Alexandra Exter – who designed both Annensky's *Famira Kifared* (1916) and Wilde's *Salomé* (1917) for the Kamerny Theatre – to a great extent predetermined the whole visual aspect of Tairov's early productions. The actors' bodies stood out in relief against the austere background of the artist's geometrically precise compositions, which clearly tended towards Cubism.

A scene from *Famira Kifared*.

Two costume designs by Alexandra Exter for *Famira Kifared*.

Before the Revolution performances of Oscar Wilde's *Salomé* were prohibited in Russia; attempts by Vsevolod Meyerhold and Nikolai Evreinov to stage it had been categorically forbidden by the censor. Immediately after the overthrow of the autocracy two directors, Alexander Tairov in Moscow and Konstantin Mardzhanov in Petersburg and Kiev, turned their attention to the play. In the Kamerny Theatre in Moscow Salomé was played by Alisa Koonen; of Mardzhanov's two productions the one in Kiev was the more successful, with Vera Yureneva in the role of Salomé and sets by Isaak Rabinovich.

Opposite, above: Model of the set designed by Alexandra Exter for the 1917 production of *Salomé* at the Kamerny Theatre. *Below*: A scene from *Salomé*, 1917.

Above: Three sketches by Rabinovich of costumes for the 1919 production of *Salomé* at the Solovtsov Theatre in Kiev. *Below*: Set by Exter for the 1917 production of *Salomé* at Moscow's Kamerny Theatre.

Salomé

Sketch by Alexandra Exter of Salomé's costume for the 1917 production of *Salomé* at the Kamerny Theatre.

Meyerhold (centre) with members of the cast of *Masquerade*.

Vsevolod Meyerhold spent over five years preparing his production of Mikhail Lermontov's *Masquerade*. The critic Alexander Kugel observed ironically that the director 'had built the production like a pharaoh his pyramid'. The première in the Alexandrinsky Theatre took place in February 1917, in the very days of Nicholas II's abdication. Alexander Golovin's dazzlingly sumptuous sets imparted a glint of threatening majesty to the whole course of Lermontov's tragedy. The production was perceived as a sombre requiem for the dethroned Romanov dynasty, a burial service for the old world that had perished in these February days.

When Meyerhold on the day of the première took a photo-call together with the participants in *Masquerade* (this recently discovered photograph is being published for the first time), he could not, of course, foresee the

A scene from *Masquerade*.

Masquerade

long life that lay in store for his remarkable creation. The production was splendidly acted by Yury Yuriev as Arbenin, Nina Kovalenskaya as Nina, Elizaveta Timé as Baroness Shtral, and Nikolai Barabanov as the Stranger. *Masquerade* remained in the repertoire right until 1941, when a German bomb destroyed the building on Rossi Street in which Golovin's sets and costumes were stored.

Three characters in *Masquerade*. *Left*: Yury Yuriev as Arbenin. *Below left*: Elizaveta Timé as Baroness Shtral. *Below*: Nina Kovalenskaya as Nina.

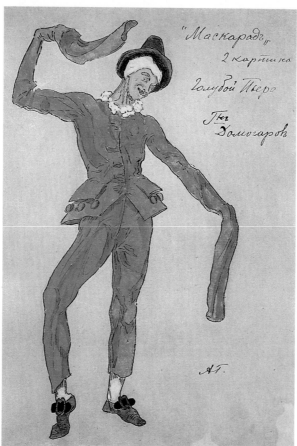

Top row: Two set designs for
Masquerade by Alexander Golovin.

Bottom row: Sketch of the costume for
Sprich; Nikolai Barabanov as the
Stranger; sketch of the costume for
the Stranger; sketch of the costume
for Nina.

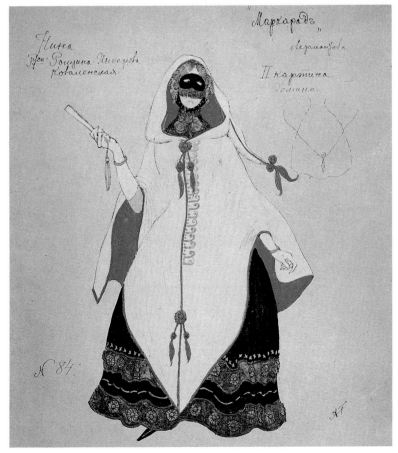

ph... A. Gubcsshewsky.

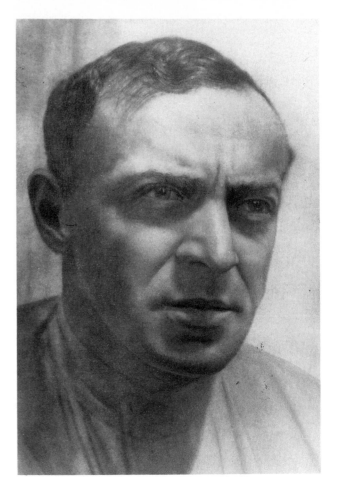

Evgeny Vakhtangov, 1920.

Alexander Tairov, 1932.

Konstantin Stanislavsky, 1923.

Les Kurbas, 1921.

38

Directors

Among the theatre directors whose portraits are shown here the most experienced was undoubtedly Konstantin Stanislavsky, who founded the Moscow Art Theatre in 1898. His pupil and rival Vsevolod Meyerhold began his career as director in 1902. Then, almost simultaneously, Konstantin Mardzhanov (Kote Mardzhanishvili) and Alexander Tairov began to try their talents at directing, to be followed a little later by Evgeny Vakhtangov. It was only after the Revolution that the following directors emerged: the Ukrainian master Les Kurbas, Meyerhold's pupil Sergei Eisenstein, and the leaders of small but very interesting experimental theatres, Nikolai Foregger and Igor Terentiev.

Drawing of Sergei Eisenstein, 1922.

Nikolai Foregger, 1922. Portrait by P. Galadzhev.

Vsevolod Meyerhold, 1925.

Alexei Popov, 1929.

Drawing of Igor Terentiev, 1927.

The Cricket
on the Hearth

After the October Revolution
the intimate productions of
the Moscow Art Theatre's
First Studio – such as the
adaptation of Dickens' *Cricket
on the Hearth* which had
opened in 1914 – continued
to enjoy undiminished
popularity with the public. All
the Studio's productions of the
Civil War years were imbued
with the same warm,
optimistic, anti-militaristic
tone.

Above: Mikhaïl Chekhov as Caleb.
Right: Two scenes from *The Cricket on
the Hearth*.

2 Theatre During the First Years of Revolution

'Everything Anew!'

In 1919 a newspaper columnist wrote, with unconcealed surprise: 'It is hardly possible to point to any other epoch when the theatre would have occupied such an exceptionally great place in people's lives, would have become such an essential part of popular culture as now in Russia. Everywhere, throughout the length and breadth of the Republic, there is an insatiable thirst for the theatre and for its stirring impressions, and this thirst is not only not diminishing, but is steadily gaining strength. Theatre has become a necessity for everyone.'[1]

A year later Viktor Shklovsky was still expressing surprise: 'All Russia is acting, some kind of elemental process is taking place where the living fabric of life is being transformed into the theatrical.'[2]

And yet another year later, in 1921, the art critic Petr Kogan stated: 'In no field of art has the October Revolution provoked such intense struggle as in the sphere of theatre. In the crucial moments of this struggle the boundaries which divide the adversaries from each other have been sharply delineated.'[3]

After the October Revolution public interest in the theatre immediately intensified. Theatrical performances occupied an unusually important role in the lives of the people. And furthermore in the field of theatre the internecine strife became so embittered that soon the headline 'On the Theatrical Front' became an almost daily reminder of this struggle from the pages of newspapers and magazines.

Lunacharsky, the first Narkom (People's Commissar) for Education, offered this formulation: 'The Revolution said to the theatre: "Theatre, I need you. I need you, but not so that I, the Revolution, can relax in comfortable seats in a beautiful hall and enjoy a show after all the hard work and battles. . . . I need you as a helper, as a searchlight, as an advisor. I want to see my friends and enemies on your stage. . . . I want to see them with my own eyes. I want also to study them through your methods." '[4]

The answer to the question of why the Revolution needed the theatre specifically, why it had not laid a similar claim to music, or perhaps painting, is as simple as ABC. It is *precisely* as simple as ABC, because approximately eighty percent of the country's population was illiterate and did not know the alphabet. 'An uncivilized country,' wrote Lenin, 'in which the masses have been *robbed* of so much in the sense of education, enlightenment and knowledge, such a country is not to be found anywhere in Europe, only in Russia.'[5] In the Revolutionary situation, when Russian history took a sharp and decisive turn, and then under the even more complex political circumstances of the bloodbath accompanying civil war,

the theatre and only the theatre could serve as primary school and newspaper for the masses thirsting for 'education, enlightenment and knowledge'. For the light which the theatre radiated could reach everyone. The language of the theatre was comprehensible to everyone. Every peasant, every worker, every soldier sought to find out on whose side the truth lay: it was a question of life or death for them. The theatre was of real help to millions of such spectators as they orientated themselves in the complex political conflicts of the period. The theatre served them (we'll repeat Lunacharsky's words) 'as a helper, as a searchlight, as an advisor'. The stage often became a kind of platform for political agitation. Time and again performances reached the pitch of mass meetings.

The audience to which the art of the theatre addressed itself had changed. If previously theatres had been the privilege of the upper and middle strata of society – the noblemen, the bourgeois and petit-bourgeois, officials and intelligentsia – and the so-called 'simple people' as a rule had not had any real opportunity to attend performances, then after the Revolution factory workers, soldiers and large numbers of yesterday's peasants, now wearing soldiers' overcoats, filled the auditoriums.

At first the veterans of the theatre experienced great difficulties in the face of this new audience to which they were completely unaccustomed. The difficulty lay in finding a common language, for the politically aroused stalls reacted to what was taking place on stage in the most unexpected ways. The following incident, reported by a journalist, was not untypical: 'In Elisavetgrad [now Kirovograd] two soldiers tried to shoot an actor performing in full dress uniform and wearing epaulettes. In the next act the actor appeared without the epaulettes.'[6] Such extreme reactions occurred frequently. But people of the theatre, like the entire artistic intelligentsia in general – writers, painters, architects, musicians, and so on – did not formulate their attitude to the new leadership, the Bolsheviks, by any means right away or without hesitation.

Several days after the Revolution the Bolsheviks invited all 'performers and socialist artists interested in the future of the State theatres' to the assembly hall at Smolny. It is known with certainty that five people responded to the call and went to Smolny: Natan Altman, Alexander Blok, Ryurik Ivniev, Vladimir Mayakovsky and Vsevolod Meyerhold. With less certainty historians cite two more – Kuzma Petrov-Vodkin and Larisa Reisner. Meyerhold was not only the eldest and most experienced of these five (or seven) but the only one from the theatre.

A relatively short time later, in August 1918, Meyerhold joined the Bolshevik Party and thereby unequivocally announced that he would devote his art to the service of the Revolution. The significance of this action becomes clear if it is remembered that throughout the Civil War none of the prominent figures in the theatre chose to follow Meyerhold's example. On the contrary, a wary mistrust, which within the walls of the old theatres was the attitude towards the new leadership, was immediately transferred also to Meyerhold. They doubted his sincerity and some associates believed he was acting opportunistically, simply adapting to the new masters of the situation.

In fact this step was not only completely natural for Meyerhold but the only one it was possible for him to take. A revolutionary in the theatre, he considered his place was in the ranks of the most radical Revolutionary party. He was as sincere as both Blok, who celebrated the Revolution in his poem *The Twelve*, and Mayakovsky, who celebrated it in *Mystery-Bouffe*.

There is a striking similarity between these two works. They both represent a turning point in the art of Blok and Mayakovsky. Moreover, the turning point is realized in exactly the same way: from the minor notes to the major, from the refined to the deliberately primitive. Formerly élitist poets, Blok and Mayakovsky almost overnight adopted the position of democratic, street poets. Over the heads of their recent, sophisticated readers and listeners, they now addressed the masses, a people in revolution.

In *The Twelve* Blok utilized and modified one of the most steadfast of Russian folkloric traditions – the tradition of the popular ditty (*chastushka*), of the short couplet, brisk, provocative and responsive to topical events. In *Mystery-Bouffe* Mayakovsky, while proclaiming 'everything anew!', also turned to the old folkloric tradition. The theatrical experience of the fairground show and the theatre of the Russian 'merrymen' were revived and restored in this play. The devices of the carnival barker – a kind of master of ceremonies, cheerful and uninhibited – join forces here with the devices of circus clowns and the language of mass meetings. *Mystery-Bouffe* was the very play of Meyerhold's dreams, finally enabling him to apply and test in battle the weapons Doctor Dapertutto had stockpiled in the Studio on Borodinskaya.

Mayakovsky and Meyerhold wanted to stage *Mystery-Bouffe* for the first anniversary of the Revolution on 7 November 1918.

This did not prove to be an easy task, for Meyerhold's attempt to offer *Mystery-Bouffe* to the actors at the Alexandrinsky Theatre, where he directed, proved a fiasco. The play plunged the former 'Imperial performers' into a state of horror. In the end Mayakovsky and Meyerhold acquired the Musical Drama Theatre for several days where they staged their production with the help of casual actors who had been the first to reply to a newspaper appeal calling for participants in a 'Revolutionary production'. The production was performed three times, on 7, 8 and 9 November 1918. It made an enormous impression but the reviews were highly contradictory – some enraged and malicious, others ecstatic.

In characterizing his play, the poet stated, 'the mystery is all that is great in revolution and the *bouffe* is its comic aspect. The verse of *Mystery-Bouffe* consists of the slogans of mass meetings, shouts from the streets and the language of newspapers. The action in *Mystery-Bouffe* is the movement of crowds, the conflict between classes and the struggle of ideas – it is a microcosm of the world within the walls of a circus.'[7]

Globality ('the microcosm of the world') in Mayakovsky's play was accompanied by the precise differentiation of social and class characteristics. The class affiliation of each character is clearly

Poster (*above*) and advertisement (*below*) announcing the first performance of Mayakovsky's *Mystery-Bouffe*, directed by Meyerhold at the Musical Drama Theatre, 1918.

indicated. They were divided into two groups: 'the clean' – the exploiters – and 'the unclean' – the exploited. While 'the clean' were strongly differentiated from each other – the Merchant could not be confused with the Negus, or the Frenchman with the Australian, and so forth – 'the unclean', representing the international proletariat, formed a unified chorus. Here, within the group of 'the unclean', similarity was more important than difference. The whole group is a collective hero, although in the chorus of 'the unclean' they have their own leader of song and action: he is 'Simply Man'.

Mayakovsky portrayed 'the clean' in placard-style satire by means of vicious theatrical caricature. And he devoted his lyrical pathos, the passion of the celebration of Revolution, to 'the unclean'. It is 'the unclean' who will create a new world, and to them the future belongs.

'The unclean' wore identical grey costumes. The artist Kazimir Malevich sought to represent them all, regardless of nationality or profession, as a unified mass of workers. Thus the idea for the actors' uniforms (prozodezhda) which had already undergone preliminary trials in Meyerhold's Studio on Borodinskaya was actualized, to be repeatedly adapted by Meyerhold on subsequent occasions.

In the first act of the 1918 production one half of an enormous globe stood on the stage; in the second the prow of a ship pointed out toward the public; in the third 'hell' was portrayed as a red and green cave with terrifying stalactites hanging down from above; in the fourth, in 'heaven', aniline pink, blue and raspberry-coloured clouds, resembling iced buns, rested on the stage; finally, in the fifth, the 'Promised Land' was portrayed as a realm of mechanization, a vision of a bright future, a mechanized world gleaming with the coldness of iron and steel.

The production had been hastily put together. On the day of the première it fell upon Mayakovsky to play not only 'Simply Man' but also Methusala and 'one of the devils'. Just as in the tragedy Vladimir Mayakovsky, he performed superbly. Even the critic Andrei Levinson, who had contemptuously called Mayakovsky the 'genius of mystification', acknowledged that when 'the author himself delivered his lines, their fabric appeared more impressive, their rhythm conquered the ear. Every short, hard line initiated a protracted resonance, like a bullet hitting a wall, and as long as his melodic and powerful voice sounded the acoustic enchantment did not fade.'[8]

Of course public opinion dwelled primarily upon the fact that the Futurists had openly and decisively supported the Bolsheviks in this production. Meyerhold was now even being called a Futurist on all sides (although this was completely unjustified), and Lunacharsky praised him for successfully 'adapting' Futurism 'to the placard and mass meeting period of our Revolution'.[9]

At the time very few realized what Osip Mandelstam had understood at once when describing Mystery-Bouffe as 'a simple, healthy school for the enlightenment of the masses'.[10] In addressing a truly broad and semi-literate audience for the first time, the Futurists, especially Mayakovsky, had immediately simplified their language and relinquished deliberately complicated vocabulary and imagery. Precision, accuracy and terseness characterize the poet's language in Mystery-Bouffe. In parodying the famous biblical legend about the Ark, Mayakovsky employed images which were familiar even to simple people and the new characters included in the parody were easily recognizable and comprehensible.

If Mystery-Bouffe can nonetheless be characterized as Futurist, then only in the primary and literal sense of the term: focus on the future and hatred of the past, of the old, outmoded system, including, of course, old forms of art. This is why Mayakovsky derided 'theatre wardrobes' in the prologue to the play and, in keeping with the poet's idea, 'the unclean' tore up the 'curtain, painted with the most cherished symbols of the old theatre'.

Meyerhold decided to simplify this in the production. The actors tore posters from the old Petrograd theatres to shreds, thus openly identifying those whom they considered to be their adversaries. It was not a question of 'old art' in general but of entirely tangible, neighbouring and celebrated theatres, well-known to everyone. The actors from these theatres were naturally offended by the proceedings of Mayakovsky and Meyerhold.

Alexander Blok attended the first performance of Mystery-Bouffe and commented in his notebook, 'a day not to be forgotten'.[11]

On the first anniversary of the October Revolution, a play entitled Stenka Razin by another famous 'Cubo-Futurist', Vasily Kamensky, was performed in Moscow. Like Meyerhold in Petrograd, the director Vasily Sakhnovsky created a 'collective' performance in the theatre of the Vvedensky People's House. Actors from various theatres participated, including Alisa Koonen from the Kamerny, (she played the Persian Princess Medran), Anatoly Ktorov from the Korsh Theatre (the Persian prince) and Nikolai Znamensky from the Art Theatre (playing Razin himself). Pavel Kuznetsov painted the scenery and Kasyan Goleizovsky choreographed the dances.

It was notable that once again the Futurists, in seizing the stage, displayed their readiness to dispense with shocking 'trans-sense language' (zaum) for the sake of intelligibility, simplicity and clarity. The figure of Stepan Razin, leader of a peasant uprising in the seventeenth century, had long attracted Kamensky. In 1915 he had devoted to Razin a strange symbiosis of novel in prose and poem in verse. Archaic vocabulary in the spirit of Khlebnikov alternated with scarcely comprehensible neologisms in this cumbersome composition. But the play Stenka Razin, composed by Kamensky in 1918, was quite different. Like Blok's The Twelve and Mayakovsky's Mystery-Bouffe, it showed a clear trend towards folkloric primitivism. 'The author himself,' reported one newspaper, 'was convinced that Razin could only be performed in the spirit of the popular print, the lubok.'[12] This admission is significant, for it directly indicates that while Blok was inspired by the popular ditty and Mayakovsky by the comic carnival barker, Kamensky's theatre was inspired by the naive little prints and cheap printed literature for the simple person, in which were depicted fairy tales, lives of saints, adventure stories and heroic exploits.

The critic Yury Sobolev, who had shown hostility to the Futurists' 'unseemly clamour' and 'publicity stunts' wrote with surprise that Stenka Razin had stirred him with its 'irrepressible spirit' and boldness as 'a very Russian and very talented work where historical truth is blended with poetic invention and authenticity of legend is interwoven with unrestrained fantasy'. The critic concluded that the director Sakhnovsky had succeeded in creating 'a production of broad sweep completely harmonizing in proportion with the style and enormous range set by the author' and that the production – perhaps precisely because the stage 'reeked of streets and circus' – deservedly enjoyed 'enormous success'.[13]

A year later Kamensky's play was staged by Konstantin Mardzhanov in Kiev.

Mass Festivals. Proletkult. Agit-plays

Only a very few professional literati, such as the Futurists, wrote plays immediately after the Revolution which celebrated the event. Nevertheless, as has already been mentioned, Russia was seized by a thorough-going theatrical epidemic during the years of civil war. Amateur and professional drama clubs, studios and more or less permanent companies sprang up everywhere like mushrooms after rain. In 1919 *Vestnik teatra (Theatre Bulletin)* wrote that 'the quantitative side is staggering. The future historian will record how throughout one of the bloodiest and most brutal of revolutions all of Russia was acting.'[14]

The amateur and semi-professional theatres enthusiastically performed the classical plays as well as they could, but their productions were usually of a propagandist character. This was primarily a propagandist theatre, and the classics did not always suit their purposes. As Lunacharsky explained, 'by propagandist theatre I mean placard theatre, a theatre of bright, witty images and situations, which issues specific appeals, sheds light on events and fights against prejudices and counter-Revolutionary propaganda.'[15]

'Mass festivals' or 'mass pageants' represent the most striking form of propagandist theatre. The 'mass festivals' are a remarkable trend in the theatrical life of the first Revolutionary years. Many hundreds, sometimes many thousands of people participated in them and not just actors but workers, soldiers and sailors as well, who not only appeared in the productions but also simultaneously, together with others, became its spectators. Thus to a significant degree, with no division between spectators and actors, the 'mass pageants' realized Vyacheslav Ivanov's dream of the 'collective action'. But the character of these spectacles did not conform in any way to Ivanov's Utopia. They were, on the contrary, militant. By the most direct means they responded to the hatred for the enemies of revolution characteristic of the entire situation of civil war. Rage directed against the former masters of this world, the wealthy, the factory owners, the landowners, the merchants, against the White Guard and interventionists, boiled within them and poured out in crude placard forms.

The mass pageants were usually organized on days marking Revolutionary holidays and enacted on city squares. In addition to the entire square, adjacent streets and moving platforms such as trams, lorries, and so on served as their grandiose 'stage'.

The mass pageant *Mime of the Great Revolution* was realized in Moscow, *Scenes from the Life of Emilyan Pugachev* in Orenburg and *The Struggle of Labour Against Capital* in Irkutsk. The monumental performance of *The Storming of the Winter Palace* was enacted in Palace Square in Petrograd.

Information has come down to us about the multitudinous festival-spectacles which took place in the open air, in Omsk and Yaroslavl, Samara and Astrakhan, as well as on the fronts of the Civil War. Sometimes the mass pageants took the form of theatricalized 'court cases'. On the southern front ten thousand Red Army soldiers participated in the *Judgment on Wrangel*.

The enormous scale and agitational aims of these productions determined their artistic features. Their stylistic shape was undoubtedly influenced by Mayakovsky's *Mystery-Bouffe*: the underlying theme was also the direct conflict between 'the clean' and 'the unclean', that is the 'oppressors' and the 'slaves', the 'Whites' and the 'Reds'. The theme of the uprising people was expressed with pathos while that of the denunciation of the 'masters', the 'bourgeois' and the 'tsars', was portrayed comically, satirically. The mass pageants, however, were distinguished from Mayakovsky's play in that they required an enormous crowd. The movement of vast numbers of people enthusiastically shouting out slogans in unison, the brightness of the placards and the simplicity of the images gave spectacles of this kind a stirring grandeur.

The well-known director Nikolai Evreinov staged the spectacle *The Storming of the Winter Palace* with the assistance of the director Nikolai Petrov and the theatre critic Alexander Kugel to coincide with the third anniversary of the Revolution. The artist Yury Annenkov erected two platforms linked by an arch-shaped bridge on Palace Square: the 'Whites' were situated on one platform and the 'Reds' on the other. About 10,000 soldiers and sailors participated in the action, which re-fought the struggle between the 'Reds' and the 'Whites' over the Winter Palace, while approximately 100,000 townspeople followed their 'performance'. Some episodes were described by Evreinov as follows: 'Silhouettes of those locked in battle were visible through the lighted windows of the Winter Palace. . . . The crackle of gunfire and rifle shots, the thunder of artillery guns . . . two to three minutes of continuous din . . . then a rocket soared up and everything instantly subsided only to be filled with the new sound of the "International" as sung by the forty-thousand-strong chorus. As the lights in the windows were being extinguished, five-pointed red stars lit up and a huge red banner was raised above the palace itself.'[16]

The mass pageant *Toward a Worldwide Commune* was also enacted in 1920, in Petrograd, on the Vasilievsky Island on the banks of the Neva, in front of the monumental Stock Exchange building. The main scenes were supposed to demonstrate the historical development of events (beginning with the Paris Commune and ending with the battles of the Civil War) leading the workers to freedom. Two groups participated in these scenes: the 'slaves' (who were located below, near the foot of the Stock Exchange entrance) and the 'masters' (who presided above). Mighty waves of crowds surged upwards along the stone steps; the unarmed crowd of 'slaves' struggled to overthrow their 'masters'. An enormous red sheet fluttered above the 'slaves'. Sombre ranks of soldiers in dark blue uniforms defended the 'masters' – fat, bald and wearing costumes and make-up in exaggerated caricature style – by firing at the 'slaves' and throwing smoking explosives, while a black smoke screen hid the sovereigns from view. The soldiers tore the red flag to pieces. The 'slaves' protested with cries of rage voiced by thousands and again charged toward the top. A huge, absurd puppet depicting Tsar Nicholas II was lowered from the Stock Exchange pediment to meet them. Lorries decked in red flags and bristling with bayonets drove across the square to the Stock Exchange. Red Guards forced the soldiers away from the entrance. When the 'slaves' gained their victory, cannon fire resounded from the Peter and Paul Fortress. Girls in fluttering red dresses with golden trumpets in their hands appeared beside the imposing columns. Cardboard crowns were scattered from the lorries as they passed through the crowd of spectators (which numbered around 45,000). The emancipated 'slaves' raised artificial sheaves of wheat, clusters of grapes and baskets of fruit upwards. The beams of the searchlights on the destroyers anchored on the Neva illuminated a poster bearing the inscription 'RSFSR' which had been raised on the Stock Exchange pediment. The black two-headed eagle fell down on to the stones of the carriageway.

The professional directors Konstantin Mardzhanov, Nikolai Petrov and Sergei Radlov staged the festival celebration *Toward A Worldwide Commune*, and the artist Natan Altman designed it.

Images of the past and present acquired an inevitably exaggerated character and an allegorical simplicity in all these productions. History, even relatively recent history, only provided an occasion and a pretext for the creation of effective, grandiose, living scenarios. Among the participants in the performance of *The Storming of the Winter Palace* there were undoubtedly many who had actually taken part in the real event which, just three years later, the director Evreinov transformed beyond recognition. They knew, if anyone did, that in reality everything had not been like that, had been different, simpler, without rockets, without choral singing, without red stars blazing above the palace windows. But this lack of correspondence with reality did not disturb them in the least, for the need to elevate and embellish reality, to impart to it visual grandeur, over-powered everyone. The enthusiasm displayed by both participants and spectators in the mass celebration was genuine, living, and was further increased by the fact that many spectators were at the same time participants.

On 1 May 1919, when the mass *Pageant of the III International* was performed, Petrograd lay in a state of siege as battles against Yudenich's armies were taking place on the approaches to the city near Gatchina. Posters along the streets declared 'There is no greater honour than to die for Red Petrograd!' Under these conditions the dramatized, theatricalized festival took on the character of a direct challenge to the enemies of the Revolution, of a collective demonstration of the city's readiness to fight.

Of course the sweep, the militant spirit and placard style of the mass pageants would not fit within the limitations of the usual theatrical scale. The festivals, organized in the open air (although often also in theatre premises or clubs), were akin to the Revolutionary rally and mass demonstration.

All these features of the mass festivals, their collectivism and large numbers of people, the participation of worker and Red Army soldiers, inspired the leaders of Proletkult to suggest that the mass pageants represented a prototype and perhaps even the ideal model for the theatre of the future.

'Proletkult' is the abbreviated form of the name of the powerful literary, artistic and cultural enlightenment organization formed in the period between February and October 1917. Up to 400,000 members, mostly workers, were counted among the ranks of *Proletarskaya kultura* (Proletarian Culture). Many of them participated in theatrical clubs and studios. The mass festivals were almost always arranged on the initiative of Proletkult, and they published more than twenty journals.

The philosopher and idealist Alexander Bogdanov, the critic and theoretician Platon Kerzhentsev and the dramatist Valerian Pletnev formed the leadership of Proletkult. They advocated a 'pure' and 'absolutely new' proletarian culture, created only by the proletariat, that is by the workers themselves, and having nothing in common with the old, pre-Revolutionary culture. 'New art,' they maintained, 'only arises with the development of new forms. A new form of theatre is not possible as long as the stalls and the stage, the actor and the spectator, the author of the play, all the elements of the old theatre still exist, even if this author has written the most Revolutionary play and the most exclusively proletarian public has filled the stalls.'[17]

It was from this point of view that mass festivals seemed an unusually alluring enterprise to the Proletkult leaders. In 1918 Kerzhentsev's book, *Tvorcheskii teatr* (*Creative Theatre*) was issued and by 1928 it had run to a fifth edition. Kerzhentsev thought that Revolutionary theatre must, without fail, unite spectators and actors, turn spectators into actors or, as he expressed it, make room 'for the creative, artistic instinct of the broad masses'. The new theatre did not require either permanent companies or professional actors. The workers themselves would create the productions, unfailingly 'remaining by the machine bench, remaining workers' and 'living in close contact with their class'.[18] And this is why, wrote Kerzhentsev, 'the principle of amateurism must be preserved as completely as possible' and the task consisted of encouraging and cultivating diverse forms of mass festivals in every way possible.

One of Vyacheslav Ivanov's crowning ideas, the idea of a 'life-forming' art capable of transforming both its creators and participants, acting as a cleansing influence on their spirit and, consequently, on the whole human community, permeated Kerzhentsev's book. 'Art,' assured Proletkult's theoreticians, 'should become an exultant labour, and not an entertainment.' They believed that a 'new generation of harmoniously developed individuals' would emerge through the process of mass festivals.[19]

The Bolsheviks took a different, more realistic line. They were not deceived by Proletkult's visionary projections. Of course Lunacharsky acknowledged that 'theatre for the broad masses, the theatre in which the masses participate, is that innovation which the Communist system has put at the forefront.' The Narkom welcomed this 'innovation', but he could not help but see that 'all subtlety', all 'individualism' is lost in the monumental performances carried out in public squares in the open air, and that the spoken word is only of secondary importance in the mass pageants. He therefore could not believe that they would 'completely transfer to this monumental theatre'. On the contrary, he declared: 'We shall not reject the indoor theatre, just as we shall not renounce the printing of books.'[20]

Lenin had the mass festivals in mind when, in conversation with Klara Tsetkin, he said, 'with regard to spectacles, there's no harm in them! I don't object. But it must not be forgotten that the spectacle is not truly great art, but only a pretty entertainment. Our workers and peasants really do deserve something greater than a spectacle.'[21]

The different evaluation of the 'spectacles' by Lenin and Lunacharsky on one side, and by the Proletkult theoreticians on the other, testifies to the serious differences between Bolshevik views and Proletkult conceptions. Lenin and Lunacharsky displayed foresight when taking into consideration all the spiritual wealth, the old and the new, to which the people had a right. The leaders of Proletkult relied on the experience of the mass spectacle as the only practical and experimental basis for their theory. All the rest of their theoretical propositions were abstract.

The Proletkult members felt that class membership as well as the class background of those occupied with creative work completely determined the social orientation of their work. 'The task of building a proletarian culture,' declared Pletnev, 'can only be resolved through the strengths of the proletariat itself,' that is by artists 'who have come from among its ranks.' The participation of the peasant, even of the poor peasant, in the business of cultural construction was considered undesirable. The proletariat alone, without any 'brilliant bourgeois actors' and 'without backward peasants' would create its own new theatre.[22]

Refusing to build on artistic traditions from the past, the Proletkult hastened to sever all threads of continuity linking the new culture with the former, pre-Revolutionary culture.

The Proletkult leaders' hostile attitude toward the artistic legacy of the past was revealed most clearly in the field of theatre. They reasoned in the following way: because, for example, Shakespeare and Molière, Gogol and Ostrovsky, Ibsen and Chekhov had written their plays under conditions of feudal and bourgeois society which the Proletarian Revolution had overthrown, then, accordingly, their works would not only not be needed by the liberated people, but would even be hostile to them. Such a nihilistic attitude to the classics looked dangerous, for the Proletkult was a popular organization and it aspired to complete power in the field of art. The leaders of Proletkult had no desire to give in to the Narkom of Education. They accused Lunacharsky of liberalism, of pandering to the old artistic intelligentsia. They demanded sharp measures: 'Theatrical politics must be imposed forcibly.'[23] According to Kerzhentsev the old, celebrated theatres were a 'pile of chaff' which must be 'dispersed by a gust of Revolutionary wind'. And therefore the only correct course for theatrical politics lay in 'the creation of a new theatre by passing through the stage of destruction of theatre'.[24]

Naturally the question arose as to what should be done with the professional actors, directors and designers. Kerzhentsev grudgingly agreed to a compromise whereby these specialists would teach the amateur workers, helping them initially in the preparation of the mass pageants. But other more radical Proletkult theoreticians regarded this compromise as ruinous since the professionals would undoubtedly taint the purity 'of the proletarian world-view', bringing a 'bourgeois tinge' to the creativity of the proletariat.

A major point remained unclear: from where would it emanate and what would it be like, this 'new', 'purely proletarian art'? The leaders of Proletkult could not give a distinct answer to this question. They hoped that a new form of art would be worked out gradually, through experimental explorations, or would take shape of its own accord.

It must be said that the participants in the great majority of Proletkult theatres and studios did not share these aspirations and regarded these theories with indifference. The companies formally existing under the auspices of Proletkult were not at all averse to the old plays, especially the classics, and readily employed the services of professional actors and directors. Theatrical practice within the Proletkult collectives was eclectic and usually simply imitated the repertoire and theatrical practice of provincial theatres. The advocates of Futurism and those who emulated Mayakovsky and Meyerhold only set the tone in a few Proletkult theatres and studios.

On 1 December 1920 a letter O proletkultakh ('Concerning the Proletkults') from the Central Committee of the Bolshevik Party was published in Pravda which contained an analysis of the situation that had emerged in the Proletkult organizations. It was indicated in the letter that the 'independence' from Soviet power which the leaders of Proletkult sought would not be granted. The letter demanded Proletkult's direct and absolute submission to the Narkompros (the Ministry of Education) and furthermore warned against nihilistic attitudes toward the artistic values of the past. Lenin spoke about this again in a speech to an audience of young

people on 2 October 1920: 'Without the clear understanding that only through a precise knowledge of the culture created by the whole development of mankind, only through its reworking, will it be possible to build a proletarian culture – without such an understanding we shall not be able to solve this problem.'[25] The same idea was formulated in Lenin's draft resolution on proletarian culture: 'not the invention of a new proletarian culture, but the development of better examples, traditions and results of existing culture from a Marxist point of view and conditions of life and the struggle of the proletariat in the epoch of its dictatorship.'[26]

Under the conditions of civil war, the leaders and participants in the many thousands of amateur clubs had neither the time nor the inclination to pursue the invention of new kinds of theatrical art forms. The amateur theatre, which at the front, in the city and in the country indeed united incalculable numbers of actors and spectators, was inspired by one idea: to defend Soviet power, to protect the Revolution. A contemporary wrote: 'These numerous drama clubs, studios, collectives and theatre workers did not have a tenth of the resources of the high theatrical culture, of the technique, craftsmanship or finance which had been at the disposal of the old-timers. But on the other hand they burned with the courage and enthusiasm of youth and of the Revolution.'[27]

During the years of civil war the Red Army's propagandist theatre acquired huge importance. By 1920 approximately 2000 amateur theatres, clubs and studios were in operation in the Red Army's divisions, brigades and regiments as well as in the Navy. They gave their performances in the immediate vicinity of the front line, in the most readily available premises – in stations, schools, colleges and barns, often holed by shells, under kerosene lighting, sometimes even by candlelight or in the open air by the light of campfires. Classical plays occupied an important place in their repertoire.

But in 1919 Vestnik teatra reported that the Red Army masses required 'a repertoire that was heroic, cheerful, bright,'[28] Revolutionary, militant. There were almost no up-to-date plays which corresponded to 'the tasks of the moment'. Thus 'in the Red Army drama clubs, in the heart of the army itself, a new repertoire was born, created by members of the Red Army themselves, genuinely proletariat, familiar and comprehensible to the masses.'[29] In other words, the plays were written by commissars and commanders of the Red Army, its soldiers and members of the drama clubs – inexperienced writers but ones who nonetheless understood very well what the audience expected from them.

During the period of civil war these 'amateur' plays appeared in enormous quantity and were very often performed by the Red Army, workers and agricultural amateur clubs. The performances almost always were either preceded by speeches by Bolshevik propagandists and agitators or concluded with rallies. The plays themselves were deliberately composed as reason and pretext for a rally and were hastily written for propaganda purposes. From this derives the expression 'agit-plays', popular in these years. The agit-plays could not boast of artistic perfection, but substituted a directness of political aim.

Two lines of development in the plays and spectacles of the propagandist theatre are immediately discernible – the down-to-earth and the romantic. The down-to-earth trend, the most widespread, was close in spirit to the poetry of Demyan Bedny, whose simple and intelligible verse enjoyed enormous, genuinely popular success at the time. Bedny's poetry reflected all the most important events of the Civil War and gave them all a Bolshevik evaluation, expressed clearly and sensibly so that even the most dense *muzhik* could understand. Equally unambiguous, clear and naive, yet honest, were the plays and spectacles of the propaganda theatre which presented 'propaganda through facts', showing genre sketches from the life of the people. The plays depicted the hard, forced drudgery of the workers and peasants during the pre-Revolutionary period, and featured familiar types of cruel landowners, factory owners and gendarmes. The reality of the Civil War was recorded in them, the selflessness of the Red Army was celebrated and the cruelty of the Whites was exposed. Of course all these plays and spectacles were characterized by a placard-style simplification in their portrayal of 'heroes' and 'villains'. Nonetheless a willingness to employ the lessons of realistic drama was perceptible in them. The writers of the agit-plays hastened to learn from Ostrovsky and Gorky, without attaining their fullness and colour of life, but seeking to remain within the boundaries of truth, even if only the truth of fact. Among the best realistic agit-plays were *Mariana* by Alexander Serafimovich, already a famous writer of the time, and *The Red Truth* by Alexander Vermishev, a participant in the storming of the Winter Palace and a commissar in the Red Army who died a hero's death in one of the battles of the Civil War.

In both *Mariana* and *The Red Truth* the action takes place in the countryside. Both plays show how the dark, formerly enslaved people break the shackles of social dependence under the influence of Bolshevik ideas. In *The Red Truth* the old, poor peasant Ipat, holder of the St George's Cross, overcomes his terror before the wealthy Polikarpov and becomes an active Revolutionary. In Serafimovich's play the downtrodden peasant Mariana breaks out of her oppressive, patriarchal lifestyle and leaves her husband in the hope of finding Pavel, the Red Army soldier with whom she has fallen in love.

The other line of development within the propagandist theatre inclined toward the allegorical and symbolic use of images and was related to Mayakovsky's poetry. Both Demyan Bedny and Mayakovsky drew on the experience of folklore, although Bedny made no attempt to renew the folklore tradition while Mayakovsky radically transformed and re-thought it. While Bedny primarily followed in the track of events, recounting them, 'as they really were', Mayakovsky hastened to explain 'how it will be', boldly drawing a picture of the future. While Bedny depicted the daily life of the majority of Russian people, Mayakovsky's eye took in the whole planet at once, expressing the ideas of the Revolution, its dream, its romance. The spectacles and plays in the romantic propagandist theatre, just like those of the realistic genre, were inspired by the spirit of poster art. But their employment of its devices created allegorical images of Capital, Freedom, Slavery, the Emancipated Slave, Destruction, and so forth. In one of the typical plays of this type, *The Legend of the Communard* by Kozlov, revolution was portrayed as the procession of oppressed peoples through an arid and lifeless wasteland to a promised land of freedom. The oppressed were led by the Communard, 'the son of the earth, son of the sun, son of wisdom, son of happiness'. The image of the Communard – other-worldly, allegorical – personifies the romantic dream of the hero-liberator.

However naive and simple-minded the agit-plays were, a number of important characteristics emerged in them which were later developed in the more mature Soviet drama of the 1920s.

'In Tune With the Revolution'

While on the fronts of the Civil War and behind the lines the amateur theatrical movement was spreading throughout the entire country, the leaders and actors of the old, professional theatres were clarifying their attitudes to the Revolution, trying to realize its scale, interpret its significance and comprehend what kind of demands the new times would place on them.

For many in the theatre world this had been no easy task, for at first the Revolution had worried some and frightened others. One of the leading actors from the Alexandrinsky Theatre, Yury Yuriev, later wrote, 'At the moment of Revolution the theatre was ill prepared for the rapid progression of events.' The development of these events 'caught the theatre unawares and reduced many of us to a state of utter confusion.'[30] Lev Prozorovsky, actor and director from the Maly Theatre, recalled that when the Bolsheviks gained power some actors 'found themselves utterly confused. . . . They did not know and did not wish to know either the Bolsheviks, or the Bolshevik politicians, the leaders of Soviet power.'[31] Confusion also reigned in the company of the Moscow Art Theatre. 'The truth must be told,' wrote Nemirovich-Danchenko. 'When the Revolution arrived we were frightened. It did not turn out as we had imagined it from our reading of Schiller.'[32]

Meanwhile the new Soviet leadership placed great hopes on the old theatres. 'If there is a theatre from the past which we should at all costs save and preserve, then it is, of course, the MAT,'[33] stated Lenin. He considered it necessary to take some care 'in order that the structural pillars of our culture should not collapse, for the proletariat would never forgive us for that.'[34]

In 1919 the Soviet government conferred the title of 'academic' on the Maly, the former Alexandrinsky, and the Moscow Art Theatres. One relatively new dramatic theatre, the Kamerny, as well as two of the country's most prominent opera theatres – the Bolshoi in Moscow and the Mariinsky in Petrograd – were added to the rank of the academic theatres. The government thereby publicly announced that it was taking the designated theatres under its protection and would make it a priority to render them financial assistance.

There were many other theatres closely allied with the academic ones, particularly the former Korsh Theatre in Moscow as well as provincial companies headed by such highly experienced figures as Nikolai Sinelnikov, Nikolai Sobolshchikov-Samarin, Alexander Kanin, Ivan Rostovtsev and others. These theatres were not officially regarded as 'academic'. The Bolshoi Drama Theatre, founded on the initiative of Gorky and Blok in 1919 in Petrograd, had also not formally been named 'academic'. Nevertheless they were all united with the academic theatres by a common position: firstly, they were orientated in the main toward a classical repertoire, readily staging plays by Shakespeare, Lope de Vega, Schiller, Griboedov, Gogol, Ostrovsky and Gorky; secondly, they attached great significance to professional acting experience and craft. From the point of view of the leaders and actors of the traditional theatres, the art forms which had been shaped long before the Revolution possessed enormous value and their greatest task consisted in ensuring that this value was neither lost nor wasted in order to introduce the proletariat to the spiritual richness which had not previously been available to either workers or peasants.

At first the most experienced actors and directors in the Russian theatre had only a very hazy idea of what kind of plays should now be produced and how they should be performed. They did not know how the 'simple' public now filling the auditoriums would react to their art. A decade later Stanislavsky said with genuine gratitude, 'when the events that were taking place found us, the older generation of the Art Theatre, in a state of some confusion, when we did not understand all that had happened, the government did not force us at all costs to change our colour to red, to become what we were not in actual fact. We gradually came to understand the epoch, gradually began to evolve, and our art, too, evolved with us, naturally and organically. If it had been any different we would have been pushed into performing simple "Revolutionary" hack work. And we wanted to relate to the Revolution in a different way: we wanted to see not only people marching with red banners, but wanted to look into the very depths of the country's Revolutionary soul.'[35]

Many others in the theatre world shared these feelings. On the eve of the Revolution the best dramatic theatres in Russia, the Alexandrinsky, the Maly and the Moscow Art, had been experiencing a protracted and profound crisis. Their contact with daily life had weakened, their repertoire had become dull and pale. They had, as it were, grown old and decrepit. Nemirovich-Danchenko said that in the years just before the Revolution the art of the MAT 'had begun to dry up . . . we were beginning to lose faith in ourselves and in our art . . . we were losing the creative courage without which art cannot advance.'[36]

Following the rapid course of events with mixed feelings of hope and alarm and experiencing difficulty in finding its bearings in circumstances of armed class struggle, a large section of the creative intelligentsia even after the Revolution still could not at first 'advance'. Under these conditions Lunacharsky, holding forth on behalf of the government in speeches and in print, acted 'calmly, cautiously and in a civilized manner' but at the same time firmly, striving not to leave the theatre world with any doubts whatsoever 'as to the power of Soviet authority over the country's artistic life'.[37] The Narkom of Education reminded the art world that the time had come to demonstrate in deeds the love of freedom and democracy on which the Russian theatre had always prided itself.

During the first days after the Revolution it became clear, to the actors' great surprise and delight, that the new audience was not only prepared to watch and listen to the great classical plays but literally craved to see them and responded to them with great rapture. The attraction of the broad masses to the classical repertoire was explained not only by the fact that the beauty and emotional richness of plays by Griboedov, Gogol and Ostrovsky, Shakespeare and Molière, Schiller and Beaumarchais and other great writers were revealed for the first time to audiences who had previously not had the opportunity of going to the theatre. Another factor was important. The repertoire of the classics subjected to uncompromising and incisive criticism the feudal, bourgeois and bureaucratic system, deriding class privileges and inspiring most lively sympathy for the heroes who were capable of defending the rights and dignity of simple people. Therefore, during the years of civil war classical plays were often performed, among them *Fuenteovejuna* and *Dog in the Manger* by Lope de Vega; Shakespeare's *Othello*; *Intrigue and Love* and *Die Räuber* by Schiller; Hugo's *Ruy Blas*; Griboedov's *Woe from Wit*; Gogol's *The Government Inspector*; *The Storm* by Ostrovsky, *The Power of Darkness* by Tolstoy, and many others. Of course all these works were far removed from the real, contemporary life of Russia at the time of civil war. Nonetheless they served, as it were, to unite the distant past with the present day and instilled in the audience feelings and ideas close to and consonant with the Revolutionary struggle.

It was here that the expression 'in tune with the Revolution' originated. Although initially it only referred to the fact that a number of classical plays, through their spirit and the ideas expressed in them, were 'in tune with the Revolution', this expression very quickly acquired another, more active meaning. The theatre world, particularly directors and actors, began consciously to select those classical works which most closely corresponded to what was at the time called the 'current movement'. Moreover, in the productions of the plays themselves, in the directors' staging, in the actors' performances, attempts were made to underline as forcefully as possible the motifs of sympathy for the enslaved people, burning compassion for the oppressed and the rebellious, and hatred and contempt towards tyrants, the oppressors of ordinary people and the enemies of freedom.

Such a stage reading of the classics in the spirit of consonance with the Revolution to a great extent predetermined all the activity of the traditional theatres throughout the years of civil war.

One of the earliest and best productions where this principle was employed to enormous effect was the performance of the drama by Lope de Vega, *Fuenteovejuna*, produced by Konstantin Mardzhanov on 1 May 1919 in Kiev just after the liberation of the city from the Ukrainian nationalist forces of Petlyura by the troops of the Red Army.

Before the Revolution Mardzhanov had worked primarily in Russian theatres, including the Moscow Art. He returned to his native Georgia soon after the Kiev production of *Fuenteovejuna*. It was as if *Fuenteovejuna* foreshadowed the romantic sublimity, passion and brightness of the theatrical work the director subsequently created in Tbilisi. Furthermore, in the Kievan production Mardzhanov expressed with exceptional power the moods governing the spectators – Kievans and Red Army soldiers.

On the stage of one of the best Russian provincial theatres, the former Solovtsov Theatre, the young artist Isaak Rabinovich, working in his typical style, created a colourful set for the play by Lope de Vega. He explained: 'I imagined *Fuenteovejuna* as the clash of two socially hostile forces: on one side the peasants (action set in the village) and on the other the feudal lord, the despot, the tyrant (in the castle). These two opposing forces also determined the nature of the production. The stage was designed to present a bright, sultry, sunny scene of a hamlet: a field of an intense orange colour and sunny towers set in bright green hills, meeting a blue sky above.'[38] The blazing colours of the rural landscape were counterposed to the gloom and dark of the tyrant's castle. The play was performed on an open stage without a curtain. However, the inner chambers of the castle were concealed by a small curtain decorated with heraldic emblems and it was drawn back when the action moved to the rooms of the Comendador.

The contrast in the transitions from the bright landscape drenched in southern sunshine to the austere, cold tone of the ruler's apartments fully echoed Mardzhanov's concept. He succeeded in organizing crowd scenes that were dynamic, seething, stormy. The insurgent peasants were led by the fiery Laurencia (Vera Yureneva). In the pre-Revolutionary period Yureneva had been celebrated as a 'decadent' actress, performing in plays by Przybyszewski, Artsybashev and Andreev. The role of Laurencia forced her, she said, 'to cast aside many of the devices I had previously used for several of my heroines: the broken voice of their fading intonations, the intricate lacework of feelings, fine as a spider's web. . . . And I replaced all this with others: deep notes in my voice, a golden tan on my face and bare feet, health; energetic gestures and strong, honest, clear feelings.'[39]

According to Lope de Vega's text the play concludes with the just King don Fernando forgiving the peasants who have killed the Comendador. This ending, however, did not suit the director, who, in keeping with the principle of consonance with the Revolution, rejected the idea that the insurgent people should depend on a monarch's mercy. Mardzhanov's dénouement was therefore different – a general, triumphant cry in unison from the crowd of rebels: 'There are no more tyrants!'

Later, when Mardzhanov returned to his native Georgia, he abandoned the Russified form of his name and reverted to its Georgian form. Heading the Rustaveli Theatre he – now already Kote Mardzhanishvili – staged a new version of *Fuenteovejuna* with Georgian actors, in which Tamara Chavchavadze played Laurencia.

While Mardzhanov's production of *Fuenteovejuna* was the most vivid, it was by no means the only attempt by a provincial theatre during the Civil War to interpret a classical play in the Revolutionary spirit. Nikolai Sinelnikov, a director who had always sought to establish the principles of realism on the provincial stage and who derived much from the founders of MAT, directed a very strong company in Kharkov. Here he worked with the first-class actors Mikhail Tarkhanov, Viktor Petipa, Stepan Kuznetsov and others. He produced Schiller's *Intrigue and Love*, Beaumarchais' *Le Mariage de Figaro*, Tolstoy's *The Power of Darkness* and Gorky's *Enemies*. Sinelnikov sought to stage all these plays so that the productions were responsive to the Revolution, so that the motifs of rebellion and the love of freedom rang out triumphantly.

The other major theatrical figures in the provinces remained faithful to the same programme: they primarily staged the classics, becoming ever more conscious that 'the words of the old plays', as one actress from Saratov expressed it, 'were acquiring new meaning'.[40] The old established directors treated the classical plays with respect and did not introduce any changes to their text. The younger generation acted more daringly, and, just as Mardzhanov had deleted the king's role at the end of *Fuenteovejuna*, so the finale to one of the productions of Schiller's drama *Intrigue and Love* was also 'simply changed': the scene of 'the reconciliation of the dying son with his evil father' was eliminated entirely in order to replace a 'Christian moral' with a social moral.[41]

The principle of consonance with the Revolution initially determined the entire creative programme of the Bolshoi Dramatic Theatre (BDT) which had been created in Petrograd at the end of 1918 with the active participation of Lunacharsky, Maxim Gorky, and Maria Andreeva, a former MAT actress. Prominent figures from the arts world were concentrated at BDT: the artists Vladimir Shchuko, Mikhail Dobuzhinsky and Alexander Benois; the composers Boris Asafiev and Yury Shaporin. The management of the theatre was headed by the poet Alexander Blok. In Blok's words it had been conceived as a theatre for 'Shakespeare and Goethe, Sophocles and Molière, great tears and great laughter,' that is, a theatre where only classical works would be performed. Blok was categorical on this issue: 'We must base ourselves firmly on the classical repertoire,' because 'we must not bury twenty-five

centuries of art.' With regard to the classics, the poet continued, 'a new inner approach must be found'. In practice the search for these 'new approaches' meant the attempt to achieve consonance with the Revolution in the selection of plays and their stage interpretation. Blok believed that theatre had been called upon to become a 'great school of noble liberty'.[42]

As distinct from such theatres as the former Alexandrinsky, where the Russian classics were primarily produced, Blok directed the collective toward a repertoire of Shakespeare and Schiller.

The Bolshoi Dramatic Theatre opened on 15 February 1919 with Schiller's tragedy *Don Carlos* directed by Andrei Lavrentiev. The tragedy's central tyrannophobic concept was expressed in monumental and majestic form. The stage was framed by a semi-circular stone arch. Bright, quickly changing backdrops contrasted with the dark, sombre tones of the costumes designed by the artist Shchuko. The action developed rapidly with true Schillerian energy.

All three of its best actors – Yuriev, Monakhov and Maximov – had arrived at the BDT with rich, but diverse theatrical experience.

Yury Yuriev, a rather cold actor but possessing an extraordinarily expressive range of gestures and a sonorous and beautiful voice, had appeared previously at the Alexandrinsky Theatre in roles such as Romeo, Uriel Acosta, Karl Moore and Don Juan. Yuriev's personification of romantic nobility as the Marquis Posa in *Don Carlos* brought him acclaim. Lunacharsky wrote, 'in this, according to Schiller's idea, first apostle of the idea of freedom, we, the people of the Revolutionary avant-garde, can in a sense recognize our predecessor. . . . Not for one moment does the audience doubt in the final triumph of Posa's idea, a triumph which Posa himself, of course, could never have foreseen.'[43]

Nikolai Monakhov, who played the part of King Philip, had previously been famous as a highly gifted musical comedy actor, so his participation in the company of the dramatic theatre and his appearance in the tragic role was a complete surprise to the audience, especially when he gave such a powerful performance. 'He gave Philip tightly compressed lips, lowering eyebrows, deeply sunken eyes and an unbending back. He endowed him with the commanding, heavy, thick but also wheezy and creaky voice of old age. He not only brought out the terrible and cruel side of the gout-stricken old man, the despot king, but the unhappy side as well,' wrote the critic Stefan Mokulsky.[44]

Yuriev soon left the BDT and returned to the former Alexandrinsky Theatre, but Monakhov remained in its company until the end of his life.

Before the Revolution Vladimir Maximov had enjoyed success as a film actor and as a performer of neurasthenic roles in salon melodramas. In the role of Don Carlos he, in Lunacharsky's words, came across to audiences as 'very young, attractive and very passionate'.[45]

While *Don Carlos* can be counted among the highest achievements of heroic-romantic art, BDT could not attain other victories of the same scale. Schiller's *Die Räuber*, as staged by Boris Sushkevich, also enjoyed significant success, but this production only developed the motifs of *Don Carlos*. Lavrentiev's Shakespearian productions, however – *Othello* and *King Lear* – did not make much of an impression (*Don Carlos* had 195 performances, *Die Räuber* 93, *Othello* 32, and *King Lear* 18). Part of the reason for this lay with the directors at BDT who, aspiring to strike romantic chords in the productions, 'Schillerized' Shakespeare with all their might.

From the point of view of consonance with the Revolution Schiller, and not Shakespeare, exemplified one of the most suitable writers. The magnetic force of Schiller's plays for the audiences of those years is recorded also in the contemporary fiction: we read about a production of *Die Räuber* at the front in Alexei Tolstoy's novel *Khmuroe utro* (the first volume of the trilogy *The Road to Calvary*); and one of the heroes in Konstantin Fedin's novel *Neobyknovennoe leto* (*The Extraordinary Summer*), the actor Tsvetukhin, stages *Intrigue and Love* in an amateur theatre.

As distinct from the new Bolshoi Dramatic Theatre, the other, old, traditional theatres were slow to take advantage of the possibilities now open to them.

The company of the former Alexandrinsky Theatre (called the State Theatre of Drama from 1917 onwards) was the most conservative and distrustful towards the Revolution and Soviet power. At first the company announced that 'as long as Petrograd remains under Bolshevik power it will not perform.' Lunacharsky exerted much effort in assuring the Alexandrinsky actors that no one would infringe upon their artistic freedom and tried to persuade them to call off their boycott and resume their performances. 'Some of the company soon felt all the grandiose significance of the events which had taken place'[46] and gradually the actors came to understand that it would be appropriate to heed the Narkom's advice. After a ten-day boycott daily performances were resumed, and on 3 February 1918 it gave its first free performance, *The Government Inspector*, for the Red Guard and the workers of Petrograd. Lunacharsky made an introductory speech before the performance and the newspaper *Petrogradskoe ekho* (*The Petrograd Echo*) reported that 'Performances such as the one given on Saturday at the Alexandrinsky Theatre are exhilarating, like a festival of rebirth. . . . The Alexandrinsky Theatre is not hostile or alien to the masses. It was joyously radiant this evening.'[47]

Contact with the audience was established and from this day Gogol's *The Government Inspector* ran very frequently. Many productions which had been staged before the Revolution were systematically presented. In addition to the rich Russian repertoire the Alexandrinsky Theatre could also offer Shakespeare's *The Merchant of Venice* and Molière's *Don Juan*.

In 1918 new productions of Griboedov's *Woe From Wit*, Ostrovsky's *The Forest*, Gogol's *Marriage*, Molière's *Le Médecin malgre lui*, Schiller's *William Tell*, and Beaumarchais' *Le Mariage de Figaro* were staged. *Le Mariage de Figaro* and *William Tell* enjoyed the greatest success (the première of *William Tell* coincided with the first anniversary of the Revolution on 7 November 1918). It is understandable that these two plays proved particularly in tune with the mood of the Revolutionary audience.

Less successful were attempts by the Alexandrinsky Theatre to stage Gorky's plays. Under the tsar it had been generally forbidden to produce Gorky's plays on the Imperial stage. After the February Revolution (1917) the former Alexandrinsky Theatre had performed *The Philistines* once, then after the October Revolution the production was revived but only shown six times in two seasons. The actors could not express Gorky's sharp social criticism. The play came across as a family drama with the conflict between 'fathers and sons' in the forefront. In 1919 the première of *The Lower Depths* took place, yet even although 'all the theatre's old guard'[48] took part and the celebrated character actor Kondrat Yakovliev (he was called 'Kondrat-Simplicity' because of his amazingly natural and lucid acting) appeared in the role of Luka, the company as a whole was not equal to the occasion. Nevertheless this readiness on the part of the actors of yesterday's Imperial stage to perform plays by 'the stormy petrel of revolution', in itself indicated that the theatre was changing course.

At the Maly Theatre in Moscow during the first months after the October Revolution, the prevailing conviction was that no matter what events occurred in the country, the actors had one task: to preserve their high art intact and in its pure form. Only a few of the company's leading figures (in particular, Osip Pravdin) called for co-operation with the Bolsheviks. Immediately after the Revolution the highly experienced actor Alexander Yuzhin took up the position of defending celebrated traditions from 'politics'. He had always appeared to great acclaim in heroic roles of the romatic type and from 1918 was virtually the sole leader of the Maly Theatre. Very quickly, however, he realized that the traditions would only survive in a revitalized form, that theatre develops 'along with the life around it, at its tempo, and is its involuntary and inevitable reflection.'[49] Yuzhin consciously led the Maly Theatre to meet the demands of the popular audience. If the Maly Theatre had previously regarded the director with scepticism, placing their trust in the power of the actors, Yuzhin now admitted Stanislavsky's former comrade-in-arms, the experienced director Alexander Sanin, to cross the threshold of the 'home of Ostrovsky'. In the Maly Theatre greater concern than previously now began to be shown for the ensemble and for the design of productions.

The great strength of the art of the Maly Theatre lay in its old productions of the classics, in which the leading lights of the Russian stage continued to play: Olga Sadovskaya, Maria Ermolova, Elena Leshkovskaya, Alexander Yuzhin. The classics dominated the repertoire: in the 1917–18 season classical plays comprised sixty-nine percent of all performances and in the 1918–19 season up to ninety-eight percent. Plays which enjoyed the greatest success included many by Ostrovsky and comedies by Turgenev, Molière, Lope de Vega and Beaumarchais. When reviving earlier productions, the Maly Theatre introduced a number of new touches as dictated by the times. Notable in this sense was their very first production after the October Revolution (on 21 November 1917), *Woe from Wit*, in which Yuzhin played the role of Famusov. Yuzhin's Famusov was distinguished from its predecessors by a particularly strong emphasis on his great, far-sighted intellect and his lust for power. His Famusov was a prominent dignitary with a strong-willed, hard, arrogant personality – one of those people who quite consciously had created the whole former 'quality of Russian life'. 'On the foundation of such intellects,' maintained Yuzhin, 'the old Russia rose up and prospered.' They 'created their world', they 'struggled for its power' and deliberately 'suppressed free thought'. Yuzhin's new interpretation of the role was motivated by the necessity of providing, 'in its full stature', 'the most solid and truthful figure of the past'[50] exposing not only the humorous but also the terrible traits in the comic character.

However, the Maly Theatre did not limit its activities to old or newly revived productions. Striving to respond somehow to the Revolution even if only in a historical production, Sanin staged Alexei Tolstoy's historical tragedy *The Governor*, with a set designed by Anatoly Arapov, for the first anniversary of the Revolution. The play was dedicated to the defence of free Novgorod from an enemy army in the thirteenth century.

Previously, as critics justly remarked, the Maly Theatre had been somewhat afraid 'of the onslaught of the innovator-director'. In this case, however, Sanin was granted great freedom and 'introduced into Tolstoy's play crowd scenes the likes of which the Maly Theatre had never before been able to achieve.' The seething, surging Novgorod crowd swamped the stage to such an extent that 'at moments the audience forgot about the main characters.' But if the two large-scale and spirited mass scenes were unquestionable achievements for Sanin, an experienced organizer of crowd scenes, then the main roles, performed by Yuzhin and Sadovsky, depended less on the director – and not because 'these actors were too distinguished for an ensemble theatre'[51] as the *Izvestia* critic believed, but simply because in the Maly Theatre the authority of the director had not yet been extended to the leading actors. Nonetheless the production possessed definite stylistic coherence: both the director and the actors had been animated by a common idea.

Like the Alexandrinsky Theatre, the Maly Theatre made an attempt to turn to Gorky, but it did not start with his popular plays, *The Philistines* or *The Lower Depths*, but with *The Old Man* which had never been performed before at all and the complexity of whose structure defeated the understanding of both the director Ivan Platon and the actors.

The actors of the Maly Theatre felt much more confident when they started work on Lunacharsky's historical melodrama *Oliver Cromwell*. This play lay close to the romantic tradition that had always lived in the art of the Maly Theatre and which was so vividly embodied by Yuzhin in his performances.

Lunacharsky's drama reconstructs the events surrounding the English bourgeois revolution of the seventeenth century. The conflict within the play is constructed not only on the decisive clash between the revolutionary leader Cromwell and King Charles I, but also on the complex and conflicting relations between the leader and the people. While admiring Cromwell's love of freedom, courage and heroism, the writer at the same time implies that the rebel leader is distant from the people and in no position to rely on the support of the destitute, simple labourers.

The production, devoted to events from the remote past of English history, was angled towards the Russian present and celebrated the insurgent people as a decisive force in history. The strong will and vivid temperament of 'the iron man' Cromwell (Yuzhin) was revealed through the contrasting comparison with the weak spirit of King Charles I, played by Prov Sadovsky as wallowing in idleness.

The Moscow Art Theatre, always expressing the views and frame of mind of the progressive Russian intelligentsia, had reason to be proud of the deep humanism and psychological subtlety of the directorial and acting art which had grown on the basis of the dramas written by Chekhov and Gorky. But the problem of Revolutionary violence, which it was inconceivable to ignore during the Civil War, troubled and disturbed the artists of MAT. 'In 1917, after the interruption in our theatrical life brought about by political events,' wrote Olga Knipper-Chekhova, 'the first play which we performed was *Three Sisters*. Everyone had the feeling that previously we had played it thoughtlessly, without conveying the significance of its ideas and feelings and most of all of its dreams. And indeed the whole play began to resound differently, to reveal that these were not simply dreams, but some kind of foreboding and that "a mighty event had descended on all of us, a fierce storm had blown from our society the laziness, the indifference to work, the rotten

tedium" . . . although of course it was not of such a storm that Chekhov's fine soul had dreamed.'[52]

The 'interruption' which Knipper-Chekhova recalled lasted less than one month. Performances did not run from 27 October to 21 November (by the old calendar). As soon as performances were resumed the auditorium filled to capacity and it became clear that just as before the plays of Griboedov, Ostrovsky, Turgenev, Chekhov and Gorky aroused lively interest among the public. The new audience, in Stanislavsky's words, 'did not come to the theatre in passing, but with trembling and anticipation of something important, not seen before.'[53] On 20 February 1919 at a general meeting of the MAT company Stanislavsky uttered the significant statement, 'I see the salvation of the theatre and its revival in what life itself gives us.'[54]

However, at this time MAT selected what for it was a difficult direction in its search for a repertoire: from the motifs which were natural and close to it as the company of Chekhov and Gorky, it moved towards works of a quite different style, to the romantic tragedy *Cain* by Byron, to *Prometheus* by Aeschylus and the Symbolist drama *The Rose and the Cross* by Blok. The company did not succeed with these plays, which demanded open pathos and loftiness of tone and style. Stanislavsky himself had said 'we are not able to play this but we must try.'[55] The attempts dragged on for a long time and with depressing results. *The Rose and the Cross* never even opened, although it had been rehearsed for several years.

A severe blow, a 'catastrophe' in Stanislavsky's definition, hit the Art Theatre in the summer of 1919 when a group of actors, headed by Kachalov and Knipper-Chekhova, while on tour in Kharkov, was cut off from Moscow by the advance of Denikin's troops and then, after a long period of travel in Southern Russia, ended up abroad, whence the group was able to rejoin the collective only in 1922.

In the years when every season at the Maly and the former Alexandrinsky Theatres was marked by new, although not always successful, productions, the Art Theatre presented only old ones. It seemed that MAT had lapsed into silence, that it had nothing to say. It was only in April 1920 that MAT presented its first new post-Revolutionary production – Byron's *Cain*. Byron's interpretation of the biblical legend of Cain and Abel appealed to the theatre because it could enable them to respond to contemporary events and express the militantly atheistic spirit of the Revolution in theatrical form. But the task of encapsulating the monumental tragedy written in verse proved insurmountably complex for a company raised on the drama of Chekhov and Gorky. 'The MAT system, in its form at that time, diminished the tragic image. . . . The art of the MAT actors hardly touched Byron's poetry and was brought to a halt in bewilderment before its complexity.'[56] This time the theatre itself recognized defeat: *Cain* was only performed eight times. The Byron mystery play progressed at a sluggish pace and against the musical background of orchestra, organ and chorus, it breathed a solemn grief and icy grandeur. Meanwhile everyone understood that the triumphant ending of the Civil War was not far off, news conveyed from the front was reassuring, and the auditorium was least of all inclined toward Byronic grief.

The Government Inspector, as revived by Stanislavsky in 1921 in a new directorial version, proved more comprehensible to the audience. As compared with the Art Theatre's old 1908 production of the play, this one had noticeably changed. Now the MAT was not interested in naturalistic details of the provincial life of Gogol's characters, in the slovenly provincial offices and that dirty little room in the inn where Khlestakov, lolling about on the sagging divan, squashed bedbugs on the wall with his foot. The new set by the painter Konstantin Yuon transformed the place of action, making the Mayor's rooms cheerfully colourful. The action progressed more quickly and with greater liveliness. Several changes which Stanislavsky made were very sharply satirical, such as the scene of the Mayor's ceremonial dressing when Dobchinsky and Bobchinsky crawled around his feet on their knees fastening the spurs to his boots. In the finale of *The Government Inspector* Stanislavsky employed a consciously theatrical device: the Mayor's words 'What are you laughing at? You are laughing at yourselves!' were delivered by Ivan Moskvin with his foot placed on the prompting box and directly addressing the audience, while at this moment all the lights in the auditorium were turned on full.

The production was dominated by Khlestakov, played by an actor from the First MAT Studio, Mikhail Chekhov. His performance stunned with its unbelievable improvised ease and unrestrained imagination. Chekhov's Khlestakov now dived underneath the table three times in search of money, now skipped across the stage like a young goat, now lusting for the Mayor's wife, gnawed the leg of a chair, now mocking Khlopov, moved a burning candle about right under his nose. Countless mischievous, eccentric pranks followed one after another, forming themselves into the dodging, confused line of behaviour of the unprepossessing, snub-nosed official from Petersburg, the silliest, emptiest man, gripped by a great flight of imagination.

Mikhail Chekhov as Khlestakov in Gogol's *The Government Inspector*, directed by Stanislavsky at the Moscow Art Theatre in 1921.

Despite the success of *The Government Inspector*, the Art theatre for a relatively long time remained in a state of creative apathy. In 1922 Yury Sobolev, a critic close and loyal to MAT wrote: 'A Revolution occurred in Russia, it swept by in blizzards and storms, shattering and headlong, but the Art Theatre remained just as it was under the pressure of the threatening waves. It gave very few signs of its participation in Revolutionary contemporaneity. Too quickly it has become a sort of museum, a monument to past culture, carefully preserved and protected.'[57]

Many thought this. It was difficult to anticipate the changes in the art and life of the Art Theatre that would soon occur. All the same, these changes were approaching. To a significant degree they had been foreshadowed by the explorations conducted in the four young studios of the Art Theatre, especially in the Third Studio of Evgeny Vakhtangov and the First Studio headed by Mikhail Chekhov. If the principal MAT company carried twenty years' experience of artistic life on its shoulders after all, the artistic youth gathered in the Studios were much more receptive to innovation. Stanislavsky's young students quickly sought to test his 'system' in new theatrical forms and most of all to link art with the life which had been transformed.

The Studio students not only began to appear more frequently in the old MAT productions but, more importantly, the Studio was now presenting its productions on the principal stage of the Art Theatre, on Kamergersky Lane. *The Cricket on the Hearth* by Dickens and *The Flood* by Berger (productions of the First Studio) were publicized on posters side by side with *The Government Inspector* or *The Hamlet of Stepanchikovo*. However the Studios, while coming closer to the MAT company, did not actually link up with it but developed as independent collectives, exploring their own direction in art.

Vakhtangov

The most outstanding and brilliant director from the MAT studios was Evgeny Vakhtangov. As early as 1911 Vakhtangov, who had begun his theatrical career in the provinces, became one of the devoted and consistent advocates of Stanislavsky's 'system'. When the First Studio opened Vakhtangov entered as an actor and director, and together with Sulerzhitsky he maintained the ideals of the good and the humane, remained close to the Tolstoyan world view and followed the path of maximum rapprochement between theatrical truth and truthfulness to life.

One would think that the abstract humanitarian world view of the First Studio, the closeness and intimacy of its 'sincere realism' would inevitably have hampered Vakhtangov's acceptance of the Revolution. However, the opposite occurred; he accepted the October Revolution quickly and without reservation.

In April 1919 in an article entitled 'C khudozhnika sprositsya' ('The Demands on the Artist') Vakhtangov wrote passionately and persuasively: 'The red line of Revolution divided the world into the "old" and the "new". . . . If the artist wants to create the "new", to create after the Revolution has arrived, then he must create "together" with the people. Neither for them, nor on their behalf, not apart from them, but together with them. In order to create the new and to obtain victory, the artist needs the firm ground of Anteus. The people – they are this ground. . . . And of what people do we speak? All of us are the people. We speak of the people who are the creators of the Revolution.'[58]

Theatre During the First Years of Revolution

Reflecting on the nature of an art directly addressed to the people, Vakhtangov searched intensely for new theatrical forms which would exert a more clearly pronounced and active influence on the audience. Romain Rolland's book *Le Théâtre du Peuple* made a great impression on him. Furthermore, during these years he tried also to apply Meyerhold's experience which, in Vakhtangov's words, 'provided the roots for the theatre of the future'. Vakhtangov's 'new programme' was in practice expressed through his aspiration to give art sharper outlines without falsifying its 'truthfulness to the life of the human spirit' or breaking from Stanislavsky. From this derives Vakhtangov's particular interest in the grotesque, the comic and the tragic. From this also derives his readiness to transform and apply in his own way theatrical forms which had been tested by Meyerhold. And finally, from this derives Vakhtangov's own particular system of imagery which took shape in his work after the Revolution. Every Vakhtangov production of this period embodied an important principle.

Strindberg's *Eric XIV* became the turning point in the work of the First MAT Studio. The disturbing and dark tragedy came to take the place of the compassionate intonation of *The Flood* by Berger and the calm lyricism of *The Cricket on the Hearth* by Dickens. In Vakhtangov's directorial work the theme of the doom of an autocratic power resounded. The royal palace appeared deathly, shifted to the edge of an abyss, ready to collapse. The artist Ignaty Nivinsky clearly understood Vakhtangov's idea. In his set patches of royal gold were weakly and impotently washed over the walls alongside the great areas of rust which were corroding the palace. The columns were leaning and bent. Against the black backdrop angular streaks of lethal lightning flickered ominously. A labyrinth of passages and short flights of stairs and landings in the displaced perspective of the broken playing area all created an impression 'of something mid-way between palace and prison (a prison for Eric)'. Nikolai Zograf, in his study of Vakhtangov's work, has written that the director created 'a new theatrical world far removed from the realistic verisimilitude of depiction', a world 'of the anti-everyday'.[59] The inhabitants of this death-like world, the courtiers, ghost-like apparitions with white, lifeless, mendacious faces twisted by flattery, envy, greed and thirst for power, silently glided round Eric, the madman on the throne.

Mikhail Chekhov played Eric as a man who has heard the firm, inevitable tread of fate, who knows that his demise is inescapable, and this is why he seems indifferent to everything, apathetic, as if transfixed in his cumbersome silver attire, then suddenly driven into furious activity by terror, the impotence of rage. The tragic was conveyed in the spare, graphically incisive and outwardly cold figure. Abnormally dilating eyes, dropping intonation and the nervous movement of his thin hands betrayed suffering and anguish. At the moment when Eric threw the magnificent royal mantle from his shoulders with one short, quick movement, his boyish thinness, his frailty immediately became apparent. Eric personified weakness itself, impotence itself.

Vakhtangov further intensified this feeling in the static, protracted staging that contrasted the fragile figure of the king with the sullen, threatening crowd of common people. The people, wearing dark, greyish-green and brown cloaks and wide-brimmed hats invaded the inner sanctum of the palace. They could not help Eric and did not want to help him, for in their eyes he was the embodiment of the hated power. The social theme of the conflict between the people and the courtiers was presented extremely sharply and, increasing in intensity, was propelled by means of repeated shocks with the characteristic Expressionist intonation first sensed by Vakhtangov as early as the war years in Berger's *The Flood*. On the side of authority, apart from the weak Eric, appeared the strong, majestic and embittered Dowager Queen – one of Serafima Birman's first significant performances – and the red-bearded courtier Göran, resourceful, shrewd, cynical and ruthless, played by Boris Sushkevich.

Markov wrote, 'it is impossible to separate [this production] from Moscow of the period, from destroyed buildings, red flags, street posters, Red Army detachments on the march, searchlights stabbing the night sky above the Kremlin, solitary automobiles cutting through the streets and rumours flying from flat to flat.'[60]

Each of Vakhtangov's last productions possessed this pointed relevance to the contemporary.

In January 1922 Vakhtangov directed the play *Hadibuk* by An-sky (S. A. Rappoport) in the Jewish 'Habima' Theatre which at that time was headed by the actor Naum Tsemakh. As in *Eric XIV* this production demonstrated purely Expressionistic means of theatrical projection, which in this case were derived from the naive material of a sentimental melodrama, shot through with compassion for the wretched, hopeless life of the inhabitants of a Jewish settlement. The work on this play presented Vakhtangov with great difficulties for several reasons. First, the inexperienced actors of the 'Habima' rehearsed in Hebrew, which he did not know; second, in the studio a strong Zionist mood prevailed, which was both incomprehensible and alien to him; and third, the melodrama required submersion in a way of life unknown to him, that of a Jewish settlement.

Nonetheless Vakhtangov surmounted all these obstacles with surprising ease. With the help of the artist Natan Altman he created a stifling, gloomy and barren little world on the studio's tiny stage. Alexander Kugel wrote that there was no sun, no fresh air and no life in the production. 'There is something oppressive, as if the lid of a coffin constantly presses down on you. There isn't a single character from whom the joy of laughter would reach you, on which a shaken spirit could rest. Fate, terrifying and implacable, moves throughout the whole play, you endlessly hear its iron step, hear its breathing.'[61]

However, through this gloominess, through this fatal oppression, the theme of protesting love, doomed yet thirsting for life and happiness, broke out again and again in powerful shocks with a repetitiveness typical of Expressionist structure, articulated in the ecstasy of the dance, the nervous angularity of gesture and the flickering candle flames.

Khana Rovina played the heroine, the poor bride Leah. Her deathly pale, waxen face and her white silk dress stood out clearly against the red and green background of Altman's scenery and the black background of the long gabardines worn by the Hasidim who crowded round the lovers. Another actress, Mira Elias, played the part of the hero, the poor bridegroom Khanan. The force of passion in the scenes between Leah and Khanan, of the sensual attraction the lovers felt for each other, insistently, hopelessly and nonetheless unyieldingly resisted the orthodox religiosity of the Hasidim and the prim stupidity of the settlement's petit-bourgeois womenfolk.

Three motifs set in a complex counterpoint of alternating group scenes created an intense and disturbing atmosphere. A group of women wearing bright, gaudy dresses, heavily made-up, over-dressed, haughty and stiff, periodically emerged at the back of the stage. These women stood motionless, like mannequins, and gazed at the lovers with unconcealed contempt. The Hasidim, in their long, black gabardines, were, on the contrary, fussy, animated, and in their threatening dynamics could be felt a sense of community, achieved by means of a very simple, yet strong directorial device: all the movements of the Hasidim were synchronized, yet they each moved their arms individually. One bent his arm at the elbows and held out his open palms, another spread his arms out to the side, a third raised his hands over his head. 'This play of hands,' remarked Zograf, 'forms the basis of the image of the Hasidim.'[62] The third group was the most turbulent and frenzied: a grotesque crowd of beggars who danced at the wedding. Vakhtangov transformed the crowd of beggars into a crowd of monsters and freaks: hunchbacks, the blind, lame and cross-eyed. The critic Georgy Kryzhitsky wrote that in *Hadibuk* all these 'beggars, the blind and deformed, with their writhing arms and crippled torsos, consumptive and crazy hunchbacks, straight out of an engraving by Goya, these terrifyingly grey clumps of contorted bodies, this swarming mass of half-beasts resembling delirious, nightmarish apparitions, were moved about and grouped by Vakhtangov with endless diversity, imparting a monstrous, sinister awfulness to their grimaces.'[63]

In a leaflet published immediately after the director's death, the critic Nikolai Volkov wrote that in the beggars' dance in *Hadibuk* Vakhtangov revealed 'how cruel his talent was, how close to his soul lay the beauty of ugliness'. This observation was, however, rash and was refuted very simply in *Hadibuk* in the beggars' dance itself. Into the round-dance of chimeras there entered, 'like a white ray', the luminous, slight, delicate Leah, who also started to dance. Her appearance attests to another, rather truer, characteristic of Vakhtangov's, whom the same Volkov called 'a master of contrasts', 'a first-class painter of chiaroscuro on stage'.[64] In his ability to play with contrasts of light and shadow, the dynamic and the static, tragedy and comedy, Vakhtangov was truly inimitable.

In the Third Studio of the Moscow Art Theatre which he himself had created, Vakhtangov worked even more intensely than he had in either the First Studio or the 'Habima'. In 1920 the Third Studio acquired premises in Berg's private residence at 26 Arbat (where the Vakhtangov Theatre is now located). The small hall, with a seating capacity of three hundred, opened its doors to the public for the first time on 13 November 1921 with a performance of *The Miracle of Saint Anthony* by Maurice Maeterlinck. The Studio students had already performed Vakhtangov's production of this play earlier, in 1918, and now the director created a second version of it, introducing changes which completely transformed it.

An atmosphere of meekness and all-forgiving love dominated the first version of the production. In the play the saint, who has appeared in the world in order to perform a miracle, is taken for a madman or rogue and sent to prison. In 1918 Vakhtangov brought to the fore the servant Virginie, a simple woman, the only person to believe in Anthony's saintliness. At that time Vakhtangov pitied rather than condemned smug citizens who were unable to recognize the homeless tramp as a saint: they are blind and thus deserve sympathy. The warmth of tenderness and kind-hearted humour showed through in the 'emotional realism' of the production.

In 1921 Vakhtangov rewrote this entire tableau with the angry pen of a satirist. 'Now,' he wrote, 'the theatrical means which we use in *Anthony* to brand the bourgeois have coincided with the demands of life, the demands of contemporaneity.'[65] Dull, insolent and greedy monsters crowded around Anthony whom the Studio student Yury Zavadsky played as an inspired ascetic, a sage with a high forehead, with long white hair thrown back, a lucid wanderer cloaked in coarse rags belted by a rope. To embody the little world of the French bourgeois,' wrote the critic Nikolai Volkov, 'Vakhtangov did not resort to the static, as he had done with Eric's courtiers, but to the dynamic. The inwardly dead Gustave, Achille, their wives, aunts, the doctor, priest and guests were given a highly animated outward appearance. Intensifying Maeterlinck's irony, pushing it to satire, Vakhtangov loosened the actors' movements, caricatured their faces, emphasized the senselessness and inertia of the actions.'[66]

The same denunciatory motifs appeared again in Chekhov's *The Wedding* which in 1921 was also performed in a second version, renewed by the director. Audiences perceived *The Wedding* as a disgusting Devil's reel of coarse provincials and petit-bourgeois who were raging round an insulted and oppressed old man, the 'nuptial general' Revunov-Karaulov.

Both *The Miracle of Saint Anthony* and *The Wedding* were shown to the directorate of MAT. Stanislavsky and Nemirovich-Danchenko thought highly of both of these Vakhtangov productions and proposed that the Studio students perform them on the principal stage of the Art Theatre.

No one, however, could have foreseen that several months after the opening of the Third Studio a genuine theatrical miracle would take place on its Arbat stage in the form of the première of a production, the name of which would be recorded for all time in the chronicles of the Russian theatre. Such a miracle occurred on the day of the première of *Princess Turandot*, by Carlo Gozzi, on 28 February 1922.

Gozzi's naive and undemanding fairy tale provided Vakhtangov with an occasion for the creation of a unique work, the fundamental and overall theme of which was the joy of creativity. The principle of composition was pre-determined by the rule dictated by Vakhtangov at the outset: the actors do not simply perform Gozzi's fairy tale, they show how they perform it. During the performance each participant was constantly supposed to 'get into character' and then 'get out of character' again, to conduct complex, capricious and merry play with the character, simultaneously demonstrating the technique of transformation, the joy of metamorphosis and the ability to look at one's hero with irony 'from the side', that is to express 'an attitude to the character'. According to Vakhtangov's concept, which was fully realized in the show, irony did not undermine but, on the contrary, made the authentic truthfulness of feeling more prominent, emphasized and intensified it, restoring its original freshness to the old and touching fairy tale.

Nivinsky built an empty platform for *Princess Turandot* which tilted toward the back. On the left side a large oval opening, either a window or a door, was visible and to the right stood a wall with a wide, square embrasure. As a whole the grey-coloured construction seemed like a laconic sketch for a hastily delineated space intended for performance and ready for any transformation. The production began with a drawn curtain, when four maskers from the Italian Commedia dell'Arte appeared on the forestage – Tartaglia, Pantalone, Brighella and Truffaldino. They announced the title of the performance. Then the entire troupe from the Studio filled the proscenium. Actors wearing tails and starched white shirts and actresses in *décolleté* evening dresses arranged themselves along the footlights. The curtain rose and before the audience's eyes the actors

Poster for the second performance of Gozzi's *Princess Turandot*, directed by Vakhtangov in the Third Studio of the Moscow Art Theatre in 1922.

The major difficulty lay in the Vakhtangov production plan which required first, the strict and precise observance of the form set once and for all by the director (that is the intonational and sculptural shape of the role, the rhythm and tempo of movement) in combination with complete improvisational freedom and apparent ease of play; second, the instantaneous shift from comic or ironic intonation to genuine lyricism and sincere feeling; third, a natural simplicity of interaction not only among the characters themselves, but between the performers and public.

'All these situations in which Vakhtangov placed the actors,' wrote Ruben Simonov, 'sharpened the theatrical tasks, made the characters' simplest actions expressive.'[67] Furthermore, as Markov justly observed, 'it was not only "playing at theatre" that was embodied in the spectacle but "the celebration of the victor". Within it shone "the smile cast at mastered material".'[68]

The concept of 'festive theatricality' is indissolubly linked with *Princess Turandot*. It signifies that the spectacle is conceived and executed as a celebration demonstrating the joy of theatrical play itself and capable of conveying this joy to the audience.

It was as if the festive beauty of the merry spectacle refuted the everyday reality of Moscow life in the early 1920s, still cold, dark and half-starved. The production delighted Stanislavsky, Nemirovich-Danchenko, Kachalov, and Lunacharsky, who all expressed their opinions in writing[69] since Vakhtangov himself had not been able to attend the première. With only weeks to live, on this evening he was bedridden in his room on Denezhny Lane, only five minutes walk from the theatre which was already out of his reach. He had been given morphine injections to alleviate his agonizing pain. During the intervals excited messengers gleefully ran to him from the Studio and reported the triumphant success of the first performance of *Princess Turandot*.

Vakhtangov's production outlived its creator by many decades. It clocked up more than one thousand performances, then in 1971 was revived and to this day is preserved in the theatre's repertoire.

The Transformation of Melodrama

Not long before the October Revolution, the leader of the Kamerny Theatre, Alexander Tairov, stated in 'Deklaratsii khudozhnika' ('An Artist's Declarations') that there should not be any kind of special 'art for the people'. 'Surely art is not a train with sleeping cars for the 'clean' public and goods vans for the ordinary people?' he exclaimed. 'No, art is unified and has its own worth, art is for everyone in whose soul lies a conscious, or unrealized, thirst for beauty.' He was roused to indignation by the very idea that 'it is necessary somehow to reduce, to adapt art for the people.'[70]

Tairov had no desire to adopt a simplified form of theatre as in the practice of the Proletkult, nor was he capable of doing so. Equally unacceptable to him was the entire system of bright, placard allegories manipulated by Mayakovsky and Meyerhold and followed by the organizers of the multitudinous 'mass pageants'.

Tairov sincerely wanted to create 'genuinely Revolutionary theatre'. 'But,' he said, 'not the placard Revolutionary' and not the 'propagandist Revolutionary!'[71] Still insisting on the 'theatricalization of theatre', he was convinced that only 'self-sufficient mastery' held significance. He repeated, 'the cult of this mastery and the striving for it as the goal itself form the basis of our inner work.'[72]

spontaneously changed their clothes, naturally, lightly tossing coloured pieces of fabric to each other in time with the music and draping themselves in an off-hand manner. When they had completed their costume change the stage was transformed to 'China' with the aid of the same coloured fabric drapes which, in two strokes, 'dressed' the set. The 'zanni', the stage attendants, spread out a bright sheet revealing the large inscription 'Peking'. However, in the midst of 'Peking' stood the most ordinary bentwood chair. This kind of juxtaposition of fantasy with the commonplace permeated the entire score of the spectacle – its props, its staging, its text. Prince Calaf wound round his head a turban made from a towel; instead of a beard Khan Timur tied on a scarf; the musicians, like children in a Moscow courtyard, played on combs with cigarette papers and the maskers mocked the latecomers among the audience.

Tsetsilia Mansurova played Princess Turandot; Osip Basov, her father, the Emperor Altoum; Yury Zavadsky, Prince Calaf; and Anna Orochko played the Princess Adelma. Boris Shchukin as Tartaglia and Ruben Simonov as Truffaldino were the most notable of the maskers. The spectacle's complex score required refined and agile virtuosity of the young Studio students and displayed their potential to great effect.

But all the same, while cultivating mastery, the leader of the Kamerny Theatre was obliged to win over the auditorium quickly. Virtuosity had no point before an empty theatre. The company could not wait for the time when the public would be ready to enjoy 'self-sufficient mastery'. 'Tomorrow' meant almost the same as 'never'. And the question of what direction to take today remained frighteningly open.

As often happens, the solution came about by chance. For it is inconceivable to assume that Tairov was guided by some kind of far-sighted, strategically formulated plans when he undertook the melodrama *Adrienne Lecouvreur* by Eugène Scribe and Ernest Legouvé. The sentimental play, which Eleonora Duse had already introduced to the Russian public in 1908, attracted him as a 'box-office' piece since it promised fair takings, although it did not seem to be either topical or consistent with his programme. The production was arranged hurriedly while he was touring in Smolensk in 1918. The actor Boris Ferdinandov made a fairly simple set with screens, and the costumes were hired from the wardrobe of a local theatre. Major, important productions are prepared differently. When *Adrienne* was performed for the first time and its success immediately surpassed all conceivable expectations, it suddenly became obvious that a 'box-office' play can have great scope. Tairov avidly scrutinized the faces of the spectators and listened attentively to the unrestrained, incessant thunder of applause. At this moment in Smolensk the Kamerny Theatre awoke, came to life as if reborn.

Once back in Moscow Tairov again – this time fervently and in earnest – set to work on *Adrienne Lecouvreur*. He worked furiously and painstakingly. It opened on 25 November 1919 and proved to be one of the most crucial events in the history of the Kamerny Theatre.

In the kaleidoscope of theatrical exploration in the post-Revolutionary years, outwardly this show appeared distressingly traditional. The production did not conform with Tairov's reputation as the innovator, as 'the furthest left' of directors. There were neither surprises nor extremisms in it. It was only possible to discern 'a kind of Cubist Rococo' in Ferdinandov's set if there was a great desire to do so. The critic Abram Efros had such a desire, and he even wrote about a kind of 'abstracted materiality'. But he was annoyed, for Ferdinandov 'gave the set too great a flourish and lightness', 'mixed up his Louis' and 'slid into the atmosphere of another style'.[73]

Meanwhile the capricious delicacy of Rococo corresponded not only to the real biography of the actress Lecouvreur but to Tairov's aims as well. It was important for him to create an atmosphere of vicissitude, of the ephemeral, of the instability of all values, both material and moral, of gold and love. Furthermore, historicity in Tairov's production really was a very relative concept. Style had been observed without pedantry. Which Louis, this one or that one, was of no importance. Tairov consciously sought to inform the action with a subtle, barely perceptible, faded scent of history, a hundred times filtered through the theatrical sieve.

In so far as the play counterposed artistry to aristocracy and the power of art challenged the mightiness of the court and the palace, to that extent in Tairov's production 'sense of place' and 'sense of costume', long familiar to the stage, appeared both as an echo of history (approximate) and, simultaneously, as an attribute of theatrical play (irrefutably exact). Mischievously and in its accustomed manner, theatre played with history. History, reflected in the mirror of Tairov's stage, lost the precision of stylistic outlines and the concreteness of details. Ignoring the requirements of authenticity, Tairov presented the audience with a monarchy in general, an aristocracy in general, and indeed the past in general. This entire system of casual references revolved around the main role, around Adrienne, setting off her independence from everything historically concrete, and, therefore, from the transient, the more or less conventional. The main role was presented as if above the palace intrigue. The Scribe-Legouvé melodrama unerringly relied on the audience's sympathy for the unfortunate Adrienne, but neither Tairov nor Koonen, who was playing the leading role, were content with sympathy. Their Adrienne did not evoke pity. And Ferdinandov's construction had been intended not for a salon melodrama, but for a tragic play.

Ferdinandov erected a semi-circular acting surface in the centre of the stage high above the main stage floor. Three wide steps led up to the top of it. Two additional semi-circular inclined acting planes (of a slightly smaller size) were attached to the main surface along the left and right. At the back, up-stage, glided mobile screens, tarnished gold, faded blue and greyish-black. The actors' poses and gestures stood out clearly against this monochromatic, lightly stained background. The affectation of the movements, the ladies' aspen-like waists, the cavaliers' ceremonial bows, the tawdry splendour of the clothing, the quivering of fans, the fantastical multi-colours of the wigs, the narrow slippers with shining buckles, the bird-like chirping, suddenly ceasing then suddenly starting up again, everything indicated that in the immediate proximity of the throne, the centre of capricious and dangerous power, there was careless play with fire taking place. Tairov's Rococo had no opulence about it, just pure affectation. In the staging that lightly parodied court etiquette, in the puppet-like prettiness, porcelain coldness and disturbing rhythm, there was presentiment of the tragedy towards which Koonen was leading Adrienne.

In this play Tairov was interested in the possibility of poeticizing artistry, of declaring the particular rights of talent. He staged not the clash of the honest plebeian with the dishonest nobility (and by no means did Koonen play the plebeian; there was not a single plebeian note in her monologues) but the unequal struggle of solitary talent against the united mediocrity of power. And it is here that the 'tragic pathos, inspired by the spirit of Corneille and Racine,'[74] was highly appropriate, since Lecouvreur in the course of the play declaimed Corneille, Racine and La Fontaine. The concern was not so much the demise of a person, struggling for a place under the sun, as the demise of a great talent, by its very nature incapable of adapting either to prevailing manners or to any kind of common standard whatsoever.

During this period all director-innovators – everyone except Tairov that is – considered that to democratize art meant compelling it to use a language comprehensible to all, bringing it close to the popular spectacle, to the forms of the fairground and the circus. This explains the unjustifiedly great hopes which Gorky and Lunacharsky then placed on melodrama, on its easily accessible 'colourfulness' and on its characteristic play of the sharp contrasts between heroism and villainy. Tairov however dealt with melodrama in his own way. His method was not one of adaptation, but of complication. He concentrated on refinement rather than popularity, tragedy rather than melodrama, as if having sensed (it was a genuine revelation which also later struck the poet Boris

Pasternak) that simplicity 'is most necessary to people, but the complex is more comprehensible to them'.

In line with this presupposition that the complex is more comprehensible, he selected the most refined means of expression. The image of Adrienne was not placed at the intersection of Scribe's crude co-ordinates of truth and deceit, love and hatred. Koonen's Adrienne, pensive and calm at the beginning of the performance, knew in advance that she would not see happiness. Passionately in love, she did not believe in the possibility of an idyll. Furthermore, her love did not require reciprocation. Count Maurice of Saxony, a handsome man, a military leader, the hero, played by Nikolai Tseretelli, was needed by Adrienne not as an ardent lover, but only as inspiration, as a more or less accidental 'object' which had imparted a living impulse, a contemporary sense to the monologues of Corneille and Racine. His presence, and equally his absence, his loyalty, and equally his disloyalty, all became a pretext for the tragic performance, taken far beyond the limitations of the Scribe love triangle.

Koonen, playing an actress, and hence playing an actress acting, demonstrated the agonized but happy split of personality: the split between the effeminacy of the century of powdered wigs and the austere force of great talent that is cramped in the salons and boudoirs; the split between her own female nature fired by love and her tragic essence, recognizing not love but passion. The entire role was built on such overspill from the noble naturalness of feeling to the tragic excesses of passion. Instantaneously shooting upwards from Adrienne's lyrical tenderness to the thunderous roar of Chimène, Phèdre or Hermione, Koonen's voice vibrated and surged with power.

Pavel Markov wrote that in Koonen's Adrienne 'there was a kind of astonished bewilderment at life. She distanced herself from love and at the same time obediently and submissively went to meet it. She waited for it and summoned it from somewhere deep inside herself . . . she lived in a bewitched world.'[75] This astonished bewilderment and bewitchment rose out of the split between her earthly love for the count and the immortal strength of the poetry inspired by this love, the split between the woman who did no more than live and suffer and the actress who created the miracle of art from her life.

It is known that Scribe and Legouvé wrote their play for Rachel, and it is known that in Rachel's performance the final scene was the strongest – the death of Lecouvreur conveyed with chilling details, right up to the hiccups and spasms in the final throes of death. This final scene was also Koonen's most powerful, but she had no need for such details. 'The classical verse, with its regular rhythm,' asserted Leonid Grossman, 'brings shapeliness and proportion to the stormy finale.'[76]

The triumph of *Adrienne Lecouvreur* confirmed Tairov's conviction that the course begun by the Kamerny Theatre in the pre-Revolutionary years could be successfully continued, that he had been right to move forward without betraying himself. Immediately after *Adrienne* Tairov decided to stage Racine's *Phèdre*. His programme of the 'theatricalization of theatre' was bringing him closer to the traditional, as if to prove that Lunacharsky had not been mistaken when he placed the Kamerny Theatre in the category of 'academic' theatres.

But in Tairov's hands this very 'academism' acquired features of astonishing originality.

Sergei Radlov's 'Popular Comedy'

The young director Sergei Radlov, who in 1920 created a little theatre in Petrograd under the name of 'Popular Comedy', believed that a genuine contemporary theatrical art form could be achieved only in one way – by means of 'the actor's verbal improvisation'. This would transform each performer into an independent creator, into the author of a text spontaneously delivered and modified in each performance. 'Here, and only here,' assured Radlov, 'can the living life of the future national theatre take refuge. . . . leaving behind the reconstruction of the style of various past epochs, the irritating pettiness of realism in the portrayal of the present, we shall aspire to sense, to feel and to forge the style of our epoch.'[77]

Radlov's great hopes for actors' improvisation apparently arose as early as the years from 1913 to 1916 when he was studying in Meyerhold's Studio on Borodinskaya, where the methods of the Commedia dell'Arte were being cultivated. Meyerhold encouraged silent improvisation in gestures and even presented excerpts from *Hamlet* in mime. His student, Radlov, transferred the emphasis to verbal, textual improvisation. After Meyerhold left Petrograd to settle in Moscow, Radlov became the most noticeable innovator on the Petrograd theatrical scene and immediately steered towards a type of comedy where the actor would be entirely free to chatter 'in his own words', that is, towards a crude, clowning comedy.

It is impossible to deviate from the 'fixed text' in melodrama, drama or least of all tragedy without running the risk of confusing and destroying the whole storyline. In serious genres too much depends on the construction of the dialogue as set in advance. In farce or buffoonery, however, fairly free manipulation of speech is possible, as the actors of the Commedia dell'Arte proved in their day. Radlov thus decided from the very beginning that the range of genre in his theatre would be narrow and exclusively comic. He himself usually composed and directed the half-comedies, half-scenarios which encouraged actors' improvisation. He proposed a chain of amusing situations to the actors, precisely designating the essential action, but only roughly indicating what kind of dialogue was desired and what kind of tirades and banter were possible.

Every member of the cast was allowed, and in fact obliged, to say everything that came to mind. The main criterion for success lay in the audience response: the more often and the more loudly they burst out laughing, the better. Topical jokes about current events, remarks unexpectedly directed at the audience and informal, familiar banter with spectators were encouraged.

Radlov remained entirely consistent in his antipathy to 'drama with a fixed text'. He would say ironically that it is 'a very peculiar variety of theatre, "a verbal ballet", so to speak, where the actor is bound to every given word, as the ballet dancer is to gesture.' The obligation to deliver 'someone else's' words rather than his own completely atrophies the actor's initiative, transforming an independent artist into an obedient and passive performer, practically a marionette, controlled by the writer's will. Radlov therefore declared that it was necessary 'to destroy that pernicious being, the armchair literary man who writes words for the theatre in the tranquillity of his flat.'[78]

Radlov's mandate on verbal improvisation immediately drew him closer to compèring and clowning, to those devices which had already been legitimized in the art of the circus. He made no mistake on this score and immediately invited professional circus artistes into his troupe – clowns, acrobats and jugglers. It was the first time this had happened in Russia, but Meyerhold and Eisenstein were later to follow suit. Radlov had jugglers and conjurers working for him as well as the clown Georges Delvari and the aerial gymnast and acrobat Serge who had previously been well known to visitors to Ciniselli's Petrograd circus. Radlov highly valued the 'divine ease and perfection of Serge's acrobatic technique and the irresistible comicality of Georges Delvari, who directed the crowd's laughter as the conductor does an orchestra.'[79] Radlov also invited the compère, Konstantin Gibshman, who had previously worked with Meyerhold in the little theatre, The House of Interludes; Stepan Nefedov, a singer of satirical ballads containing topical allusions; and several other performers from the area of light entertainment. There were also dramatic actors in the company but they formed a minority and usually appeared in secondary roles.

The performances of the 'Popular Comedy' took place in the so-called 'Iron Hall' of a large club situated in a section of Petrograd where primarily workers and minor officials lived. The hall had been named 'iron' because the metal construction work in the interior had been left dauntingly exposed and the floor had been covered with grey asphalt. The director liked the overall appearance of the space, ascetic and even rather dismal, as the hall's bare outlines contrasted well with the loud, bright colours of the actors' costumes. The most ordinary, undemanding public gathered in the hall – workers, who brought their wives and children; soldiers and sailors; caretakers; postmen; and stallholders from the neighbouring market. 'The intelligentsia is alien to our theatre,' wrote Radlov. 'I feel that a gulf is being created between myself and the intelligentsia.' He felt proud of this 'gulf', for he was quite consciously ccreating a 'barbaric'[80] theatre orientated round the primitive taste of its unsophisticated and naive audience.

The artist Valentina Khodasevich built a permanent stage in the Iron Hall. It was a shallow, open platform with a proscenium brought out in front and a light, three-level constructional rigging divided into nine cage-like boxes. Six of these had their own curtain which enabled the director to move the performance from one box to another and to conduct action in several cages at once. There were neither footlights, borders or wings. But on the other hand the sets were painted boldly and brightly and the costumes were visually pleasing with their many cheerful colours.

Design for the stage of Sergei Radlov's 'Popular Comedy' Theatre.

The actor/circus-performer was always the centre of attention, 'tirelessly demonstrating jumps, tumbling, somersaults, juggling with fire, conjuring tricks, verbal wittiness, musical clowning and other wonders banned from the serious theatre.'[81]

Plays by Radlov himself were staged one after another on these platforms: *The Dead Man's Bride*, *The Monkey-Informer*, *The Banker's Second Daughter*, *The Sultan and the Devil*, *The Foster Child*, *The Bear and the Sentinel*, *Love and Gold* and others. At first the dependence of Radlov's 'circus comedies' on Meyerhold's variations of themes from the Commedia dell'Arte was striking, then Radlov began experimenting in the spirit of the detective thriller with the chases, investigators and other devices canonical to the genre. In his *The Foster Child* the gymnast Serge, playing the role of a thief who had stolen a certain document and escaping from his pursuers, jumped into and over barrels, clambered up a rope beneath the ceiling of the Iron Hall, then swinging from the rope flew above the audience's heads. The performances became progressively more dynamic, the circus stunts progressively more sensational. Fairly soon, however, two things became apparent. First, all these merry little sketches were far removed from both politics and contemporary life. Their attitude to 'the current movement' could have been characterized as peaceful neutrality, and their 'consonance with the Revolution' as a kind of formality. Secondly, the performances of the 'Popular Comedy' highly resembled circus divertissements broken down into separate 'numbers'. Yury Annenkov wrote that 'the circus artiste came onto the stage with prepared stunts, each served on a special platter with the usual circus flavour.' And 'there was no electricity between Delvari and Gibshman [the circus clown and the music-hall compère] – they met and separated, cold, unnecessary to each other and strangers to one another.'[82]

The Radlov 'theatre-circus' was still more circus than theatre, and the 'numbers' related to each other not so much through theme and action as through verbal compèring.

The critic Adrian Piotrovsky wrote that Radlov's formally inventive 'Popular Comedy' 'does not satisfy through its content – now is not the time for playing silly games' and that the verbal attacks against the Entente did not disturb anyone. Calling upon Radlov to engage in 'political satire', Piotrovsky advised him 'to leave the Entente in peace' and 'address the internal affairs of the country'.[83]

Radlov only tried to do this once, when Gorky wrote a script for him, *The Hardworking Slovotekov*. The idea of actors' improvisation had attracted Gorky for a long time, and in this play he provided Radlov with a good foundation for a witty, satirical improvisation with topical allusions. At the centre of the Gorky lampoon was the new style of bureaucrat, a chatterbox who when in a state of panic was afraid to take any kind of concrete decisions and always avoided the slightest personal responsibility, pleading the need to 'co-ordinate', 'organize' or 'discuss collectively'. Whatever problem had been addressed to him, whatever the matter, whether it was a burst water-pipe, the lack of soap, or even how to crush a louse, Slovotekov at once began to utter endless, empty tirades about co-ordination, organization and collectivism. Finally, the ceiling collapsed above him, large chunks of plaster fell down on his head, dirty water poured from the newly formed hole in the ceiling and Slovotekov – undoubtedly the precursor of Pobedonosikov in Mayakovsky's *The Bath-house* – carried on talking and talking throughout.

Theatre During the First Years of Revolution

Radlov directed this piece with enthusiasm. Slovotekov was played by one of his best performers, the clown Georges Delvari. But the inertia of feckless slapstick, which the Radlov actors had already adapted themselves to, carried them away from satire to farce. Valentina Khodasevich recalled that Delvari's improvisations were 'crude and vulgar' and that Gorky had been disappointed by the production. 'Rarely have I seen him so sullen.'[84]

After this failure Radlov changed direction and began to stage classical plays 'with a fixed text'. He produced Shakespeare's *The Merry Wives of Windsor*; *La Jalousie du Barbouillé, Le Médecin Volant, Monsieur de Pourceaugnac* by Molière; *The Village Judge* by Calderón; Gogol's *The Gamblers* and *Le Voyage de Monsieur Perrichon* by Labiche. Now he declared that 'in order for comedy to be popular, it must turn to the popular theatre of past centuries.'[85] Changes occurred in the company: the dramatic actors drove the circus performers into second place and the circus artistes abandoned Radlov one by one in order to return to Ciniselli's circus ring.

In 1922 Lunacharsky observed sadly that 'the theatre of buffoonery directed by Radlov which started out so well seems to be folding in its multi-coloured wings.'[86] In the spring of 1922 the 'Popular Comedy', having first lost its actors then its audiences, indeed closed.

However, the idea of the 'circusization' of theatre had not died. In the same year, 1922, it was revived in Moscow in productions by Meyerhold and Eisenstein and in Petrograd in the productions of FEKS ('Factory of the Eccentric Actor').

'Theatrical October'

In the autumn of 1920 Lunacharsky appointed Meyerhold head of the Theatrical Department (TEO) of the People's Commissariat of Education. Meyerhold then took full control over the premises of the former Zon Theatre on Sadovo-Triumfalnaya Square (now called Mayakovsky Square) in Moscow and created a theatre company, composed chiefly of young actors, which he named the RSFSR (Russian Socialist Federal Soviet Republic) Theatre No. 1.

Both of these actions produced important consequences.

Meyerhold's appointment to the authoritative post of leader of TEO immediately strengthened the position of those artists – and not only theatrical figures, but painters, poets and musicians as well – who had been regarded as revolutionaries in art before the October Revolution and who, after it, had declared without hesitation their readiness to place art at the service of the liberated people. They called themselves 'the left', distinguishing themselves from artists of the traditional mould whom they labelled 'the right'. By implication 'leftists' were 'revolutionaries' and 'rightists' were 'reactionaries'. This demarcation was drawn particularly sharply within the theatre. From the 'left' point of view, to which the Proletkult leaders also adhered, all traditional theatres and particularly the academic theatres (popularly known as 'aky') represented the bastion of aesthetic reaction and conservatism.

The 'leftists' were essentially guided by a very simple criterion: whatever is new is good. Everything old, everything which existed before the Revolution, all the plays, traditions, methods and skills of the craft, must, in their opinion, be discarded and destroyed, and the sooner the better. If the theatrical traditions of the Maly, Alexandrinsky or Moscow Art Theatres had been formed in tsarist Russia then it followed that once having thrown off the yoke of

tsarist oppression it was necessary also to throw off the yoke of these traditions as quickly as possible. It was assumed that art which had previously 'served' the ruling classes contained nothing other than an ideology hostile to the proletariat.

The 'leftists' found themselves in the public eye immediately after the October Revolution. The programme 'Theatrical October', advanced by the 'leftists' as its name suggests, presupposed that theatrical 'revolution' should directly follow the social revolution, that the old art must be destroyed without delay and a new art created on its ruins. Since the tsarist government had fallen, argued the 'leftists', then all the old theatres, in their opinion thoroughly 'feudal' and 'bourgeois', should also fall. It seemed to the 'leftists' that the worker-peasant government was wrong in protecting these theatres hostile to the proletariat.

The name 'Theatrical October' appealed to Meyerhold very much. So much so, in fact, that he was inclined to interpret the abbreviation TEO in two ways – as *teatralnyi otdel* (Theatre Department) and *Teatralnyi Oktyabr* ('Theatrical October').

The newspaper *Vestnik teatra*, inspired and virtually edited by Meyerhold, became the herald of 'Theatrical October'. Until Meyerhold's appointment to TEO, *Vestnik teatra* had been content to report general information about the latest events in the theatrical world. After his accession, its articles immediately took on a tone of unprecedented sharpness, even aggressiveness: the term 'civil war in the theatre' was used, and time and again the expression 'theatrical front' appeared. The newspaper alleged that the old theatres, the 'aky', were quite simply 'nests of reaction', shelters for both overt and covert enemies of the Revolution, and maintained that the Revolution would not tolerate the existence of such 'nests' for long.

The slogans of 'Theatrical October' declared war on the apolitical character of the old stage art and demanded the most swift and thorough-going renovation of the theatre from top to bottom. The 'leftists' wanted the stage to become a platform for Revolutionary ideas right there and then and to celebrate the victory of the proletariat.

But the conviction of the 'leftists' that old, traditional forms of art are alien to a Revolutionary people pushed them to unjustified extremes. While it was easy to proclaim 'Theatrical October' in words, in reality it proved immeasurably more difficult to oppose the art of the old theatres with new forms of theatrical art, especially since these new forms still existed more in theory than in practice. The attempts of the 'leftists' to find a common language with the new audiences were by no means always successful.

It is understandable that the leaders of the old, traditional theatres were seriously alarmed when their art was declared 'dead' or 'unnecessary' in newspaper articles or in public debates. The threatening expression 'theatrical front' essentially placed such experienced figures of the theatre world as Stanislavsky or Yuzhin, Yuriev or Nemirovich-Danchenko on nearly the same footing as the generals of the White Guard whom the Reds were fighting at the real fronts.

Under these conditions much depended on the position of the Commissar of Education, Lunacharsky. In 1920 Lunacharsky had declared that 'in the field of theatre the policy of the Soviet leadership' has two main tasks. The first of these – 'the revolutionary-creative formation of new theatre' – suited the 'leftists'. But they did not like the second; the Narkom insisted on 'the preservation of the best theatres of the past, which unconditionally deserve the state's concern as custodians of artistic traditions.'[87]

The 'leftists' could say – and they said, and they wrote – that theatres such as the former Alexandrinsky and the former Mariinsky, the Maly and the Moscow Art, belonged entirely to the past, were unnecessary and even hostile to the Revolution, that all those 'bastions of reactionary values' must be 'destroyed'. They were not, however, permitted either to 'destroy' or to close a single one of these 'feudal' or 'thoroughly bourgeois' theatres.

Even Meyerhold's power as head of TEO did not extend to the academic theatres, since they remained 'under the direct authority of the People's Commissar of Education', that is, they were subject not to Meyerhold but to Lunacharsky. Furthermore, in order to enable the representatives of the 'aky' to defend themselves publicly, the journal *Kultura teatra (Theatre Culture)* was created in which *Vestnik teatra* was calmly, weightily and convincingly refuted.

Meyerhold proved to be a bold but poor administrator. Sometimes he sanctioned actions which were to say the least unreasonable, such as the seizure of the Nezlobin Theatre building by members of the Red Army amateur company. He rashly ordered all theatre tickets to be exchanged for special tokens that were supposed to be distributed to audiences through factories and military units. The system of tokens was so complicated that not one theatre adopted it. Further, he planned to create an entire system of 'RSFSR Theatres', progressive and with a Revolutionary repertoire.

His own theatre would be called RSFSR No. 1; the former Nezlobin Theatre – RSFSR No. 2; the former Korsh Theatre – RSFSR No. 3. All these theatres would stage plays recommended by TEO. Various theatres obeyed and, for example, Nizhnii Novgorod named its theatre RSFSR No. 4, just as Meyerhold required. However, the change of name altered neither the repertoire nor the nature of productions.

Gradually Meyerhold came to understand that it was far easier to proclaim 'Theatrical October' than to implement it. The Proletkult idea of the 'invention' of hitherto unprecedented forms of art did not gain Meyerhold's sympathy for the simple reason that he, as a practising director, sensed no reality behind it. The more philosophical the Proletkult theoreticians became, the further their imaginations departed from reality. Meyerhold brushed them aside in disappointment. He could not inhabit the realm of clever, verbal constructs; he wanted to direct productions.

The agit-plays popular during the Civil War years could not satisfy this director, nor could they suggest to him any direct route to new art forms. While fully sharing the militant political zeal of the agit-plays, he was faced with the problem of creating new means of theatrical expression, aesthetic forms which could contain and express the spirit of Revolution.

Such an attempt was made in the production of *The Dawn* at the RSFSR Theatre No. 1. This theatre, according to Meyerhold's plan, was to stage plays of two extreme genres: 'Revolutionary tragedy and Revolutionary buffoonery.'

Vakhtangov had also dreamed of producing Verhaeren's *The Dawn*. The Belgian poet's Symbolist play contained much that was, in the parlance of the time, 'in tune' with the ideas of the Revolution. War was transformed into a people's uprising, and there was the particularly relevant motif of the fraternization of soldiers and people on both warring sides and their union in a revolutionary struggle against their rulers and military commanders.

The premises of the Zon Theatre on Sadovo-Triumphalnaya Square, which Meyerhold acquired, were cold and derelict. 'The stage area is stripped,' wrote Viktor Shklovsky. 'The theatre resembles an overcoat with its collar ripped out. It is neither cheerful nor light.'[88] But Meyerhold did not in fact want it to be cheerful or light, nor did he intend to impart to the space the usual comfort or the festive air of a theatre interior. The spectacle, conceived in the style of a political rally, fitted naturally into a hall which was neither comfortable nor in the least bit ceremonial. 'The doors to this theatre knew no ticket-collectors,' recounted Meyerhold's associate, Boris Alpers. 'The railings had been torn from the boxes. The seats and benches for the audience had been poorly constructed and ruined the regularity of the rows. You could crack nuts and smoke shag in the corridors. . . . Everyone felt like the master in this theatre. The Revolutionary atmosphere of the streets had broken into the theatre.'[89] There were female busts and male torsos on the walls – the remains of vulgar, hastily decorated sculptures, relics of the half theatre and half café-*chantant* which had been here previously. The curtain, however, was very striking: a red circle against a black background, with a yellow area cut into the circle bearing the inscription 'RSFSR'.

Meyerhold threw the old scenery of the Zon Theatre into a shed, stripped the stage and exposed the building's brick walls. He destroyed the footlights. The stage was joined to the auditorium by boards. The walls of the corridors were covered with posters, slogans and cartoons.

The hope of finding a common language with the mass of Red Army soldiers and workers who filled the theatre prompted Meyerhold at that time to be bold in subordinating the literary basis of the production to the demands of 'the present experience'. 'If,' Meyerhold declared to his company, 'up to 1917 we treated the literary work with a certain caution and care, then today we are no longer fetishists, we do not kneel and call out in prayer "Shakespeare! Verhaeren! . . ." Now we are no longer protecting the interests of the author, but of the audience.'[90]

Meyerhold and his co-director Valery Bebutov therefore introduced into Verhaeren's text numerous alterations prompted by 'the current moment'. They brought the play nearer to the situation of the Civil War. Their characters spoke of 'the power of the Soviets' although Verhaeren, of course, had not had this in mind. Verhaeren's hymn of the imaginary 'Great City' was replaced by the 'International'.

The première of *The Dawn* took place on 7 November 1920, three years after the October Revolution. The form of the production clearly recalled the shape of the Revolutionary rally which had emerged in real life during those years. The actors appeared without make-up, without wigs and were, in essence, orators at a political meeting. Their very manner of speech, their gestures and even their 'hoarse voices, as if they had caught a cold', provoked sarcasm among seasoned theatre-goers; everything was 'just like at a mass meeting'. At times two orators addressed the public at once. The lights in the auditorium were not turned off during the performances but the beams of two military searchlights, placed in the boxes, were directed straight on the actor/orators' faces.

Actors seated among the public were to react to the action on stage and thus draw the audience into direct interaction with the heroes. They would applaud one speaker then interrupt another's speeches with booing and hissing.

'The actors,' reported an eye-witness, 'not only perform in the area where the footlights used to be, but descend on a wide staircase to the space which the orchestra previously occupied. A crowd speaking the author's lines is hidden below in a corner of the orchestra pit, creating the impression that these mass responses are coming from the audience, to whom the heroes of Verhaeren's tragedy turn at such moments. This inflames, it excites. . . . The solemn and awesome sounds of a funeral march are heard over the coffin of the slain leader. I saw Red Army men in the audience instinctively take off their hats. You can feel the beating of a common pulse, a common rhythm. And when, over the coffin, the workers smash the pillar of power of the old world with hammer-blows, the entire audience and the actors join together to the sounds of the "International" in a vow to build a new world.'[91]

Outwardly the performance-meeting was decked out quite extravagantly. A student of Petrov-Vodkin, the young artist Vladimir Dmitriev, erected silver-grey cubes, cylinders, prisms and triangles on a bare stage against a background of two plywood circles, one red and one gold. The scenery was made from iron, wood, rope and wire. A shiny piece of tin-plate resembling the shape of a piano lid hung above the geometric forms.

Dmitriev's design somewhat puzzled the audience. Lunacharsky wrote that the workers, who were 'embarrassed and nearly sweating from awareness of their lack of culture, pointing at one or another detail in the sets', asked him, 'what does it all mean?'[92]

Verhaeren's text was equally bewildering. Mayakovsky noted with irritation, 'the actors spoke about some kind of chimera for two hours, but this chimera did not take part in the action.'[93]

Contradictions, particularly noticeable in the performance of the leading roles, permeated the entire structure of the production. The actors' passionate and sometimes howling declamations did not relate to the austere, grim military bearing of the show. The ascetic stage design of The Dawn breathed readiness for battle. Meyerhold arranged his silvery-grey extras in strict semi-circles or in straight lines frontally deployed. They framed the performance-meeting, solemnly and silently viewing its development. Their movements were accompanied by a barely perceptible but yet distinct rustling of the red flags. Taut lines of rope trembled as if ruling off the stage from bottom to top, from the stage floor to the flies. However, the rather cold, militarized statuesqueness of the production disturbed to some degree a rally-like style of interaction between stage and auditorium.

The desired contact with the audience did not always happen. Sometimes, for example, the applause which Meyerhold predicted would interrupt Hèrènien's speech three times did not occur. The audience remained silent, without supporting the clapping of the 'chorus' from the orchestra pit and those actors specially seated among the audience.

The production had a very mixed reception.

From N. K. Krupskaya's point of view, Meyerhold's experiment was decidedly unsuccessful. 'Someone,' she wrote, 'conceived of adapting The Dawn to Russian conditions at the wrong moment. . . . To cast the Russian proletariat in the role of a Shakespearian crowd which any conceited idiot could lead wherever he pleases – this is an insult.'[94] The politically imprecise portrayal of the Revolution incensed Krupskaya. And she was not alone in her annoyance with Meyerhold's production. Tairov said that The Dawn was 'a vulgar popular print'. Ferdinandov called the production 'a concentration camp for actors'.

Arguments about The Dawn did not disturb Meyerhold or his co-director on the production, Bebutov. Both readily and aggressively responded to their opponents, even such authoritative ones as Lunacharsky and Krupskaya. Bebutov's reply to Krupskaya contained a comprehensive explanation of the basis for almost all the ideas behind the production of The Dawn and promised, instead of a return to Verhaeren, 'to embark on a path of even more radical alterations'. Mayakovsky argued with Lunacharsky, Osip Brik with the public, Samuel Margolin with Brik, Alexander Mgebrov with Margolin. It had been expected that the performance-meeting would have this kind of follow-up in discussion and debate.

But at one of the discussions Lunacharsky suddenly placed the very idea of a performance-meeting in doubt. 'In all probability,' he said, 'there are few people in Russia who attend mass meetings as frequently as I do, and I am regarded as an expert and master in this field. . . . And I will say: the mass meeting has become so tedious that there is no need to drag it on to the stage!' Tairov readily supported Lunacharsky on this point. 'It is high time to say,' he quipped, 'that propagandist theatre after the Revolution is like mustard after dinner.' Here the chairman interrupted Tairov and said that his time had run out. An argument ensued as to whether or not the speaker's time should be extended. The nature of the discussion is revealed in the minutes taken by a confused stenographer: 'Unbelievable shouting . . . terrible shouting . . . so much noise and uproar that you can't tell what is being said, everyone is hollering, almost coming to blows. . . .'[95]

Although the theatrical passions did not abate, it soon became clear that Lunacharsky was correct. All the same there was much about the production that Lunacharsky liked. 'If you ask whether this production is a success or a failure, I would say that it is a success. . . . This is indeed a real, genuine step forward.'[96]

Mayakovsky resolutely declared that theatre had embarked 'on the exclusively correct path', that the staging of The Dawn heralded 'the first Revolutionary trend in theatre'.[97] According to Pavel Markov, The Dawn was The Seagull of Meyerhold's theatre.

During the performance of The Dawn on 18 November 1920 the news of the taking of Perekop was announced. The telegram about the victory over Wrangel was delivered to Meyerhold who at once decided to read it from the stage, to substitute it for the Herald's line announcing victory over the foe.

'It is difficult to describe,' recalled an eye-witness, 'what occurred in the theatre when this historic telegram was read out. Such an explosion of shouts, exclamations, applause, such a universal, delighted, I would say, frenzied roar has never been heard within the walls of a theatre.'[98]

From this time onward the ROSTA (Russian Telegraph Agency) communiqués were no longer posted in the corridors but were each time read out from the stage.

The success of the news insertions into the text of The Dawn during the performance appealed to Meyerhold so much that he even planned a production of Hamlet in which the gravediggers' scene would be a contemporary political review. He wanted Illarion Pevtsov as Hamlet and Georgy Yakulov as the designer. Mayakovsky was to re-write the gravediggers' scene in order to give it political relevance. However, Marina Tsvetaeva, who had initially wanted to retranslate the tragedy's verse text, later categorically refused to take part in this work. Evidently Meyerhold's activities at this time were not at all to her liking.

Meanwhile Mayakovsky brought Meyerhold a new version of *Mystery-Bouffe*, which opened at the RSFSR Theatre No. 1 on 1 May 1921. The success was so great that *Mystery-Bouffe* was then performed every day until the close of the season on 7 July.

In this production Meyerhold rejected the front curtain, along with Futurist and Cubist design principles and the whole idea of scenery altogether as a background to the actors' performance.

The scenery was replaced with a system of staircases and gangways devised by the sculptor Anton Lavinsky and the painter Vladimir Khrakovsky. It surrounded a relatively small hemisphere, the upper half of a globe, on which was inscribed 'Earth'. 'Earth' lay to the bottom right, near the audience's feet. The stage was united with the auditorium.

'The principle of the box stage was broken,' recalled the actress Maria Sukhanova, who performed in the production. 'The action was carried out into the auditorium, for which purpose several rows of seats had been removed from the stalls. In front, in the foreground, a globe or rather a section of a globe had been constructed. The wings had all been cleared away. "Paradise" was stacked on top of a construction beneath the ceiling at the very back of the stage. Those of us in "Paradise" (I was an angel) stood, with our arms raised, and with every movement our white wings, made of thin wire covered with gauze, quivered behind us. The devils were allotted a place near the base of the globe. The objects and machines were located in the boxes of the stalls. "The Man of the Future" appeared in the right-hand-side of the stage (as seen from the auditorium) at the very top near the ceiling on a platform specially built for this purpose.'[99]

The action spilled into both stalls and boxes while on the stage itself it was enacted on several 'levels'.

The large wooden structure which occupied the stage resembled the deck of a ship, with its gangways and stairs. An Eskimo was seated on top of the globe inscribed 'Earth', plugging the hole with his finger, saving the world from the flood. When it was necessary to show 'Hell', the 'Earth' rotated and merry devils jumped out of a trap door cut out of it 'like a hunk of bread'. Meyerhold had specially invited the circus performer, satirical clown and acrobat Vitaly Lazarenko, who slid down a rope from the flies onto the stage dressed as a devil, to take the most active part in the general devilry.

At this point the interaction between actors and public achieved maximum freedom and easiness. The experiments from the Studio on Borodinskaya were at last producing results. What they had previously been attempting – enthusiastically, but uncertainly and through guesswork – suddenly became coherent and not just possible, but essential.

Later Meyerhold was to say, 'Mayakovsky knew what theatre is. He had a command over the theatre.' Memoirists who recount how Meyerhold reshaped plays by other dramatists are unanimous about his careful treatment of Mayakovsky's texts, his thorough execution of all the – sometimes almost impossible – stage directions given by the poet. This seems odd when you re-read *Mystery-Bouffe* and realize that while some scenes are barely outlined, others are precisely and fully delineated, some parts are written while others are only conceived but not written, and some are not really parts at all but opportunely placed outcries, and so forth.

Meyerhold believed that Mayakovsky 'was brilliant in the field of composition . . .'.[100] He particularly admired the poet's characteristic principle of multi-episodic dramatic construction, which extends as far back as the Shakespearian theatre. In structuring the play as a

Sketch by V. Kiselev of the Menshevik's costume in the 1921 production of Mayakovsky's *Mystery-Bouffe*.

series of individual episodes, Mayakovsky in no way strove for continuity of development. On the contrary, by presenting separate 'numbers' and placing them together (a method which Eisenstein later called 'montage of attractions'), Mayakovsky offered Meyerhold theatrical forms that corresponded, in terms of their general conviction, to the demands of the time. In the second version of *Mystery-Bouffe* circus and carnival elements were even more prominent than in the first version. At the same time the features were more clearly revealed that link *Mystery-Bouffe* with the new form of political revue, a form which had just come into being and which showed great potential. All these innovations appealed very strongly to Meyerhold.

If Verhaeren's *The Dawn* was used by Meyerhold as 'a pretext for a mass meeting' and was 'filled with allusions to contemporaneity', then the second version of *Mystery-Bouffe* was a ready-made text for

Theatre During the First Years of Revolution

Sketch of the Devil's costume for *Mystery-Bouffe*, directed by Meyerhold in the RSFSR Theatre No. 1.

a topical spectacle, a political revue incorporating passionate celebration of the Revolution and comic mockery of its enemies.

In the second version of the play Mayakovsky added a whole new scene – 'The Land of Debris' – in which the theme of the struggle against devastation dominated and where there was a character named 'Devastation'. This and various other changes made it more sharply up-to-date. The theme of electrification was introduced in 'The Promised Land'. 'Simply Man' became 'The Man of the Future', the Russian Merchant became the Speculator. Masks of Clemenceau, Lloyd George, Lev Tolstoy and Jean-Jacques Rousseau appeared, deriding not only the political opponents of the Revolution but also thinkers whose ideas at that time were perceived as hostile. The Student became the Intellectual, the Hysterical Lady, the Lady With the Cardboard Boxes (the personification of emigration). There was even the Conciliator who tried to reconcile everyone and

therefore, like a circus clown, was forever being beaten up by everyone.

The Conciliator was Igor Ilinsky's first theatrical success. He performed in a dishevelled red wig with a tangled red beard and strongly resembled a red-haired circus clown, only with spectacles crammed onto his nose and clutching an umbrella. For a long time thereafter these glasses and the umbrella became the requisite theatrical attributes of various political renegades and capitulators. 'The actor who plays the Menshevik is brilliant,' remarked Lunacharsky, who did not yet know Ilinsky's name.

'The clean' were dressed whimsically in costumes created by the artist Viktor Kiselev, who was inspired by the 'ROSTA windows' (window displays of cartoon-like posters on social and political themes issued by the Russian Telegraph Agency, ROSTA) and Picasso's paintings. Devils' horns protruded from beneath crumpled bowler hats and cuirasses, and the 'particularly business-like' devils flaunted false shirt fronts. 'The unclean' appeared in identical blue blouses, that is, once again in uniform 'overalls' (*prozodezhda*). Meyerhold wanted them all to merge together into a single placard image of the victorious class.

Subsequently the costumes of 'the unclean' from *Mystery-Bouffe* passed into political revue and became the uniform of the numerous 'Blue Blouse' theatre groups.

But the monolithic character which both poet and director sought was considered monotonous, and the declamations of Valery Sysoev as 'The Man of the Future', the leader of the entire group of 'the unclean', sounded dispassionate and cold.

'*Mystery-Bouffe*,' maintained the critic and director Margolin, 'is a spectacle of maximum theatrical excessiveness. Its power is indisputable, the production is forged from steel, its range is undoubted, it swallows whole people then ejects them from its vast interior. . . . Its frenzied movements are compelling. The style of a new theatrical writing is embodied in it, the rhythm of a new theatrical progress.'[101]

Another critic, Emmanuel Beskin, recounted, 'There is no stage and no auditorium. There is a monumental platform projecting halfway into the auditorium. There is the feeling that there is not enough space for it within these walls. It calls for a city square, a street. It needs more than these several hundred spectators which the theatre accommodates. It calls for the masses. It has broken away from all the machinery of the stage, has elbowed out the wings, the grid, and has soared up to the very roof of the building. It has torn down the hanging backdrops of a lifeless decorative art. It is all fitted up, fitted up lightly, with conscious theatricality, as in the fairground booth: everything is made of wood – benches, trestles, boards and painted screens and panels. It does not imitate life with its swaying curtains and idyllic crickets. Actors come and go on the platform-stage. Before the spectators' very eyes the workers shift, fold, dismantle, collect, nail together, take away and bring in. The author and director are here too. The performance ends and some of the actors in costume mingle with the audience. This is no "temple" with its great myth of the "mystery" of art. This is the new proletarian art. . . .'[102]

The cited review, by a herald of 'Theatrical October', reveals the polemical intention in Meyerhold's work against the 'theatre-temple' and against the stage becoming a 'picture of life'. The spirit of polemics was also manifested in the production's programmes where it was explained that 'it is possible to enter the auditorium even during the performance. Expressions of approval (applause) and protest (whistles) are permitted. Actors respond to calls both after each scene and throughout the course of the performance.' This declaration called for art which is born and lives in simple, free and easy interaction with its audience.

In his diary the writer Dmitri Furmanov spoke disapprovingly of Mayakovsky's play, while highly praising Meyerhold's work. 'This is the embryo of a completely new concept of theatre,' he wrote. 'The new theatre leaps out at the audience with body and soul. . . . The staging is splendid, it creates an impression of something great, significant, powerful.'[103] The 'bouffonade' *Mystery-Bouffe* did not, however, suit Demyan Bedny's taste. He responded to the production with the poem 'Tsar Andron', where Mayakovsky was depicted under the obvious nickname 'The Futurist Poet Yatakovsky', who has composed 'an absurd fable'. Bedny considered the new proletarian art was always, under all circumstances, obliged to speak simply and he equated the simple with the Revolutionary. Mayakovsky and Meyerhold did not want simplification.

In the heat of the controversy that accompanied the premières of *The Dawn* and *Mystery-Bouffe*, the term 'the civil war in theatre' was heard more often and more insistently.

Meanwhile the real Civil War ended, and history drew a line under the brief period of war Communism. The victory over the enemies of the Revolution which *Mystery-Bouffe* celebrated meant the art which had arisen under the conditions of armed class struggle must now change.

Sketch of the Worker's costume for the 1921 production of *Mystery-Bouffe*.

No one in the 'Theatrical October' camp comprehended this yet. Meyerhold himself was the first to realize it, or in any case, to feel the inevitability of change since he was always acutely sensitive to the shifts of the times. But the blows which the new times immediately dealt to 'Theatrical October' were unexpected even to him.

As early as February 1921 Meyerhold was removed from his post as head of the Theatrical Department of Narkompros and soon after he left TEO altogether.

On 6 September 1921 performances of the RSFSR Theatre No. 1 ceased.

The newspaper *Vestnik teatra*, the mouthpiece for the ideas of 'Theatrical October', closed down in August 1921.

Later, explaining the reasons that had prompted him to relieve Meyerhold of his duties as head of TEO, Lunacharsky wrote, 'The enthusiastic Meyerhold immediately mounted a Futurist warhorse and led the advocates of 'Theatrical October' in an assault against the bastions of academism. With all my love for Meyerhold, I had to part with him since such a one-sided policy sharply contradicted not only my views but also the views of the Party. . . . I had to recognize Meyerhold's extreme line as unacceptable from the point of view of state administration.'[104]

It is important, however, to point out that as soon as Meyerhold acquired his theatre and began to work on *The Dawn*, his interest in the affairs of TEO diminished. Absorbed by rehearsals, he willingly began to delegate responsibility to his assistants and deputies. Even before Lunacharsky decided to remove TEO from Meyerhold, he had essentially already exchanged both 'Theatrical October' and the Theatrical Department for a single, yet on the other hand, quite real and concretely existing theatre.

As for the slogans and declarations of 'Theatrical October', they quickly lost their popularity. The movement had exhausted itself. Its circle of supporters grew narrower from day to day. They spoke out just as fervently and categorically, but they were listened to half-heartedly, impassively and without enthusiasm. Their claims to represent a revolution in art had not been confirmed by the Revolution.

In 1921 Lunacharsky wrote: 'Mayakovsky is recognized (and it is good that he is recognized) by certain sectors of our youth and our proletariat. He is, of course, a very great phenomenon, but in no sense a standard-bearer. . . . The Party as such, the Communist Party, which is the major forger of the new life, regards not only Mayakovsky's former works with coldness and even hostility, but also those in which he appears as the trumpeter of Communism.'[105]

There were reasons for this 'coldness and even hostility'. Futurism, wrote Lunacharsky, 'had not been able to provide a picture, had not been able to provide a drama.' It still only offered placards and mass meetings and propaganda shouted at the top of its voice. 'Meanwhile the Revolution had grown stronger, been victorious and moved on to construction. And then it was as if a general cry resounded throughout the entire country: 'Comrades, look around you! Comrades, study your country, your enemies and friends and your own selves! Comrades, get closer to reality, to the issues at hand! And when the corresponding mood had finally taken hold, it became clear that Futurism was out of step with this mood, that it created a strange dissonance in this respect.'[106]

Thus, with the utmost simplicity and clarity, Lunacharsky presented the objective causes which led to the crisis and end of 'Theatrical October'.

Three sketches by Mayakovsky of costumes for the Shoemaker (*left*), the Priest (*below left*) and the set (*below*) for the first performance of *Mystery-Bouffe* in 1918.

In the art of the stage new, quite different notes soon made themselves heard. Mayakovsky's politically tendentious *Mystery-Bouffe* was twice produced by Vsevolod Meyerhold, in collaboration with the poet – in 1918 in Petrograd and in 1921 in Moscow. In the years of relentless civil war that engulfed the whole country the very direct art of Mayakovsky and Meyerhold, which willingly adopted forms of theatrical caricature or political poster, inspired the spectators and instilled in them contempt for the enemy and faith in victory.

Mass Festivals

After the October Revolution mass theatrical festivals, organized in city streets and squares, soon began to enjoy widespread popularity. At times their participants numbered thousands, mostly workers and soldiers. These mass pageants were usually organized by experienced directors and designers – such as Konstantin Mardzhanov, Sergei Radlov, Nikolai Evreinov, Natan Altman and Yury Annenkov. Some of the subjects were taken from history – for example the rebellion of the gladiator Spartacus or the peasant revolts of Emilyan Pugachev and Stepan Razin – but more often quite recent battles of the Revolution and Civil War were re-enacted.

Left and opposite, below: Four scenes from a mass pageant called *The Hymn of Freed Labour*, 1920. *Opposite, above*: Scene from Ada Korvin's mime entitled *They Were Executed*, at the Proletkult Arena in 1919.

The Storming of the Winter Palace

In Petrograd the mass pageant 'The Storming of the Winter Palace' was an attempt to reproduce the events of October 1917 after a lapse of three years, in that same Palace Square. Just as in Mayakovsky's *Mystery-Bouffe* the 'Reds' and the 'Whites', the 'clean' and the 'unclean' were depicted in opposition to each other with placard-style directness. Many images of the mass pageants were in the nature of naive allegories. This tendency towards allegory was a general characteristic of the art of the period – in particular of some amateur productions of the Proletkult theatres, such as Petr Kozlov's *Legend of the Communard* (1919).

Two scenes from *The Storming of the Winter Palace*.

Opposite: General plan (*above*) and stage design (*below*) by Yury Annenkov for *The Storming of the Winter Palace*.

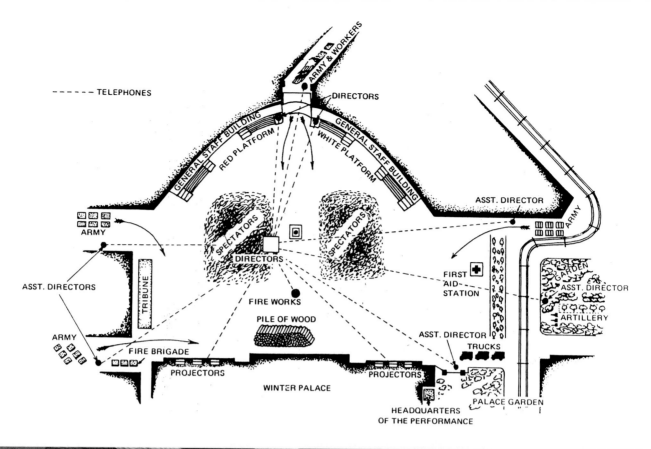

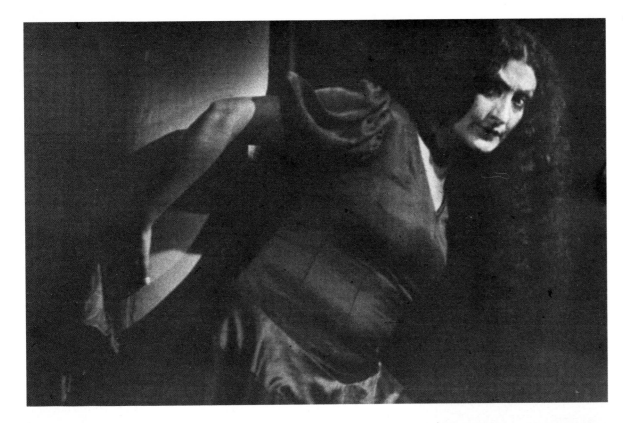

T. Chavchavadze as Laurencia in the 1922 production of *Fuenteovejuna* at the Rustaveli Theatre in Tiflis.

Vera Yureneva as Laurencia in the 1919 production of *Fuenteovejuna* in Kiev. Drawing by K. Fonvizin.

The idea of 'the theatre as mass meeting' was alien to the directors and actors of the professional stage. They, as a rule, avoided placard-style grossness and primitive allegories. But they certainly instigated some changes to accord with the transformed times. Addressing themselves to the classical repertoire – to such plays as Lope de Vega's *Fuenteovejuna*, Gutzkow's *Uriel Acosta*, Alexei Tolstoy's *The Governor* – the directors,

actors and designers strove to make these plays 'consonant with the Revolution', that is to express in their productions sympathy for the insurgent masses and hatred for tyranny and despotism. Konstantin Mardzhanov achieved these aims in his Kiev production of *Fuenteovejuna* (1919), where the role of Laurencia was played by Vera Yureneva, and the colourful set was designed by Isaak Rabinovich.

Opposite: A scene from *Fuenteovejuna* in Tiflis, 1922.

Fuenteovejuna

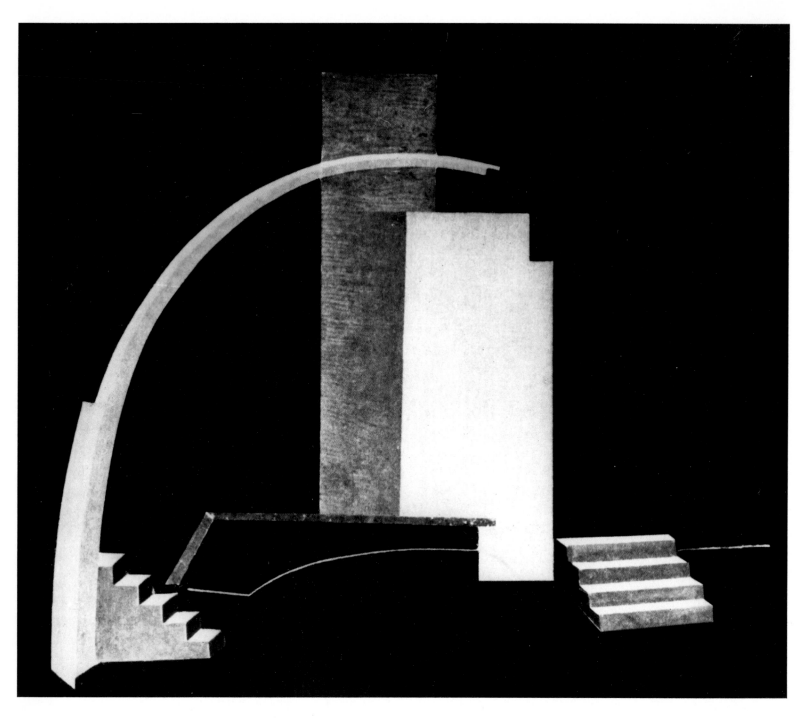

Uriel Acosta

From the earliest days of the Jewish State Theatre (GOSET) Alexei Granovsky commissioned experienced artists to design the productions, so they were often extremely original in form. Gutzkow's *Uriel Acosta* was staged in 1922 with a cheerful, abstract set designed by Natan Altman, which brightened up the cramped, plain space of the hall in Malaya Bronnaya Street in Moscow.

Model of Natan Altman's set for *Uriel Acosta*.

Opposite: Sketch by Natan Altman of the set for *Uriel Acosta*.

Don Carlos

Three characters in *Don Carlos*. *Left*:
Nikolai Monakhov as Philip. *Below
left*: Yury Yuriev as Posa. *Below*:
Vladimir Maximov as Don Carlos.

Sketch of Vladimir Shchuko's set for *Don Carlos*.

In the Civil War years the plays of Friedrich Schiller enjoyed huge popularity. Their freedom-loving spirit, their characteristic opposition of heroism and villainy, their wealth of dramatically effective situations – all this guaranteed success with an unsophisticated audience. *Intrigue and Love* and *Die Räuber* were enthusiastically acted by amateurs in numerous clubs. The Bolshoi Dramatic Theatre in Leningrad, led by Alexander Blok, Maria Andreevna and Maxim Gorky, opened in 1919 with a production of Schiller's *Don Carlos*. The sets were designed by Vladimir Shchuko and the main roles were played by Yury Yuriev, Nikolai Monakhov and Vladimir Maximov. The artists of the 'World of Art' group – Alexander Benois, Mikhail Dobuzhinsky – had close affinities with the Bolshoi.

A scene from *Don Carlos*.

Above and opposite: Two sketches of Ignaty Nivinsky's set for *Eric XIV*. *Right*: Sketch by Natan Altman of a costume for *Hadibuk*.

After the October Revolution the directorial talent of one of Stanislavsky's most interesting and most insubordinate pupils, Evgeny Vakhtangov, burst forth with unexpected strength and vividness. Vakhtangov was working at this time in several theatrical studios, with the artists Ignaty Nivinsky and Natan Altman, who were very responsive to his ideas. In the sets for Vakhtangov's productions there arose a strange mixture of the authentic and the fantastic, the real and the unreal. In such productions as *Eric XIV* (1921) or *Hadibuk* (1922) the overall tone was sombre; in *Princess Turandot* (1922) it was one of festive high spirits.

Vakhtangov's artists

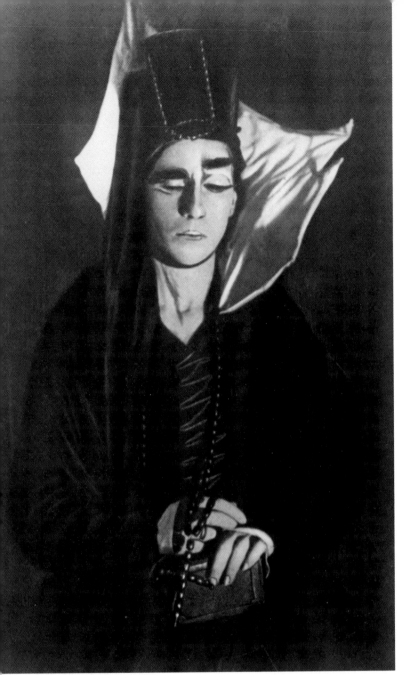

Two characters in *Eric XIV. Above:*
Serafima Birman as the Queen. *Above
right:* Mikhail Chekhov as Eric.

Right: Sketch by Ignaty Nivinsky of
the costume for Eric.

Expressionist motifs could be
clearly felt in Vakhtangov's
art. Expressionist highly
wrought nervousness
characterized both his
production of Maeterlinck's
The Miracle of St Anthony (in
the Moscow Art Theatre's
Third Studio in 1921, with
Yury Zavadsky in the role of
Anthony) and, in particular,

the production of Strindberg's
Eric XIV (in the MAT's First
Studio in 1921, with Mikhail
Chekhov in the role of Eric).
In the sets and costumes for
Eric XIV, the artist Ignaty
Nivinsky successfully
conveyed the outer rigidity
and inner tension of the lives
of this dying kingdom's
inhabitants.

Left: Two scenes from *The Miracle of
St Anthony*.

Yury Zavadsky as Anthony.

Hadibuk

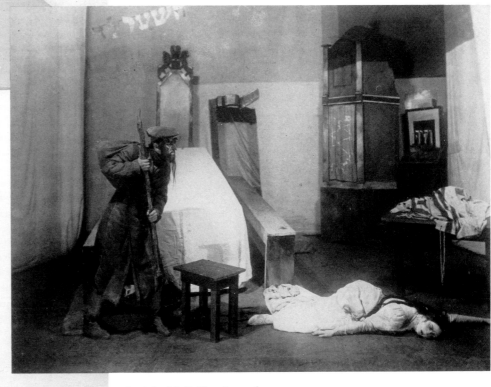

Inset, far left: D. Khendler as the Hassid.
Left and above: Two scenes from *Hadibuk*.

The melodrama *Hadibuk* (or *Between Two Worlds*), written in Hebrew by the little-known writer An-sky (S. Rappoport) and produced in the Jewish 'Habima' Studio in 1922, acquired a tragic resonance in Vakhtangov's interpretation. The Jewish environment, Jewish rituals, dances and songs all began to take on a hallucinatory, nightmarish aspect in the highly sophisticated production. In the words of the critic Akim Volynsky, Vakhtangov created 'a whole symphony of visual signs that assisted the arguments and twists of thought'.

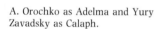

A. Orochko as Adelma and Yury Zavadsky as Calaph.

Boris Shchukin as Tartalaya.

Princess Turandot

In *Princess Turandot* Vakhtangov to some degree anticipated the later Brechtian idea of the actor's 'alienation': Vakhtangov's actors maintained an ironic attitude both to the subject of the fairy tale and to the characters they were playing, moving now 'into' and now 'out of' character and freely improvising as they communicated with the audience. The mortally ill Vakhtangov was already too weak to attend the première of *Princess Turandot* in 1922.

But the pupils of his Studio (the Moscow Art Theatre's Third Studio, which was usually called 'Vakhtangov's') – Yury Zavadsky, Tsetsilia Mansurova, Boris Shchukin, Ruben Simonov and many others – celebrated total success that evening. Subsequently the Third Studio became the Vakhtangov Theatre, which exists to this day. *Princess Turandot* remained constantly in this theatre's repertoire for more than half a century.

Adrienne Lecouvreur

Above: Alisa Koonen as Adrienne,
G. Yanikovsky as Michonet and
N. Chaplygin as Maurice in a 1932
revival of *Adrienne Lecouvreur*. *Inset*:
Alisa Koonen as Adrienne in the
1919 production.

Opposite: Two scenes from *Adrienne
Lecouvreur*.

One of Alexander Tairov's
most remarkable productions,
Scribe and Legouvé's *Adrienne
Lecouvreur*, which opened in
1919, turned out to have a
very long stage life, remaining
in the Kamerny Theatre's
repertoire for three decades –
right up to 1949 when the
theatre was closed. The
unique feature of this theatre
was the way in which
Tairov's productions always
gave total freedom to the
enormous talent of the tragic
actress, Alisa Koonen. It was
in *Adrienne Lecouvreur* that the
full power of such an alliance
of equals was demonstrated
for the first time. The graceful
form that Tairov devised for
this production served as a
vehicle for the heroine, who
turned an old-fashioned
melodrama into genuine
tragedy.

The Dawn

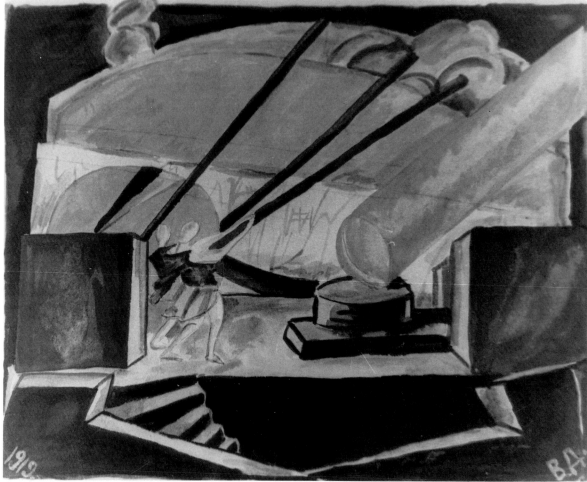

Model (*above*) and sketch (*below*) of
the set by Dmitriev for *The Dawn*.

A scene from *The Dawn*.

During the Civil War Meyerhold experimented in the RSFSR Theatre No.1 with various ways of organizing 'the theatre as mass meeting' and 'performance meetings'. His free adaptation of Emile Verhaeren's tragedy *The Dawn* (1920) was staged in sets by the young artist Vladimir Dmitriev, and was distinguished by the austerity of its abstract contours and the militarized geometrical shapes of the crowd scenes. The second version of the production of *Mystery-Bouffe* (1921), by contrast, tended towards circus clowning and buffoonery. The RSFSR Theatre No.1 also contemplated a new production of *Hamlet*: a translation had been commissioned from the poet Marina Tsvetaeva; Mayakovsky was going to turn the gravedigger's scene into a sharply topical political review. But these plans came to nothing for Tsvetaeva was not attracted by the idea of working with Meyerhold and Mayakovsky.

Sketch by Nikolai Andreev for
Lucifer's make-up in *Cain*.

Cain

Three sketches by Andreev of sets
for *Cain*.

In the Moscow Art Theatre
Stanislavsky decided to
respond to the events of the
Revolution and Civil War
with a production of Byron's
tragedy *Cain* (1920). This step
signalled a change in
direction: he was in fact
demanding the complete re-
orientation of the intimate
psychological theatre of
Chekhov, Gorky and Lev
Tolstoy, a theatre which had
never really been able to
perform tragedy successfully
and to which romantic
tragedy was completely
unfamiliar. But despite
Stanislavsky's stubborn and
even frantic rehearsals,
despite the impressive sets by
Nikolai Andreev and despite
the fact that the whole
external appearance of the
production was majestically
monumental, Stanislavsky's
ambitions were not realized
and the production turned
out over-rationalized and
heavy.

3 Theatrical Expansion

NEP, LEF and Theatre

In March 1921 the Soviet leadership announced the New Economic Policy (NEP) and began to carry it out. Within certain limitations, NEP permitted private initiative, private trade, private ownership, and it provided for new relationships between city and country. At the same time it dictated the strict economy of state resources.

The prominent critic Nikolai Efros noted that 'the New Economic Policy cut off State finances for the majority of theatres'; moreover, it required theatres to show profit. Free performances, including the 'mass pageants' with scores of participants that required great financial outlay, became an impermissible extravagance. Theatre tickets became more expensive. Efros declared that 'all the uproar with which "Theatrical October" was proclaimed and all the fervour with which it was carried out, turned out to be in vain.'[1]

This was, of course, an exaggeration, yet even Meyerhold's most zealous supporters understood the necessity for changes. Only a few refused to yield. The critic Vladimir Blyum, for instance, would not be reconciled to the prospect of any kind of compromise: 'We have nothing to repent. We have made no mistake whatsoever, and there can be no talk of any concessions,'[2] he wrote, insisting that the ideas of 'Theatrical October' must still be realized to their full extent.

Meyerhold's voice, however, was less confident: 'With the departure of the RSFSR Theatre No. 1 from the theatrical front, we do not see who in practice could continue the monumental and heroic principle.'[3]

In actual fact it was no calamity that the RSFSR Theatre No. 1 had ceased to exist. Meyerhold soon resumed his activities, very energetically, under a new banner. But he was obliged to make radical changes.

'Those new spectators, fresh, unspoilt, innocent and open to impressions, who seemed to encourage all that was best in our theatre,' wrote Efros, 'are now turning away from it.' Efros's judgment was over-hasty but he was right in believing that the theatre was again beginning to depend on 'those who pay'.[4] And, of course, those who paid were the so-called NEP-men, that is the proprietors of shops, restaurants, cafés and various small industrial enterprises, businessmen, and so forth.

The concept of NEP was internally extremely contradictory and very dramatic. Soon it was supplying both the new Soviet literature and Soviet theatre with subjects for novellas, novels and plays that were expressive and in some cases quite 'intoxicating'. During 1921 and 1922, however, many thought, like Nikolai Efros, that NEP would mean a move backwards for the arts, 'a return to the old, pre-Revolutionary days.'[5] Artists loyal to the ideals of the Revolution, who called themselves 'leftists', thought otherwise.

The LEF (Left Front of the Arts) headed by Mayakovsky, constituted a sort of successor to 'Theatrical October'. But whereas that had been a spontaneous movement without formal organization, LEF represented an ideologically united group which published its own journal – also called *LEF*, and later *Novy LEF (The New LEF)* – and which formulated its aims quite precisely, firmly and resolutely. It is true that LEF's programme was primarily a programme for the renewal of literature. It is also true that members of LEF regarded the theatre with a certain reserve, preferring the cinema and especially documentary films. However, it soon became clear that many points of contact existed between LEF theories and theatrical practice.

Theatre of any kind – even the avant-garde, even the one-hundred-percent Revolutionary – inspired mistrust in the members of LEF, for the simple reason that the events which took place on stage were imaginary and so were the characters represented. From the point of view of LEF doctrine and from that of the LEF theoreticians Sergei Tretyakov, Osip Brik and Boris Arvatov, any artistic invention was a heresy, any fantasy was sedition.

Apart from Mayakovsky, the constituent members of LEF included such famous poets as Nikolai Aseev, Vasily Kamensky and Boris Pasternak, yet this group, at least in theory, rejected and censured true poetry in favour of utilitarian, 'life-building' and 'industrial' art, and the 'literature of fact'. They considered a newspaper story to be much more important than a poem or novel, a documentary film more necessary than an art film and applied art (ceramics, design) more useful than easel painting. In their view art should be used to make all human activities more intelligent, rational, functionally precise and economical. When the members of LEF called for 'revolution of form', they had in mind the creation of aesthetic forms which could be infused into everyday life and which would then quickly change that life. Art was seen as an instrument capable of transforming both man and society in accordance with 'clear thinking and intellect'.

This programme derived, on the one hand, from the modernized ideas of Vyacheslav Ivanov (passed on to LEF theoreticians by the Proletkult theoreticians) and, on the other hand, from the scientific systemization of labour propounded by the American engineer Frederick Taylor, which aroused very great interest in the Soviet Union during the 1920s. It is, incidentally, worth noting that in 1924 Taylor's book was published in Russian translation with an introduction by Platon Kerzhentsev. One of the leaders of Proletkult, Kerzhentsev promoted 'the Taylorized gesture', economical and functionally expedient, 'the Taylorized movement', efficient and precise, and so forth.

Nikolai Aseev wrote that 'LEF was declaring war on invention, fantasy and generally any "artistic" approximation which misrepresents and distorts fact.' Therefore 'the centre of gravity in LEF's work is transferred to the journal, reportage, *feuilleton*, to the "low" literary forms of newspaper work which LEF considers the most modern.' 'After the invention of printing and then of cinema and radio,' believed Aseev, the theatre no longer had any social value and 'continued to exist only through inertia, alongside the forms of human culture which have already replaced it.'[6]

Although the leaders of LEF – Mayakovsky, Aseev and Pasternak (who broke with LEF in 1927) – were in their creative practice far removed from the dogmas of LEF theory and although the film-makers close to LEF, such as Sergei Eisenstein and Lev Kuleshov, did not always respect its theory, it was nonetheless a very influential group. So influential, in fact, that several other significant groups virtually adopted the LEF programme with minor amendments and observed LEF practice.

This applies above all to the Constructivists. Like the members of LEF, the Constructivists declared their 'love for figures, business-like speech, quotation from documents, the functional fact and description of the event.'[7] Moreover, in some senses the Constructivists were 'further left than LEF': in principle they entirely rejected art as such. 'We, the Constructivists, renounce art because it is not useful. Art by its very nature is passive, it only reflects reality. Constructivism is active, it not only reflects reality but takes action itself.'[8]

It is understandable that to the Constructivists theatre seemed a waste of time. Boris Arvatov asserted with vexation: 'Our everyday life is disorganized. People don't know how to speak, walk, sit down, lie down, arrange their surroundings, conduct social life, receive guests or go to funerals. . . . It is not we who control everyday life, but everyday life which controls us – controls us with its elementality, its fragmentation.' The Constructivists would have liked to counterbalance this shapelessness with order. But the theatre that 'teaches speaking, lying down and paying visits', in Arvatov's view, was not suited to this purpose, for its aesthetic organization of everyday life could not be transferred into real life. And Arvatov urged directors 'to abandon stages and theatrical performances'. He called on them to 'Go into life to re-educate yourselves and others. Be the engineers, the orchestrators of everyday life.'[9]

It may seem strange that people concerned with the arts, poets, came out so resolutely against art, against artistic invention, against fantasy. (Among the Constructivists were Ilya Selvinsky, Eduard Bagritsky, Vladimir Lugovskoy.) But if one remembers that both these groups, LEF and the Constructivists, emerged soon after the Civil War in conditions of devastation and chaos, one can understand their dreams of the future focussing on a worship of technology. Both the members of LEF and the Constructivists made a fetish of the machine. 'The machine,' assured Osip Brik in all seriousness, 'is more like an animate organism than is usually thought.'[10]

Their attitude to the theatre brings us to an amusing paradox. All of them, unanimously, dismissed it as useless. Yet all, one after another – Sergei Tretyakov, Sergei Eisenstein, Ivan Axenov, Ilya Selvinsky and Liubov Popova – were drawn into it. The dismayed Arvatov attempted to justify this paradox. He expressed the hope that theatre would be turned into 'a factory turning out people qualified for life' and that 'the results achieved in the theatrical

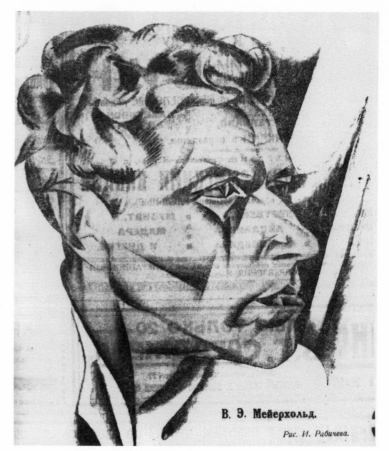

В. Э. Мейерхольд.

Рис. И. Рабичева.

Portrait of Meyerhold by I. Rabichev, 1922.

laboratory' could be 'transferred into life, recreating our real, everyday social life'.[11]

In other words, a utilitarian, social function was found for theatre: to teach the workers how to conduct themselves, how to control their bodies. This idea soon acquired the elegant forms of 'biomechanics'. However, biomechanics did not live up to the hopes of the Constructivists, for it never in fact served all of society, but only the theatre.

In Soviet industry and architecture of the early 1920s Constructivism asserted itself primarily through declarations, designs and models, and in poetry through manifestos. Only in the theatre could it claim any real achievement.

Meyerhold led the zealots of Constructivism out of the studios where they were drawing plans for enormous buildings, towers and entire cities of the future or composing geometrical patterns from squares, circles and triangles, and on to his brightly illuminated stages. 'Theatre,' wrote Ivan Axenov, 'gave Constructivism the first opportunity to manifest itself in large forms and to make its brilliant entry into society.'[12]

To put it more briefly: Meyerhold gave Constructivism its big chance.

Why?

Firstly, because the Constructivists did not yet have any other realistic prospects. The young Republic was too impoverished to erect the Constructivist towers, skyscrapers, glass palaces, spiral clubs and so on; the period of new construction had not yet arrived. In the theatre, however, the Constructivists' ideas could be achieved with ordinary planks and ordinary nails (although at that time there was a shortage of them too).

Secondly, and this is the main thing, in the early 1920s theatre showed a vigorous tendency to take over other aesthetic territories. The theatre was 'music-hallized', 'circusized' and 'cinematographized'. This capacity of the theatre to absorb and appropriate the means of expression of other, allied arts, in the 1920s, although only for a brief period, made it a much more important factor in the spiritual life of society.

In theory it was entirely possible to ridicule the theatre as 'pathetic contemporary histrionics' surviving only through inertia or some kind of strange misunderstanding. In practice, however, no-one managed to ignore it. Anyone who wanted to be in the public eye (and who did not?) went to work in the theatre.

The confrontation between the 'leftist' avant-gardists and the defenders of traditions was aggravated by the appearance of LEF on the theatrical scene. In 1923 the director Nikolai Petrov wrote, 'theatre is sharply split into two camps. In one the old is rotting in respectable routine (having lost all its freshness and vitality), and in the other the new is making a fool of itself with its stridency, obscurity and silliness.' Attacks on the old, coming from Petrov, a student of Meyerhold's, surprised no-one. But his description of 'the new' as strident, obscure and silly testified that the 'left' was, to say the least, not entirely confident of itself. And indeed the theatrical practice of the 'leftists' told the same story. Their former unity had been replaced by fragmentation. While still totally rejecting everything old, they now, in their search for the new, were growing increasingly apart from each other and each was experimenting in his own way.

The Denuding of Theatre

After the closure of the RSFSR Theatre No. 1 Meyerhold quickly rallied round him a large group of talented, young students, including Maria Babanova, Igor Ilinsky, Vasily Zaichikov, Mikhail Zharov, Dmitri Orlov, Erast Garin, Sergei Eisenstein, Sergei Yutkevich, Zinaida Raikh, Nikolai Bogolyubov, Nikolai Okhlopkov, Lev Sverdlin, Ilya Shlepyanov, Nikolai Ekk and Vladimir Yakhontov. Although all these people subsequently became famous, their names did not mean anything to anyone at that time. 'The Master' (as they called Meyerhold) worked in the studio with his inexperienced pupils. The name of the studio changed several times over the years and was abbreviated to rather ugly acronyms: GVYRM, GVYTM, GEKTEMAS, GITIS.[14]

Apart from Meyerhold himself, lessons were given by the poet and translator Ivan Axenov, the director Valery Bebutov and the specialist in theatrical movement, Valery Inkizhinov. Compulsory lessons in rhythmical gymnastics, dance and acrobatics were included in the programme. Vladimir Mayakovsky, Sergei Tretyakov, Andrei Bely and, later, Nikolai Erdman, Vsevolod Vishnevsky and Ilya Selvinsky came to the Theatre Workshop and read their poetry and plays.

The Master's theatrical guard were still very green – some only seventeen or eighteen years old – but they were burning with desire to re-build the theatre anew, from top to bottom. Inspired by the fighting spirit, fervour and courage of their teacher, they wholeheartedly and unquestioningly followed him through the turbulent sea of theatrical explorations.

As the critic Boris Alpers observed, 'the main dynamic, life-forming centres of the theatrical universe were at that time found in the Moscow Art Theatre and Meyerhold theatrical systems, and the principal nuclei were Stanislavsky and Meyerhold.' It was 'between these principal sources of illuminative energy within the theatre world that all remaining theatres of that time were situated.'[15] In the early 1920s the relationship between these two systems – the avant-garde and the traditional – was still antagonistic.

Meyerhold believed that the old theatres had completely lost their former democratic traditions. 'I accuse those,' he wrote, 'who shelter behind the fetishism of spurious traditions, not knowing how to preserve the genuine traditions of Shchepkin, Shumsky, the Sadovsky family, Rybakov and Lensky.' This accusation was directed at the Maly Theatre. Meyerhold declared that at the State Theatre of Drama (the former Alexandrinsky) 'the key to the doors of Shakespeare, Calderón, Lermontov and Pushkin has been lost.'[16] In 1921 Meyerhold (in co-authorship with the director Valery Bebutov) published a sensational article, 'Stanislavsky's Solitude', in the pages of Vestnik teatra, attempting to place Stanislavsky in radical opposition to the Moscow Art Theatre as a whole. The article portrayed Stanislavsky as one who was born for 'theatre of exaggerated parody and tragic suspense', in the tradition of 'cloak and dagger' drama.[17] Stanislavsky was apparently required to renounce the methods of the Moscow Art Theatre which he himself had created, methods which had, in Meyerhold's view, become obsolete, too 'domestic', 'indoor', everyday and intimate in a way that was inappropriate for the time. He called realism 'naturalism', psychology 'psycholatry' and derided 'verisimilitude' which 'empathizers strive in vain to squeeze out of themselves'.

Meyerhold's tirades against the MAT were supported by Mayakovsky's stentorian voice. In the prologue to the second version of Mystery-Bouffe, the poet sarcastically wrote that for theatres such as MAT 'the stage is a keyhole. . . . You look and you see – Aunt Manyas and Uncle Vanyas whimpering on the settee. But neither uncles nor aunts concern us – you'll find aunts and uncles at home. We'll also show real life, but transformed by theatre to a most extraordinary spectacle.'

For Mayakovsky it was the promise of the 'most extraordinary' spectacles which the 'leftists' intended to – and indeed did – organize, that was most vital for the future.

Meyerhold, however, was sceptical of these 'mass pageants' and asserted that 'now there cannot be a genuine merging of auditorium and stage'. He saw the immediate future of the theatre in 'simplicity, schematization, intensity, dynamism of action and ability to capture the rhythm of the epoch'. This was the origin of his idea of 'the denuding of the theatre' – ridding the stage of showy, colourful scenery, large casts and magnificent costumes and the auditorium of moulding and gilding, and so forth. Instead of theatre that was outwardly rich but inwardly bankrupt, he was proposing a theatre that would be outwardly poor but strong and robust in spirit. 'The Italian comedy of masks, the theatres of Shakespeare and Molière were effective popular theatres, struggling against the glittering opulence of the aristocracy's theatres' (which, Meyerhold said, corresponded to 'the contemporary academic theatres'). The present task consisted of 'putting propaganda into forms which will make theatrical action engaging' – here 'the experience of the popular theatres of past epochs' will become useful, here there will be a need for 'the clowns typical of Shakespeare and fairgrounds'.[18]

The struggle with 'the theatre of the aristocracy' began with the struggle against opulence of the kind which had only recently been characteristic of the collaborations between Meyerhold and Golovin on *Don Juan*, *The Storm* and *Masquerade*.

The first herald of the 'denuding of theatre' was in Ibsen's *The Doll's House*, produced hurriedly in five days and performed on 20 April 1922. Rehearsals with the actors were crammed into only three days. 'I have met many people in my day . . .' wrote Eisenstein many years later, going on to enumerate Chaplin, Chaliapin, Stanislavsky, Mayakovsky, Shaw, Pirandello, Douglas Fairbanks, Marlene Dietrich . . . and then concluding: 'but not one of these impressions could ever erase from my memory those that were made on me by the three days of rehearsals for *The Doll's House* in the gymnasium on Novinsky Boulevard. I remember constant trembling. This was not cold; this was excitement, it was nerves tightly wound to the limit. . . .'[19]

Meyerhold's students created chaos on the stage. A fantastic array of furniture was jumbled together. Old scenery was turned back to front, signifying the 'disintegration of bourgeois life', the collapse of the milieu against which Nora was rebelling.

In *The Doll's House* the removal of the dramatic situation from the everyday environment was hastily and crudely executed. One of the reviews of the performance concluded with the rhetorical question: 'What is this production? Parody or hoax?'[20]

However, Meyerhold was not parodying or deceiving anyone. He had simply hurried to seize the premises of the former Zon Theatre which had been taken away from him and which were now once again available. Immediately after the première of *The Doll's House*, his students began to knock together something unprecedented on the stage which they had taken over: a construction.

The idea of a Constructivist theatrical production occurred to Meyerhold after visiting the exhibition of Moscow Constructivist artists entitled $5 \times 5 = 25$ in autumn 1921. Five artists participated in this exhibition: A. Rodchenko, L. Popova, the brothers V. and G. Stenberg and K. Medunetsky, each of whom exhibited five items.

Two months after the thunderous success of Vakhtangov's mischievously festive *Princess Turandot*, on 25 April 1922 Meyerhold showed Muscovites his production of Fernand Crommelynck's *The Magnanimous Cuckold*, the first, if not the only, performance in which the principles of theatrical Constructivism were realized. Scenery was replaced by a machine created by Liubov Popova.

Popova, who had been giving lessons in Meyerhold's Theatre Workshop on 'objects in staging', carefully studied Crommelynck's stage directions concerning the set for the action and then discarded all of them one after another. She and Meyerhold did not need the garden in blossom or the well-built, prosperous country house, or the brand-new furniture glistening with a cheerful yellow glow or the earthenware crockery. After Popova had carried out the 'subtraction' of the unnecessary, the 'remainder' represented only what the play required for practical performance – doors, stairs, windows, landings.

It was from these elements, reduced to stylized forms, that the construction was created. There was no need for walls. Two wooden machines, one a little higher than the other, were linked together by a bridge. Two staircases descended to the stage floor on the left and right. The entire apparatus, made from planks and beams, looked deliberately schematic and possessed the clarity of a blueprint. But it had to be a moving blueprint.

So three rotating wheels of varying sizes, one black, one white, one red, were placed between the two machines. On the upper left-hand side was perched an object that resembled a windmill, although its 'sails' were left in a skeletal state, latticed rather than solid. Finally, a smooth, inclined plank descended from the machine to the stage floor so that the actors could suddenly slide down it.

Thus emerged a strange structure adapted to the actors' performance, yet evoking the most varied and unexpected associations: perhaps a windmill, although it might be a flying machine. If the construction had taken off no one would have been surprised.

The wheels rotated, sometimes quickly, sometimes slowly, sometimes separately, in turns, sometimes all together, reflecting the rhythm and tempo of the acting. During the show the construction itself performed, lived. In order to convey how significant this movement really was, we may reveal a secret that has been kept for half a century: it was Meyerhold himself who rotated the wheels during the first performances.

The construction represented, in the words of the critic Alexei Gvozdev, 'a spring-board for the actor, comparable to those contraptions and devices used by circus acrobats.'[21] Axenov noted that 'it was possible to play with this set as with a fan or a hat.'[22]

'The keyboard for performers' built by Popova gave a feeling of impetuosity, vigour and dynamism. There was a lightness, spareness and clarity in everything. The construction was not fixed to the stage. It could be transferred to any other space, as it was for the theatre's tour in 1923, when Popova's construction was set up on open-air summer stages in the parks of Kiev and Kharkov.

As a Constructivist-'Productivist', Liubov Popova considered work in the theatre admissable only if it completely renounced the 'artistic', the 'aesthetic'. She regretted that the conditions of the stage forced one side of the construction to face the audience and that to a certain extent the desired utilitarianism yielded to an effect of an 'aesthetic nature'. According to the ascetic principles of the monastic order of Constructivism, this was a sin. Popova's orthodox colleagues in the group of 'Productivists' were so shocked by her 'betrayal', by her participation in 'theatrical deception', that they even summoned her to a comradely tribunal. In her defence she might have said that she had struggled for a long time, had hesitated and had only decided to have her name on the poster on the eve of the première. What she actually said that day, according to her own account, was that when she saw the construction for *Cuckold* from the balcony, illuminated by the bright beams of the military searchlights (Meyerhold had placed them in the side boxes), it was the happiest day of her life.

As for Meyerhold, he was delighted with Popova's work, and – a rare thing for him – he publicly acknowledged that 'much in the tone of the performance', in all its directorial invention, had been prompted by 'the Constructivist set'.

Throughout his entire artistic career Meyerhold attached exceptionally great importance to this staging of *The Magnanimous Cuckold*. From this moment the artist was essentially banished from the theatre. In his place entered the engineer, the constructor. With the artist the costume designer too was banished, for the actors performed in identical blue *prozodezhda*, also 'constructed' by Popova: loose-fitting shirts, trousers whose cut combined the principles of bell-bottoms and jodhpurs, cloaks and peaked caps made from black oil-cloth.

Igor Ilinsky, however, observed that Meyerhold's urge to free the actor completely from false theatricality, from 'artificial colours' ('Here, on the bare platform-constructions, in blue canvas *prozodezhda*, without make-up, the young actors will reveal their mastery in pure form, without the aid of theatrical illusions'), this urge 'unexpectedly, to some extent even for Meyerhold himself,' suddenly acquired 'yet another significance.'[23] What was this? Why did all this machinery captivate the audience?

The answer is simple: the stage, transformed by the Constructivists, seemed to presage the swift transformation of life itself. It was as if the dream of mechanization, of electrification, of a finely organized world had materialized in the construction. And this is why Meyerhold's intention of turning the stage into the ideal 'working place' for the actor immediately acquired an aesthetic function. Meyerhold wanted the stage 'to portray nothing', utterly to reject the illusory. But the engineers and constructors, the 'fitters' who replaced the artists, immediately created, first in Meyerhold's theatre and later in others, a compelling image of the future.

Biomechanics

The principle upon which Meyerhold's actors based their performing technique became known as 'biomechanics', and it was in *The Magnanimous Cuckold* that the new method was revealed to the public for the first time.

When the word came into use, it was assumed that the ideas behind it were indissolubly linked with the projects of LEF and the Constructivists, and that it stood for the mechanico-technological reconstruction of man's everyday life. The human body was perceived as a machine: man had to learn to control that machine. It was the theatre's function to demonstrate the fine tuning of the human 'mechanisms', as an example and an encouragement to all others. In Ippolit Sokolov's article 'The Industrialization of Gesture' it is stated categorically that 'on stage the actor must become an automaton, a mechanism, a machine.' He is required to master 'the culture of industrialized gesture', that is 'the gesture of labour, built on the principle of economy of effort', the gesture is 'linear, of a geometric order'.[24]

Meyerhold did not deny this sort of fantasy, but his biomechanics had another object, another sense. 'The art of the actor,' he said, 'is the art of sculptural forms in space.' This means that the art of the actor is the ability to utilize the expressive potential of his body. The path to the image must begin not from emotional experience, not 'from within', but from without, from movement. Moreover, any movement, the tilt of the head, the turn of the body, the smallest gesture, even the fluttering of eyelashes, should ideally involve the whole body of the performer, who possesses musical rhythm and quick, reflexive 'excitability'. What was necessary was an actor who could 'do everything', a truly all-round actor. The virtuoso actor's body becomes for him an ideal musical instrument.

As for 'soul' and psychology, Meyerhold asserted that these could only be found through specific physical positions and states ('points of excitability').[25]

In expounding biomechanics, Meyerhold contrasted it with the Moscow Art Theatre's system for training actors. Although the polemical sharpness of this contrast gradually faded, the methodological principle remained unchanged: from the external (which is easily caught, grasped and may be fixed) to the internal (which even if understood to the end, is not always caught and in practice cannot be consolidated for repetition). As it evolved and entered into new relationships with the changing reality, biomechanics became ever more versatile, more capacious.

Meyerhold's conception of biomechanics brought the actor to the very centre of the director's composition. In the Meyerhold archive there is the following note: 'Biomechanics is man-movement, man-speech; man-speech-movement; man-space; man-collective (the masses).'[26] That is, biomechanics allows the actor, perfectly controlling his body and movements, firstly, to be expressive in dialogues; secondly, to be the master of the theatrical space; and, thirdly, in integrating with the crowd scene, the grouping, to impart to it his energy and will.

According to biomechanical theory, every movement, then, must be not simply realistic, or lifelike (many bodily movements in real life are simply accidental or fortuitous) but deliberate, reduced to essentials and – this was particularly emphasized – responsive to the movement of the partner.

Drawing of biomechanics exercises by V. V. Lutse, 1922.

The 'biomechanics exercises' which are frequently demonstrated nowadays (based on what happens to have survived on film) are the most elementary, primitive ones and do not give a real idea of Meyerhold's methodology, for they do not convey the most important element: rhythm. Through biomechanics Meyerhold turned rhythm into a component of the performance which created form and also gave it content. The rhythmic organization of a role entailed the impulsive-reflexive link between thought and movement, emotion and movement, speech and movement.

In *The Magnanimous Cuckold* rhythm was everything. When the actors first stepped onto Popova's machine they found themselves in a completely unfamiliar environment, cut off from all help. There was no décor, costumes or make-up for them to fall back on. They stood on the bare, inclined planes and ladders of the machine, on the empty stage floor. Every movement, whether they intended it or not, acquired sculptural form and significance. They had therefore to strive for the most subtle expressiveness of outline and gesture, to move with the ease of dancers and the dexterity of acrobats. The artistry took on an athletic character. The gracefulness of the sculptural image entailed the ease of each line's delivery, a sonority and clarity of intonation.

All this, taken together, created a system of performance which highlighted above all the joyful demonstration of confident and co-ordinated mastery. Emotion revealed its dynamic framework: the moment of appearance, the development (rising and falling), the culmination, the exhaustion. Dynamism was stressed, passion abolished. Herein lies the secret of the purity and health, freshness and youth which coloured the crude farce on the Meyerhold stage.

Suddenly, in the third act of the performance, some totally extraordinary, cheerful and assertive music rang out. For the first time in the Soviet Union a jazz band performed, conducted by the poet Valentin Parnakh who had just arrived from Paris.

Three Meyerhold students celebrated a triumph in *The Magnanimous Cuckold*: Igor Ilinsky, Maria Babanova and Vasily Zaichikov. All three had mastered ideally the requirements of biomechanics.

'It is difficult to find more perfect consonance than in the triad Ilinsky-Babanova-Zaichikov,' wrote Gvozdev. 'The swiftness and suppleness of Ilinsky finds its continuation in the exceptional rhythm and musicality of Babanova, while Zaichikov creates a peerless accompaniment for them with the absolutely precise reinforcement of every gesture. Like the chorus in a Greek tragedy, he accompanies and elucidates in mime everything that happens to his partners in the turbulent exchange of passions.'[27]

Some, like Gvozdev, Tretyakov and Mayakovsky, were delighted by *Cuckold*, but many others were bewildered. 'There is absolutely no Revolutionary content whatsoever in this production,' said one speaker at a debate on the production. Another asked: 'Surely all the storms that have passed over our country and through our theatre in the course of five years have not come down to this – to biomechanics? Meyerhold's vaunted revolution is only the revolution of the ankle!'[28]

Its neighbours in the Moscow theatrical repertoire of 1922 included Vakhtangov's *Princess Turandot*, Tairov's *Phèdre* and Granovsky's *The Sorceress*. Against the diversity and bold colour of these productions, *The Magnanimous Cuckold* could seem dryly austere, indifferent to and even contemptuous of the eternal human passions which seethed in some theatres and mischievously played in others. It was obviously of a different, unforeseen and unexpected complexion.

In its marvellously co-ordinated liveliness, in its purity of line, in the dynamism which ran through all the acting, in the rhythmic mechanization and circus-like athleticism of Meyerhold's whole creation could be seen a prototype for the future, cleansed of passions not subject to the intellect.

The production mocked – derisively and condescendingly – those uncontrolled instincts and passions before which man has been powerless from time immemorial. In *The Magnanimous Cuckold* theatre heralded harmony and ease in human relations and in daily life.

It soon became clear that the break with the past in the sphere of feelings and passions was impossible to realize. But the aesthetic prognosis of *The Magnanimous Cuckold* proved to be far-sighted. Theatrical art absorbed the ideas of *Cuckold* avidly and quickly, and their numerous echoes are heard in the theatre to the present day.

'Circusization'

The attempts begun in Sergei Radlov's 'Popular Theatre' to cross theatre with circus either by involving professional circus artistes in theatrical action or by teaching young actors circus stunts were soon continued. By a strange twist of fate the young people who first took up Radlov's initiative were in the future destined to become major figures in the art of cinema – Sergei Eisenstein, Grigory Kozintsev, Leonid Trauberg. In Petrograd Kozintsev and Trauberg organized something akin to a studio called the 'Factory of the Eccentric Actor' (FEKS): the word 'studio' seemed unbearably old-fashioned to its founders, who would not, under any circumstances, call themselves directors, but 'engineers of the spectacle'. Participants in FEKS included the clown-acrobat Serge, the Japanese juggler Takashima who had previously worked with Radlov, and the new (subsequently famous) actor Sergei Martinson. The first thing they decided to stage was *The Marriage* by Gogol, although – as the poster intriguingly communicated – 'not according to Gogol'. And indeed there was literally not a single word from the classic Gogol text in the performance.

As was often the case in those years, the Gogol title and barely noticeable rudiments of the Gogol theme were only used by the organizers for shock value. The FEKS programme proclaimed its aim as 'art that is exaggeratedly crude, which jolts, batters the nerves, is openly utilitarian, mechanically precise, instant, fast.' The eccentric show is 'the rhythmical battering of the nerves'. The eccentric performance is 'not movement but affectation, not mime but grimace, not speaking but shouting'. The eccentric play is 'a conglomeration of stunts'.[29] Striving toward the 'Americanization of theatre', Kozintsev and Trauberg named Charlie Chaplin as their ideal and idol and claimed that their 'parents' were circus, jazz, café-chantant, cinema and even boxing.

It is therefore not surprising that among the characters in *The Marriage* appeared Chaplin, Einstein and even Gogol himself (who turned up at the end of the show to express his indignation at what he had seen). There were mechanical characters besides: a Steam Bridegroom, an Electric Bridegroom and a Radioactive Bridegroom, three robots who entered on roller skates. The chaotic action was accompanied by numerous light and sound effects. Garlands of multi-coloured electric lights could be seen through the fabric of

Kozintsev's scenery flashing on and off to the sounds of the two-step and Ragtime, while in the meantime hooters, rattles, bells and whistles 'assisted' the pianist. Serge's somersaults and tumbling, executed against a background of a large portrait of Chaplin, gave way to the cancan, the cancan in turn to cheeky satirical couplets with topical allusions. 'It could probably best be called a kind of fantastic ballet,' Kozintsev would recall with a smile in his later years. It is interesting, however, that Kozintsev also recalled Eisenstein, then still completely unknown, being present at a rehearsal and murmuring with dissatisfaction: 'Slow! Too slow!' and recommending maximum acceleration of the tempo.[30]

FEKS existed for a very short time: *The Marriage* was staged on 25 September 1922, and the second (and last) production, *Foreign Trade on the Eiffel Tower*, was on 4 June 1923. However, Eisenstein's theatrical experiments did last rather longer; he did not arrive immediately at the 'circusization' of theatre, but only after FEKS and his teacher Meyerhold had done so.

In the same year, 1922, that Kozintsev and Trauberg performed *The Marriage* 'not according to Gogol' in Petrograd, Meyerhold presented the 'circusized' play *Tarelkin's Death* by Alexander Sukhovo-Kobylin to astounded Muscovites. This time too the production's design was Constructivist, but the very idea of Constructivism underwent essential changes in the hands of Varvara Stepanova. If in *The Magnanimous Cuckold* Popova had offered an integrated form – 'a machine for acting' – one single, large and intricately constructed contraption, then Stepanova divided the construction into portable and mobile mechanisms, into separate 'apparatuses', each of which had its own function.

The action of Sukhovo-Kobylin's play soon takes its characters into a police station. In order to point out that people are tortured and tormented by the police, Stepanova erected a structure which was a frightening combination of a barred cage and a mincing machine. All who fell into the clutches of the police were put into the cage and then 'cranked' through the mincer. A table and chairs were necessary props for the interrogations. But the chairs gave way when sat upon and bounced back when people stood up. One chair – 'the shooting one' – reacted to any attempt to sit on it with a pistol shot. Another collapsed. A third spun like a top. The table gave way at its joints whenever anyone so much as leaned his elbows on it, and then, as if nothing had happened, snapped up onto its legs again. There was a screen which Tarelkin got stuck in during the second act. There was a tall box with a lid that kept opening suddenly, and then an actor's head would stick out. The lid would be slammed down, the head would disappear.

Stepanova's 'furniture', painted white, was basically a set of various circus props, which did not attempt to conceal their circus nature. Numerous truncheons, clubs with inflated bull's bladders on the end, and bottles in the form of skittles were there for the players to belabour each other with.

A central feature in this production was the fact that the actor performed with mobile, living objects which themselves were able (or were supposed to be able) to perform. And if it is borne in mind that the main content of the action is physical torture, then an even more pointed formulation appears: instruments of torture comically corresponded to a tortured body. In comedy of this kind tragic notes were clearly heard.

Acting also changed because it was now spread over the entire stage floor. The centrifugal impetus of *Tarelkin's Death* contrasted with the centripetal impetus of *Cuckold*. The performance burst out toward the audience and into the audience – unlike *Cuckold*, the dynamics of which were confined within the limits of the stage.

The desire to draw the action nearer to the audience induced Meyerhold to illuminate the foreground exceptionally brightly with two floodlights which stood to the left and right in the front wings. But the back of the stage area remained darkened and when Meyerhold's *comédiens* went to the back of the stage they seemed to dissolve in darkness. The contrast between the bright resplendence of the forestage and the gloom lurking in the background, behind the actors, immediately struck the spectators. *The Magnanimous Cuckold* looked cheerfully ahead; *Tarelkin's Death* looked back, with horror, to the past.

The actors again performed in identical *prozodezhda*, without make-up and wigs, although the costumes of blue material and cotton duck, made according to Stepanova's designs, recalled either prisoners' clothing or hospital gowns. 'The clothing of the condemned' was how Vasily Sakhnovsky expressed it. He also gave the most concise definition of the production: 'a terrifying circus'.[31]

Every act concluded with the audience being shot at with a gun from the stage, and a director's assistant yelling, 'In-terrr-val!' During the intervals merry distractions entertained the whole auditorium. Enormous multi-coloured balls flew through the stalls, and the audience eagerly threw them to each other along the rows. Enormous fake apples were lowered from the dress circle and the audience enthusiastically tried to grab them.

When the interval ended, the audience observed the prompter, dressed in the same *prozodezhda* as the actors, sitting in the first row of the stalls and from time to time very loudly 'cueing' the performers. The *comédiens* poured water over each other, fought with sticks, truncheons, bulls' bladders and struggled with the whims and caprices of the bouncing, skipping and shooting 'furniture'. As befits the circus, the actors did not speak, but bawled, did not walk but skipped. Moreover, the reviewers noted, with some embarrassment, 'indecent' stunts such as 'sniffing each other's backsides'.

During rehearsals for *Tarelkin's Death* Meyerhold involved his students in a competition: he challenged everyone to devise stunts and stagings. It was the most gifted of the young pupils – Sergei Eisenstein – who fantasized most boldly. He proposed two stagings. Ivan Axenov commented: 'There was no way that Eisenstein's stagings could be called bad, but to acknowledge them as good meant to introduce them into the performance. . . . The stagings were rejected because they were executed in a style different from that of the coming performance.'

Several days later Zinaida Raikh sent Eisenstein a little note. It read: 'Seryozha, when Meyerhold felt ready to be a director, he left Stanislavsky.'[32] It only remained for Eisenstein to heed the advice – or the order.

As a matter of fact, before this significant episode and before his departure from Meyerhold, Eisenstein, together with the director Valentin Smyshlyaev, had staged a play adapted by Valerian Pletnev from Jack London's story 'The Mexican' at the First Workers' Theatre of the Proletkult. Eisenstein's theatrical début was very extravagant. Suffice it to say that the two rival boxing clubs were represented geometrically – one in the form of cubes and squares throughout, the other in the form of spheres and circles. 'This,' recounts Yutkevich, 'was expressed not only in the form of the furniture, but also in the way that he turned all the characters into either spheres or squares with the help of costumes and even of make-up.'[33] According to the play the boxing match took place behind the scenes. Eisenstein, however, built a ring on the forestage and the fight took place in an electric atmosphere, right in front of the audience. Nevertheless there were still no purely circus stunts in *The Mexican*, perhaps due to the influence of Eisenstein's co-director, the relatively moderate Smyshlyaev.

To make up for this, in April 1923 Eisenstein presented his true opus – Ostrovsky's comedy *Enough Stupidity in Every Wise Man* which, together with Sergei Tretyakov, he re-worked and turned into a scenario for a circus revue.

This production by the First Workers' Theatre of the Proletkult was performed in the premises of an ornate mansion, built at the very end of the nineteenth century at the whim of the millionaire Morozov. (The building, with all its intricate embellishments, has been preserved to the present day, and is now Friendship House located at 16, Prospekt Kalinina.) The poster advertising the première of *Wise Man* announced: 'Montage of Attractions (staging, direction, arena lay-out, costumes, props) by Sergei Eisenstein.'

The stage was replaced by a circus ring covered with a carpet. The action was broken up like a circus programme into different 'acts' of aerial and floor gymnastics and musical eccentricities. Acrobatics and clowning were offered instead of acting, and a series of 'attractions' replaced the play. The characters walked the tightrope, climbed a pole, executed circus 'dives', flying somersaults and tumbling; they performed satirical songs mocking the White Guard generals, White *émigrés*, and the politicians of the Entente. (General Joffre appeared in place of Krutitsky and Lord Curzon in place of Mamaev.) The participants included Maxim Shtraukh, later to become a famous actor, and Ivan Pyriev and Grigory Alexandrov, later to become famous film directors. The performance was concluded by a short film of stunts, *Glumov's Diary* (this was the first film that Eisenstein ever shot). During a relatively brief period of rehearsals (six months in all) Eisenstein had succeeded in teaching his young performers circus technique.

As for the text, he did return briefly to Ostrovsky in some places (unlike the FEKS production of *The Marriage* which bore not the slightest relation to Gogol whatsoever); but the play was still only seen as an occasion and pretext for topical political satire and circus eccentricism. Meyerhold observed that even though there remained 'only bits and pieces' of Ostrovsky in the Eisenstein spectacle, on the whole the enterprise did have a point: 'Eisenstein did not set himself the task of showing Ostrovsky; he was getting into his director's stride.'[34]

The stride was a long and firm one, and Eisenstein promptly, abreast with Tretyakov, stepped into modern times. The Eisenstein-Tretyakov tandem, which enthusiastically headed the First Workers' Theatre of the Proletkult, was internally torn with conflicts. Eisenstein was attracted to eccentricism, to the grotesque, to 'circusization', while Tretyakov was drawn to the documentary and the agit-play. In their collaborative work Eisenstein's living fantasy suppressed and overcame Tretyakov's factual account. 'Circusization' prevailed over politicization.

Tretyakov's 'agit-Guignol', *Do You Hear, Moscow?!*, was an attempt to respond sympathetically to revolutionary upheavals in Germany. In this short play the German Communist workers waged a bitter struggle against the Count-Governor, the prefect of police,

Yudif Glizer as the Courtesan in Tretyakov's *Do You Hear, Moscow?!* directed by Eisenstein at the Proletkult Theatre, 1923.

the bishop and Mister Pound, 'the representative of the American banks'. Eisenstein, however, totally disregarded the entire dramatic situation: in his production the Count's lover, the courtesan Marga (played by Yudif Glizer) came out on stage riding a live camel, completely nonsensical in Germany. The caricature and buffoonery overflowed over the whole stage; the mime, very dynamic and fast, took up much more time and space than Tretyakov's dialogue and the circus numbers – diving from great heights, flying through the air, tightrope walking, and so on – excited the audience more powerfully than the character's primitive lines.

In the next production, *The Gas Masks*, the dramatist attempted to take revenge. The action of this play was set in a Moscow factory, in an atmosphere of 'the heavy uneventfulness of everyday life'[35] (Eisenstein's description), and Tretyakov persuaded the director to stage the show on the shop floor of a Moscow gasworks rather than in the theatre. A wooden platform for the actors was built alongside the immense turbo-generators which, as the director subsequently admitted, 'with the glistening blackness of their cylindrical bodies completely swallowed up the small theatrical appendage, humbly sheltering next to them.'[36] Circus was inappropriate here: theatre was trying to close ranks with real industry, acting with real industrial work. From Tretyakov's point of view these conditions were ideal, and he could not have wished for better: it seemed that the concept of 'industrial art', of theatre without invention, without fantasy, had finally been realized. Three years later Tretyakov wrote, 'the discrediting of the theatrical prop was taken to the limit by Eisenstein who transferred the action of *The Gas Masks* to its natural setting, to a gasworks.' But, alas, 'theatre failed to dissolve its aesthetic essence in practice.' And Tretyakov came to the bitter conclusion that theatre is not made 'to be an instrument of direct practical influence (of life-building)'.[37]

The ideas of LEF failed to be realized.

The idea of 'circusization of theatre' also quickly exhausted itself. FEKS' production of *The Marriage* and Meyerhold's *Tarelkin's Death* were presented in 1922, Tretyakov and Eisenstein's *Wise Man* and *Do You Hear, Moscow?!* in 1923. Then the circus began to leave theatre stages and return to its own rings.

Meanwhile one more avant-garde idea was being tried out in practice – the idea of merging theatre with music hall.

'Music-hallization'

Nikolai Foregger was the pioneer and enthusiast of the 'music-hallization' of theatre. In Moscow in 1921 he organized a little theatre called The Foregger Theatre Workshop (Mastfor) and initially gave performances in the hall of Printing House on Nikitsky Boulevard, then later made his base in his own tiny premises on the Arbat. Foregger began with a series of witty and gleeful parodies. At Mastfor agit-plays were scorned (their parody of agit-plays was entitled *Don't Drink Unboiled Water!*) alongside the operas of the Bolshoi Theatre (*The Tsar's Mother-in-Law* parodied Rimsky-Korsakov's *The Tsar's Bride*), the Kamerny Theatre, MAT and even Meyerhold's productions of *The Dawn* and *The Magnanimous Cuckold*. Perhaps the most comic and telling was the parody of *The Dawn*: Chekhov's vaudeville *The Proposal* was executed in an exaggerated form of the performance-meeting. Foregger was able to extract maximal comic effect from the absurd incongruity of form and content.

Theatrical parody had been a mocking companion to the history of the Russian stage as far back as the nineteenth century. In the early twentieth century, however, small theatres emerged which specially cultivated parody, such as Nikita Baliev's The Bat in Moscow, and The Distorting Mirror in Petersburg where Nikolai Evreinov operated. At first it seemed that Mastfor would also advance along these lines, relying primarily on its 'own', artistic audience. Soon, however, Mastfor's shows began to attract a wider public, and Foregger started to prepare original productions as well as parody.

In many respects his ideas were akin to those of Eisenstein and the founders of FEKS. Like them, Foregger was under the spell of technology and like them he believed the circus stunt should serve as the main element of the modern show. But in his view it was absolutely essential that any performance should be set to music and organized musically. Borrowing acrobatics from the circus and dynamics of action from cinema, Foregger was quite explicitly orientated towards the aesthetic of the music hall. 'The future,' he stated, 'belongs to the cinema and music hall,' for the theatre, in its former, 'non-musicalized' form 'is living out its last days and soon won't be needed by anyone.'[38] In Foregger's programme, 'avant-garde art' was obliged to combine American tempo with circus dexterity and the bravura of dance. In appealing to performers to emulate circus acrobats, in the control of their bodies 'as supple, obedient, expressive instruments', Foregger meant not so much the expressiveness of circus as that of dance. Special significance was attached to pose and gesture. 'The transition from one pose to another,' he taught, 'is the gesture. Gesture leads the melody, the pose sets it off, theatrical action is revealed in the sequence of gestures and poses.'[39] A certain, simplified similarity to Meyerhold's principles of biomechanics was cultivated in Mastfor, only with the proviso that movement obeyed the rhythm of dance.

The plays for Mastfor were written by the witty dramatist Vladimir Mass, and the music was composed by the talented Matvei Blanter. The collaborative creations of Mass and Blanter were commonly called 'parades'. A 'parade' was essentially a sort of comic revue, lightly peppered with satire which touched in passing on certain fashionable themes and topical issues. At that time, for example, the question of 'marriage or free love' was being hotly debated – and on Foregger's stage there appeared a dashing woman in a leather jacket caricaturing Alexandra Kollontai, an ardent propagandist of love without marriage. The Imagist poets Esenin, Mariengof and Shershenevich, were notorious as 'Moscow dandies', and so on Foregger's stage a corresponding character emerged: in tails, but with a Russian peasant shirt and coarse country breeches, with a shiny patent-leather ankle-boot on one foot and an old bast shoe on the other.

All such caricatures were relatively good-natured, and although Mass later claimed that he 'openly imitated' Mayakovsky's *Mystery-Bouffe*,[40] and although sometimes Lloyd George, Kerensky and other politicians were derided in his 'parades', the Mastfor 'bouffonades' did not possess either political bite or satirical vehemence. The text of the 'parades' contained no independent significance, its function was a linking one: dialogues and monologues led from one dance number to another, from tango to foxtrot, from shimmy to cakewalk, from Charleston to Russian folk dance.

Sergei Eisenstein and Sergei Yutkevich worked enthusiastically for Foregger as designers. When the best and most sensational of the Mastfor programmes, *Kind Treatment of Horses*, was being prepared, Eisenstein devised a stunning costume for the theatre's leading lady, Ludmilla Semenova: an enormous hat, small brassière and a lampshade-skirt, an enormous wire frame resembling a crinoline but only lightly covered with multi-coloured ribbons. 'The ribbons were placed at intervals,' wrote Yutkevich, 'so that the actress's shapely legs were exposed beneath them to the astonished gaze of the puritanically conditioned spectator of the Moscow of those years.'[41]

Barely six months later the artist Georgy Yakulov employed roughly the same costumes in Tairov's production of Lecocq's *Giroflé-Girofla* and, to Eisenstein's great annoyance, without acknowledgment. However, there was much at Mastfor that was new for Moscow and much that was later borrowed by others. In particular, Foregger was the first to show Muscovites the synchronized movement of chorus girls – the latest 'rage' in Western music-hall fashion. But the Foregger 'singers wearing nothing but "chic" instead of costumes'[42] were far from being to everyone's liking. Their bare, high-kicking legs plunged moralists into a state of commotion. 'They dance,' gloomily prophesied one reviewer, 'on the last night before the dawn of a new revolutionary culture.'[43]

Two sketches by P. Galadzhev of S. Savitskaya and L. Semenova in *Kind Treatment of Horses*, directed by Foregger at Mastfor, 1922.

During a dispute concerning the production *Kind Treatment of Horses*, the critic Vyacheslav Polonsky became indignant. 'You,' he accused Foregger, 'are cultivating the thoroughly rotten bourgeois café-*chantant* under the mask of Revolutionary satire and parody!' The leader of LEF, Mayakovsky, unexpectedly stood up in support of Foregger. 'Yes,' he declared, café-*chantant* and music hall!... Give us dancing ideology, merry and uproarious cascades of propaganda, sparkling Revolutionary theatricality!' The poet in fury called Foregger's opponents 'petit-bourgeois philistines in art'.[44]

Foregger responded immediately to Mayakovsky's demand to provide 'dancing ideology' without delay by staging a programme called *Machine Dances*. It was a fairly typical music-hall dance show. To an accompaniment which imitated the swelling noise of a factory, a similarity to a complex mechanism was created from human bodies. 'The combined action of the rhythmic movements created the impression of working machines, of piston, gears, transmission, and soon even an entire blacksmith's shop appeared,'

wrote the historian of light entertainment, Elizaveta Uvarova.[45] The Moscow magazine *Zrelishcha* reprinted an article from *The New York Times* which said that 'the dancing machine is delighting Moscow' and that the ballet which creates the illusion of a functioning mechanism through 'acrobatic movements' is making a great impression.[46] The ballet-master Kasyan Goleizovsky also praised *Machine Dances*, considering that it 'liberated' the dramatic performers and equipped them with perfect technique of gesture and pose, with the feeling of rhythm, of musicality.[47]

Nonetheless there was a sense of something second-hand in all Mastfor's performances: everywhere either parody slid into imitation or imitation turned into parody. But when Foregger tried to do something original and turned his hand to melodrama (d'Ennery's *The Baby-Snatcher*), operetta (Lecocq's *The Mysteries of the Canary Islands*), and Expressionist drama (Toller's *Eugene the Unlucky*), his theatre immediately faded, became banal. One after another Foregger's best workers abandoned him — first Eisenstein

Theatrical Expansion

Sketch by S. Yutkevich of A. Senderov, the compère at Mastfor.

Sketch by P. Galadzhev of the singer P. Baburina at Mastfor.

Sketch by S. Yutkevich of 'The Walk Scene' in *Machine Dances*, staged by Foregger at Mastfor, 1923.

left, then Yutkevich and Mass. The end of Mastfor was hastened by an unfortunate accident when in January 1924 a fire destroyed all the scenery and costumes. But those critics who believed that 'an artistic crisis' had overtaken Foregger well before this fire were evidently correct. 'Foregger,' wrote Pavel Markov, 'for the time being remains the creator of small pieces. And it is not accidental that the artistic and the material end of his Theatre Workshop coincided.' A critic asked: 'Will Foregger succeed in finding new rhythms and forms for that musical theatre which he has always created? . . . Who knows?'[48]

History answered this question in the negative. Foregger's experiments ceased. 'The dilettante master and the expert dilettante'[49] (Markov's expression) subsequently became an ordinary professional, working in opera, in ballet, in circus, but working like everyone else. As for the idea of 'the music-hallization of theatre', however, it was recalled time and again, most often in Meyerhold's political revues, such as *The Earth in Turmoil* and *D.E.*

Sketch by S. Yutkevich of a set for Lecocq's *The Mysteries of the Canary Islands* directed by Foregger at Mastfor, 1923.

Expressionist Drama and Constructions

Attempts to 'circusize' or 'music-hallize' theatre were invariably accompanied by the urge to impart a mechanized appearance to the production. Under Meyerhold both *The Magnanimous Cuckold* and *Tarelkin's Death* were staged with Constructivist sets. Eisenstein and Tretyakov, as we already know, tried presenting productions on factory floors, and Foregger asserted that his *Machine Dances* was 'an experiment of Constructivism in form and movement'.[50]

Subsequently the writer Alexei Tolstoy, reflecting on the reasons for the general enthusiasm of theatre people for all kinds of machinery, came to the conclusion that 'for us the machine and technology are linked with the idea of the movement to socialism. The machine is a conditioned reflex that evokes images of the struggle, the achievements, the desired future.' In an article entitled 'The Moon Which Was Replaced by a Tractor', Tolstoy spoke with some degree of irony about productions where 'the actor stood in *prozodezhda* by a paste-board machine', and he said that the theatre required neither these 'wooden gears nor hammers made of papier mâché' but something quite different: what was needed was 'passion', what was needed was 'keen perception of life'.[51] These common-sense ideas, however, only occurred to the writer in the early 1930s. In the 1920s Tolstoy had himself paid considerable tribute to the fetishization of technology. His play *Mutiny of the Machines*, staged in 1924 by Konstantin Khokhlov at the Bolshoi Dramatic Theatre, was a free adaptation of Karel Čapek's drama *R.U.R. (Rossum's Universal Robots)*, with little to distinguish it from the theatrical attempts, typical of that period, to reinterpret the works of Western (usually German) Expressionist writers.

Expressionist plays such as *Die Maschinenstürmer*, *Masse Mensch* and *Hoppla, wir leben!* by Ernst Toller and *Gas* by Georg Kaiser attracted Soviet directors primarily because the portents of coming world revolution could be heard clearly within them, the angry protests against the power of big business that numbs, suffocates mankind and tramples freedom. Moreover, much in these plays was related to 'leftist theatre': composition was broken into short,

striking episodes, and frequently there was a mighty surge of aroused and indignant crowds over the stage.

However, beyond this point there emerged highly characteristic differences. Technology, industrialization and the machine instilled fear in the Expressionist dramatists, for they perceived mechanization as a means of depriving mankind of individuality, of turning him into a spineless, spiritless adjunct of the machine, a robot obedient to the capitalist boss. Soviet directors, on the contrary, regarded technology with admiration and hope since only industrialization could lead the country out of devastation.

The crowds which the Expressionists depicted did not evoke special sympathy in the authors of these plays. Most often the masses were featureless, obtuse, hostile to the inspired hero, a solitary intellectual-rebel. Such schematically drawn inter-relationships between hero and crowd were in no way congenial to the Soviet directors. They, on the contrary, were inclined to glorify the rebelling masses and were mistrustful of the lone intellectual whom the authors of Expressionist dramas had defended.

Finally, the spirit of pessimism and despair, the terror before the almighty power of machinery and the lack of spiritual content in petit-bourgeois life that permeated Expressionist drama was also alien to Soviet producers of these plays. The tragic conclusions of the majority of the plays did not satisfy them at all, and they usually tried to substitute a triumphant, cheerful finale in place of a depressing one.

The Theatre of the Revolution in Moscow and the Bolshoi Dramatic Theatre in Leningrad staged Expressionist plays more readily than others. In their productions the structure of Expressionist drama was modified. New emphases were established: dynamic crowd scenes portrayed the insurgent people as a conscious and victorious force, while the solitary intellectual-hero was drawn as a backward, naive idealist, incapable of understanding the will of the mighty collective. While industry frightened and urbanization horrified the Expressionist dramatists, while hatred for the machine and machinery was intensely felt in their plays, the Soviet directors, on the contrary, admired machinery. On their stages Constructivist artists eagerly constructed mechanized worlds fully in the control of man the creator.

In other words, the principal themes of Expressionist plays were turned upside-down in the productions of the Theatre of the Revolution and the Bolshoi Dramatic Theatre. The writer Konstantin Fedin correctly observed that 'transferred to Russian soil, the backbone of Expressionist drama collapses completely.'[52]

During the brief period (1922 to 1924) when Meyerhold was chief director of the Theatre of the Revolution, he turned his hand to staging Expressionist dramas. The set for Ernst Toller's *Masse Mensch* was designed by Viktor Shestakov. 'Bridges made of wood and iron suspended from steel cables and supported by heavy girders' could be seen on stage. These bridges 'cut through the proscenium in all directions', and between the acting platforms situated 'at various heights', 'steel trolleys' dashed about, crashing and clanging, their movement followed by the dazzling beams of the searchlights, picking out the contours of the construction.

As to the general interpretation of Toller's drama, the tendencies which guided the director are made evident in a sympathetic review by Boris Alpers. The critic wrote: 'the style of the urban propaganda spectacle is firmly establishing itself. Bankers, like wind-up puppets in top hats and tail coats, fly about in a stock-exchange flurry along the construction's split-level platforms, scattered about the stage. The stock broker cries from high above. The electric figures showing the share prices flash in the air. Variety show girls dance. The movements of this dandified herd of profiteers and speculators are whipped up by the disturbing rhythms. Gold jingles, music roars. The "Big Wheel" of the stock exchange in post-war speculators' Germany revolves manically. A sudden stop, silence, the knife-switch cuts out the light, and, picked out on stage by the narrow beam of a searchlight, the face of the Woman, the tragedy's heroine, appears. Groups of workers in blue-black *prozodezhda* are placed on the high bridges and platforms. In solemn and elevated tones a dialogue is conducted between the Woman and the Masses about the ethics of the struggle. The theatre ironically presents Toller's naive yet profound arguments and the pretentious tragic pose of the philosophizing, divided intellectual that so patently shows through all these earnest dialogues. The class nature of the Woman's "lofty" humanitarian morality is unmasked for the audience through her sing-song declamatory reading, her prayerful movements and gestures. In the production this hypocritical morality is contrasted with the sober morality of the masses, who are not that faceless, doctrinaire crowd of the author's text and scenario, but masses whose movements are filled with action, urgency and anger, deployed by the director as a conscious, rational force that moves events. The masses take the platforms and bastions of the construction by storm, spreading over the stairs, splitting into separate groups, again gathering together into a whole, emphasizing through their movements the meaning and character of the individual episodes in the social conflict that is being enacted. The mass scenes are the strongest parts of the spectacle.'[53]

The director Khokhlov likewise struggled with the 'author's text' when he staged the plays of Toller and Kaiser at the Bolshoi Dramatic Theatre with designs by Yury Annenkov. In the production of Kaiser's *Gas*, Annenkov 'erected on stage entire industrial cities which stretched up under the grid, fantastic interlacings of bridges, girders, ladders and hoardings,' wrote the critic Adrian Piotrovsky.[54] Alexei Tolstoy's adaptation of Čapek's play *R.U.R.*, entitled *Mutiny of the Machines*, needed no directorial reinterpretations for Tolstoy had himself met the demands laid down by the theatre. The play portrayed an uprising of Robots (Čapek actually invented the word 'robot') against the proprietors, so naturally all the sympathies of the author, director and public were on the side of the animated machines. The Robots joined in the 'class struggle' and were endowed with Revolutionary consciousness; the proprietors, yesterday's owners of these machines, abandoned their factories and plants in panic.

However, such devoted enthusiasm for the rebelling machinery inevitably entailed a reconsideration of the ideas behind theatrical Constructivism. In Annenkov's theatrical works industrialism and urbanism acquired an independent significance. Machinery displaced actors. The audience, busy examining all this complex machinery, illuminated from one side then the other, gleaming, crashing, paid almost no attention to the people who were glimpsed against the mechanized background. For 'actors were neither visible nor audible among these rotating, sputtering, hissing, creaking discs and cranes.'[55] Annenkov's construction had nothing in common with the original Constructivist idea of the set which was intended for the actor's performance. The construction essentially became self-sufficient mechanized scenery. In his review of *Mutiny of the*

Machines, the critic Alexei Gvozdev wrote, 'There is plenty to look at here: electric posters, bright light-effects on coloured hoardings, revolving turbines, a real automobile, strange people-machines, mass fox-trotting scenes. . . . the framework of the play provides wide scope for the fantasy of the director and artist.' However, within their work 'a compromise is concealed: the construction is turned into a beautiful stage *picture*, revived scenery, essentially just as static as the old.' The outer dynamism 'does not reinforce the dynamism of the dramatic action'.[56]

A slightly different impression was created by Viktor Shestakov's Constructivist design for Alexei Faiko's play *Lake Lyul*, staged by Meyerhold at the Theatre of the Revolution. This time the construction did not strike anyone as being static, not only because Shestakov stunned the audience by equipping the stage platforms with moving lifts, but also because the play itself was an entertaining melodrama. *Lake Lyul* was set, according to a stage direction, 'in the Far West or, perhaps, in the Far East,' in a kind of theatrically stylized centre of 'civilization and cosmopolitanism'. Its hidden theme, however, was highly relevant to Moscow of the early 1920s: there were disturbing images of the 'high life', notoriously wanton and inaccessible, and thus all the more alluring.

Reviewers reproached both Faiko and Meyerhold for 'cheap vulgarity' in imitation of Hollywood films. The critic Yury Sobolev spoke ironically of 'the romanticism of the Revolution', combined in Faiko with an attraction for 'the detective story, the adventure novel'. Nonetheless he acknowledged that *Lake Lyul* at the Theatre of the Revolution was 'one of the most biting, brilliant and interesting spectacles', that Meyerhold 'had constructed a production whose dynamics can compete with cinematography'. Sobolev liked 'the ascending and descending lifts, the crowd of shoppers moving up and down in the department store, the staff of the hotel coming running at the sound of the gong, ringing telephones, the workings of the telegraph machines, the lights of the semaphores, and so on'.[57]

The public flocked to *Lake Lyul* and the production brought in record takings. Alexei Gripich, a student of Meyerhold, tried to extend this success: one year later, also in the Theatre of the Revolution, he staged Vladimir Bill-Belotserkovsky's play *Echo*, which is set in the Far West. Viktor Shestakov's Constructivist set raised suspension bridges, steps and the lights of advertisements high up beneath the very grid of the stage. The walls moved, the café floor revolved, the lights flashed on and off. The subject of the play, however, did not touch at all upon the temptations of the 'good life' – the play was about dockers' strikes, their skirmishes with police and strike-breakers. A street rally, an episode involving the lynching of a black docker, the reviewers warmly approved of all this. 'The first play without foxtrotting vulgarity,' reported Beskin in *Izvestia*. But he had to admit that the actors, including both Babanova and Martinson, performed 'without joy, without love, without spirit'.[58] The play was poorly attended.

Having encroached upon circus and music hall, in *Lake Lyul* and *Echo* theatre now attempted to appropriate the expressive means of cinematography as well. This expansion was carried out with the full armament of Constructivist aesthetics.

As it turned out, the potential of theatrical Constructivism was great, and its range sufficiently broad. This message will be reinforced when we look at the achievements of the directors Alexander Tairov and Les Kurbas in the early 1920s.

Model of the set by V. Shestakov for Faiko's *Lake Lyul* directed by Meyerhold at the Theatre of the Revolution, 1923.

But the period of time granted by history to the Constructivist theatrical form was relatively brief. In the second half of the 1920s, constructions 'in pure form' had already become obsolete: theatre, wrote Sergei Tretyakov, 'entered its own aesthetic channel, constructions became good old wooden sets.'[59] This transformation first occurred in the Kamerny Theatre, in the Tairov production of *The Storm*.

Political Revues

There were not, as yet, any new plays which even partly conformed to the theatrical principles realized by Meyerhold in *The Magnanimous Cuckold*. At this time his attention was drawn to *La Nuit*, by Marcel Martinet, being staged by another director at the Theatre of the Revolution. As head of this collective, Meyerhold scrutinized the production before its première. The director Zinovy Daltsev recalled that he 'didn't make a single criticism. I could see that he couldn't find fault with anything – everything was polished.

But surely Meyerhold wasn't contemplating putting on such a slick production himself?'[60]

Indeed, having approved the 'slick' production at the Theatre of the Revolution, Meyerhold promptly staged *La Nuit* in a completely re-worked adaptation by Sergei Tretyakov re-titled *The Earth in Turmoil* at his own theatre on Sadovo-Triumfalnaya Street. From 1923 this theatre was called The Meyerhold Theatre (TIM).

In taking the Theatre of the Revolution under his aegis, Meyerhold had assumed that, 'at home', in TIM, he would experiment, explore new directions, while in the Theatre of the Revolution the tried and tested means of theatrical expression would be presented before a mass audience. In other words, TIM was perceived as a kind of (relatively large) studio and the Theatre of the Revolution as a theatre for the masses. The Theatre of the Revolution had been conceived as a profit-making commercial enterprise; meanwhile Meyerhold wanted to save TIM, his laboratory for new explorations, from the influence of the 'box office' altogether.

Meyerhold did not like Martinet's play at all, which is why he commissioned Tretyakov to alter it, to 'stuff' the melodrama with the gunpowder of biting satire. Tretyakov retold Martinet's long-winded verse in coarse and laconic prose, squeezing and compressing the text, giving it urgency, stridency and a folkloric simplicity. The thematic lines linking the individual scenes were casually severed. Martinet's melodrama disintegrated into individual 'numbers', almost independent of each other, and was turned into a modern political-propaganda revue. This revue, performed for the first time in 1923, consisted of episodes of pathos and satire: 'Down with War!', 'Attention!' 'The Truth of the Trenches', 'The Black International', 'All Power to the Soviets!', 'A Knife in the Back of the Revolution', 'Shearing the Sheep', 'Night'. The performance took place without a curtain on an open platform, on a construction illuminated by searchlights. Slogans and photographs flashed onto a screen at the back of the stage. Liubov Popova's construction was proudly called 'machine-photo-placard'. The action repeatedly moved into the auditorium, to the centre aisle between the rows of the stalls.

'The Earth in Turmoil', wrote Stefan Mokulsky, 'is a superb propagandist show realized in the pure form of the mass meeting.... For all this, it still contains a number of compromises with the old theatre.'[61] The compromises arose because the days of The Dawn were over. The performance-meeting could no longer take place. While trying to remain faithful to his former principles, Meyerhold was compelled to resort to the most striking and forceful means. They worked. From the entire production of The Earth in Turmoil, both the audience and the critics liked two episodes best – a farcical and a tragic one. All the rest were viewed with interest, but nothing more.

The farcical episode was crudely executed. The Emperor, Vasily Zaichikov, dressed in uniform coat, helmet and longjohns, presided on a chamber pot. The orchestra thundered 'God Save the Tsar!'. Then the Emperor's servant examined the contents of the pot through binoculars and, holding his nose, ran, to the laughter of the audience, through the entire auditorium carrying the pot which bore the heraldic crown.

In the tragic episode of the hero's death, Meyerhold composed a bleak picture – in the centre was the body of the slain warrior, lying on a bench, hand hanging down. To the left and right were two groups of war comrades frozen into immobility. The atmosphere of death permeated the entire scene; it was stern and majestic, like the bas-relief on a tombstone. But this was only the beginning of the director's development of the theme. 'Slowly, to the steady sound of a motor, a lorry drives onto the stage. A pause. The close friends bid farewell to the body of the deceased; the coffin is loaded onto the lorry. The motor runs softly during the pause, as if to replace the funeral march with its humble sound. The final farewell. The lorry slowly begins to move, the motor's rhythm changes, and the lorry disappears from the stage with a roar of the motor that continues to be heard in the distance off-stage. Those attending the coffin freeze in place. With this the episode concludes, but the hypnotic sound of the motor lingers in the ears of the spectators gripped by the scene's dramatic effect.'[62]

It was these two episodes that brought success to the production. Meyerhold 'welcomes the destructive force of civil war,' wrote P. Markov, 'which brings to the fore great social disturbances in place of minor and ordinary feelings.'

The difficulty, however, for all leftist art lay precisely in the fact that 'minor' and 'ordinary' feelings could no longer be brushed aside: 'the personal and the minor' had again become significant, important. On the contrary, direct political propaganda now concerned or interested hardly anyone. Thus the form of the political revue, scarcely having emerged, promptly underwent substantial changes.

One year after The Earth in Turmoil, the première of D.E. (Give Us Europe) took place in the Meyerhold Theatre. A rather confused amalgam of two novels – Trust D.E. by Ilya Ehrenburg and Der Tunnel by Bernhard Kellerman – served as the literary basis of the production.

The naive plot outline of the dramatization, the fantastic struggle between a certain American trust which thirsts to annihilate Europe (on the one hand) and the international proletariat, headed by the workers of the USSR (on the other), was regarded as a vehicle for the glorification of the coming world revolution.

The play, said Mayakovsky with unconcealed irritation, 'is an absolute zero. The language in it, its stage material is wretched.'[63] The poet, however, missed the main theme of the production which attracted lively interest in the performances of D.E.

Under the influence of the New Economic Policy Moscow life had changed radically. In the evenings people danced the Charleston, the foxtrot and the tango in restaurants. Moscow women, imitating the Western fashion, cut their hair in short bobs, wore little round hats pulled down low to their eyebrows and skirts with hemlines above the knee. Cinema posters displayed the names of Conrad Veidt, Harry Piel and Lya de Putti. A kind of front line emerged in the sphere of everyday life. On one side were lads in Russian blouses and shirts with turn-down collars and girls in red kerchiefs, and on the other, young men wearing ties and girls wearing hats. It is here, along this new line of fire, that the real battles of the production of D.E. developed. Its true content was the opposition between robust athletic spirit, physical culture, military marches and the dynamism of the foxtrot and languid rhythms of the tango.

Biomechanics was very appropriate here, while Constructivism began to disintegrate literally before one's eyes. During the performance one of the actors displayed some absurd and enigmatic drawing. 'What is it?' he was asked. 'Constructivism!' he declared importantly. Thus, with a smile, theatre admitted to its betrayal of Constructivism.

The moving walls constructed by the artist Ilya Shlepyanov formed the basic structural element of the production. They were the object of Meyerhold's pride and the critics' admiration. Meyerhold asserted that in place of the fixed construction, dynamic construction was being offered in D.E. for the first time. And indeed, through the use of moving walls the stage was instantly transformed: what had just been a street became a hall of Parliament, the mouth of a tunnel, a stadium or a suite of rooms. However, this function of the moving walls directly contradicted the fundamental principle of theatrical Constructivism – to portray nothing. The red walls, placed on castors, moved with a great din, but very quickly. The chase and escape scenes, which delighted the public and moved critics to comment that Meyerhold was successfully competing with the cinema, were conducted as follows. The actor ran from the front to the back of the stage, where two walls were rolling toward each other from either side. The actor managed to slip between them before they converged, making it seem as though he had instantaneously disappeared. Nevertheless Mayakovsky noted sceptically: 'The struggle with the cinema can not achieve its goal.'

There had been a cinema screen in *The Earth in Turmoil*. In *D.E.* Meyerhold installed three whole screens: in the centre and along each side of the stage. Slides and captions were projected onto them. The side screens reported the actions of the two opposing forces. The central screen gave the titles of the episodes and also served as the 'means of revealing the director's attitude to what was taking place on stage': slogans flashed up on the main screen, warning the audience that they would now see 'A Fossilized Creature From the White Emigrés', and so forth.

Ilya Shlepyanov's design for *D.E.* already contradicted the functionalism and severe ascetic nature of Constructivism, but did not yet pretend to a coherence and unity of style. The political revue acquired features of music and dance revues. Jazz took on itself the theme of 'the decaying West'. Moscow audiences heard both familiar and totally new foxtrots, tangos and shimmies. Tremolos, wheezes, whistles, unexpected crashes of the gong, banging of the drum – all this was stunning. Even more surprising was the unrestrained behaviour of the orchestra members, who came galloping up in time to the music, grimaced, struck the drum with their foot, used their shoulder to bang the gong. So that there could be no doubt that the *dernier cri* in fashion was being demonstrated, the programme stated that the leader of the jazz band, Valentin Parnakh, 'has invented a number of new dance movements which he has performed (solo) in Paris, Rome, Seville and Berlin'. None other than the well-known ballet master Kasyan Goleizovsky staged the foxtrots and shimmies. Boris Romashev wrote in *Izvestia* of the oppressive impression created by 'the stiflingly frenzied shimmy of a rotten civilization exhausted in lascivious dance.'[64] These were strong words.

The critics wrote with much less enthusiasm about those episodes which 'show the health and will to work of our Red youth'. If the good old accordion could still somehow contend with the new-fangled jazz, then the real Red Army men and sailors marched about the stage much less effectively than Goleizovsky's dancers and Meyerhold's actors. 'Bringing the Red Army men and seamen onto the stage is ridiculous,' said Mayakovsky, typically forthright. And he added: 'It's some kind of theatre institute for playing at soldiers.'[65] The show made an entirely 'dispiriting impression' on him.

In *D.E.* Meyerhold widely employed the technique of actors' quick change: Garin, Ilinsky and Babanova performed several roles each, instantaneously transforming themselves between them. Seven inventors came in turns to the Steel King, Mister Jebs, and all of them were played by Erast Garin, demonstrating the art of lightning-quick changes. Ilinsky (who himself played seven characters in *D.E.*) observed that in other roles the transformation 'was accomplished less convincingly' since the audience simply did not manage to grasp 'whether these were new characters or old'.[66]

On the whole the actors got lost in *D.E.* Audiences had begun to like some of the performers and regretted it when they were swallowed up by the dynamic revue.

Although nearly all the critics agreed that *D.E.* 'is the most propagandist of all the productions in the USSR', and that Meyerhold 'had revealed himself here not only as a brilliant director, but also as a brilliant agitator', nonetheless the 'brilliant agitator' himself evidently felt that the time had come to change course.

Many conjectured as to what direction the Master would take. The air was particularly rich with prognoses in 1923 when, ceremoniously and militantly, Meyerhold's double jubilee was marked: twenty years as director and twenty-five years as actor.

On 28 March 1923 *Izvestia* published a resolution of the Council of People's Commissars: 'In view of the twenty-five years of outstanding artistic activity of Vsevolod Emilevich Meyerhold, the title of People's Artist of the Republic is to be conferred on him.' Before then such honours were rarely awarded, but in October 1923 Stanislavsky and Nemirovich-Danchenko also received this title. An anniversary publication dedicated to Meyerhold contained articles championing him in the most impassioned terms, naming him 'the great master', 'the great artist'. The collection included a poem by the young Turkish poet Nazim Hikmet, 'Glory to Meyerhold!'. Hikmet loved Meyerhold's art throughout his life and in the late 1950s and early 1960s spoke just as enthusiastically of him.

'Toward the sun, onto the square, to the masses goes Meyerhold,' exclaimed Emmanuel Beskin. 'The theatrical earth must arise in turmoil. And it will arise.'

Nikolai Semashko, on the other hand, supposed that time would bring correctives 'to Meyerhold's revolutionary destructiveness'. Perhaps, observed Semashko carefully, much will have to be 'corrected and supplemented', much 'softened'.[67]

Foregger compared Meyerhold to Picasso. 'The eyes of Meyerhold,' he asserted, 'are fixed only on tomorrow. Meyerhold is to theatre what Picasso is to painting. Their task is to search, to experiment, to project new paths. . . Meyerhold must discover!'[68]

But voices were also heard that were irritated by 'the cult of Meyerhold, the canonization of Meyerhold, the elevation of Meyerhold to sainthood'.[69] Nemirovich-Danchenko, who had been in the Kremlin not long before Meyerhold's jubilee, left feeling certain that 'the attitude to theatres has changed substantially: Meyerholdism has lost not only prestige but any interest,' yet on the other hand the Moscow Art Theatre had apparently gained esteem.[70] Furthermore, Alexander Tairov's Kamerny Theatre was gradually winning for itself a more prominent place in Moscow's cultural life.

Tairov's Harlequinades and Tragedies

Theatres responded to the New Economic Policy with joyful productions. The 'leftist' director, Vladimir Tikhonovich, who gloomily asserted that NEP 'sets the limits on further experimentation'[71] was mistaken, for theatrical experimentation continued and spread, meanwhile becoming ever more light-hearted. Lunacharsky expressed his views on the subject: 'We are experiencing a period of some relaxation after that nervous fit in which everyone lived during the heroic years of the Revolution. . . . People want to laugh and seek relief in impressions far removed from that which has disturbed, tormented and enraptured them. Russian citizens have the basic right to a pleasant, cheerful hour of light, carefree amusement.' He welcomed the theatrical achievements 'in the field of bright and carefree humour'.[72] There were a considerable number: the string of comic productions of 1922 – Vakhtangov's *Princess Turandot*, Granovsky's *The Sorceress*, Meyerhold's *The Magnanimous Cuckold* and Tairov's *Giroflé-Girofla* – showed that directors were full of optimism and seemingly competing with each other in the sphere of sparkling humour.

Granovsky, the leader of GOSET, had studied with Max Reinhardt and advocated the methods of 'mass direction'. But unlike Reinhardt, who operated freely with the movements of whole crowds in circus rings, in enormous cathedrals or in the open air, Granovsky had to be content with an ordinary, poorly equipped stage and cramped hall on Malaya Bronnaya Street in Moscow. Nevertheless he obstinately swore by 'the mass tragic spectacle' and 'the mass popular comedy', believing that only such forms 'are comprehensible to the modern audience',[93] that intimate, indoor, 'conversational plays' had become hopelessly out of date. He therefore very frequently and contrary to the stage directions 'broke up the interior', took the action out of the room onto the street and forced 'the mass body of the company' (one of his favourite expressions) to race around 'skipping, jumping, tumbling along the open spaces, roofs and stairs of a fantastic Jewish settlement'.[94] The poor, wretched settlement life, realistically recorded by such Jewish writers as Mendele Moicher-Sforim, Avraam Goldfaden, Yitzhak Leibush Peretz and Sholom-Aleikhem, acquired in his productions a distinctly Hoffmannesque element. The commonplace became unreal.

To a certain extent Granovsky's devices resembled the manner characteristic of early Chagall where a powerful sweep of fantasy lifts the settlement characters from the ground and elevates the poor and humble folk, together with their fiddles, goats and loved ones, straight up to the skies. This likeness was noticed straight away: as early as 1922 the critic Abram Efros called Granovsky's The Sorceress 'a variation on Chagall themes'.[95] But he immediately went on to mention the rationalism which prevented Granovsky from surrendering to ecstatic poetry in the spirit of Chagall.

Granovsky was known as 'brains', a name which held a grain of truth, for his excessively methodical tendency prevented him from becoming a great artist. A confident professional rather than a true performing artist, he consistently and pedantically tried to convey the technique learned in Reinhardt's school to his young actors. They were quite inexperienced and even the most gifted among them, Solomon Mikhoels and Veniamin Zuskin, took their first steps in theatre under Granovsky's leadership. Not surprisingly they initially obeyed the director's will passively and without complaint. However, apart from rehearsals with Granovsky, they also had access to the performances (and sometimes the rehearsals) of Stanislavsky, Vakhtangov, Meyerhold and Tairov. Moscow's intense and diverse theatrical life drew them in, and fairly soon these two actors, Mikhoels and Zuskin, at first cautiously, then more boldly, began to introduce amendments into Granovsky's rigid production scores that were paced by a metronome. Without violating the structure of the mise-en-scène as prescribed by Granovsky and obediently following his outline sketch, they embellished the director's plan with bursts of sudden comic improvisations. Granovsky was intelligent and experienced enough to appreciate the merits of these performances. He saw that both actors were infinitely talented and did not restrain them.

Already by 1922, in The Sorceress, in a free directorial interpretation on Goldfaden's theme, the duo of Zuskin and Mikhoels predetermined the show's success. Zuskin appeared in the main female role of the Sorceress herself, a wicked old witch, and led the development of the entire plot. Mikhoels in the role of the cunning street merchant Gotsmach, on the contrary, bore virtually no relation to the plot whatsoever; his role was to lead the settlement crowd, a dancing, singing and expressively gesticulating human chain. In the picturesque, richly coloured sets of Isaak Rabinovich the naive tale passed, in the words of one critic, 'from splendour to splendour, from dance to dance, from song to song' and in fact constituted a skillfully organized divertissement where mass 'numbers' predominated, choral songs and group dances taking over the entire performance area erected by the artist: ladders, roofs, little streets, corners and alleyways. All this, taken together, was highly reminiscent of Tairov's Princess Brambilla. But in this chorus, in this settlement corps de ballet, time and again two soloists, Zuskin and Mikhoels, advanced to the forefront. They each had different missions and different functions: Mikhoels brought scepticism, irony and a philosophical quality to Granovsky's production while Zuskin introduced bright humour, radiant lyricism, musicality and poetry.

Their acting duet rang out with particular beauty and strength in the 1927 production of The Journey of Veniamin III, after Mendele Moicher-Sforim. Granovsky defined the genre of the production with the phrase 'poignant epic'. The sets for The Journey of Veniamin were among Robert Falk's first theatrical works and, as distinct from the stage design for The Sorceress where the picturesqueness concealed a solid, multi-stage Constructivist set, they modestly framed the bare stage floor. Falk considered it his task to create a peaceful, slightly melancholy background for the actors' performance. The set, make-up and costumes 'must serve primarily to create a distance in time', to remove the action into the far and misty past.

As for Granovsky, whose 'Reinhardtism', as Efros aptly described it, 'had begun to sink into café-chantant'[96] and whose previous productions, Night in the Old Market after I. L. Peretz and M. Le Trouhadec by Jules Romains had not enjoyed success, on this occasion he also seemed to retreat into the shadows, granting freedom to his best performers.

Mikhoels as Veniamin and Zuskin as Senderl took full advantage of this freedom, creating a variation on a Cervantes theme. Veniamin was the settlement Don Quixote, his friend Senderl the settlement Sancho Panza, the only difference being that Mikhoels invested his comic hero, a fantasizer and dreamer, with an inclination toward the philosophical, and to the earthbound realism of the sensible Jewish Sancho, Zuskin added a quiet, melancholy resignation. Zuskin's adroit improvisational acting ideally accompanied the solid, impressive structure of the role characteristic of Mikhoels' acting style. Zuskin's lyricism accompanied the indefatigable energy of Mikhoels' thought, his humour, his all-penetrating irony.

This correlation between two such enormous talents subsequently, in 1935, brought great success to the production of King Lear where Mikhoels played Lear and Zuskin played the Fool. Gordon Craig stated that for him King Lear at GOSET proved to be 'a completely unexpected experience and, without any exaggeration, a shock'.[97]

This Shakespearian production was a shock for theatrical Moscow as well, and a difficult one to explain. For not only did the magnificent performance of Mikhoels and Zuskin enrapture and not only did the highly original form discovered by the artist Alexander Tyshler delight, but even the direction was exciting. This was the most suprising element. Sergei Radlov was cited as the director, although at that time in the 1930s no one had thought him capable of surprising or startling anyone: it was a long time since any of his other work had been distinguished by originality. Only now, half a century later, has an explanation been found for this longstanding enigma. It has been discovered that the directorial interpretation of *King Lear*, in its fundamental, original outlines, was created by the marvellous Ukrainian director Les Kurbas, one of the boldest theatrical innovators of the 1920s.

Radlov had only completed and 'signed' Kurbas's last work.

Les Kurbas

Before the October Revolution of 1917 the theatrical art of the numerous peoples and nationalities which inhabited the former Russian Empire existed 'on a hand to mouth basis', persecuted by the representatives of the tsarist autocracy. The Imperial power in the multi-lingual country officially recognized only one language – Russian. The peoples of the Ukraine, Belorussia, the Caucasus, Central Asia, Povolzhye or Siberia had no rights to any form of national autonomy whatsoever, and where there were professional, semi-professional or just amateur theatres, their activity was by no means encouraged. Frequently these companies gave performances in secret, without publicity and, even more frequently, their performances were prohibited.

Immediately after the Revolution the situation changed fundamentally. 'We have given *all* non-Russian nationalities,' stated Lenin, '*their own* Republics or Autonomous Regions.'[98] The Soviet Union was formed as a multinational state, actively interested in the development of national cultures and in particular, liberal with finance for theatres of all peoples, of populations large and small. National theatrical organisms appeared very quickly both right in Moscow itself (where there were Georgian, Belorussian, Latvian, Uzbek, Armenian and Jewish studios) and in the capitals of the newly formed Republics – in Kiev, Minsk, Tbilisi, Baku, Yerevan, Kazan, Ulan-Ude and others. Usually the leaders of these collectives sought to transfer to a professional basis the theatrical art that had previously existed only in amateur or folkloric forms. However, in those Republics where theatre, despite all persecution, already possessed relatively stable and long-standing traditions, conflicts often arose, just as in Russia, out of the fierce confrontation between traditional art and new art, between avant-garde innovators and senior authoritative masters who felt that if their creative work, semi-legal and out of favour before the Revolution, was now legitimized and encouraged by the state, then their task was to reveal the riches that had formerly been hidden, to create space for the acting talents finally to realize their full potential. But to experiment, to explore new forms and new means of expression was pointless.

The directors and actors who had participated in Russian and Western European culture, however, such as Konstantin Mardzhanov (Mardzhanishvili) in Georgia or Levon Kalantar in Armenia, reasoned otherwise. They would not be content with a repetition of what had been done before and did not want to be locked into the confines of national tradition.

In the Ukraine the young director Les Kurbas took upon himself the mission of the renewal of the national theatre.

Like Granovsky, as a student in Vienna Kurbas had come under the strong influence of Max Reinhardt and this influence was patently obvious in his earliest works. As early as 1916, Kurbas created the experimental Molodoi Theatre ('Young Theatre') in Kiev and in 1918, openly imitating Reinhardt, staged Sophocles' *Oedipus*

Rex. But Granovsky and Kurbas had absorbed Reinhardt's lessons in different ways. Granovsky was captivated above all by 'mass direction', while Kurbas, even from his youth, tried to transfer to Ukrainian soil the Reinhardt concept of theatre as magic, his sense of pageantry and poetry of form. This task was complicated by the fact that Kurbas had to overcome the long-standing Ukrainian tradition of conscientious but naive everyday realism in shows that were usually melodramatic or light-heartedly comic, but in all cases accompanied without fail by folk singing and dancing.

The so-called 'theatre of stars' which had existed in the Ukraine before the Revolution abounded with great acting talents and enjoyed enormous popularity, although it was content with an extremely shallow, didactic repertoire and eschewed classical plays, both Russian and Western. The 'theatre of stars' had narrow horizons, its subject-matter was monotonous and its level of culture low. The public's steadfast love for this conservative theatre was explained primarily by the fact that the 'stars' – the most popular of whom were the marvellous actors Maria Zankovetskaya and Panas Saksagansky – performed in the native Ukrainian language (at that time it was called 'Little Russian') and thereby defended the independent national culture which the tsarist authorities did not recognize and persecuted. The distinctive ethnographic enthusiasm for traditional festive costumes, ancient songs, folk rituals and dances, all this naive aestheticization of age-old customs afforded the public great pleasure.

After the Revolution, which proclaimed and established in practice the equality of nations, the historical mission of the 'theatre of stars' was essentially exhausted. Their prestige, however, was as great as it had been previously, and Kurbas's attempts to create a theatrical art in the Ukraine which could rival the Russian and Western European theatre on an equal basis, were for a long time to come perceived as pretentious and of no interest to a wide public. Kurbas, however, worked energetically. He declared that he wanted 'to break completely with vulgarized traditions' and establish 'new values in both the art of the theatre generally and in the art of the actor in particular.'[99] Following Sophocles he presented Kievans with Molière's *Tartuffe* and Shakespeare's *Macbeth*, he staged Goldoni, Grillparzer and original plays by contemporary Ukrainian dramatists and, most importantly, experimented ever more boldly with the renewal of theatrical form. A group of young supporters rallied round him who subsequently were to become major figures in Ukrainian theatre. Among them were the actors Amvrosy Buchma, Gnat Yura, Natalia Uzhvi, Valentina Chistyakova, Liubov Gakkebush, Marian Kruzhelnitsky and Vasily Vasilko and the artists Anatoly Petritsky and Vadim Meller.

The characteristics of Kurbas's directorial style were established very quickly and remained distinctive to him throughout the entire period of his creative life, even featuring in works which at first glance seemed completely dissimilar to each other. Perhaps because Kurbas was committed to wage the struggle against the mellow lyricism and bright picturesqueness of the 'theatre of stars', his direction invariably revealed a predilection for a hard graphic quality of contours, economy and simplicity of groupings and a spareness and clarity of line in the *mise-en-scène*. The various theatrical frolics, which often attracted Vakhtangov and Tairov, were completely alien to him. The dynamism in Kurbas's productions possessed characteristic sharpness, expressiveness and nervous pulsation of rhythm. Not infrequently he was called the

'Ukrainian Meyerhold', but even this comparison is inaccurate, for it prevents an understanding of the originality of style and special qualities in the development of the Ukrainian director. At times converging with Meyerhold, but sometimes also with Tairov, Kurbas forged his own completely original path in art.

In *Oedipus Rex*, following Reinhardt, in a relatively impoverished staging where the synchronization and coordination of all the small chorus's movements and the severe monumentality of the sculptural expression stunned the audience, he managed to create a tragic tension which was not at all inferior in power to Reinhardt's production. Kurbas himself played Oedipus. Then in 1920 *Haydamaks*, after the poem of the same title by Taras Shevchenko, exhibited a completely new type of directorial approach in which traditional songs and dances of the Ukrainian theatre became integral, component parts of the tragic action. In previous Ukrainian productions songs and dances had been linked with dialogue according to the principles of the divertissement. It was Kurbas who first managed to create an integrated structure, taking national tradition and decisively transforming it.

As the historian of Ukrainian theatre Natalia Kuzyakina writes, he 'staged *Haydamaks* in an entirely stylized manner: a bare stage, four steps at the back of the stage area between oblique wooden platforms, the front curtain and backdrop made of coarse unbleached linen. The poetry was embodied on stage in the form of "The Poet's Ten Words", a chorus composed of ten beautiful young women dressed in grey linen dresses with modest, everyday ribbons in their plaits. The girls divided into two half-choruses at different ends of the stage, then anxiously gathered together; they joined in the action in turns.' To the severe 'masculine' show, the subject of which was the uprising of rebellious Cossacks and the finale their heroic death, the director, according to the law of romantic contrast, gave 'a troubled feminine soul in the shape of a lyrical chorus,' an original transformation of the chorus of an ancient tragedy.[100]

In 1922 Kurbas's Molodoi Theatre was renamed the Berezil Theatre (in Ukrainian *berezil* means 'March' – the name symbolized spring) and soon moved from Kiev to Kharkov, the capital of the Ukraine at that time. Here Kurbas's most notable works were *Gas* by Georg Kaiser and *Jimmy Higgins* after Upton Sinclair. Both these premières took place in 1923 and both were stamped with the mark of Expressionism. Kurbas said then that Expressionist drama opens to theatre 'the most interesting possibilities', for in it is 'the fusion of mime and dialogue, sounds of speech and liturgy, sculptural expression and music.' For a time he even proudly 'counted' himself 'among the Expressionists'[101] and, of course, paid due respect to the Constructivist solutions obligatory in those years, to the imitation of various mechanisms, at the same time widely employing the technique of 'light painting' from the beams of searchlights which from below, above and the side illuminated the mass crowd scenes and Vadim Meller's urbanist set, slipping along its rectangular contours, intersections and stairs.

Like other Soviet directors, Kurbas shifted the emphases in Expressionist drama, trying to turn the spectacle into a sort of hymn to machinery, to convey in the theatrical action the thrill of technology and of rationality in the movement of the mass. In every possible way he 'underlined the dynamic value of the new gesture, dictated by light and rhythm', and Vadim Meller 'tried to unite the feeling of space, depth and volume, taken from Cézanne, with a Constructivist form prompted by Picasso.'[102] Small groups of actors

– in one place four, in another six – were situated on various levels of the construction and with synchronous movements they imitated the work of rationally regulated mechanisms. Evidently this was very similar to Foregger's 'machine dances', but it did not have independent significance, being only one of the parts in the complex visual shape of the production.

The adaptation of Upton Sinclair's novel *Jimmy Higgins* supplemented these typical Constructivist staging devices with the use of cinema stills. More importantly, Kurbas brought the actor Amvrosy Buchma to the forefront of the production; he played Jimmy Higgins with the liberal emotionalism traditional to the Ukrainian stage but also with a mastery of sudden shifts from tragic pathos to grotesque eccentricity, something which had never been seen before in Ukrainian theatre. In his work with this actor, Kurbas's new method celebrated its first significant triumph.

Buchma's Higgins was a stooping, outwardly completely unremarkable worker in grey overalls. His sad fate was expressed through the deliberately flat intonations of his falling voice, suddenly broken by a piercing cry; at the moment when the cry resounded, a close-up of Buchma's face, distorted with pain, would appear on the cinema screen. Then the actor performed an expressive tragic dance on the forestage. In the finale this expression reached its climax: Buchma was able to convey magnificently the divided personality of the demented hero, his choked laughter, his wailing, his moans. The clash between the 'little man' and the powerful machinery of the state acquired enormous poignancy.

The writer Mikola Bazhan recalled that Buchma as Higgins stunned him 'with his mighty talent'.[103]

Osip Mandelstam, in a review of the Leningrad tour of the Berezil Theatre, observed that all the remaining actors in *Jimmy Higgins* were cruelly 'oppressed by the unlimited despotism of the modern director'. The poet wrote with irony: 'sleepwalkers in overalls speak in sing-song voices, rush, dash around, clamber onto crates depicting America, and onto ladders: everything follows the most strict, purely rational plan. In these Tollerized and Kaiserized cages, in Sinclair with trimmings of Toller, the Ukrainian actors suffocate like hunted mice,' and if 'the tragedian Buchma acts so that a chill runs down the spine,' then 'the rallying theatrical crowd' looks quite unconvincing.[104]

These reproaches were probably fair. But a year later, in *Macbeth*, Kurbas proved that his despotic style of direction was beneficial not only to Buchma.

Shakespearian Productions

The characteristic diversity of direction in the explorations of the early Soviet theatre is particularly evident in the Shakespearian productions of the initial post-Revolutionary years. The stylistic pendulum swung widely and the stagings of Shakespeare were often located at the extreme points of its swing.

The Theatre of Tragedy, under the leadership of the actor Yury Yuriev, opened in Petrograd in the spring of 1918 and existed for a very brief period (by 1919 it had joined the new Bolshoi Dramatic Theatre). Its performances were given in Ciniselli's circus ring. Alexei Granovsky directed, and the circus ring provided a fine opportunity for him to display the mastery he had acquired in Reinhardt's school. *Oedipus Rex*, with which the Theatre of Tragedy opened, was performed on the stage boards which remained in the

Poster advertising the opening of the Theatre of Tragedy in Petrograd, 1918, with a production of *Macbeth* directed by Granovsky.

circus after the recent tour of Reinhardt's company with Moissi as Oedipus. It was intended in the future to stage Shakespeare's tragedies *Macbeth*, *Richard II* and *King Lear*, and Byron's *Cain* with the famous singer Fedor Chaliapin as Lucifer. Of all this programme, only the first item was realized: the staging of *Macbeth*.

In the unusual conditions of the circus ring the artist Mstislav Dobuzhinsky built a set in banal Victorian style. The only new thing about it was that two castles were placed in the circus ring: on one side Dunsinane, on the other Inverness, with a hill in the centre where the tragedy's principal episodes took place. Macbeth was played by Yuriev, Lady Macbeth by Maria Andreeva. Both attached great importance to costume, and the designer gave them regal attire.

Several years later when Yuriev had returned to the familiar walls of the former Alexandrinsky Theatre (now the Academic Theatre of Drama), he performed together with Elizaveta Timé in *Antony and Cleopatra*. On this occasion the architect Vladimir Shchuko designed the production. The contrast between the severity of Rome and the sultry languour of Egypt was felt in his sets. Timé, primarily a comic actress, played Cleopatra vivaciously, elegantly and with cunning coquetry, while Yuriev as Antony, on the contrary, declaimed

pompously and without passion, in the classical manner, repeatedly adopting haughty poses. But neither he nor she possessed true vigour.

At that time *Macbeth* was staged more frequently than Shakespeare's other plays because it was easily interpreted, in the spirit of 'consonance with the Revolution', as anti-monarchical. Theatrical conservatives and innovators alike turned to it. In 1922 the young avant-gardists Sergei Eisenstein and Sergei Yutkevich produced designs for the sets and costumes for *Macbeth* under the direction of Valentin Tikhonovich. Tikhonovich headed the Central Educational Theatre in Moscow, which existed for only a few months. Not the tiniest shred of evidence showing how *Macbeth* was performed has survived. Only the drawings by Eisenstein and Yutkevich have been preserved, enabling us to see that there was one set which served throughout the production – a system of acting areas of varying heights inter-linked by stairways and illuminated by the flickering light of candles. The designers wanted to cover the whole set with grey canvas so that the silhouettes of the characters in black, gold or deep crimson costumes would be distinctly outlined against the neutral background. As for the costumes themselves, judging from the designs they were startlingly reminiscent of the militarized aspect of the semi-robot, semi-people engendered by Kazimir Malevich's fantasy as far back as 1913 in the Futurist staging of *Victory Over the Sun*.

Such motifs appeared more than once in the costumes for *Macbeth*. They were also characteristic of the 1924 production by Les Kurbas which enjoyed enormous success at the Berezil Theatre in Kiev. Kurbas staged *Macbeth* as a vicious tragi-farce, freely moving from blood-soaked Guignol to coarse 'bouffonade'. Both the director and his designer, Vadim Meller, felt deep antipathy toward the opulent pageantry of the traditional 'costume Shakespeare'. The outer form of the production was on principle spare and harsh. The performance was conducted on a bare stage floor against the background of a black horizon. A change in the place of action was designated by large screens with captions – 'A Heath', 'The Castle', 'The Gates to the Castle', and so on – which were let down from above, thereby reviving a device characteristic of the Elizabethan theatre. Chairs, wooden benches and small platforms were also let down from above on ropes, as required, and then later raised up under the grid.

The actors all appeared in identical militarized *prozodezhda*, but each of the characters received in addition a short, cape-like mantle decorated with simple and bright geometric shapes.

'The story of Macbeth's downfall,' writes an expert on Kurbas's art, Natalia Kuzyakina, 'was grotesquely, farcically reduced and treated as a parable about unintelligent, common criminals.'[105] So to a certain extent, in both meaning and style, it anticipated the Brechtian *The Resistible Rise of Arturo Ui*. Moreover, in Kurbas's directorial work on *Macbeth*, portents and some devices typical of Brecht's political theatre can easily be seen; in particular, Kurbas repeatedly resorted to the device of alienation. For example, in the first scene the witches, in red wigs and wide blue trousers, were 'electrified': while they were uttering their prophecies with pathos and sinister grimaces under surreal violet lighting, mysterious little lights twinkled in the folds of their clothing. But as soon as their scene concluded and the screen with the caption 'A Heath' disappeared from sight above, all these effects were revoked, the calm light of day flooded the stage, and the witches unhurriedly

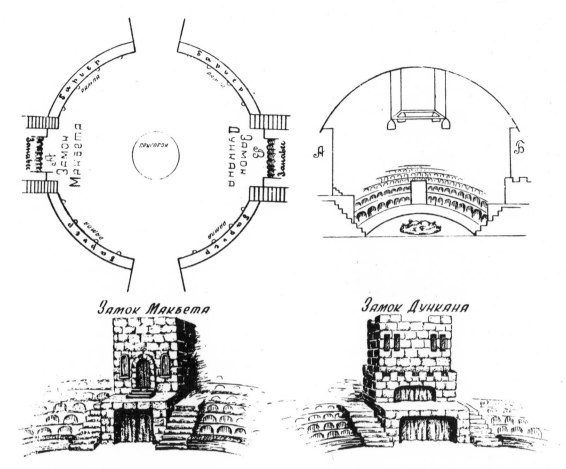

Plan of the circus arena (*above*) and a sketch of the set by M. Dobuzhinsky (*below*) for Granovsky's production of *Macbeth* at the Theatre of Tragedy, 1918.

Sketch of a set by Eisenstein and Yutkevich for Tikhonovich's production of *Macbeth* at the Central Educational Theatre in Moscow, 1922.

exited into the wings with the businesslike step of actresses who have done their 'number'.

In exactly the same way Liubov Gakkebush, before playing the sleepwalking scene, calmly proceeded to the centre of the stage, mounted a low platform, took off her mantle and, left only in a white shirt, shook her head so hard that her long golden hair tumbled down around her shoulders; then only after this did she pronounce in agonized hysterics, 'Out, damned spot! . . .'

Ivan Maryanenko played Macbeth as a limited, dull, straightforward army man, clothed in service jacket, helmet and clumsy ankle boots with puttees. The culmination of the role was the moment when Banquo's ghost appeared before Macbeth at the banquet. Instead of a ghost Kurbas used the beam of a searchlight which fell onto the stage from above and, passing by the other characters, moved towards Macbeth. When the blinding shaft of light caught up with Macbeth his face was twisted with terror. He rushed away, ran to the back of the stage. But lowered screens blocked his path; he flung himself to the left, to the right, trying to weave a way round these obstructions, and the beam followed him relentlessly. All the remaining characters also leaped up from their places and raced from corner to corner. Only Gakkebush as Lady Macbeth remained completely calm and motionless.

Amvrosy Buchma played two roles in the production – the fool-porter (here Kurbas deviated from the tragedy's specified text: for the fool, who had a crooked mouth and bulbous nose, topical political lines had been written in. provoking Homeric laughter from the audience) and the bishop in the finale, in Malcolm's coronation scene. The bishop entered on buskins in a white soutane and gold tiara, but with the same comic make-up on his mockingly grinning face. As soon as he placed the crown on the head of the new king, the next pretender to the throne promptly ran this king through with a dagger. Buchma's bishop, unperturbed, lifted the fake crown from the floor and repeated the coronation ceremony a second time, a third, a fourth. . . . This Kurbas 'line of kings', as the actor Vasilko

noted at the time in his diary, produced 'the effect of an exploding bomb'.[106] Subsequently many other directors copied this innovation by Les Kurbas in the finale of *Macbeth*.

Working on *Macbeth*, Kurbas feared, like fire, any sort of splendour. A pictorial quality of gesture was hostilely rejected. The director sought a deliberately prosaic, even mechanistic, style for the actors' gestures and poses.

Tairov chose completely the opposite path, and his production of *Romeo and Juliet* assumed invariable grace of movement and poetic gesture and pose. The culture of the 'emotional gesture', to which the Kamerny Theatre always attached great significance, was this time, despite Tairov's aspiration toward a chemically pure genre (either 'mystery' or 'harlequinade'), too complicated, for the director wished to conduct a 'mystery' against the background of a 'harlequinade'. He declared that he would obtain a sharp contrast between 'the symphony of the audacious and passionate, powerful and all-consuming' love of Romeo and Juliet on the one hand and the foolish, petty enmity of the Montagues and Capulets on the other.[107]

Tairov was apparently attracted to the idea of combining in one theatrical work the sublime beauty of *The Veil of Pierrette* with the carnival motley of *Princess Brambilla*. He wished to conduct the theme of free, selfless love through the empty and amusing jostle of a small town torn by feuds and fights, through a life where merry feasts were interrupted time and again by bloody murders and weddings were replaced by funerals.

His interesting plan, however, proved to be too unwieldy. In the production's design Alexandra Exter attempted to achieve a kind of synthesis of Cubism and Baroque, but her sets, which in maquette form created a light and airy impression, appeared heavy as soon as they were installed on the stage. Instead of 'Cubist Baroque' they turned out as something highly mannered in the style of 'Art Nouveau'. Everything that Tairov had intended to convey in the register of a 'harlequinade' (in particular, Lorenzo was supposed to be the 'harlequin'), came out too coarse, too thick, and the 'harlequinade', instead of serving as the background for the 'mystery', in actual fact rudely elbowed it out and crushed it.

Nonetheless the scenes between Alisa Koonen (Juliet) and Nikolai Tseretelli (Romeo) had a truly poetic quality. The balcony scene where Juliet, visually elevated by the powerful rising lines of inclined silvery surfaces, met Romeo who had climbed to her on a rope ladder, and also the final scene where the lovers were picturesquely laid out on the steep steps leading to the deathbed, drew applause from the audience every time. But these little islands of poetry drowned in the brightly coloured turmoil and clamourous hurly-burly of Tairov's Verona. Only Boris Ferdinandov (Tybalt) was good: in him, wrote E. Beskin, 'there was something of Verona's sunniness, of the brightness of the Italian Renaissance.'[108]

Subsequently Koonen, explaining why Juliet did not number among her 'particularly favourite roles', acknowledged that in the acting 'unity was not attained'.[109] Exter took her failure particularly hard: after *Romeo and Juliet* she left the Kamerny Theatre and refused to engage in any theatrical activity. As for Tairov, the failure spurred him to further effort, and only six months after the Shakespearian production he achieved a triumph with *Phèdre*.

In 1924 in Moscow, in 1925 in Tbilisi and in 1926 in Baku, one after another, three premières of *Hamlet* took place. Two of them, the Moscow and Tbilisi productions, were undoubtedly linked to the

Poster advertising the première of *Hamlet* in the Second Studio of the Moscow Art Theatre, 1924.

renowned Craig-Stanislavsky *Hamlet* of 1911. Mikhail Chekhov, who now played Hamlet, had in 1911 performed the modest part of one of the courtiers, and Kote Mardzhanishvili, who now staged *Hamlet* in Tbilisi, had been assistant to Craig. The success or failure of *Hamlet* was of enormous importance at this time for Mikhail Chekhov, who headed the former First MAT Studio which had separated from the MAT in 1922 and become the Second Moscow Art Theatre. Mikhail Chekhov's great acting talent was already universally recognized. His authority as a director and the head of a theatre was, however, a different matter. Chekhov did not possess great directorial talent, something even he himself acknowledged, and therefore he often relied on collective direction, that is he created a group of three or four directors to work on each play. 'Collective direction' did not prove its worth; a lack of co-ordination was sensed in the productions. Those young directors who believed (and at times with full justification, as in the case of Alexei Diky) that they could say something new in art, naturally, grumbled. Quite a few actors were unhappy with the theatre's repertoire, far removed from contemporaneity. And although the Studio's company was entirely composed of Stanislavsky's pupils, including such gifted ones as Ivan Bersenev, Serafima Birman, Leonid Volkov, Sofia Giatsintova and Lydia Deikun, there was no harmony amongst them. Internally the theatre was fraught with tension. Gradually a small group of convinced opponents to Chekhov formed, with Diky as its head.

Three directors (Valentin Smyshlyaev, Vladimir Tatarinov and Alexander Cheban) staged *Hamlet*, and all the shortcomings of the method of 'collective direction' were clearly displayed in their work. Each actor performed in his own way, and all differently: the figure of Gertrude gravitated to the nervous grotesque, that of Claudius to sinister monumentality, the role of Ophelia was conducted with tranquil sorrow, that of Laertes with deliberate impetuosity and the role of Polonius was expressed with rather crude satire. The stage set recalled a Gothic cathedral with narrow windows, through the stained glass of which the light fell on something akin to a truncated pyramid placed in the centre of the stage. The artist Mikhail Libakov's opulent costumes, knights who ceremoniously measured out their pace, banners fluttering high above, sounds of trumpets – all this was more or less routine. Only Mikhail Chekhov as Hamlet

Two sketches by Mikhail Libakov of costumes for the Ghost (*above*) and Polonius (*below*) in the 1924 production of *Hamlet* in the Second Studio of the Moscow Art Theatre, directed by Valentin Smyshlyaev, Vladimir Tatarinov and Alexander Cheban.

struck some previously unknown chords. Straight locks of ash-coloured hair framed his stern, frowning face; melancholy filled his eyes. He passed among the tragedy's characters like a dark shadow, all dressed up in velvet and silks, dragging his heavy sword behind him. In appearance not a prince at all, but rather more a warrior, much experienced in his lifetime and prepared for the worst, Chekhov's Hamlet delivered soliloquies with anxiety and pain, a pain that was abundantly clear to the audience.

Stanislavsky said of Chekhov: 'He is a mighty talent, and there is no artistic task whatsoever which he could not fulfil on stage.'[110] The mightiness of his talent revealed itself in his ability to justify internally the sharpest break in a character's behaviour. His Hamlet, strong-willed and mournful, quickly, without any special reflections, came to the conclusion that violence, bloodshed and murder could be justified by high ethical motives – the necessity of cleansing the world of its terrible vices and restoring the integrity of the time which was 'out of joint'. With a weak hand he firmly gripped the sword of retribution. The tragedy of his fate was that by fulfilling the recognized mission, he acted against his own nature. This strong-minded and active Hamlet agonizingly overcame his humaneness, goodness and compassion for those he punished.

Such an interpretation of the tragedy inevitably coloured the production with a bitter pessimism. Some critics were perplexed: why were there no 'triumphant silver trumpets of Fortinbras' in the finale, why was the tragedy 'concluded hopelessly'?[111] In a production where Mikhail Chekhov played Hamlet it could not have been concluded otherwise.

The critic Mikhail Zagorsky perceived this Hamlet as 'a modern city-dweller whose nerves could not endure the turbulence of the times'. To the question as to 'whether or not we need such a Hamlet now', Zagorsky categorically responded, 'no, we do not.'[112] Such a conclusion from a zealous proponent of 'leftism' was entirely in the spirit of LEF. But other opinions were voiced: Pavel Markov, for instance, considered that in the Chekhov Hamlet, 'like a lyrical underwater stream, lives a love for people and for every real, individual person', including Gertrude, and that although 'the actor seems to bring the personal tragedy to the fore', Chekhov nonetheless 'permeates Hamlet with the will and thirst for action'.[113]

Debate surrounding the production spread, while Mikhail Chekhov's success grew with each performance.

Kote Mardzhanishvili achieved an even more resounding success at the Rustaveli Theatre in Tbilisi. If in Hamlet as played by Mikhail Chekhov the link with theatrical Expressionism was unquestionably felt, particularly with *Eric XIV* in which Chekhov had appeared two years earlier, then Mardzhanishvili's production, much more consistent than that of the Second MAT, was confidently sustained in romantic tone. This was explained in part by the particular qualities of the Georgian theatrical tradition which Mardzhanishvili sought and achieved, in part due to the individuality of a most interesting actor, Ushangi Chkheidze, who played Hamlet, in part due to the characteristic style of the artist Irakly Gamrekeli, but most of all due to the ineradicable passion of the director himself for bright pageantry, the romantic play of contrasts between dark and light, lofty spirituality and base sensuality, heroism and villainy.

While in many respects imitating Craig's devices, in particular readily adopting Craig's screens, Mardzhanishvili placed the set on a revolving disc (which Craig had never done) and in place of Craig's

Theatrical Expansion

Sketch of a set by Irakly Gamrekeli for Mardzhanov's production of *Hamlet* at the Rustaveli Theatre, Tbilisi, 1925.

abstract form he suggested the artist erect on stage the bleak shape of Elsinore and, most significantly, an enormous stairway which ascended to the castle. On this stairway, perceived as the symbol of 'all the life and movement of a man, his ups and downs',[114] almost all of the tragedy's principal scenes took place. Tchaikovsky's music often accompanied the action.

Ushangi Chkheidze invested Hamlet with nobility of soul, a vulnerable conscience and physical good looks and conducted the entire role with turbulent, raging spirit. His hatred for Claudius and Gertrude exploded at once, and the soliloquy 'To be or not to be' signified his clear realization of the need to avenge the murder. All this Hamlet's doubts and hesitations were dictated solely by his love for Ophelia. But what is more, and on this point Mardzhanishvili differed with Craig, under no circumstances did he wish to 'diminish' Ophelia, so he gave the part to the company's best actress, the young Veriko Andzhaparidze, lyrical, graceful and poetic.

The visual imagery in the production was of the utmost simplicity, at times even, perhaps, an oversimplification – the sublime and inspired heroes, Hamlet and Ophelia, entered into deadly battle with the sullen, vile and cruel power of Claudius (Akaky Vasadze), Gertrude (Elena Donauri) and Polonius (Niko Gotsiridze). Such simplification, however, enabled the director to make the Shakespearian tragedy accessible and comprehensible to the Georgian public.

In Baku, where the Russian director Alexander Tuganov staged *Hamlet* at the Azerbaidzhan State Theatre, the desire to bring Shakespeare close to the local, national audience inspired him to undertake an unusual experiment: to transfer the tragedy's action to a kind of abstract Oriental country, to give its heroes (everyone, except Hamlet and Ophelia) Muslim names and to design the set in a style mid-way between the Persian and the Turkish.

The Azerbaidzhan dramatist Dzhafar Dzhabarly, who translated and edited *Hamlet* in accordance with the idea of making the tragedy 'Oriental', was sincerely convinced that he was guided by Goethe's words 'about the necessity of applying the works of Shakespeare to the conditions of a given stage' and, in a letter to the director, expressed his complete satisfaction that 'the play was performed against a background of the East and everything down to the most minor detail was oriental.'[115] The Baku critics supported this idea: 'there is no sense whatsoever in portraying the life of Danish Elsinore; this would make the tragedy uninteresting, would reduce to nought its universal significance.'[116]

It is difficult to judge how consistently the plan of Dzhabarly and Tuganov was realized, for nothing has been preserved – neither sketches (even the name of the designer has not come down to us) nor photographs of the production, apart from photographs of individual characters taken later, several years after the première. Only one thing is incontestable: the most talented Azerbaidzhan actor, Abas Mirza Sharifzade, appeared as Hamlet, and he performed this role 'with fiery spirit'. In Baku the romantic actor Sharifzade, like Chkheidze in Tbilisi, deprived Hamlet of 'Hamletism', of doubts and hesitations, and with assured mastery brought to the fore the sacred loyalty to the oriental law of blood revenge. 'He was dressed,' recalled Dzhabarly, 'not in the traditional black costume of the Danish prince, but in dark violet-blue silk attire, and his performance conveyed great inner strength, the readiness to restore justice at any cost.'[117]

Subsequently historians of Azerbaidzhan theatre were inclined to regard this entire venture as a kind of curiosity, even as a mistake of principle. But if it is remembered that *Hamlet* was being performed on the Azerbaidzhan stage for the first time, that the Muslim religion denounced theatre altogether, which is why the art of theatre had been subjected to cruel persecutions in the Muslim East before the Revolution, that, consequently Shakespeare's tragedy was performed before audiences totally naive in relation to theatre, then one must recognize Tuganov and Dzhabarly's aspiration, to bring the play as close as possible to the people, as both logical and sensible. For a long time the role of Hamlet was confirmed in Sharifzade's repertoire, and subsequently he performed it with great success, not in an extravagantly 'Oriental', but in a very ordinary production where the usual Laertes had already replaced Sokhrab, the usual Polonius Logman, the usual Guildenstern Gyulchina, and so forth.

'Back to Ostrovsky!'

For the jubilee of the Russian dramatist (in 1923 the one-hundredth anniversary of his birth was officially celebrated), Lunacharsky promoted a slogan, 'Back to Ostrovsky!', that many found puzzling. The Narkom of Education called upon the masters of the stage to examine modern life more intently, to take from Ostrovsky the ability to record the characteristic traits of everyday life, to turn the theatre into 'a living mirror of surrounding reality'.[118] In his extensive article he also broached the question of how classical plays should be staged, to what extent they can serve the aims of political agitation and propaganda and how far the director may go in interpreting classical works and giving them a contemporary resonance.

The 'leftist' theatres, striving 'to modernize' the classics, adopted a highly unceremonious attitude towards them. The traditional theatres treated the staging of the classics more cautiously, although they also realized that the task of finding a modern reading of the old plays, their new interpretation, must be resolved urgently.

Meyerhold's experiments with the classical Russian repertoire were the centre of attention – and they provoked the most conflicting responses. He was continuously presenting the public and critics with surprises. If the avant-garde director had turned Sukhovo-Kobylin's *Tarelkin's Death* into a sort of fusion of circus and fairground show, then in his staging of Ostrovsky's *A Profitable Post* at the Theatre of the Revolution in the same year, 1923, contrary to all expectations, there was no 'circusization' whatsoever, the actors did not wear *prozodezhda* and the text had not been modified. However, in his design the artist Viktor Shestakov offered for the first time the combination of historically authentic costumes (the characters were dressed according to the fashion and customs of the mid-nineteenth century) with a functional, austerely delineated stage area, set outside history and noticeably modernized. Old civil servants' uniforms, frock coats, tavern waiters' white shirts belted with a cord, crinolines, wasp-waists tightly cinched, ladies' hairstyles with little bows and ribbons, officials' side-whiskers and bald spots – all this was as in Ostrovsky's times. However, solidly black plywood walls sealed off the stage, and from the stage floor small, steep spiral staircases resembling ships' gangways soared upwards. Instead of comfortable seats and period chairs, tables, benches and stools knocked together from rough boards jutted up everywhere.

The characters' historically precise costumes were introduced into an environment indifferent to history, they acted against the stylized background which seemed to have pushed them out of the distant past into Moscow of the 1920s.

In their acting Dmitri Orlov and Maria Babanova complemented one another. Orlov gave Yusov the pre-possessing affability of a man confident that he has grasped all wordly wisdom and, in becoming rich, is in no way devoting himself to vice but to virtue itself. His gait was slow and dignified, with a slight sway, his voice unctuous, his gestures imperious and commanding. Babanova set off Yusov's stateliness with Polinka's gracious vitality and changeability, his slowness with her quickness, his self-satisfied satiety of speech with her capricious patter. The actress concealed from the audience neither Polinka's bourgeois narrow-mindedness nor her naivety. But through the mockery in Babanova a sympathy for Polinka was perceptible, in her clear childlike voice was heard the lyricism of an innocently pure soul. 'Playing the bourgeois "little fool",' wrote Gvozdev, 'Babanova leaves Polinka with some grain of sound humaneness. She retains the ability to speak the simple and sincere word of love.'[119] This humanity sharply contrasted with Yusov's cynicism, the iron grip of the briber and embezzler of public funds.

In the same way the production contrasted the figures of Zhadov (who sets out as an uncompromising idealist) and Belogubov (a brisk predator in civil servant's uniform who grows in impudence before one's eyes). Zhadov's capitulation was marked simply and graphically: over a white shirt with a turn-down collar, he put on an official uniform jacket and thus promptly moved out of the present into the past.

Meyerhold's staging metaphors in *A Profitable Post* were sharp in their visual expressiveness: Belogubov (Vasily Zaichikov) ran up the spiral staircase and at every turn of the spiral bowed low to Yusov; Yusov (Orlov), entering the boss's office gradually shrank, bent at the knees and seemed to become shorter; Polinka would repeatedly go down the stairs toward Zhadov, then back up again, moving away from him, and Babanova danced with capricious wilfulness. Zhadov and Polinka's little room, reminiscent of a bird-house, was in itself a 'materialized metaphor': the director Vladimir Soloviev wrote that it signified that the young people live wantonly and carefree, like 'birds in the skies'.[120] The focal point of the great scene in the tavern was the episode when the tipsy Yusov, swaggering, burnt a newspaper on a tray: the yellow flames danced in the dark, symbolizing the bureaucrat's hatred of the press and of freedom of thought.

The entire composition was graceful, fluent and coherent.

The directorial plan for *The Forest*, another Ostrovsky comedy staged at the Meyerhold Theatre a year later, in 1924, had quite a different character. This play, chosen for a radical experiment, had previously been produced frequently and was considered the *plat du jour* on the posters of the Imperial theatres.

Sharply changing course, Meyerhold provided a contrast to the outward austerity of his previous works with the joyful, colourful and deliberately bright costumes of *The Forest*, where low buffoonery was fused with elevated lyricism. Once again the most ordinary everyday objects appeared on stage, and in great quantity: bentwood chairs, icons, freshly laundered linen, even a dovecote with live pigeons. All these changes had been implemented because Meyerhold was trying to overcome the distance separating 'leftist art' from the wide, mass audience with one stroke, one powerful blow. He wanted to create a spectacle that, even if crude, was on the other hand topical, at once both satirically biting and cheerful.

The task was resolved by means of a bold combination of the most diverse means of expression: in the production the devices of the fairground show, circus and cinema stood side by side and alternated with one another, that is the devices of very different but completely democratic spectacles, comprehensible to anyone. If in Meyerhold's preceding productions circus stunts and clowning had often been exhibited for their own sake, then in *The Forest* they functioned in service of the comic subject, contributing directly to the theme of the show. In precisely the same way Meyerhold used devices from the silent cinema to work actively for the production's central theme, in particular captions and parallel montage.

In the cinema when scenes showing events which occur at one and the same time but in different places succeed each other, this kind of montage is known as parallel. Before *The Forest* this method of conducting one action parallel to another had not been used in the theatre. Meyerhold employed it very simply. He divided the stage into two parts: on the left was a curving spiral, a road shooting upwards along which Schastlivtsev (the Comedian) and Neschastlivtsev (the Tragedian) walked; on the right, on the flat stage floor, lay the estate of the landowner Gurmyzhskaya. On the left – liberty; on the right – bondage.

A beam of light illuminated first one, then the other half of the stage, producing a purely cinematic effect of successive frames. This was further emphasized when the captions flashed on the screen above the stage before each episode. They not only announced or clarified events but also provided an unambiguous appraisal of them, for example: 'Cheat and pray, pray and cheat' or 'Arkashka against the petit-bougeoisie,' and so forth.

The plan of the production swung it swiftly round to meet modern times. Ostrovsky's play was deliberately simplified. The logic behind the simplification roughly corresponded to the words which at the same time, in 1924, Mayakovsky addressed to Pushkin: 'I could even entrust agit-poems to you.' That is just what Meyerhold did: he subcontracted political agitation to Ostrovsky. The will of the director threw into sharp prominence class interests and the class identity of each of the play's characters. The comedy's kaleidoscopic, complex and mobile system of imagery acquired the character of the direct opposition of 'two camps' – the exploiters and the exploited, the oppressors and the oppressed. From the very beginning a hostile attitude was declared with complete frankness toward the landowner Gurmyzhskaya, her confidante and informer Ulita,

Milonov whom Meyerhold made a 'priest', Vosmibratov whom he made a 'kulak', Bodaev whom he made a 'police chief' and so on. Also immediately identified were those 'fighting against exploitation' to whom all the sympathies of the theatre belonged – Aksyusha, Petr, Schastlivtsev and Neschastlivtsev.

Class characteristics dominated, subordinating and crushing everything else. The play was transformed into a kind of arena where the class struggle was conducted combatively and merrily.

In place of Ostrovsky's distinctive and wayward characters the theatre offered a selection of types designated in a placard style, 'social masks' replacing live portraits. The social mask says nothing about the individual attributes of the face that it covers, but fixes and caricatures only the social, class identity of the dramatis personae.

Such an aggressively sociological approach, which absolutely scorned individual distinctions and was always prepared to evaluate any of the characters exclusively along class lines (a merchant or landowner means a scoundrel or villain; a peasant or impoverished actor means a hero, a rebel), subsequently spread very extensively and acquired the name 'vulgarized sociology'. In many theatres the old plays continued to be dismantled and reconstructed for a long time, everywhere tracing class interests and bringing them forward as major, exclusively important. But this emphasis on politics and class usually resulted in very boring, schematic productions.

The naive and straightforward sociology of *The Forest* was not boring, primarily because Meyerhold utilized the merry language of the fairground show (with digressions into circus and cinematography) and fully exploited all the potential of audacious buffoonery and ingenuous lyricism.

The performance commenced in emptiness, on a bare stage. And at once, in this neutral, cold space, there started up an unrestrained 'play of colours', burningly bright, and a 'play of objects' of the most diverse sort. No *prozodezhda*, no uniform, but, on the contrary, gaudy, colourful costumes, coloured wigs (gold, green, red), coloured beards tied round the faces of some. The colours clashed with each other, vying to drown each other out. The cacophony of colour stormed on stage, accompanied by a cacophony of sound (chiming bells, piercing whistles, the thump of the linen-beater plus many other sudden and loud noises). This comic and satirical outburst was matched by an exceptional outpouring of lyricism, which elevated Petr and Aksyusha in their love duet and made them superhuman in scale.

The exaggeration, which informed both the satire and the lyricism, gave inner unity to the composition of *The Forest* and although the play was broken into thirty-three individual episodes they seemed to interplay, as if winking at one another. Two waves rolled through the performance: the wave of satire, crude and contemptuous, and the wave of lyricism, triumphant and inspired.

Among the actors-participants in *The Forest*, Igor Ilinsky as Arkashka Schastlivtsev was brought to the forefront. In flat black hat, ragged baggy checked trousers and a jacket that was too short, Arkashka behaved like a real circus clown, at times recalling the capers of Charlie Chaplin. On stage he acted like a clever and mischievous emissary for the present-day public, thrown onto the stage by the audience itself in order to turn everything upside down, to place the past 'on end'. An intimate relationship of mutual solidarity was immediately established between Arkashka and the spectators: for the audience this mischievous, dissolute comic was 'one of them', as were also his majestic travelling companion, the tragedian Neschastlivtsev and the persecuted but defiant lovers, Aksyusha and Petr. But all the others seemed like enemies, like 'strangers', and to jeer at them was highly satisfying.

Just as Meyerhold had hoped, the staging of *The Forest* brought 'leftist' art one of its most resounding and major triumphs. The show's success surpassed all expectations. In a relatively short period (less than half a decade) *The Forest* sustained a record number of performances – 1328 in all.

The lively public interest in the production was explained to a significant degree by the fact that Meyerhold had 'modernized' the play: the landowner Gurmyzhskaya, as performed by Elena Tyapkinaya, resembled a Moscow NEP-woman; Bulanov (Ivan Pyriev), the son of an NEP-man, who at that time were contemptuously called 'georgies'; Aksyusha (Zinaida Raikh), the fighting young Communists of the 1920s, and so forth.

The audience easily deciphered and eagerly picked up the topical references in both *A Profitable Post* at the Theatre of the Revolution and *The Forest* at the Meyerhold Theatre.

Alexander Tairov, at this time one of the most energetic rivals and opponents of Meyerhold, in 1924 also turned to Ostrovsky, although not to comedy but to tragedy. His choice was *The Storm*.

There was considerable risk involved here. The Kamerny Theatre, now almost ten years old, had never staged a single play from Russian life before *The Storm*. 'On the theatre's stage,' wrote Stefan Mokulsky, 'Indians, Jews, Greeks, Spaniards, Italians, French and English have filed by: everyone but the Russians.'[121] But *The Storm* is steeped in everyday Russian life, Russian speech creates all the play's 'music'. Tairov, together with the three designers (the brothers Vladimir and Georgy Stenberg and Konstantin Medunetsky) devised a highly distinctive theatrical form for the play. On stage a deliberately unwieldy, vaulted construction was built from squared beams which conveyed the heaviness of the patriarchal order of life gloomily hanging over the characters' heads and, contrary to tradition, uprooted the drama from the countryside and enclosed it in cramped, beamed cages.

Alisa Koonen as Katerina strove to give the heroine an accentuated peasant-woman look. She appeared in a red *sarafan* (a Russian peasant woman's dress without sleeves, buttoning in front), white shirt with wide sleeves and with a plain *povoinik* (a kind of kerchief worn on the head by married Russian peasant women). K. Derzhavin noted 'her provincial accent, the cheerless submissiveness of her eyes,' and wrote that from the very beginning of the performance Koonen's Katerina seemed doomed to defeat, incapable 'of dispelling the oppressive darkness'.[122] In the finale when Koonen exchanged the red *sarafan* for a pale blue one and unloosed her dark plait, her hair spilling out and falling over her shoulders, Katerina's submissiveness to her bitter, woman's fate was felt ever more poignantly. The actress searched persistently for historically concrete signs of the heroine's everyday characteristics, and other performers also moved in this direction. The result, in Lunacharsky's words, was unexpected: a strange mixture 'of completely realistic acting, in the style of the Maly Theatre, and somewhat artificial Constructivist scenery.'[123]

Tairov strove for the 'pathos of simplicity' and 'sought new forms of expressive means', in particular, 'melodiousness in intonation', thereby leading the actors not so much to the comprehension of the essence of the tragedy as to the reconstruction of a style of Russian drama to which they were unaccustomed. And the Kamerny

Theatre's actors obediently followed 'the path of the traditional performance of Ostrovsky'.[124] One German critic wrote that Koonen 'endows this Russian petit-bourgeois with the grandeur of an ancient heroine'.[125] The Russian critics, however, did not have such a high opinion of her performance.

At the Moscow Art Theatre Stanislavsky set to work on Ostrovsky after Meyerhold had already shown *A Profitable Post* and *The Forest*, and Tairov *The Storm*. Stanislavsky's production of *A Passionate Heart* sharply altered traditional opinion on the style, manner and resources of MAT. The previous view had been that the art of the MAT, tuned to the Chekhovian tuning fork, was, in its best productions, melancholy, mournful. The 'deliberately muted tone' was accepted as characteristic.[126] The striking thing about Stanislavsky's new production was the riot of colour, the energy and irrepressible impetus of the comic spirit.

The artist Nikolai Krymov's design broke with the previous customs of the MAT where, as a rule, the most minute historically authentic details of everyday life were valued and an exact 'picture of life' was sought. This time intentionally exaggerated tableaux appeared on stage. The trivialities of life were banished. The scenery presented exaggerated features of merchant life, sarcastically correlated to the poetry of the Russian landscape. The most vivid example was in the third act of the play, at the country residence of the merchant Khlynov: absurd, blue columns twisted like pretzels, crowned with gold balls; between the columns – wide steps of a marble staircase; to the right and left of the staircase – the enormous snouts of bored heraldic lions; on the forestage – Khlynov's massive armchair and by it a stuffed bear holding a tray in his paws. And behind this flashy merchant opulence loomed the tall and melancholy wall of the Russian forest.

The artist established such contrasts everywhere, as Stanislavsky had wanted. Against the background of peaceful birch groves and spacious sky jutted out gloomy fences, milestones and absurd gnarled clump-like structures; the characters paced about in glaringly loud costumes. Stanislavsky wanted to present satire in the forms of 'folk buffoonery' and carnival-like mischievousness while nowhere foregoing the truth of the characters' psychology.

Three characters appeared in the forefront – Kuroslepov, Gradoboev, Khlynov. The specialist on Stanislavsky's art, Marianna Stroeva, has written that, according to the director's idea, these 'three bigwigs, crushing the city, all of grimy, sleeping Russia beneath them, seem to have everything; their life is full to capacity, replete. However, for them it is still not enough, something is lacking. And, feeling some sort of inner emptiness, discontent, they crave totally unrestricted power.'[127]

Kuroslepov (Vladimir Gribunin), bloated and dulled from lethargy, wearing a long, loose, rose-coloured shirt, with feathers and down in his dishevelled hair, a soured and vacant expression on his face, through his entire appearance expressed the most complete indifference to everything in the world.

In contrast, Gradoboev (Mikhail Tarkhanov), a beast-like swindler whose eyes burned with impatience and an administrative rapture, was, as the director Sakhnovsky expressed it, a fierce 'extortionist and profiteer', 'indefatigable as a contagion, as the plague'.[128]

One of the most gifted actors of the MAT, the multi-talented Ivan Moskvin, who felt equally at home in both tragedy and comedy, played the role of Khlynov, an irrepressible petty tyrant in the grip of tedium, eternally drunk, gone mad from idleness, unbridled and unbelted to the point of savagery. This red-faced, sweaty merchant with a spade-shaped red beard, wiry red hair parted down the centre and a chest covered with clattering gold medals, did not know a moment of peace. The enormous energy which found no intelligent application whatsoever forced Khlynov to rush about the stage in a drunken frenzy. His legs, in striped trousers, skipped eternally, his narrow eyes glistened excitedly. 'The image of Moskvin,' wrote Sakhnovsky, 'is genuinely terrible and cruel. In Moskvin's performance the humour and powerful embodiment of the "popular element" cause waves of such devastating force to roll from the stage that that kingdom which Ostrovsky had intended to destroy is smashed, demolished by the powers of Moskvin's talent.' Sakhnovsky, an experienced director and recognized expert on Ostrovsky's drama, was delighted by the way in which 'invention' and 'truth that touches the heart' were woven together in the MAT production. 'This,' he asserted, 'was the very boldest position which the theatre had risked taking.'[129]

Moskvin was the soul of the performance, its moving force. The theme of 'brutocracy' and 'fantastic outrage' that had enticed Stanislavsky was raised to the level of the tragi-comic grotesque in Moskvin's performance. Equally exaggerated were the caricatures of Gradoboev, Matrena (Faina Shevchenko), Narkis (Boris Dobronravov) and others. Satire raged on the MAT stage, relentless and unerringly targeted.

Such a sharp perception of Ostrovsky in the productions of Stanislavsky and Meyerhold corroborated Lunacharsky's urgent appeals to study this writer's 'unusual simplicity and cogency of form' and 'inflammatory advocacy of new truths'.[130] And with every year it became clearer that, however interesting the directional variations on the themes of the plays of past centuries, wide audiences would nevertheless not be content with them. They expected uncompromisingly truthful pictures of present-day life.

'On the Issue of the Day'

One of the first Soviet plays dedicated to modern times, written 'on the issue of the day', came from the pen of Lunacharsky himself. He had previously composed a considerable number of historical 'costume' plays, some of which – Faust and the City, Oliver Cromwell and The Chancellor and the Locksmith – had been staged and enjoyed success. In 1925 with the melodrama Poison, he accomplished, as a reviewer expressed it, 'the first leap from the clouds of history to the land of reality'.[131] It can not be said that this leap was successful. Wishing to show how pernicious were the seductions of NEP to the young generation, Lunacharsky had heavily over-emphasized, depicting the temptation of an honest but weak-willed youth, Valery Shurupov, by all possible kinds of prostitutes, cocaine addicts, charlatans and even demonic villains, like the spy and murderer Nickel Poluda. The pictures of the 'moral disintegration' of the unstable young people were presented with frightening vividness, and the characters who were attempting to resist the 'intoxicating fumes of NEP' seemed pale by comparison. Nonetheless, the very fact that contemporary life was shown proved enough to attract the attention of the audience, and Nikolai Petrov's production at the Leningrad Academic Theatre of Drama aroused great interest.

Among the young writers whose first attempts inspired hope in the hearts of directors, Boris Romashov had already, in the very

early 1920s, drawn attention to himself. At one time he had worked as a reviewer, then later he composed topical, humorous sketches for the cabaret theatres and in 1925 he wrote the comedy The Soufflé which Meyerhold's student, Alexei Gripich, staged at the Theatre of the Revolution.

The main character in The Soufflé is the crafty wheeler-dealer, Semyon Rak. Romashov succeeded in skilfully portraying the inexhaustible inventiveness, resourcefulness, insolence and aggressive energy of this entrepreneur for whose initiative the conflict of NEP offered wide scope. There was considerable boldness in Romashov's satire. In particular, the comedy depicted a prominent Soviet economic planner, a man with a fighting Revolutionary background, Ilya Koromyslov, who is entangled in a net cast by speculators and swindlers. In Koromyslov the audience detected a real figure, the bank chairman Krasnoshchekov, the hero of a recent scandalous court case that had exposed corruption and embezzlement on a grand scale. The publicist Mikhail Koltsov, defending Romashov's play, wrote in Pravda: 'We have nothing to fear of the strong episodes in The Soufflé. We are not innocent schoolgirls who must lower our eyes bashfully before any dark sides of Soviet life.'[132] The director Gripich thought likewise: he wanted to turn in a new direction, 'to create a production depicting modern life'.[133]

Dmitri Orlov played the part of Semyon Rak with thrust and bravura. His character wore smart, well-cut suits, stylish checked shirts and, as a sign of collaboration with the new leadership, a red handkerchief peeping out of his jacket pocket. In him, rapacious cupidity and inexhaustible energy were the dominant forces. The actors made it clear that Semyon Rak was not some ordinary swindler but a kind of devotee, a 'poet of speculation' hatching out global plans, dreams of all Russia's return to the times of private enterprise, of transactions and speculations on an international scale. However, there was also a feeling that things were getting too hot for him. Alexei Gripich later recalled how subtly Orlov indicated the precariousness of Semyon Rak's situation: 'In the midst of turbulent action he would suddenly stop, pause very briefly as if listening to something, then go on. Quickly, almost imperceptibly, he would glance back over his shoulder or, like a dog, look in fear into the eyes of his partner and turn away. And now the smile would fade from his face and his teeth would gnash, fury in his eyes.'[134]

Economic planners, office workers, wheeler-dealers as well as 'the newspaper sellers, porters, waiters, policemen, plain-clothes detectives, Red Army soldiers, café-goers and people on the boulevard' listed in the programme were transferred onto the stage with the accuracy of an official record so that the audience could easily recognize all of them. The 'official recordism' (the expression of the critic B. Alpers) of Gripich's direction and Viktor Shestakov's stage designs sharpened the point of the satire. Many of the genre scenes in the production looked like completely authentic sketches from life, like animated photographs.

At almost exactly the same time, in 1925, another comedy was shown at the Meyerhold Theatre – The Warrant by Nikolai Erdman – which contained immeasurably greater energy of social generalization and satirical wrath than The Soufflé. In The Warrant 'yesterday's men' came under the magnifying glass of comedy, spiritually barren philistines who seven or eight years after the victory of the Revolution could not and would not acknowledge the reality of its victory. They perceived what had been accomplished as a bad dream, a nightmare just about to end. The most distinctive quality of Nikolai Erdman's play lay in its collection of 'human dust' that had fallen into the satirist's field of vision: not people but the husks of people. Not one of them was capable of being compared even with Semyon Rak in scale, energy or enterprise. The behaviour of the residents of the petit-bourgeois swamp whose 'old brains', according to the mournful admission of one of the characters, 'cannot endure the new regime,' was held up for examination and ridicule. Scared half to death by the Revolution and unable to adapt themselves to it, they secretly cherish the impossible hope that 'the good, old' times will return.

Erdman stated both these themes – the futile attempts to cling on to the new life and the absurd dreams that history will move backwards – in the form of two skilfully interwoven storylines. The story of how the petit-bourgeois Pavel Gulyachkin, frightened by the Revolution, has falsely declared himself a Communist in order to marry off his old-maid sister to Valerian Smetanich, the son of a wealthy NEP-man, crosses in the play with the story of the cook Nastia who has by a chance concatenation of circumstances been taken for the Grand Duchess Anastasia Nikolaevna Romanova. Consequently the wealthy Smetaniches face a tormenting alternative. A choice between the two fiancées must be made: either Varvara Gulyachkina who has a brother, ostensibly a Communist with 'a warrant', or Anastasia, apparently the relative of the Emperor himself, ostensibly the heiress to the throne. Between these two spurious possibilities all the 'inhabitants' of the comedy begin feverishly to rush about in the Gulyachkins' cramped apartment.

The two stories are unified by the general theme of the inauthenticity, the unreal quality of the petit-bourgeois existence. Gulyachkin is no Communist and he has no 'warrant'; Nastia Pupkina is no duchess, but a servant.

Meyerhold greeted Erdman's play with delight. He asserted that *The Warrant* is 'a modern comedy of daily life written in the true traditions of Gogol and Sukhovo-Kobylin.'[135] The director took care to ensure that all the characters received authentic costumes, similar to the everyday dress of Muscovites of the 1920s down to the most minute details. But Erdman's comedy did not prompt him to return to the principles typical of MAT's 'picture of life' or resort to the 'photographs from life' which Gripich had created in staging *The Soufflé*. In Meyerhold's production unquestionably real characters, familiar to anyone and everyone, existed in an openly stylized, moving and changing, 'flowing' space.

The innovation in *The Warrant* was the artist Ilya Shlepyanov's mobile, dynamic stage, the outlines of which instantaneously changed before the audience's eyes. In the centre of the stage floor there was a small stationary disc around which revolved two flat rings, each a metre in width (Meyerhold called them 'moving pavements'). The concentric rotation, jointly or in opposite directions, of these two 'pavements' intersected time and again with the movement of three tall plywood screens which rolled on wheels parallel to the footlights.

The empty space of the stage was transformed with magical speed enabling the director to make rapid changes of the most diverse arrangements (though always on a single, horizontal level). The characters rode out onto the stage, obstinately clutching their trunkloads of possessions. 'We are presenting the characters,' explained Meyerhold, 'in the midst of the real objects with which they have become inextricably intertwined.'[136] The objects – standard lamps, with orange lampshades, domestic altars, horn-gramophones, and so on – embodied in themselves the power of the past, the petit-bourgeois attachment of 'yesterday's men' to property, to acquired 'goods'.

Meyerhold managed to attain truth here, to show the ordinary in the incredible foreshortened perspective of the tragi-comic grotesque. An eccentric manner of performance was required of the actors which demanded exceptionally sharp character acting, to the point of caricature, invariably combined with excruciatingly sincere veracity in the character's behaviour when they found themselves in highly improbable, anecdotally absurd situations. The eccentricism demonstrated the sharp breaks in the psychology of the ordinary, 'little' person at historical turning-points that are too abrupt and incomprehensible for him.

Two young actors, Erast Garin in the main role of Pavel Gulyachkin and Sergei Martinson as Valerian Smetanich, exhibited the potential of eccentricism most successfully. An out-at-elbows bourgeois, in his threadbare jacket and coarse cloth shirt from the collar of which stretched his long, thin neck, Gulyachkin, a man with a confused and distraught face, was perceived as the living embodiment of a petit-bourgeois disorientated by the Revolution. The comic in this figure was allied with the tragic, with a sense of the irreparable. Gulyachkin, a self-proclaimed 'Party man' who is himself frightened to death by his own lies, was nonetheless unbelievably hilarious. Garin's rather slow nervous gestures contrasted with the jerky dynamics, all in broken rhythms, of Martinson who, in *The Warrant*, played a vacant and stupid young man whose interests extend no further than stylish trousers and fashionable dances.

In the play's finale, the wedding ball (Valerian Smetanich has been married to the supposed heiress to the throne) rolls toward catastrophe to the thunderous accompaniment of a brass band. It transpires that Nastia is not the Grand Duchess but a cook, that Pavel Gulyachkin is 'an impostor and not a Communist at all' and that the police have already been informed of all these deceptions. But the worst news is saved for the very end: 'they have refused to arrest you.' The shattered Gulyachkin inquires: 'Mama, if they don't even want to arrest us, then, mama, how can we live? How can we live?'

The characters stood frozen, rooted to the spot, and the revolving circles slowly carried them away into emptiness, into non-existence.

If such works of Meyerhold's as *The Magnanimous Cuckold* had provoked arguments, delighting some, shocking and angering others, then *The Warrant* was met with general approval. The public joyously howled with laughter (during one performance the laughter in the hall rang out more than 350 times); the reviewers responded with enthusiasm.

A. V. Lunacharsky said of the production's realism, 'Erdman's *The Warrant* as produced by Meyerhold towers above all the realistic plays of the last season,' and he evaluated the director's satirical hyperboles as 'profoundly realistic'.[137]

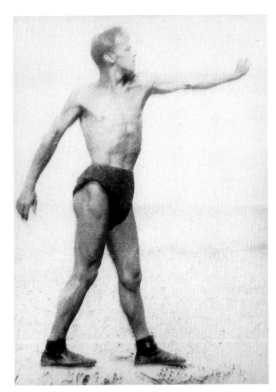

Biomechanics

As a counterweight to Stanislavsky's 'System' Meyerhold created his own system of actors' training, which he called 'biomechanics'. Photographs of biomechanics exercises like those shown here can give the false impression that in practice this system was similar to ordinary gymnastics. In fact it developed the actor's ability consciously to direct his body and voice (that is both visually and intonationally); it provided an acute sense of tempo and rhythm in acting, a musical responsiveness of gesture; and, last and most important of all, it stressed a constant awareness of the acting partner. Besides this, biomechanics incorporated elements of acrobatics and demanded athletic lightness of movement.

Scene from *The Magnanimous Cuckold*.

Liubov Popova's construction for *The Magnanimous Cuckold*.

Maria Babanova as Stella.

The Magnanimous Cuckold

Two sketches by Liubov Popova of a costume and the construction (*below*) for *The Magnanimous Cuckold*.

Scene from *The Magnanimous Cuckold*.

Biomechanics brilliantly passed its first public test with the première of Crommelynck's *Magnanimous Cuckold* in 1922. For this production the stage of Meyerhold's theatre was set not with scenery but with a construction by Liubov Popova. All the actors performed without make-up, in identical uniforms (*prozodezhda*) and all of them – Maria Babanova, Igor Ilinsky and Vasily Zaichikov with particular success – played out Crommelynck's crude farce on the bare planks and ladders of the construction, giving the action a soundness, a purity and a freshness. Nonetheless Lunacharsky was extremely shocked. 'I consider the play a mockery of man, woman, love and jealousy,' he announced, adding that he 'felt ashamed for the audience who roared in animal laughter at the slaps, falls and salaciousness'.

The 'Factory of the Eccentric Actor' (FEKS) was created in Petrograd in 1922 by two young people later to become famous cinema directors, Grigory Kozintsev and Leonid Trauberg. Trauberg, in answer to the question why he and Kozintsev had chosen Gogol's *The Marriage* for their first production, recently protested: 'But it was written in black and white on the poster that this was "not according to Gogol"! We wanted to create a show in which a series of tricks would unite the elements of circus, jazz, sport and cinema. Our ideal actor was Chaplin. We considered that eccentricism was the surest way to "Americanize" theatre, to give the theatrical action the dynamics required by the twentieth century – the century of unheard-of velocities.' Kozintsev's sketch for the set is published here for the first time.

The Marriage

Opposite, above: Two sketches by Kozintsev of costumes for Kochkarev (*left*) and the Matchmaker (*right*).

Opposite, below: Poster for the première of *The Marriage*, 1922.

Right: Sketch by Kozintsev of the set for *The Marriage*.

125

Tarelkin's Death

Meyerhold continued to experiment in the sphere of 'circusization of theatre', and he produced Sukhovo-Kobylin's gloomy play *Tarelkin's Death* (1922) in a spirit of light-hearted clowning. The artist Varvara Stepanova proposed, instead of the one whole 'machine' that Popova's construction for *The Magnanimous Cuckold* had represented, a collection of different 'apparatuses', large and small, which were placed separately on the stage area. They imitated ordinary furniture, but the chairs collapsed or fired a shot every time they were sat upon and jumped up whenever the sitter arose again. A huge meat-grinder was the metaphorical depiction of a police torture-chamber. The actors (who included Mikhail Zharov, Nikolai Okhlopkov and Dmitri Orlov) wore identical *prozodezhda* and conducted themselves with the free-and-easy swagger of clowns, throwing large multi-coloured balls into the auditorium, fighting amongst themselves with sticks and bulls' bladders and swinging out on swings over the first rows of the stalls.

Mikhail Zharov as Brandakhlystova.

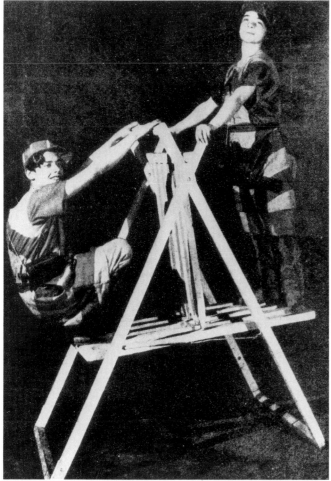

A scene from *Tarelkin's Death*.

ВАРРАВИН

МАВРУША

Varvara Stepanova's 'apparatuses' for *Tarelkin's Death*.

Left: Two costume designs by Varvara Stepanova for *Tarelkin's Death*.

The Mexican

Three sketches by Eisenstein of costumes (*left*) and make-up (*below*) for *The Mexican*.

Among Meyerhold's assistants in the production of *Tarelkin's Death* was the young Sergei Eisenstein. He had already worked independently in the Proletkult theatre, where along with Valentin Smyshlaev he had staged an adaptation of Jack London's story *The Mexican*. Eisenstein had many talents: a gifted artist and theatre director, he later became one of the greatest directors in the history of cinema besides being a penetrating theoretician of the art. But at the beginning of the 1920s, in his *Mexican*, it was sporting imagery that dominated: the centre of the show was an exciting boxing match. His 1923 production *The Wise Man* (based on Ostrovsky's play *Enough Stupidity in Every Wise Man*) was, however, the apogee of the 'circusization of theatre', with tight-rope walking, acrobatics and somersaults on the ground and in the air, executed with full professional panache.

Three sketches by Eisenstein of the set (*above*), the make-up (*left*) and a costume (*right*) for *The Mexican*.

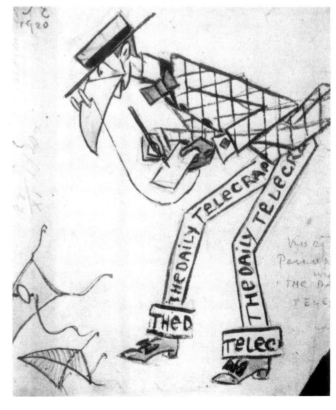

Two scenes from Georg Kaiser's *Gas*, at the Bolshoi Dramatic Theatre in 1922.

In the repertoire of Soviet theatres in the first half of the 1920s a significant mark was made by the plays of the German Expressionist dramatists – Georg Kaiser, Ernst Toller, Franz Werfel and also the Czech writer Karel Čapek. All these works were permeated with fear at the growing urbanization and mechanization of life and at the faceless, spiritually vacant masses of workers whom the writers represented as numbed adjuncts to their machines, almost as robots.

Soviet directors readily staged Expressionist dramas but they had a very different attitude to machinery and to crowds of workers. To Soviet directors mechanization, far from being a threat, represented a rapid improvement of life and the restoration of the economy after the Civil War, and the popular masses mattered to them far more than the solitary intellectuals who were the heroes of Expressionist drama.

Productions of Expressionist plays in the Bolshoi Dramatic Theatre in Petrograd, where they were most often designed by Yury Annenkov, therefore turned into a kind of parade of machines. Theatrical Constructivism found its essential metier in the loving 'aestheticization' of factory workshops, conveyor belts, lifts and so forth.

Gas

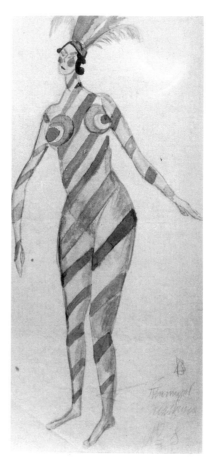

Three costume sketches by Dmitriev for *Eugene the Unlucky*.

Sketch by Dmitriev of the set for *Eugene the Unlucky*.

A scene from *Hoppla, wir leben*.

The artist Vladimir Dmitriev, in his sketches of the sets and costumes for the 1923 production of Ernst Toller's *Eugene the Unlucky* in the Petrograd Academic Theatre of Drama, tried to comply with the wishes of the director Sergei Radlov and create the image of a displaced world keeling over on the edge of a precipice, a world inhabited by very extravagant characters. The result, however, was not a great success. Konstantin Mardzhanov's 1928 production in Kutaisi of another of Toller's plays *Hoppla, wir leben* was also not a complete success, although the director had attracted the talented artist Elena Akhvlediani to work in his theatre. The audience did not particularly enjoy the satirical outbursts against the bourgeoisie. They were much more impressed by the mobile constructions that occupied the stage.

Plays by Toller

Constructivist sets

A scene from *Echo*.

When images of Western civilization sprang from the pens of Soviet dramatists it was usually with the aim of exposing the worthlessness of bourgeois customs. This did not, however, by any means prevent the creators of these productions giving themselves and their audiences enormous aesthetic pleasure. In Vladimir Bill-Belotserkovsky's *Echo*, staged by the Moscow Theatre of the Revolution in 1924, the director Alexei Gripich and the designer Viktor Shestakov distributed the action over several levels of a theatrically effective construction. The Constructivists poeticized, almost idolized, the machine. Mayakovsky's friend Osip Brik asserted: 'The machine is more like an animate organism than is usually thought. . . . More than that even, today's machines are far more alive than the people who build them.'

Alexei Tolstoy's play *Mutiny of the Machines*, staged at the Bolshoi Dramatic Theatre in 1924 by Konstantin Khokhlov, was a loose adaptation of Karel Čapek's drama *R. U. R.* (*Rossum's Universal Robots*) and an enthusiastic tribute to the cult of the machine.

A scene from *Mutiny of the Machines*.

134

A scene from *Lake Lyul*.

Model of the set by Shestakov for
Lake Lyul.

Alexei Faiko's melodrama
Lake Lyul, staged by Vsevolod
Meyerhold in 1923 at the
Theatre of Revolution with
sets by Viktor Shestakov,
enjoyed a loud and stormy
success. Here the construction
was used not in order to
reproduce factory machinery
but to show an imagined
Western town in all its
beauty, with hotels,
advertisements in lights,
moving lifts and, most
importantly, the sumptuous
evening dress of the
inhabitants. In Moscow at this
time, as throughout the whole
country, private trade and
entrepreneurial activity were
permitted under the New
Economic Policy. The get-rich-
quick 'NEP-men', their wives
and mistresses, went to *Lake
Lyul* as to a show of the latest
Parisian fashions. Of course
Meyerhold was irritated by
the heightened interest of this
public and soon he radically
altered the direction of his
experiments.

A scene from *Lake Lyul*.

Poster for the première of *Lake Lyul*,
1923.

The Earth in Turmoil

Sergei Tretyakov's drastically altered adaptation of the French dramatist Marcel Martinet's play *La Nuit* was called *The Earth in Turmoil*. Using this as a basis, Meyerhold created a political revue devoted to the First World War and the beginning of the Russian Revolution. Several episodes in the production, which opened in 1923, were performed in the style of farce and buffoonery; others were poignantly tragic in mood and content. Liubov Popova's Constructivist set was partially reminiscent of a collage: beneath red wooden supports which imitated the mechanism of a crane, authentic items of a military environment appeared – carts, hospital stretchers, rifles, machine-guns, motorcycles. In one of the episodes a real army lorry even drove out on to the stage. Illuminated slogans and captions flashed up on a screen. The stage was lit by the powerful beams of military searchlights.

Above: Liubov Popova's set for *The Earth in Turmoil*.

Right: Two scenes from *The Earth in Turmoil*.

Model of the set by Shlepyanov

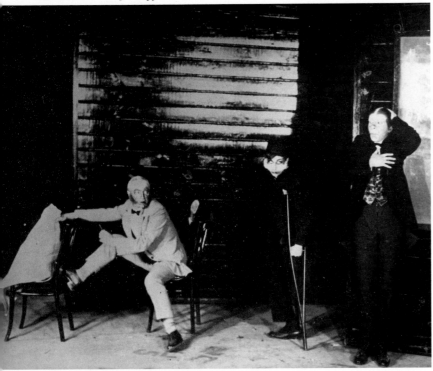

Five scenes from *D.E.* (*Give Us Europe*)

D. E. (Give Us Europe)

The next experiment in the genre of the political revue was Meyerhold's 1924 production *D.E.* (*Give Us Europe*), based on the novel of the same name by Ilya Ehrenburg and Bernhard Kellerman's novel *Der Tunnel*. Here, as in *The Earth in Turmoil*, satirical episodes alternated with episodes of poignant pathos. The satire attacked the vicious morality of 'fox-trotting' Europe, parodying its fashionable dances, while the serious episodes celebrated the healthy Soviet environment and the ethos of physical excellence. The chief surprise of *D.E.* was the effective 'quick change' acting device. In the first episode Erast Garin, rapidly changing masks and costumes, played seven characters, all of them inventors. (Some sketches for his costumes, executed by the artist Ilya Shlepyanov, are shown overleaf.) Igor Ilinsky and Maria Babanova also played several roles each. The production included a jazz band led by Valentin Parnakh, and the risqué dance numbers (foxtrot, charleston, tango, shimmy and rumba) were choreographed by the famous ballet-master Kasyan Goleizovsky.

Constructions
and Characters

ИЗОБРЕТАТЕЛЬ
№ 3
1ый ЭПИЗОД.

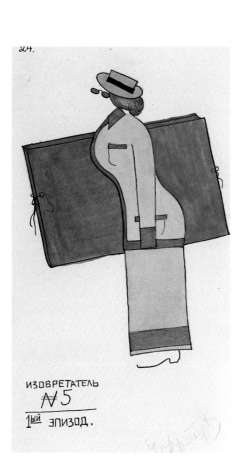

ИЗОБРЕТАТЕЛЬ
№ 5
1ый ЭПИЗОД.

ИЗОБРЕТАТЕЛЬ
№ 7
1ый ЭПИЗОД.

Three costume designs by Ilya
Shlepyanov for Meyerhold's
production of Ehrenburg and
Kellerman's *D.E.* (*Give Us Europe*),
staged at the Meyerhold Theatre in
Moscow in 1924.

Right: Alexandra Exter's plan for a
sports revue that was never staged,
1924.

143

Four scenes from *Princess Brambilla*.

Princess Brambilla

Meyerhold's art changed swiftly and suddenly, Tairov's slowly and gradually. In the Kamerny Theatre experiments in the sphere of tragedy and comedy (or, as Tairov preferred to call them, mystery and harlequinade) proceeded doggedly and consistently. Step by step but with ever-increasing confidence the company mastered the requirements of intonational and sculptural expressiveness that the director was demanding of it. *Princess Brambilla* (1920), conceived as a 'capriccio on motifs by E. T. A. Hoffmann', was one of Tairov's most entertaining harlequinades. This was a truly sparkling, infectiously merry and irresistibly dynamic spectacle, at the heart of which lay the joy of metamorphosis, the happy thrill of comic performance.

Sketches by Georgy Yakulov of
carnival masks (*above*) and a costume
(*below*) for *Princess Brambilla*.

Sketch by Georgy Yakulov of the set for *Princess Brambilla*.

Georgy Yakulov

The set for Tairov's *Princess Brambilla* (1920) was designed by Georgy Yakulov as a spiral which occupied the whole stage floor. This worked particularly well in conjunction with the circular movements of the carnival crowd. The vivid, colourful painting of the set enhanced the joyful atmosphere of the performance, of which A. Efros said: 'This was one of the most brilliant spectacles that we have ever been fortunate enough to see.'

Alisa Koonen as Giroflé and Nikolai
Tseretelli as Maraskin.

Three scenes from *Giroflé-Girofla*.

Giroflé-Girofla

In his 1922 production of Charles Lecocq's *Giroflé-Girofla*, Tairov had his dramatic actors playing, dancing and singing. The main roles were played by Alisa Koonen (as Giroflé), and Nikolai Tseretelli (as Maraskin). Their dances and duets were usually performed near the footlights, and the actors took the opportunity to address the spectators, joking and flirting with them.

149

Model of the set by A. Vesnin for *Phèdre*.

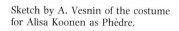

Sketch by A. Vesnin of the costume for Alisa Koonen as Phèdre.

A scene from *Phèdre*.

Tairov's 1923 production of Racine's *Phèdre* made a tremendous impression in Moscow, in Paris and in Berlin. The theatre reviewer of the Paris newspaper *L'Eclair* wrote: 'The audience was struck, and slightly stunned, by the originality of this company which has come to us direct from a country where one can expect, along with Bolshevism, all sorts of extravagances.' These 'extravagances' did indeed embarrass the veteran of the French stage André Antoine: he considered that Tairov had not only 'barbarously distorted' Racine but was also 'threatening the destruction of our whole dramatic art which has been created by a slow evolution over several centuries'. The conservative Antoine was passionately contradicted by Jean Cocteau, who was enraptured both by Tairov's production and the performance of Koonen in the main role. Cocteau appreciated to the full that unique combination of the archaic and the avant-garde which had been Tairov's aim in this production: the actors in buskins moved about on the sloping planes of Vesnin's Cubist construction; in Koonen's fiery and harrowed soliloquies there trembled the soul of contemporary woman.

Poster designed by Vladimir and Georgy Stenberg for the Kamerny Theatre's tour to Berlin in 1923.

L'Annonce faite à Marie

Tairov had turned to the drama of the French writer Paul Claudel for the first time in 1917 when he staged a production of *L'Echange*. Later, in 1920, the première took place of Claudel's tragedy *L'Annonce faite à Marie* with sets by Alexander Vesnin. The main role of the blind Violaine was played by Alisa Koonen. The actress said that for her this heroine evoked associations with Joan of Arc, and the stern and sombre spirit of the Middle Ages penetrated throughout the production.

In 1923 the Kamerny Theatre went on tour to Paris and Berlin. (See the poster on the previous page.) This tour was a significant success. But whereas in Paris Tairov's predilection for a French repertoire (Racine, Scribe, Claudel, Lecocq) had delighted both spectators and critics, Berlin at that time was unsympathetic to such 'Francophilia'. To Tairov's great amazement, on the Berlin posters *Adrienne Lecouvreur* was re-titled *Maurice of Saxony* and the author of *Phèdre* was given not as Jean Racine but . . . the translator Valery Bryusov.

Opposite: Sketches by A. Vesnin of the set for *L'Annonce faite à Marie*, and of the costume for Alisa Koonen as Violaine.

Scene from *L'Annonce faite à Marie*.

The Man Who Was Thursday

Persistently continuing his self-imposed task of acquainting Soviet audiences with contemporary Western literature, Tairov staged an adaptation of G. K. Chesterton's novel *The Man Who Was Thursday* at the Kamerny Theatre in 1923. He was clearly inspired by the idea of creating an urbanist spectacle to rival the Meyerhold *Lake Lyul*. Alexander Vesnin erected a massive construction that occupied the whole proscenium, installed moving lifts, built pavements and lit the whole structure with the flashing multicoloured lights of advertisements. The characters of the show, as they had in *Lake Lyul*, demonstrated the latest Western fashions. But the actors felt crowded on a stage that was piled high with constructions and the action moved sluggishly. In this competition with Meyerhold, Tairov was the loser.

Four costume sketches by A. Vesnin for *The Man Who Was Thursday*.

Right: A scene from *The Man Who Was Thursday*.

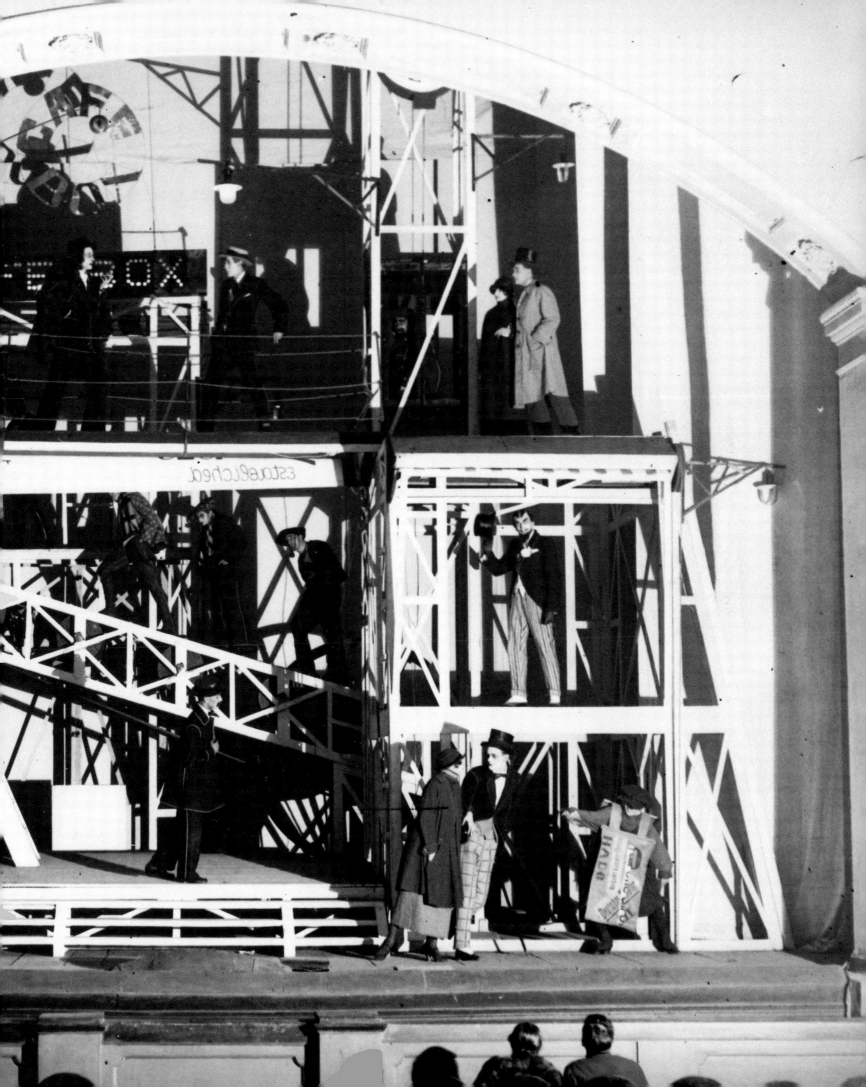

A scene from *Oedipus Rex*.

Molodoi Theatre

Opposite: Scenes from *Tartuffe* (*above*) and *Haydamaks* (*below*).

The Ukrainian theatre was one of the most notable of the many national theatres that had previously dragged out a miserable existence on the fringes of the Russian empire but after the Revolution immediately took heart and began to assert themselves. The young director Les Kurbas at once embarked on the great classics in his Molodoi Theatre in Kiev: among his first productions were Sophocles' *Oedipus Rex* (1918) and Molière's *Tartuffe* (1919). These productions showed no particular originality and still bore the stamp of apprenticeship and imitation, but in the 1920 production *Haydamaks*, based on the epic poem of the same name by Taras Shevchenko, Kurbas presented a completely independent, innovative approach to the staging, based upon the imagery of Ukrainian folklore. In 1922 the Molodoi was renamed the Berezil Theatre and some remarkable acting talents emerged – such as Amvrosy Buchma, Natalia Uzhvi and Gnat Yura.

A scene from *Gas*.

Berezil Theatre

Like other Soviet directors, Les Kurbas went through a period of enthusiasm for Expressionist drama. One of his greatest successes was a production of Georg Kaiser's *Gas* (1923). The play was perceived by Kurbas as a 'poignantly lofty tragedy' and he staged it with sets by Vadim Meller, devoting particular attention to the rapid and nervous movements of the masses over the sloping planes of the construction.

Expressive dynamics also predetermined the general contours of Kurbas's 1923 production *Jimmy Higgins*, based on the novel of the same name by Upton Sinclair.

Kurbas's innovative activities represented a sharp break with the traditional, sentimental and melodramatic Ukrainian theatre of the pre-Revolutionary epoch, and were in many ways close to the experiments of Vakhtangov, Meyerhold and Tairov, although Kurbas at that time had not yet seen their productions. The poet Osip Mandelstam observed that in Kurbas's work there was 'something in common with that of every builder of foundations: he tries in the shortest time to give samples of the most diverse genres, to mark out all the possibilities, consolidate all the forms.'

Three scenes from *Jimmy Higgins*.

State Jewish Theatre

The State Jewish Theatre (GOSET) was led by a pupil of Max Reinhardt's, Alexei Granovsky. Unlike the Jewish 'Habima' studio, GOSET gave plays not in the ancient language of Hebrew but in the comparatively modern language of Yiddish. In the repertoire were plays by Maeterlinck and Gutzkow, and Granovsky frequently staged works by Sholom-Aleikhem. Many well-known artists worked there – Natan Altman, Isaak Rabinovich, David Shterenberg, Robert Falk.

The turbulent action of *The Sorceress* took place in a small Jewish settlement. This 1922 production, composed of motifs taken from Avraam Goldfaden's works, was turned by Alexei Granovsky into a motley and festive carnival. The reviewers compared *The Sorceress* with the two princesses – Vakhtangov's *Princess Turandot* and Tairov's *Princess Brambilla* – but the critic Abram Efros accurately observed that in *The Sorceress* the irony was sharper and the actors more emotionally expansive: feelings were expressed openly and the performances were more energetic. Crowd scenes predominated in the production but even here GOSET's best actors, Solomon Mikhoels and Veniamin Zuskin, set the tone. On the steps and platforms of Isaak Rabinovich's construction GOSET's elated company walked up and down, sang and danced, creating an apparently random hubbub and gesticulating extravagantly.

In *The Journey of Veniamin III* (1927), after Mendele Moicher-Sforim, the Mikhoels and Zuskin acting duet was particularly successful. Robert Falk created a tranquil, bare set, to suggest a time in the distant past.

A scene from *The Journey of Veniamin III*.

Overleaf: Granovsky's production *Three Jewish Gems* ('An Evening of Sholom-Aleikhem') at the State Jewish Theatre marked the theatrical début of Marc Chagall in 1921. It is a sad fact that almost the entire GOSET archive was destroyed by fire at the end of the 1940s, and those costume sketches by Chagall shown here (hitherto unpublished) were preserved almost miraculously. Some of them are scorched around the edges, having been snatched from the flames at the last minute. They give a sufficiently clear idea of the mocking irony with which the artist regarded Sholom-Aleikhem's entertaining and colourful characters. Indeed the whole production, in which Mikhoels and Zuskin took part, was a witty parody of the narrow petit-bourgeois world of a small settlement inside the Pale, beyond whose boundaries Jews were not permitted to live before the Revolution.

V. Zuskin as the Witch and M. Stehman as Marcus in *The Sorceress.*

Model of the set by Isaak Rabinovich for *The Sorceress.*

Overleaf: Three costume sketches by Marc Chagall for *Three Jewish Gems.*

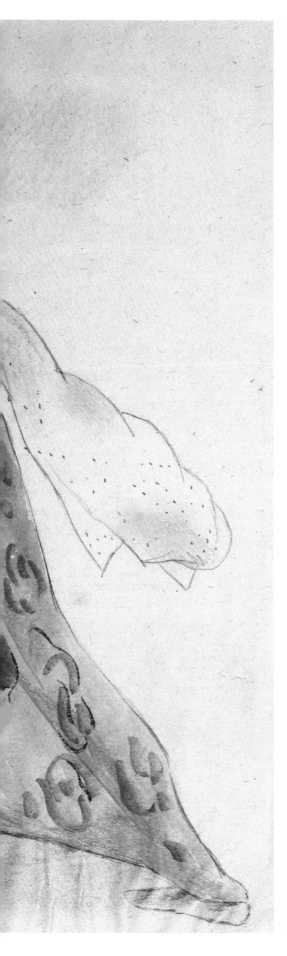

Macbeth

The interest in Shakespeare that was shared by nearly all Soviet directors in the post-Revolutionary years found very original expression in Les Kurbas's 1924 production of *Macbeth*. The director tried to combine the principles of the Elizabethan theatre (changes of location were announced by captions on large screens) with those of the propaganda theatre (all the characters wore the same militarized uniform) and with a sharp denunciation of tyranny.

In his sketches for a production of *Macbeth* directed by Vladimir Tikhonovich in 1922, Sergei Eisenstein tried to show both the hero and Lady Macbeth as figures forged out of cold steel and thereby underline their inhumanity.

Two sketches of the costumes by
Eisenstein for *Macbeth*, 1922.

A scene from the 1924 production of
Macbeth.

A. Buchma as the Fool, 1924.

Antony and Cleopatra

The designer Vladimir Shchuko chose a very stylized appearance for the production of Shakespeare's *Antony and Cleopatra* which was presented on the stage of the Petrograd Academic Theatre of Drama in 1923 (with Yury Yuriev as Antony). The free interpretation of ancient Egyptian motifs clearly interested him more than the ancient Roman motifs linked in the tragedy with the theme and figure of Caesar. The overall result was a very presentable but internally static spectacle.

Three sketches by V. Shchuko of costumes for *Antony and Cleopatra*.

A scene from *Antony and Cleopatra.*

Two sketches of the set by
V. Shchuko for *Antony and
Cleopatra.*

Romeo and Juliet

Alexander Tairov's choice from the Shakespearean repertoire was *Romeo and Juliet* (1921). Much of Tairov's *mise-en-scène* – for example the balcony scene and the tragedy's finale – was pictorially beautiful although there was too much Art Nouveau-style mannerism. But the tragic tension of the enmity between the Montagues and the Capulets was weakened – partly, it would appear, because the director wanted the crowd scenes to look festive and picturesque. Koonen as Juliet and Tseretelli as Romeo tried to express the poetry of the young lovers but did not achieve truly Shakespearean passion and fire.

Opposite: Alisa Koonen as Juliet and Nikolai Tseretelli as Romeo in 'The Balcony Scene'.

Left: A scene from *Romeo and Juliet*.

Below: The Final Scene.

Exter's costume and set designs for *Romeo and Juliet*.

The Stenbergs' set design for *Saint Joan*.

Exter and the Stenbergs

The costumes designed by Alexandra Exter for Tairov's 1921 production of *Romeo and Juliet* at the Kamerny Theatre represent one of her greatest achievements. The sets, however, which appeared light and vivid in her sketches, became quite heavy and stylized when installed on stage. Disappointed by the failure of the production, Exter stopped practical work in the theatre from that time. Her place in the Kamerny Theatre was taken by the brothers Vladimir and Georgy Stenberg. Tairov's turn away from Exter's colourful turbulence towards the Stenbergs' geometric spareness heralded significant changes in his art.

Top row: The 1924 production of *Hamlet* in the Second Studio of the Moscow Art Theatre, with Mikhail Chekhov in the title role; designed by Mikhail Libakov.

Middle row: The 1925 Rustaveli Theatre production in Tiflis with Ushangi Chkheidze as Hamlet; designed by Irakly Gamrekeli.

Hamlet

The productions of *Hamlet* that took place in 1924 in the Second Moscow Art Theatre, in 1925 in the Rustaveli Theatre in Tbilisi and in 1932 in the Moscow Vakhtangov Theatre, demonstrated three completely different approaches to the tragedy. The supremely gifted Mikhail Chekhov, who played Hamlet in the Second MAT, endowed the Prince of Denmark with a stern will and a deeply rooted melancholy, carrying out his task resolutely but without any hope of changing the world for the better.

In Tbilisi in the production by Konstantin Mardzhanov (Kote Mardzhanishvili) the young Georgian tragedian Ushangi Chkheidze gave the role of Hamlet a more romantic inspiration. This was a hero who did not doubt in his ultimate victory.

The most paradoxical interpretation of Hamlet's role was presented in the Vakhtangov Theatre by the young producer Nikolai Akimov. In his colourful spectacle the Hamlet, Anatoly Goryunov, was bursting with health and had no lofty aims at all, not even vengeance for his father's death. He had only one motive: to seize the throne, take possession of the royal crown. Such an interpretation brought the tragedy close to comedy and provoked wrathful protests from the critics.

Bottom row: Anatoly Goryunov as Hamlet in the 1932 production, designed by Nikolai Akimov, at the Vakhtangov Theatre.

Scene from *The Storm*.

Productions of Shakespeare were rare in comparison with those of Ostrovsky's dramas and comedies, which were staged by almost every Soviet director in the 1920s. In 1924 Alexander Tairov directed Ostrovsky's *The Storm* in the Kamerny Theatre, with Alisa Koonen in the leading role of Katerina. The wooden vaulted construction designed by the Stenberg brothers was intended to evoke the idea of the heroine's lack of freedom and her oppressed spirit. But Koonen was not really able to come to terms with the part of Katerina and Tairov's first venture into the Russian classic repertoire was not crowned with success.

Alisa Koonen as Katerina.

Sketch of the set by the Stenberg brothers for *The Storm*.

Dmitri Orlov as Yusov.

In 1923 Meyerhold achieved a great success when he directed Ostrovsky's *A Profitable Post* in the Theatre of the Revolution. This work had the restraint and dry-point precision of a master hand. Against the background of a Constructivist set by Viktor Shestakov the actors performed in costumes of Ostrovsky's period and nineteenth-century-style wigs. The acting of Dmitri Orlov as Yusov and Maria Babanova as Polina was particularly good.

Scene from *A Profitable Post*.

Maria Babanova as Polina.

Scene from *A Profitable Post*.

Igor Ilinsky as the Comedian and
Mikhail Mukhin as the Tragedian.

Below right: Ivan Koval-Samborsky as
Petr and Zinaida Raikh as Aksyusha.

Mikhail Mukhin as the Tragedian.

The Forest

Meyerhold's wilful and
cavalier version of Ostrovsky's
The Forest (1924) turned out
to be one of the most famous
productions of the 1920s.
Meyerhold broke the play up
into thirty-three episodes,
changed their order,
completely disregarding the
sequence established by
Ostrovsky, and confidently
adapted the classical play to
contemporary issues and
topical problems. His work

Igor Ilinsky as the Comedian.

Ivan Koval-Samborsky as Petr and
Zinaida Raikh as Aksyusha.

was strongly influenced by
the tradition of popular
fairground theatre, and he
also incorporated devices of
the circus and the cinema. In
The Forest there emerged a
cheerful 'theatre of social
masks', where the attitude to
each character was
completely determined by that
character's class origins.
Landowners, merchants,
clergymen were mocked
furiously, but the poor folk

(Aksyusha played by Zinaida
Raikh, Petr by Ivan Koval-
Samborsky) and the penniless
actors (the Comedian played
by Igor Ilinsky and the
Tragedian by Mikhail
Mukhin) evoked sympathy.
The satirical hyperboles
in *The Forest* went hand in
hand with lyricism, crude
comedy coexisted in easy
harmony with poetry. The
production had over 1300
performances.

179

Sketch by Nikolai Krymov of a set for *The Passionate Heart*.

The Passionate Heart

Lunacharsky, on seeing Ostrovsky's play *The Passionate Heart* (1926) at the Moscow Art Theatre, remarked 'The grey-haired Stanislavsky, the great master of theatrical art, has not been afraid of adopting some of Meyerhold's techniques from *The Forest*.' There was indeed much in Stanislavsky's approach that was reminiscent of Meyerhold's *Forest*. He turned away from the Art Theatre's customary attention to psychological and realistic detail, creating an exaggeratedly forceful and bitingly satirical production. Nikolai Krymov's sets were crudely cheerful, blazing with bright colours. The actors threw themselves into the performance with a passion and even rough energy that was unusual for the Art Theatre.

Left: A scene from *The Passionate Heart*. *Above*: Sketch of V. Stanitsyn as Kuroslepov. *Below*: F. Shevchenko as Matryona.

181

A scene from *The Warrant*.

Opposite: Two scenes from the finale of *The Warrant*.

Erast Garin as Pavel Gulyachkin.

The Warrant

One of the first Soviet satirical comedies, Nikolai Erdman's *The Warrant*, was staged in 1925 at the Meyerhold Theatre. In this production Meyerhold was able to unite authentic sketches of contemporary life with grotesque exaggeration. The hangers-on of the petit-bourgeois world were examined as if they were specimens under a magnifying glass, and everyday small-minded reality took on the character of a tragi-comic phantasmagoria. It was in fact *The Warrant* that made

Stanislavsky reassess the possibilities of Meyerhold's art. He was enthralled by Ilya Shlepyanov's combination of a revolving stage disc with moving screens: this device allowed the director to alter all the spatial contours very rapidly, to manipulate freely the sequence of tempos and rhythms and to transfer easily from soliloquies or two-handers to crowd scenes. 'Meyerhold,' said Stanislavsky, to the great amazement of his followers, 'has here achieved what I have dreamed of.'

182

Two scenes from *Poison*.

Poison

Anatoly Lunacharsky's melodrama *Poison* (1925) was one of the first plays in which attention was focused on phenomena characteristic of the NEP period: corruption, moral instability, the debauchery of those intoxicated by the possibilities of the good life, so particularly seductive after long years of hunger and devastation. The play was performed at the Leningrad Academic Theatre of Drama in a production by two directors, Nikolai Petrov and Konstantin Khokhlov, with sets by Mark Levin which cleverly gave colour and a picturesque quality to the mobile Constructivist set.

4 Extremes Converge

In Search of a Hero

The satirical attacks which Meyerhold and Gripich directed at the open and covert adversaries of the new life impressed audiences. However, there remained an unsatisfied craving for the heroic, a need to see characters on stage who embodied the will and purpose of the Revolution. In the search for a hero, playwrights of the mid 1920s turned to the relatively recent past, to the difficult period of the Civil War. The plays of Vladimir Bill-Belotserkovsky, Konstantin Trenev and Boris Lavrenev, and the adaptations of stories by Lydia Seifullina, Mikhail Bulgakov and Vsevolod Ivanov, for the first time brought onto the stage recent events that the spectators could themselves remember. What was represented on the stage was immediately recognizable. Writers completely dissimilar, even diametrically opposed, to each other stylistically were all trying to do the same thing – to show ordinary, average people who were not heroes, who did not speak or behave heroically, but who were nevertheless capable of rising to the heights of heroic action.

The inclination toward utmost authenticity inherent in *Storm* by Bill-Belotserkovsky, *Virineya* by Seifullina, *Liubov Yarovaya* by Trenev, *The Days of the Turbins* by Bulgakov, *The Break* by Lavrenev and *Armoured Train No. 14–69* by Vsevolod Ivanov, made all these works attractive and accessible to the traditional theatres, long since confident masters of the techniques of realistic drama and the portrayal of integrated human characters. It is worth noting that the above-mentioned plays, which 'created the climate' of theatrical life in the mid 1920s, had no effect on the 'leftist' theatres. They did, however, have a beneficial effect on theatres such as the Maly, the Moscow Art Theatre, its Third (Vakhtangov) Studio, the Leningrad Academic Theatre of Drama (the former Alexandrinsky) and a number of other young companies which had no connections with either 'leftism' or LEF. By the very nature of these Civil War plays that they staged, the traditional theatres began to 'move to the left', taking over from 'leftist art' some characteristic avant-garde devices.

The extension of the territory of drama to encompass scenes of battles, Revolutionary rallies and rural assemblies, to show both the heroes of the Revolution and its opponents in action, set completely unprecedented tasks for directors, actors and artists alike.

One of the first to succeed in this direction was the young Moscow Trade Union Theatre, which became famous in 1925 for its production of Bill-Belotserkovsky's *Storm*. This theatre, which opened in 1923, was headed by Evsei Liubimov-Lansky, an experienced actor but a relatively inexperienced director. He displayed no interest whatsoever in innovations in theatrical form and was, on the contrary, rather conservative, but he was able to appreciate the full merit of *Storm*, which other theatres had fastidiously spurned.

Sharply tendentious, written in a dry, almost official manner, Bill's play had all the distinctive qualities of the Civil War's propagandistic mass-meeting theatre: ardent political spirit and the direct, unsubtle division of characters into two opposing camps – Reds and Whites. The masses are drawn into the confrontation between these two forces. The 'positive' characters (Reds) and the 'negative' characters (Whites) are identified immediately: the dramatist does not conceal his attitude to them. But the heroes of the play are real people, precisely described, and it was their unmistakable truth to life which constituted the principal innovation in *Storm*.

The great majority of the characters in *Storm*, however, are given neither surnames nor first names; they are defined in the cast list only by social functions. The most notable are the Chairman of the Ukom, that is the leader of the district Party organization, and his assistant, The Sailor, alias Swabbie. Only during the course of the play does the audience learn that Swabbie's surname is Vilenchuk and that the Chairman of the Ukom is Vasya. The drama deals with a whole range of themes topical during the years of 'war Communism' – the struggle against sabotage and epidemics, the organization of the first people who did voluntary unpaid work on Saturdays, the fight against speculation and gangsterism and so forth. Characters appear episodically, some of them to be immediately eliminated. In rehearsal many actors doubted its suitability for the stage, saying, 'This is not theatre', everything in the play is 'dull and dismal'; nothing but 'lice, typhoid, sheepskin coats and dirty boots' and 'no plot, no action. It's boring! . . . The audience won't like it at all.'[1] Their sceptical forecasts proved false – audiences greeted the show with rapturous enthusiasm.

Boris Volkov's laconic sets reproduced the uneasy, disrupted life of the Civil War. Slogans written in large, bold, white lettering on red calico banners were prominently displayed in every scene. The designer did not clutter the stage with superfluous objects but made do with the most primitive furniture (a crudely knocked-together table likewise covered in red calico, two or three benches, a few plain chairs) thus leaving the director space to organize the turbulent crowd scenes. From this large, seething crowd emerged heroes cast in a new mould. The Chairman of the Ukom, played by Alexander Andreev, and Swabbie, Vasily Vanin, skilfully and firmly impose the will of the Bolshevik Party upon the chaotic energy of the people.

Vanin, dressed in sailor's cap and leather jacket carelessly thrown over a striped jersey, gave the character of the lame Swabbie a sort of triumphant gaiety, hopping and thumping around the stage with his wooden leg, a warm smile lighting up his manly features. The author admired Vanin's performance so much that he called him 'my brother-in-arms and almost my co-author'.

'The first scenes stunned you with their crude strength,' wrote Nikolai Pogodin, 'and led you mercilessly into the true life of Revolutionary Russia. It was a new kind of art that we were watching, with a message that was strong and irresistibly significant.'

The premières of Seifullina's *Virineya* and Trenev's *Liubov Yarovaya*, which took place almost simultaneously in other theatres, confirm Pogodin's opinion. *Virineya* was staged at the Third MAT Studio by the director Alexei Popov, one of Stanislavsky's most talented pupils. He was fully aware of how difficult it would be to create a truthful picture of remote, benighted rural life on the Vakhtangov stage, with a company justifiably proud of its showy *Princess Turandot*. The uncouth, grim background had to be reproduced as conscientiously as possible, yet in such a way that the action did not get bogged down by trivialities, or suffocate in the stuffy atmosphere of the peasant hut. It was also necessary somehow to get over the excessively disjointed, fragmented nature of the play. Popov solved this by putting the maximum emphasis on the protagonists and sharpening the dramatic conflicts. This meant that the main burden fell on Alexeeva, Shchukin and Tolchanov. All three proved worthy of the director's confidence.

The role of Virineya came easily to Elizaveta Alexeeva, an actress of 'wholesome straightforward feelings', ideally suited to play a peasant woman who is passionate and spiritually strong, ready to face a woman's hard fate yet revitalized by the dawn of a new life. Lunacharsky wrote: 'This Virineya is one of the brightest, most enlightening figures that post-Revolutionary art has given us. . . . Thanks to Alexeeva's superb performance with her clever, energetic and purely Russian face, Virineya at once stands before you as a model of purity and strength, a woman fully prepared to put herself in the forefront of the Revolutionary cause.'[4]

Boris Shchukin invested the Bolshevik Pavel Suslov not only with strength of character but also with a kind heart, gentleness, intelligence, contempt for prejudice and a rather rough tenderness for Virineya. As a soldier back from the front, he naturally understands the political situation much better than his fellow villagers. Shchukin emphasized the character's firmness and strength of will – an ordinary soldier in a grey overcoat with a simple face and calm, attentive eyes – but he was not at all afraid of introducing a note of lyricism, of protective masculinity into his scenes with Virineya. Alongside Pavel she seemed to blossom. . . .

Suslov also brings about a complete change in the life of Magara, a slow-witted, benighted muzhik who had almost made up his mind to die. As portrayed by Iosif Tolchanov, Magara was sluggish, stooping; his arms hung like ropes, he walked with a limp, dragging one foot, and he spoke in a toneless voice; from under his knitted grey brows his anxious eyes looked out distrustfully. But even Magara's distrust is conquered by Suslov's life-affirmative will.

All three of these roles conveyed a genuine sense of real life, as did the crowd scenes skilfully organized by the director on the tiny stage, round the cramped quarters of a rural hut. Alexei Popov possessed a unique talent for staging crowd scenes with the greatest authenticity and vigour. In this particular case, however, he was confronted by an exceptionally complex problem: to portray the movement of a raging crowd with only eighteen to twenty actors at

ГОСУДАРСТВЕННЫЙ АКАДЕМИЧЕСКИЙ
МОСКОВСКИЙ
МАЛЫЙ ТЕАТР

В среду, 22 декабря 1926 г.

ПРЕДСТАВЛЕНО БУДЕТ В ПЕРВЫЙ РАЗ

„ЛЮБОВЬ ЯРОВАЯ"

Poster for the première of Trenev's *Liubov Yarovaya* directed by Platon and Prozorovsky at the Maly Theatre in 1926.

his disposal. Popov succeeded by concentrating all of them in three areas: the doors of the hut, its windows and by the wattled fencing next to it. The separate little groups of angry peasants burst the seams of the confined space created deliberately by the director and thereby produced the impression of a turbulent 'human sea'.

The poignant refinement and grace for which the Third MAT Studio had previously been renowned suddenly gave way in *Virineya* to the new social realism.

At the Maly Theatre in the early 1920s intensive work proceeded on new productions of classic Russian plays by Gogol, Turgenev, Ostrovsky and Sukhovo-Kobylin. There were many performers in the company whose talents Moscow had long noted and valued, who all showed themselves to advantage in the classical repertoire. There were also, however, persistent attempts to include work by young Soviet dramatists and there were experiments too in the staging of these works written in the new spirit.

The best of these new plays, a work which answered the high demands of the company, was offered to the Maly Theatre by Konstantin Trenev. During the Civil War Trenev lived in the Crimea and had witnessed the Battle of Perekop, the crushing defeat of Wrangel and the flight of the White Guard armies. In his play, *Liubov Yarovaya*, he brought together all his impressions, trying 'above all to give the social and political background, and to set against it, tightly integrated with it, the historical events and the drama of the hero and heroine.'[5]

One is immediately struck by the number and variety of the characters. Nearly fifty are named in the cast list and in addition to them there are also 'workers, Red Army men, officers, soldiers, schoolgirls, citizens'. Trenev's play gives a powerful picture of the life of the masses stirred up by the Revolution. It is not all lofty passion and heroic pathos, however. Trenev alternates high drama with satire and comedy, a mixture that gives ease and movement to the play. Its structure is even conventionally melodramatic in the sense that the heroine is torn between love, which draws her to her counter-Revolutionary husband, and duty, which calls her selflessly to serve the Revolution. This traditional conflict at the heart of the situation made the play particularly appropriate for the Maly Theatre.

The directors Ivan Platon and Lev Prozorovsky did not fear to employ in the production a number of devices borrowed from 'leftist' theatre. In particular, the young Nikolai Menshutin's stage design had an unmistakably 'leftist' look: the scenery was a complex construction explicitly evoking the distinctive architecture of a southern town, but colourless, unpainted and mounted on a revolving stage disc. The whiteness of its lines was sharply etched against the bright blue backdrop. By turning the disc the set could be changed quickly to follow the play's many episodes. The directors arranged the large, populous crowd scenes on steep steps. The combination of stylized sets, realistic colourful costumes and irresistibly lifelike, recognizable make-up, gave the production an extraordinary freshness.

Vera Pashennaya, who played Liubov Yarovaya, the modest country teacher, adopted a rather dry, reserved manner: a simple everyday blouse with neat white collar and a long skirt. Only a cigarette constantly dangling from the corner of her mouth betrayed her. The actress rarely raised her voice and only in the play's finale gave free rein to her powerful temperament.

The lofty romantic motifs, consciously toned down in Pashennaya's performance, resounded openly and forcefully in that of Prov Sadovsky as the Commissar Koshkin. He wore a sailor's cap, pea-jacket and striped jersey, clearly wishing to associate the Commissar with his loyal assistant, the sailor Shvandya.

This colourful figure was played by the celebrated comic Stepan Kuznetsov, who gave him a captivating lightness, an inexhaustible humour and cheerful *joie de vivre*. Somehow the actor had managed to hear distinctive intonations in the material of everyday life, thrown into turmoil by the Civil War. Agile, good-looking, indefatigable, he seemed everywhere at once, this cheeky, round-faced sailor with dimpled cheeks, thin moustache and mischievous eyes, an unruly lock of hair escaping from under his sailor's cap. His performance conveyed an ecstatic joy in freedom and this is what made Shvandya the embodiment of the Revolutionary element, 'the soul of the crowd'.

The success of *Liubov Yarovaya* suddenly catapulted the Maly Theatre (which 'leftist' critics had long since buried) into the centre of the country's cultural life. Lunacharsky formulated the significance of this event in a statement which sounded like a paradox: '*Liubov Yarovaya*' he wrote, 'is a real triumph of the leftist theatre.' By declaring the production of an academic theatre an achievement of 'leftist' art, the Narkom sought to stress that the avant-gardists did not by any means have a monopoly on the Revolutionary. In the same article Lunacharsky appealed to the 'honourable critics' accustomed to showing off 'their Revolutionary credentials by attacking academic theatres,' to consider 'whether it was not time to cease their attacks'.[6]

The movement of the Moscow Art Theatre towards contemporary subject matter began with attempts to adapt for the stage several works of new Soviet prose. From 1925 the critic Pavel Markov headed the literary section of MAT, and he succeeded in attracting many gifted writers to the theatre. One of them was Mikhail Bulgakov, whose novel *The White Guard* was turned, after a long and difficult collaboration, into the play *The Days of the Turbins*.[7]

The Days of the Turbins was produced by Ilya Sudakov, whose talent for directing had been developed at the Second MAT Studio. Although professionally highly competent and extremely energetic, his direction did sometimes lack subtlety, psychological refinement and imagination. Stanislavsky himself corrected, clarified and, most significantly, enriched the rendering of some of the production's most important scenes. The artist Nikolai Ulyanov, well known from pre-Revolutionary times, produced modest yet expressive sets that evoked the atmosphere of a lifestyle that had only yesterday been both comfortable and peaceful but was today disturbed by bitter street battles just outside the door.

The première on 5 October 1926 provoked very stormy arguments. Despite the theatre's assurance that it sought 'to show how the Revolution changes people',[8] the reviewers alleged that the play amounted to 'a justification of the White Guards', 'a rehabilitation of White Officers' and 'a crudely cynical distortion of the historical situation of the Civil War'.[9]

The auditorium seethed at the first performances of *The Days of the Turbins*. Some applauded energetically and cried 'bravo!', but others stamped their feet and whistled. It was the first time in the entire history of the Moscow Art Theatre that disparaging whistles had resounded in the auditorium.

Such strong reactions were partially explained by the fact that the 'leftist' critics and the young people fired by their sharp, aggressive articles, automatically regarded the MAT as a bulwark of 'the bourgeoisie', of 'enemy ideology' and expected no good from it. But the main reason for the angry reactions was that *The Days of the Turbins* did not present the White Guard officers, in the gold epaulettes that were so hated, as confirmed enemies. The theatre of the initial post-Revolutionary years had always portrayed them in this way, not wishing to examine their feelings and experiences. But in *The Days of the Turbins*, officers and members of the 'White movement' were portrayed not as fiends from hell but as honest and decent people whose tragic mistake merits attention, whose historical defeat deserves close analysis, both social and psychological. To make hasty, premature judgments ran counter to the MAT's aesthetic principles.

Glavrepertkom (the state censorship body) wavered for a long time in deciding whether or not to authorize the production, which was ready and waiting. Lunacharsky too was assailed by doubts: he thought the play was far from perfect. But he did not under any circumstances wish to cancel an MAT première and therefore he insisted on authorization for *The Turbins*.

In the history of the Moscow Art Theatre, the first encounter with Bulgakov was of tremendous significance. Mikhail Bulgakov had by this time shown himself to be one of the most talented of the young prose writers. His novel, *The White Guard*, completed in 1925, related the destinies of the Russian officers who had fought in vain against the Revolution. In the play *The Days of the Turbins*, written according to the themes of *The White Guard*, the sense that the 'White movement' was historically doomed came across much more distinctly than it had in the novel. The play's artistic form, created by Bulgakov from the images of his own prose, testified to both his great talent as a dramatist and to the fact that in Bulgakov the MAT had found an author ideologically and stylistically suited to the theatre. Bulgakov mobilized the refined tradition of Chekhovian writing in the service of the modern stage, and his characters were certainly spiritually related to the Chekhovian intellectuals.

The principal events of the drama are all seen from a domestic viewpoint. Although the action is not confined to the family circle (there are scenes, for instance, in a school building where an artillery batallion is billeted, in the hetman's palace and in the Ukrainian camp), it is the Chekhovian tone, which came naturally to the MAT, that predominates. The contrast between this tone as heard in the conversations of educated characters and the tense, threatening atmosphere of Kiev, constantly changing hands according to the fortunes of war, created a particularly dramatic effect.

Nearly all the parts in *The Days of the Turbins* were given to young actors who, like the director Sudakov, had come from the Second MAT Studio. Stanislavsky was fervent in his support for the youth of the theatre, for the MAT was at that juncture faced with the acute problem of renewing the company and, simultaneously, its art. The MAT's so-called older generation – Moskvin, Kachalov, Leonidov, Tarkhanov, Knipper-Chekhova, Lilina – were still in their prime. But Stanislavsky calculated that the arrival of young reinforcements indissolubly linked with the new life would also serve as a powerful creative impetus to the older generation. His courage in bringing what was an entire young company on stage in *The Days of the Turbins* was rewarded immediately. The whole cast 'woke up famous' the day after the première.

As Alexei Turbin, Nikolai Khmelev revealed from the outset his characteristically painstaking attention to detail. He wore his uniform with debonaire ease, spoke calmly and with an air of command, lisping very slightly. Officer to the very core, his firm hand, confident gait and intelligent eyes indicated integrity and strength of spirit. Steadfast and noble, he inspired respect. When such a person was compelled publicly to acknowledge defeat, it meant that the 'White idea' had outlived its time. The scene on the stairs of the school where Alexei dismisses his soldiers to their homes and then dies was, in Khmelev's performance, a moment of truly tragic insight.

Myshlaevsky was played by Boris Dobronravov, an extrovert actor of great theatrical charm. Tall, with light brown hair and blue eyes, Myshlaevsky appeared rather simple and rough beside the smart, composed and markedly intellectual Alexei Turbin. He was noisy and demonstrative. He had the air of a front-line soldier, an army man accustomed to life in the trenches.

Vera Sokolova as the red-headed 'golden' beauty Elena introduced into the production the theme of poetic and fragile femininity, kind-heartedness and warmth. Elena was essentially the moral centre of

the Turbins' home, the soul of the family. Shervinsky, the frivolous lieutenant who falls in love with Elena, was played by Mark Prudkin with such energy and ardour that real strength of feeling broke through the dandyism, foppishness and bragging.

The note of comedy which came through in the love scenes between Shervinsky and Elena sounded completely natural in the complex polyphony of the production which seemed to comprehend every level of existence – joy and grief, love and death, cosy tea-drinking and firing squards, carefree song and the thunder of shells. The whole strange atmosphere, the incompatibility of war and humaneness, is embodied in the naive Lariosik, created by the gifted actor Mikhail Yanshin. Yanshin's Lariosik had round, child-like eyes, his speech was rhapsodic and bookish, and he looked odd: noble, like Werter, luckless, like Epikhodov, utterly ill-adapted to life, but sincerity itself, goodness itself.

The storm caused by the première of *The Days of the Turbins* rocked the newly rigged ship of the Moscow Art Theatre for a long time. The play was withdrawn from the repertoire twice. With Lunacharsky's assistance Stanislavsky obstinately defended it. Glavrepertkom finally gave a limited and exceptional authorization – *The Days of the Turbins* could be performed only by the Moscow Art Theatre, where it played continuously to full houses right up to 1941, running to nearly one thousand performances in fifteen years.

One year after *The Days of the Turbins* the MAT presented an adaptation of Vsevolod Ivanov's tale *Armoured Train No. 14–69*. This adaptation, like that of Trenev's *Liubov Yarovaya*, had a large cast – nearly fifty characters – and the crowd scenes occupied an even more prominent position within it. The general tone of the work, however, is more severe. The humour which overflows in *Liubov Yarovaya* is rarely heard in *Armoured Train No. 14–69*.

Ilya Sudakov's production was revised by Stanislavsky this time too. In the forefront were two heroes, Vershinin and Peklevanov. Vershinin was played by one of the company's most experienced and renowned actors, Vasily Kachalov, and Peklevanov by the young Khmelev. The play's success depended to a great extent on their mutual understanding and the harmony of their artistic views.

For Kachalov, who in the past had been Shakespeare's Julius Caesar and Hamlet, Ibsen's Brand, Chekhov's Tuzenbakh and Gaev, the role which he was to play in *Armoured Train* was unusual. Kachalov had, as Alexei Popov observed, 'an exceptionally rare *emploi* which combined the *jeune premier* and the "character" actor.'[10] Kachalov's range of experience was very wide, but it was the first time in his life that he had had to play a peasant. As a result of persistent work, he developed for the role an unhurried way of speaking, sweeping gestures and a long stride. His stately Vershinin, with pale eyes and a bushy light-brown beard, dressed in a dark-blue cotton print shirt, heavy rusty-brown peasant's coat and moss-green three-cornered hat, was clearly from the beginning a man to be reckoned with. His entire behaviour suggested that he was the boss, the 'head'; he was firm, a man of few words. Peasants had to believe in such a man. And he had the innate right to lead the partisan movement because he possessed independence of mind and strength of character.

Khmelev's Peklevanov, unlike Vershinin, did not look outwardly important. In appearance this was a typical Chekhovian narrow-shouldered intellectual, frail, short-sighted, bespectacled, quiet and modest. His jacket was too big for him, his tie carelessly tied, his trousers baggy, yet beneath the insignificant exterior a powerful

Poster for the première of Ivanov's *Armoured Train No. 14–69* directed by Sudakov at the Moscow Art Theatre in 1927.

tilted onion-domed cupola on a thin neck to the left, a primitive, peeling little belltower to the right, were outlined against a background of cloudy sky. This entire scene took place on the roof of the church where the partisans, peasant men, women with children, gathered spontaneously in picturesque groupings.

Armoured Train No. 14–69 was chosen to celebrate the tenth anniversary of the Revolution. Those primarily responsible for introducing new plays into the repertoire of the Moscow Art Theatre, Pavel Markov and Ilya Sudakov, enjoyed their success, but they did not rest on their laurels. February 1929 saw the première of another drama by Vsevolod Ivanov, *The Blockade*, also devoted to an episode in the Civil War, this time the Kronstadt rebellion. Sudakov directed, collaborating now not with Stanislavsky but with Nemirovich-Danchenko, and the production was designed not by Simov but by Isaak Rabinovich. The overall form of the production followed the intention of the dramatist, directors and designer to adhere to the proven aesthetic principles of *Armoured Train No. 14–69* with only minor amendments. Vsevolod Ivanov stated that he wanted 'to be liberated from everyday life' and 'to present some symbolic hero figures'.[12] Nemirovich-Danchenko, for his part, declared he would strive for 'monumental form'.[13] And indeed the production clearly inclined toward 'symbolism of figures' and monumentality in the *mise-en-scène*. The outcome, however, was unhappy. Despite the fact that strong actors performed in *The Blockade* – the experienced Vasily Kachalov, the young Nikolai Batalov and Boris Livanov – and despite the fact that the mass scenes were unquestionably beautiful, the result was less a moving and heroic tragedy than an imposing but cold and emotionally barren theatrical requiem.

Curiously enough, a production of *Armoured Train No. 14–69* put on in Leningrad in 1927 (at the same time as the MAT première) at the State Academic Theatre of Drama, created roughly the same effect. This was because the director Nikolai Petrov, trained in the Meyerhold manner, had remained loyal to the principles of 'leftist theatre', shunning everyday colours, seeking generalization and economy of form. The degree of everyday authenticity that Meyerhold had demonstrated as far back as *The Warrant* was too daring for some of his followers. However, the realistic individuality of the characters, the truth to life in the acting of Illarion Pevtsov as Nezelasov, Nikolai Simonov as Vershinin and Boris Zhukovsky as Peklevanov seemed to undercut the production's austere appearance. The same contradiction lay concealed in the MAT *Blockade* although for a different reason – the director's desire to move away from the Moscow Art Theatre's customary intimate tone. As often occurred in the theatrical practice of the mid 1920s, tradition and avant-garde met halfway.

Such meetings were by no means always disappointing. On the contrary, they often proved successful. The Maly Theatre's *Liubov Yarovaya* was one example of this, and another was Boris Lavrenev's *The Break*, staged by Alexei Popov at the Vakhtangov Theatre (the former Third MAT Studio) in 1927.

The author of this play, Lavrenev, was inclined to return to the traditional form of the 'indoor', conversational play, even although the action was set in the stormy days of the Revolution. He consciously strove to combine the 'epoch's romantically elevated mood with the sober, realistic portrayal of people and their characters'.[14] The centripetal composition of his drama was fundamentally different from the centrifugal compositions of Trenev

energy was concealed. Khmelev played a man consumed by the flame of the Revolutionary struggle, absolutely self-denying.

During rehearsals Ivanov noted with unconcealed amazement that the MAT actors 'want to and can portray the mass and at the same time distinguish each individual within this mass'.[11] What the dramatist found so amazing had always, from the day of its founding, been characteristic of crowd scenes at the Moscow Art Theatre. The old principle was preserved in *Armoured Train No. 14–69* only with the difference that in the crowd scenes here a leader unfailingly came forward, a character who summed up the entire atmosphere and tone of the action. In the scene 'On the Belltower' it was Vaska Okorok who became this leader of the people's chorus. He was played by Nikolai Batalov, a young spirited actor of rare charm who had also, like Khmelev, been nurtured at the Second Studio. Excitable, quick-tempered and impetuous, he personified all the partisans' spontaneous energy, his faded red shirt, dark, curly hair and flashing smile blazing among the crowd like a flame.

The production was designed by Viktor Simov who had worked at the Moscow Art Theatre since the day of its foundation. But changes were taking place in Simov's art and they are symptomatic. In the scene 'On the Belltower', for instance, the sloping surface of a roof, a and Ivanov. They composed action sweepingly, freely transferring it from place to place, easily introducing new motifs and new characters, crossing diverse plot lines. Lavrenev, however, aimed for compactness, concentration. He tied all the thematic motifs together in one tight knot. The events occurring in the play were presented in the symmetrical alternation of the 'indoor' scenes in the apartment of Bersenev, the captain of the cruiser *Dawn*, and the sailors' crowd scenes on the deck of the *Dawn*.

Together with the artist Nikolai Akimov, Popov upset this equilibrium, finding an unusual form for the production. The stage was divided into several compartments and the beam of the searchlight, picking out individual episodes of the drama from the darkness, brightly illuminated first a conference of sailors huddled in the cramped crews' quarters, then the raging crowd scene on deck, then the oblique contours of Bersenev's rooms. 'The small sections of the military ship and Bersenev's apartment,' wrote the director, 'resembled cinema frames, and only twice during the performance, during the mass scenes on the ship, was the entire stage fully revealed.'[15] Sometimes one or another dialogue was highlighted in 'close-up' by a circle of light that resembled the porthole of a ship. This 'cinematographic quality' enabled the director to eliminate superfluous everyday details and concentrated the audience's attention on the heroes' faces, their thoughts, hesitations, decisions.

Among the performers in *The Break*, Boris Shchukin as Bersenev achieved the greatest success. If as Pavel Suslov in *Virineya* the actor had been able to portray with uncommon veracity the inner world of a low-ranking simple soldier from the peasantry, then his Bersenev embodied nobleness, the high moral culture of the best part of the Russian intelligentsia.

The crowd scenes in *The Break* did not have the range and depth of colour of those in *Liubov Yarovaya* or *Armoured Train No. 14–69*. The formation of sailors in identical uniforms broke time and again, the uniformity of the pea-jackets creating exactly the same effect as the *prozodezhda* in Meyerhold's productions. The expressive groupings appeared against the background of the cruiser's steel-grey armour. The voices were bold and vehement. The re-groupings beneath the ship's gun-towers occurred quickly and suddenly. The sailor freemen submitted to no regulations whatsoever and only in the finale, when the Revolution had triumphed, did the crowd turn anew into a proudly frozen military formation.

Much in this production unexpectedly recalled Meyerhold's *The Dawn*, but with the essential proviso that at the centre of *The Break* were such realistically full-blooded characters as the captain Bersenev (Shchukin) and the leader of the sailor freemen Godun (Vasily Kuza).

The traditional theatres which turned to the subject matter of the Civil War in search of a hero, at this moment patently outstripped the 'leftist' collectives and managed, just as Stanislavsky desired, 'to look into the Revolutionary soul of the country'.[16] But under the pressure of new content tradition quickly underwent changes, assimilating and appropriating avant-garde experience. So in the area of theatrical form, tradition was renewed at the expense of the avant-garde. In its turn the theatrical avant-garde greedily absorbed traditional experience every time that it was necessary to portray not the mass, but the individual person, not a generalized type and 'class interest' but personality, character, psychology, the spiritual world of the individual. And the period dictated such tasks ever more frequently and urgently.

Stanislavsky and Meyerhold: Convergent Movement

In circumstances of unceasing polemic between the 'leftist' avant-gardists and 'rightist' traditionalists, at a time when the mutual hostility between the opposing camps was still very fierce, two significant statements were voiced which came as a complete surprise to both the 'leftists' and 'rightists'. After seeing *The Warrant* at the Meyerhold Theatre, Stanislavsky declared that the design and directorial work were brilliant and that he had particularly liked the last act of the play: 'Meyerhold has achieved in this act what I have dreamed of.' And on the day of the dress rehearsal for *A Passionate Heart* at the MAT Meyerhold briefly addressed the audience at his theatre, stating that Stanislavsky's production was 'marvellous' and that his own 'young theatre could not even dream of the brilliant mastery shown today at the Moscow Art Theatre.'[17]

This demonstrative exchange of compliments plunged both Meyerhold's adherents and Stanislavsky's associates into a state of complete confusion. Neither side could understand its leader. Meanwhile the leaders had simply realized before others that a process was taking place in theatrical life that was bringing them together. This was also realized by the most far-sighted critics, Lunacharsky and Markov. In the mid 1920s Lunacharsky astutely remarked on the tendency towards mutual back-slapping in the two theatrical movements recently irreconcilably hostile to each other. He said: 'The leftist theatre is evolving, as is the rightist.' Traditional theatre 'has taken a step toward a placard quality, accelerated tempo, a certain stylization of life,' and at the same time 'leftist' theatre 'has shifted strongly toward a specific realism'.[18] What is being observed is 'a process of some synthesis in theatrical forms.... Leftist theatre,' he repeated a year later, 'has moved strongly towards the realistic axis of theatrical art. But the right has not remained deaf to some, so to speak, placard-style achievements of the leftist theatre. And since our realism,' wrote Lunacharsky, 'does not in the least abjure hyperbole, the caricature effect, then it is natural that the so-called rightist theatre has felt it proper to assimilate some of the achievements of the very latest theatrical efforts.'[19]

At the same time Markov observed that if 'the aim of the "leftists" was a revolutionized theatre' and 'the aim of the "rightists" was unification on the basis of protecting traditions,' then 'the aims of both sides are now attained and the dividing lines have become confused,' which is why 'the mutual influence of the separate theatrical movements has begun.'[20]

The immediate future fully confirmed the observations of Lunacharsky and Markov. Stanislavsky's *A Passionate Heart* had already revealed the influence of Meyerhold's *The Forest*. Meyerhold's influence was also indirectly manifested in Stanislavsky's production of *Le Mariage de Figaro*. The very fact that as designer for Beaumarchais' play Stanislavsky commissioned Alexander Golovin, an artist celebrated during the years 1909 to 1917 for his collaborative work with Meyerhold at the Alexandrinsky and Mariinsky Theatres in St Petersburg, said much in itself, and above all was eloquent of the MAT leader's desire to make the external appearance of the new comic production something completely uncharacteristic of the Moscow Art Theatre.

Furthermore, with what was for Stanislavsky a new, free interpretation of the classical play, he changed much in the comedy. He transferred to France the action which according to Beaumarchais takes place in Spain and split the separate acts of the play into a succession of episodes set in various parts of the Count's castle: the Count's study, the Countess's boudoir, Suzanne's poor little room, the palace hall, the kitchen, the backyard, the park. In other words, in his own way he implemented the 'montage of attractions' typical of 'leftist theatre'.

Golovin loved and knew how to create opulent, majestic, colourful sets, but previously in his tragic works opulence had breathed disquiet, magnificence had foreshadowed catastrophe. In this case, however, in complete accord with Stanislavsky, Golovin gave a joyful freshness to the showy stage design. In the finale Stanislavsky, once again for the first time in the history of MAT, set a revolving stage disc into motion before the spectators' eyes, and all the park's little corners and pavilions floated past before the audience. The revolving of Golovin's structure, which had suddenly been transformed into a carousel, seemed to condense and repeat metaphorically the 'mad day's' dizzy run of events.

The sparkling beauty of the sets had to be matched by the brightness of Golovin's costumes and, most significantly, by the acting – light but vigorous, full of gusto. A carnival-like gaiety displaced the 'popular buffoonery' of the recent *A Passionate Heart*.

Nikolai Batalov as Figaro and Olga Androvskaya as Suzanne set the tone of the comic acting. Dark-haired, black-eyed, with a flashing smile and a large ear-ring, Figaro, a plebeian, a cunning schemer and rogue, had inexhaustible energy and a capacity to retain his presence of mind under any circumstances, no matter how adverse. Androvskaya countered Figaro's 'Hispanicized' temperament with Suzanne's 'Frenchified' grace, his rather rough effusiveness with her coquettish craftiness. Time and again, after exciting Almaviva's passion, driving him to ecstasy through tender glances and promising smiles, Suzanne slipped from the embraces of the master, making him look a fool.

The Count was played by Yury Zavadsky, who had moved from the Vakhtangov Theatre to MAT. Tall, well-built, refined, dressed by Golovin in an inconceivably opulent costume, Almaviva, while pursuing Suzanne, kept stumbling upon the little page Chérubin, stricken by a rash, youthful love. Chérubin was played by Alexander Komissarov. Working out the plan for this part, Stanislavsky created a whole line of purely French, extremely witty and lightly frivolous episodes in the spirit of eighteenth-century comedy. The scene where Chérubin changed into a woman's dress invariably provoked great outbursts of laughter from the audience.

Both productions of classic comedies staged by Stanislavsky in 1926 and 1927 – *A Passionate Heart* and *Le Mariage de Figaro* – enjoyed an enormous, prolonged success and were repeatedly revived.

Meyerhold's variations on classic themes reverberated with no less renown, still very much subject to the director's will but completely lacking the recent rather crude swagger of *The Forest*.

The production of Gogol's *The Government Inspector* (1926) marked fundamental changes in Meyerhold's creative work. The director replaced the comedy's canonical text with a complex composition which incorporated excerpts from drafts of the original play, phrases expunged by censors and brief episodes or lines from other works by Gogol. In the programmes and on the posters Meyerhold called himself the 'author of the production', thus underlining the full extent of the director's responsibility for the sense and character of the theatrical action as a whole, including also the compilation of the 'stage text'.

Set for Gogol's *The Government Inspector* at the Meyerhold Theatre, 1926.

Two main tendencies immediately came across clearly and powerfully in this work. Firstly, Meyerhold sought 'to avoid everything particularly comic, all the buffoonery,' and 'to hold course for tragedy'. Secondly, he determined to wipe the dust of provincialism from the play and the sets suggested a capital city rather than a small town. Both these amendments were introduced with the intention of creating a generalized image of Gogol's Russia, to stage not just *The Government Inspector* but Gogol's entire epoch, the entire past cancelled out by the Revolution.

While switching the play to the genre of tragedy, renouncing the provincialism and elevating all the characters to the rank of dwellers of a capital city, Meyerhold also enormously compressed, narrowed and confined the stage space. Wishing, as he explained, 'to show "swinishness" in the effective and beautiful, to find "brutishness" in the elegant form of a Briullov model,'[21] the director conducted almost all his vast, rich opulent production on small sliding platforms ('stage-trucks'). As the writer Viktor Shklovsky wittily remarked, 'the actors were served up in portions on little stage-dishes.'[22] Within these most modest limitations, in deliberately organized closeness, Meyerhold created a complex, colourful dynamic composition, reproducing the majesty of the Russian Empire Style, its bronze, silk and brocade, porcelain, period furniture of mahogany and Karelian birch, shimmering crystal. Dissatisfied with the preliminary designs proposed by the artists Vladimir Dmitriev and Ilya Shlepyanov, the director designed the production himself, successfully imparting to its colourful, pictorial, sculptural beauty an ever-increasing sense of alarm. 'The main scenes,' he noted, 'have been shot in close-up, to use the cinematic term.'[23] The reference to 'close-up' underlined that this time Meyerhold aimed to exploit to the utmost the expressive potential of the art of acting.

Alarm was inspired to begin with by the enigmatic, demonic personality of Khlestakov (Erast Garin). Khlestakov seemed here no 'pipsqueak' at all; on the contrary, he appeared arrogant, impressive and frighteningly changeable. The fear with which the Mayor and all the officials awaited the Government Inspector seemed concentrated and fixed in Khlestakov's chameleon-like transformations (he appeared as a formidable Guardsman, then an insolent card-sharp, a haughty official, then a cynical lady-killer). 'Khlestakov is clever, Khlestakov is head and shoulders above all those surrounding him,' is how Garin explained the idea behind this role.

The ominously slow figure of the impostor moved through the performance, ever increasing the trepidation of the officials and by the end reducing the Mayor to complete madness. Only the languid, sultry 'provincial Cleopatra', Anna Andreevna (Zinaida Raikh), and the coquettish, piquant and wanton Maria Antonovna (Maria Babanova) were not afraid of Khlestakov. On the contrary, the more grand and enigmatic he appeared, the more their sensuality burned, the more boldly the mother and daughter vied with each other in attempts to seduce him. Both of the production's principal themes, Khlestakov and the officials and Khlestakov and the women, crossed with one another in the famous scene of Khlestakov's lies. Here the hero of Meyerhold's *The Government Inspector* suddenly broke out of his sepulchral, sombre tone and cold, slow speech into a shriek, leaped onto the table brandishing a sword, jumped, skipped and waltzed with Anna Andreevna, then collapsed onto the divan in a state of intoxication and immediately fell asleep, snoring loudly. Almost dead with fear, the officials, completely dumb-founded, teeth chattering, trembled before the snoring monster.

Among the roles a particular precision of finish, wealth of nuances and satirical edge distinguished Garin's Khlestakov and Raikh's Mayor's wife. The success of these two actors, upon whom the director placed great hopes (Garin had shortly before this made his name as Gulyachkin in *The Warrant* and Raikh had first drawn attention to herself in *The Forest* as Aksyusha) was important to him as a matter of principle: they proved that the performers of GosTIM, the Meyerhold theatre, could not only confidently employ the very simplest devices drawn from the placard style of the 'theatre of social masks' but could also resolve tasks of the highest complexity, combining the subtlety of psychological portrayal with the energy of biting satire, balancing precariously on the border between authenticity and hyperbole, eccentricism and truthfulness to life.

The theme of the cold, stiff lifelessness of the past that penetrated through the entire production was particularly powerful in the finale. 'The Mute Scene', which in the majority of cases theatres do not handle successfully, was resolved by Meyerhold with the highest degree of originality: in the show's finale he deftly replaced the performers by large puppets frozen in horror. The sculptural group was immobile. Only after applause had resounded in the auditorium and the lights had gone on, did the actors come out from the wings, each one going up to his own puppet.

'With a wave of the magic wand of directorial genius,' wrote Lunacharsky on the finale, 'Meyerhold suddenly shows the terrifying automatism, the appalling lifelessness of the world portrayed by Gogol that is still alive in our midst. . . . Having broken this world down into rest and movement, Meyerhold is saying, in the commanding voice of the clairvoyant artist, "You are dead, and your movement is lifeless."'[24]

The alarming, gloomy and nervous dynamism of Meyerhold's production did not coincide with the accepted ideas about the nature of Gogol's comedy. The production puzzled many, bored many, and angered many. 'Laughter, you have murdered Gogol's laughter outright!' wrote Demyan Bedny indignantly in an epigram addressed to Meyerhold entitled 'The Murderer'.[25] But among the passionate supporters of the production, as well as Lunacharsky, were such acute critics as Gvozdev, Kugel and Markov; the poets Vladimir Mayakovsky and Andrei Bely; the actor Mikhail Chekhov; the composer Boris Asafiev and the artist Nikolai Ulyanov. Debate grew more heated and spread, acquiring unbelievable proportions. Dozens of articles were printed in newspapers and magazines, and three books were published on this single production alone. Lunacharsky dedicated a number of speeches and articles to the production, including the large and thoroughly considered work '*The Government Inspector* by Gogol and Meyerhold', which has kept its relevance to this day. He pointed out, 'the salutary turning point in Meyerhold's creative work,' is his movement toward 'the creation of a new realism'. Lunacharsky posed the direct question: 'Did Meyerhold have the right to change Gogol, to interpret him with absolute freedom?' The answer was quite unequivocal: 'Of course he had this right.' For the director's task is to present 'a modern Gogol' and not to adopt the attitude of 'museum conservatism'.

It is not of course a matter of turning everything upside down,' emphasized Lunacharsky, 'but of trying to break with tradition and provide a completely new, fresh, unused version. This is, of course, the right of any great artist.'[26] Proceeding from such an understanding of the director's tasks, Lunacharsky confirmed that *The Government Inspector* was Meyerhold's most convincing production.

Following *The Government Inspector*, Meyerhold turned to Griboedov's comedy *Woe from Wit*. Using Griboedov's drafts he again endeavoured to put together a revitalized text. The title the director gave his production, *Woe for Wit* rather than *Woe from Wit*, was extracted from one of Griboedov's drafts. In this work, too, Meyerhold's attempt 'to break with tradition and provide a completely new, fresh, unused version' resulted in some interesting solutions. He conceived the idea of portraying Famusov's Moscow as a cynical society devoid of spirituality yet replete, complacent, full of *joie de vivre* and strength. Famusov (Igor Ilinsky) was youthful, merry and lustful; Skalozub (Nikolai Bogolyubov) looked like a merry and dashing officer; Sofia (Zinaida Raikh) a bold and unblushing maiden.

The sad, mournful and solitary Chatsky (Erast Garin) contrasted with the cohort of optimists and lovers of life. 'You wouldn't even give Garin his twenty-two years,' wrote one of the reviewers. 'This is a serious, impressionable and musical boy, self-absorbed, a little absent-minded and highly sensitive, more despondent than mocking, certainly not at all sharp or eloquent. . . . The fire of Griboedov's monologues is not within the actor's range (these monologues are also completely overshadowed), but herein lies his great contribution in that the audience hears his soft, intimate speech.'[27] The confrontation of the freedom-loving but melancholy hero with the boorish world of the Moscow gentry did not, however, turn into an effective conflict. Chatsky, who played a great deal of music during the performance, time and again sitting down at the piano, was irrelevant to 'Famusov's Moscow' and it to him. Meyerhold's attempt to allude to a link between Chatsky and the Decembrists failed: the silent, frowning officers, holding books and proclamations, who at times surrounded the dreamy hero, invariably remained inactive extras. Although the production contained some successful episodes and a number of parts were performed well, it suffered nonetheless from a certain illustrative quality.

After the première a curious observation was made about the costume design. 'Ulyanov's costumes are superb. But how they resemble the costumes at MAT and how far removed from the *prozodezhda* of *The Magnanimous Cuckold*.'[28]

In 1928 the production *Woe for Wit* was greeted coldly by the critics. They decidedly preferred *The Government Inspector*, and probably rightly. But seven years later Ilya Ehrenburg raised his voice in passionate defence of Meyerhold's Griboedov production. '*Woe for Wit*,' he wrote, 'moves us not only because we see the struggle of old Russian romantics with the stupidity of bureaucrats and boorish gentry. No, if the director is capable of enthusiasm for an old play, if the actors are capable of inspiration in performing it, if the audience watching it feels that it is not at a history lecture but in the theatre, this means that the play is alive, the blind statue has recovered its sight.... Meyerhold is often accused of not treating the classic texts carefully enough, as if we are talking about an archivist. Meyerhold is in love with Gogol and Griboedov. He converses with them freely and easily; he is accepted by them; they stage their old comedies together with him in Soviet Moscow. The director does not dare to think of "precision": the play is to him what life is to the author. If a director does not engage in a creative link with the author, the production is lifeless. If he blindly follows the so-called "stage-directions" (they relate to the play like a suit to a body and are defined not so much by the writer's intention as by the resources of his contemporary stage), the production can not even be said to be lifeless – there is simply no production.'

'I once heard it said,' continued Ehrenburg, 'that Meyerhold's *The Government Inspector* is "not Gogol". On the contrary, it is the very essence of Gogol, it is everything that Gogol put into his comedy, and it is everything that tormented him from *A Terrible Vengeance* to *Dead Souls*.... "Meyerhold is not a realist." I am beginning to doubt whether these very critics who repeat the world "realism" from morning to night, and what is worse, from night to morning, really understand it. What is realism to them? A stylized provincial accent? Faded wallpaper on walls? Real eating on stage, that is with sandwiches? Or perhaps komsomol members in tennis whites? Last but not least the construction of the Belomor Canal amidst confetti and paper streamers? [This was a direct attack on the staging of *The Aristocrats* by Nikolai Pogodin at Nikolai Okhlopkov's Realistic Theatre.] It is time to understand that realism is Shakespeare and not *fabliaux*, Courbet and not daguerreotype, Tolstoy and not Boborykin. Realism presupposes a certain essence, synthesis, the idea of passions, conflicts, epochs. When this essence is diluted with water (and not very pure water at that), there emerges that kind of naturalism which is now struggling with Meyerhold's achievements.... Meyerhold is not young, but every time I see his staging, I think how much younger he is than many thirty-year-olds. Revolution for him is not only a system of ideas or concepts, it is his nature.'[29]

Mikhail Chekhov and the Second Moscow Art Theatre

After the sombre *Hamlet* with Mikhail Chekhov in the title role, *The Flea* appeared on the Second MAT stage in 1925 with a completely unexpected burst of gaiety. The creator of this production, the director and actor Alexei Diky who, like Chekhov, had developed within the First Studio, turned Evgeny Zamyatin's adaptation of Nikolai Leskov's *The Left-Hander* into an 'amusement performance',

announcing 'various dances and transformations' on the posters. The spectacle was stylized by the painter Boris Kustodiev in the manner of the colourful, crude Russian wood-cut (*lubok*). On stage the artist built a gingerbread-like tsar's palace, a tiny multi-domed church that stood knee-high to the actors and minute Tula houses with gardens and fences. The actors performed in a jesting, joking and amicable manner with rather crude, fairground mischief. 'For over three hours while the performance ran, the laughter in the auditorium did not cease,'[30] noted Yury Sobolev.

Diky later recalled that the production came out 'spiced in the popular way, with salt and pepper,' deriving 'its pedigree from the fairground show.' As distinct from productions created in this theatre by means of 'collective direction', Diky's *The Flea*, full of hilarious exaggerations, possessed a definite unity and was perhaps over-simplified. Diky himself played Platov, merrily, gallantly, 'with superb humour'; Serafima Birman, tall, thin, hook-nosed, touchingly and amusingly portrayed the overseas maiden Mary; and Leonid Volkov was Levsha, the Left-Hander, the simpleton who 'outwitted all the clever ones'. In the part of Levsha, the over-simplification of the play became apparent: Zamyatin and Diky deviated from Leskov's story, cutting the death of Levsha from the finale and deciding to let him live 'as long as the sun shines!' The dance of merry colours and the merry music of the Tula concertinas in *The Flea* prompted an optimistic ending. But many years later Diky realized there had been a reason for Leskov's interruption of 'the market-day bustle of the fairground show with a tragic outcome to the tale about the flea'.[31]

The 'market-day bustle' and earthy *joie de vivre* of *The Flea* were not to Mikhail Chekhov's liking. At this time he was directing a production of *Petersburg* by Andrei Bely and a very different tone, a melancholy disquiet was conceived for its staging. Bely's prose had more than once attracted the interest of those in theatre. In its broken rhythms, nervous spasmodic periods, it seemed to promise an unusual spectacle, but at the same time it was clear how difficult it would be to translate this prose into the language of theatrical action. Many had contemplated staging Bely, but practically no one had actually carried it through. Mikhail Chekhov was the first to venture this risky step, not so much because the main role of the senator Ableukhov attracted him but because he himself, like Andrei Bely, was a passionate advocate of Rudolf Steiner's anthroposophical ideas. The writer and actor were mutually inspired by their common faith, and Bely himself adapted the novel for the Second MAT.

Once again a whole group of directors prepared the production – Alexander Cheban, Serafima Birman and Vladimir Tatarinov; 'but of course,' wrote Bely, 'Chekhov directs through the three directors.' The inevitable condensation to which his text was subjected, becoming the 'skeleton of a drama', worried Bely, even though the process of 'collective creative work in which the author became the director and the actor the dramatist,'[32] nonetheless delighted him. It quickly became clear that the delight was premature: 'the collective creative work' was only distinguished by an individual acting triumph for Chekhov.

As played by Chekhov, Ableukhov, the highly placed tsarist official, was physically repulsive: a bare, egg-shaped cranium, protruding ears, the unsteady gait of a poorly regulated robot, stooped back, lifeless hands in grey kid gloves and hesitant speech. The figure was more terrible than humorous, fear and madness shone in his round unmoving eyes. None the less, he did arouse sympathy. 'While as always justifying his hero, Chekhov simultaneously accuses him,' wrote Markov. 'He builds an image of combined automatism and an inner strength which is killed and crushed by this automatism. The tragedy of Chekhov's Ableukhov is the tragedy of formalism and of an old man's despair. The evenness of thought conceals a yearning for life. . . . The automatism gradually reveals the ravaged face of a lonely old man. Ableukhov's death seems explicable, profoundly justified.'

While admiring Chekhov's performance, the critic did not hide his disappointment in the 'lack of directorial coordination' and observed with reason that 'by placing the production in the hands of three directors, the theatre condemned it to a lack of unity'. As a result the 'outer form of the production was ten years behind the times' and 'the tulles and veils, the deceptive lighting, the gloomy shadows' and all of the artist Mikhail Libakov's remaining contrivances 'only seemed like vain decorative ornamentation'.[33]

The production of *Petersburg* was quickly taken off, while *The Flea* staged by Alexei Diky ran for a long time, firmly consolidating its place in the repertoire. These two productions were not simply dissimilar, they stood in hostile opposition to each other. In the minor-key *Petersburg* the past, covered by a foggy haze, was frozen in mutliple significance and disintegrated into an enigmatic medley of characters: the high officials in dress uniforms glittering with medals, agents-provocateurs and terrorists wearing masquerade red and black dominos – everything was deceptive and spurious. In the major-key *Flea*, on the contrary, everything was clear, definite and unambiguous. *Petersburg*, furthermore, testified to the uncertainness of 'collective direction', while *The Flea* proved the great advantages of directorial autocracy. But at the Second MAT they were accustomed to acting autocracy, and Mikhail Chekhov enjoyed great authority in the company. Diky, inspired by the success of *The Flea*, shook this authority. The conflicts inside the theatre which had emerged as soon as the Second MAT achieved independence, became further aggravated with each day. The opposition, headed by Diky, openly spoke out against Chekhov in the press. The press widely reported 'the schism in the Second MAT,' which was finally crowned by the departure of the 'rebels' (Diky, Olga Pyzhova, Leonid Volkov and others) from the theatre.

Chekhov and his associates, Sushkevich, Bersenev, Giatsintova, Birman, had no desire to listen to the opposition, perceiving all its claims and demands as 'demagogic'. In reality the matter was more complicated. The conflict that flared up within the Second MAT was a conflict of different attitudes and aesthetic programmes. Each side did not want to note the merits of the other side and did not see the weakness of its own position. Chekhov found the dissensions in the company morally oppressive and sometimes they plunged him into deep despair. The only practical conclusion he drew was a fairly fundamental one: he renounced the idea of 'collective direction'.

In 1927 Sushkevich staged the satirical *The Case* by Sukhovo-Kobylin at the Second MAT. Boris Sushkevish had worked at MAT since 1908 and in the First Studio since the day of its conception. A gifted actor and director, he had always previously remained somewhere in the background: the brighter talents of Vakhtangov, Chekhov and Diky had eclipsed him. In *The Case* Sushkevich to some degree avenged former failures and created an austerely contoured production, the pathos of which lay in the tragic opposition of the soulless bureaucratic machinery to the living, suffering person. 'The

question of the individual and his rights,' wrote Lunacharsky, 'is portrayed on the one hand, that of the oppressive environment, or state despotism on the other.'[34] In the production Mikhail Chekhov appeared as Muromsky 'on behalf of the individual'. This role had long been considered passive and not very attractive: the typical 'noble father', delivering sad, monotonous soliloquies. But Chekhov even in this role accomplished a miracle. In outward appearance his Muromsky looked a comic figure: little, shrivelled up, a decrepit, unsteady, stiff-legged, old mannikin whose face was overgrown with side-whiskers and shaggy beard, with wandering child-like round eyes, timorous, in a thread-bare military uniform covered with hopelessly old-fashioned decorations and medals. In short, 'barely a breath in his body'. This comic disparagement of the image was cleverly calculated by the actor.

At first audiences received Chekhov's Muromsky with great bursts of laughter. Everything that this law-abiding but troubled, absurd old dotard said, and everything that he did, was funny. His naive attempts to attain justice and assert his rights before inveterate bribe-takers had no chance at all of success. All the stronger and more telling was the impression produced in the finale of the role, when the puny weakling portrayed by Chekhov, perishing in the bureaucratic prison cell, summoned his remaining strength and dared to rebel against the department and against the State itself. 'His legs still bend at the knee in these high boots, these pathetic grey side-whiskers still quaver as before, but one more word and then suddenly before us stands a man who has risen up in a last desperate effort, all his blood surging to his heart, and who with those same trembling lips, cries out about the executioners and the victims; but no, it is not a cry, simply total anguish of grief, rage and pain,'[35] wrote the critic Mikhail Zagorsky. For an instant the old weakling was suddenly transformed into one of Suvorov's heroic officers standing courageously under enemy fire and fearlessly confronting certain death. Another moment and death overtook him: measuring his pace, in heavy jack-boots Muromsky strode toward the doors past the officials paralyzed in fright and collapsed by the doors as if struck down. The role began comically, concluded tragically, and Chekhov executed the switch from comedy to tragedy with the supreme simplicity, with the apparent artlessness that only genius can achieve.

Muromsky was the last great creation in Mikhail Chekhov's artistic biography. In 1928 he left the Soviet Union. For a little while he tried to find himself again in Max Reinhardt's German company then unsuccessfully attempted to organize a Russian theatre in Paris; he performed in Lithuania and Latvia and finally moved to the USA where he appeared several times in the cinema. His films were sometimes shown in Russia, but those who had previously seen him on stage could hardly recognize him: on screen he was an ordinary actor of average ability. Chekhov himself felt that his talent, torn from its native soil and the poetry of the Russian language, was fading. Several times he initiated, then again broke off, negotiations to return to his homeland. He devoted the last years of his life to theatrical pedagogy and wrote, though never completed, some interesting memoirs. He died in America in 1955.

The 'Structural Realism' of the Kamerny Theatre

The Kamerny Theatre of Tairov and Koonen distinguished itself on the Moscow scene by an unwavering interest in Western literature.

J. M. Synge, Paul Claudel, G. K. Chesterton, Eugene O'Neill and John Dos Passos were welcome guests on this stage. Tairov outstripped other Soviet directors by a good quarter century, also turning to Brecht before everyone else. Although the repertoire was chosen consistently and firmly, there was no sureness in the means of theatrical expression. Manoeuvring between tragedy and the carnival, with excursions into operetta, now looking inquiringly into the distance of the Americanized future (*The Man Who Was Thursday* after Chesterton), then turning its gaze to the Russian past (*The Storm* by Ostrovsky), the Kamerny Theatre wandered in search of its own theatrical style. 'Every epoch has its pathos,' said Tairov. 'The pathos of modern times is simplicity.'[36] He would have liked to have managed 'without the reminiscences of obsolete naturalism,' without 'self-sufficient abstractness',[37] and initially called the style he sought 'neo-realism', later 'concrete' realism and finally 'structural realism'.

The last definition, 'structural realism', seems to be the most precise. It enables us to understand the essence of the changes that took place on the Tairov stage in the second half of the 1920s.

The principle of purity of genre, by which in its early years the Kamerny Theatre had defended its art from direct contact with modern times, was now applied with much less insistence. In place of the extremes of 'harlequinades' and 'mysteries' appeared drama which gravitated toward the tragic yet nevertheless permitted both an everyday tone and an interest in social conflicts. Quite recently a haughty renunciation of daily life had been for Tairov an indispensible law of any performance, whether in a Racine tragedy or a Lecocq operetta. Now the Kamerny Theatre ever more frequently rejected the refined, at times exotic spectacle in the name of a different, though not as refined, but strikingly intimate beauty.

To a great extent the shift to 'structural realism' was linked with the works of the brothers Vladimir and Georgy Stenberg. While previously such diverse and brilliant artists as Pavel Kuznetsov, Alexandra Exter, Georgy Yakulov and Alexander Vesnin had worked in succession with Tairov, the Stenbergs now designed nearly all his productions. This monopoly indicated that Tairov was completely satisfied with their manner, which combined a rather austere geometric outline of a production with fearlessly concrete detail of object and contemporary accuracy of costumes.

The Stenbergs bridled and tamed the Constructivist set. In their hands it lost the importunate mechanistic and fragmented quality, ceased flashing and flickering. The construction calmed down, quietened down and turned into a rigid framework that dictated an economical and clear sculptural form. This framework retained the ability to change, although metamorphoses were rarely executed and, as a rule, only during intervals and not in front of the audience. The place of action was designated honestly but sparingly. The space remained fundamentally unlived-in although its functions were not concealed: a house was a house, a street was a street, and the deck of a ship – the deck of a ship.

The Stenbergs were fascinated by the purity of the diagram, the simplicity of the blueprint, which for Tairov replaced Exter's vagaries and Yakulov's whims.

The combination of a generalized and simplified structure of the whole with the authenticity of the few striking details is characteristic of the productions of the three plays by O'Neill, *The Hairy Ape*, *Desire Under the Elms* and *All God's Chillun Got Wings*, staged one after another at the Kamerny Theatre.

Such a strong attraction to a writer hitherto unknown in Russia indicated that O'Neill had opened new doors for Tairov. The tragic perception of modern times, the tight interweaving of social, emotional and physiological motifs, the ability to penetrate into the dark depths of the subconscious of contemporary people who are still moved by the most ancient instincts of love and hate – all this stirred the director and induced him to search for theatrical forms adequate to O'Neill.

Although *The Hairy Ape*, staged by Tairov in 1926, made a great impression, it only cautiously touched the surface of the smouldering magma of O'Neill's drama. The production was conceived with a backward glance at the cliché of the contrast between rich and poor. The action began on an ocean liner portrayed, as it were, in cross-section by the Stenbergs: the upper deck, beneath it the crews' quarters and still lower the furnace room. A striking contrast emerged between the passengers' idle chatter on the upper deck and the stokers' truly hellish work in the ship's belly. In both locations, on the deck and in the furnace room, Tairov's actors confidently performed in mime. On the ship's deck, 'with refined aesthetic poses and gestures',[38] like mannequins, the elegantly dressed powerful of this world strolled idly. In the furnace room, mime demonstrated the inhuman exertion of muscular, sweaty bodies bared to the waist, illuminated by the scarlet flame of the furnace. 'No one,' wrote Lunacharsky, 'has yet succeeded in providing such sculptural and metallic rhythm of movement and sounds as are produced by Tairov . . . powerful and exhausted bodies, both the magnificent even pace of collective work and the music of machines.'[39]

At the centre of the production was the figure of the stoker Yank, played by one of Tairov's best performers, Sergei Tsenin.

Koonen did not perform in *The Hairy Ape*. But she played leading roles in the two other O'Neill plays staged by Tairov, *Desire Under the Elms* (1926) and *All God's Chillun Got Wings* (1929), into which she introduced her distinctive tragic range. Her former interest in the apogee of emotion and the incontrovertible commands of passion was filled with new meaning as soon as the actress entered O'Neill's drama. As before, passion remained the principal content of her acting but she found new ways of expressing it.

Previously Koonen's heroines had been released from the power of base, prosaic existence almost as soon as they stepped on the stage. In *Desire Under the Elms* the base and prosaic were perceived for the first time as fuel to the fire of lust, as the force provoking passion. Like Phèdre, Abbie Cabot betrayed an old husband for a stepson; like Medea, she committed infanticide. These sombre reminiscences, however, were complicated by an emotion unknown to the heroines of Euripides or Racine, by a proprietorial instinct with which Abbie was possessed to no lesser degree than by her attraction to the handsome young man.

Soon after the première Leonid Grossman wrote that Koonen 'imperceptibly passes from the cheerful and naive joy of owning the farm to a state of feminine captivity' and that 'the hypnosis of passion' reduces Abbie to 'a condition of psychological somnambulism'.[40]

Stefan Mokulsky later offered a different analysis: 'the proprietorial instinct clashes with the powerful passion of love that possesses Abbie.'[41] In actual fact there was no 'clash' here at all, but a merging, the complete unity of sensual passion and the proprietorial instinct. Having exchanged Phèdre's buskins for shoes with low heels, opulent theatrical attire for, first, the dark, buttoned dress of the young farmer's wife, then for a long nightdress with open neck and bare arms, Koonen played a woman whose life was totally enclosed within the limits of the farm built by the Stenbergs with its low ceilings, gloomy rooms, staircases and verandas.

Abbie's entire world was here, and she was a part of this world. In the stifling atmosphere the sinful passion flared up, yet it did not seek a way out from the four walls. On the contrary, it was the passion of the owner of these walls. Together with her body and affection Abbie generously offered her lover her principal treasure – the farm. In her eyes the farm acquired a highly ideal significance, encouraging sin, liberating the flesh, blessing the transgression.

Koonen recognized that Abbie had no other ideals. A woman without a dream, without the barest shadow of a thought for freedom, she acted within a stable world without attempting either to destroy or undermine it. But she acted by no means as a sleep-walker, but rather with total enterprise, with peasant cunning and American business acumen. She did not rush. She stood for a long time, tilting her head a little to the side as if sizing up the situation. Her movements were slow, her intonation long, drawn-out. Abbie contemplated first, then decided, but having decided she no longer hesitated. Reason every time found powerful arguments on behalf of passion and suggested to Abbie recklessly bold actions.

Her husband, Efraim Cabot is old, so it would therefore be fair if after his death the farm – together with Abbie – should pass to his stepson. Having reasoned thus, in the second act Koonen's Abbie threw from her shoulders the shawl which covered her nakedness, drew the timid youth to her and fell to the floor with him. Tairov's staging of this fall was much franker than O'Neill's stage directions and clearly indicated that the entire initiative comes from Abbie. She does not give herself to Eben, she takes him.

But the child born of Eben becomes the legal heir to her legal husband, the old Efraim, and therefore the farm slips from the hands of the one for whom it was destined. Reason again suggests the most simple solution, and Abbie again acts without hesitation, with the same peasant-like imperturbability. In the last act, in response to the frightened question of Eben (Nikolai Tseretelli), 'You killed him?', she answered with a slight nod of the head and the barely audible, indifferent 'Ay-eh'.

'Koonen's performance,' recalled N. Berkovsky, 'retained a certain distance between the woman and the passion that consumes her; the heroine's human face had not disappeared entirely into the black gloom, and therefore in O'Neill's drama of horrors there remained a shred of poetry and spirituality.'[42] This is not quite accurate. Koonen had not risen above the heroine and she did disappear entirely with her into the 'black gloom'. But she raised the human scale of Abbie's image, endowing the young farmer's wife with a sombre majesty, her lusts with the destructive power of a fatal passion and her spirit with fearlessness. Koonen met Abbie's death calmly.

Tairov illuminated the production's finale with the rays of the morning sun. Abbie and Eben came out of the house in handcuffs, but 'brightly and triumphantly' – in Koonen's words, 'as if not to an execution but to a wedding'.[43]

The lucid finale of *Desire Under the Elms* has led historians of the Kamerny Theatre to believe that O'Neill's social pessimism gave way to social optimism in Tairov's productions. This widespread view needs some correction. It is unquestionable that Tairov and Koonen

Model of the set by the Stenberg brothers for O'Neill's *All God's Chillun Got Wings* directed by Tairov at the Kamerny Theatre in 1929.

avoided O'Neill's crude sexuality. In Koonen's performance the base, coarse sensuality of O'Neill's heroines was ennobled, the irrational voice of aroused flesh acquired reason and clarity. But in this voice the notes were not in the major key. It is truer to say something else: as soon as Tairov and Koonen turned to O'Neill, the circumstances of place and time became more valuable to them. Henceforth their art required a solid, social foundation.

In 1929 in *All God's Chillun Got Wings* (staged by Tairov under the title of *The Negro*), Koonen played one more typical 'American tragedy' of a white girl who has fallen in love with a black youth. And of course the Kamerny Theatre's first actress also elevated this heroine; lonely, forsaken in the chaos of an enormous city, the weak Ella Downey was endowed by Koonen with great dignity and courage in order then to crown the role with the tragic chord of insanity and death.

Pavel Markov immediately noted that 'in the person of O'Neill the Kamerny Theatre has found a dramatist who suits it. . . . happily it has come across material with which it is in tune,' for, he wrote, O'Neill 'takes life from within in concentrated and vivid contours,' his drama 'forces thinking', 'induces reflection', sets Tairov on the road to 'generalized realism'.[44] Another critic, M. Zagorsky, also asserted that in the productions of O'Neill's plays the director had found 'the theatrical style of the great social production'.[45]

A similar pathos was inherent in the 1927 production of *Antigone* by Walter Hasenclever, the Expressionist dramatist, although the conflict between Antigone (Koonen) and Creon (Sergei Tsenin) was appreciably modernized: Antigone appeared as 'a revolutionary, ascetically severe, strict in her simplicity,'[46] implacable in her hatred for the tyrant; Creon was portrayed as a cowardly despot, the ancient chorus as 'a chorus of the poor' which proclaimed anti-militaristic and anti-monarchical slogans ('War on War', 'Peace to the Shacks, War to the Palaces' and so on).

Tairov's attempts to re-orientate the Kamerny Theatre's musical comedy repertoire proved less promising. For the time being, Tairov had no intention of rejecting either comedy or music. 'The comic spectacle,' he repeated, 'can be just as important as the heroic spectacle.'[47]

Extremes Converge

Scene from Hasenclever's *Antigone*, directed by Tairov at the Kamerny Theatre in 1927.

The leader of the Kamerny Theatre would also have liked to transfer both comedy and operetta to the plane of 'structural realism'. But only one of the new comic productions, *Day and Night* by Lecocq (1926), was a success, despite the fact that in it, too, as Alexei Gvozdev wrote, 'content somehow retreated to the background in the face of purely formal concerns, dwindled in the face of abstract movement on stage.'[48]

Threads of continuity linked the new production of Lecocq with the earlier *Giroflé-Girofla*. The difference, a noticeable and entertaining one, was that where in *Giroflé-Girofla* harlequinade had revelled in theatrical tinsel and operetta had been tinged with the spontaneity of cabaret and the raciness of the Folies Bergère, in the production of *Day and Night* the comic performance savoured the 'latest rage' in Western fashion with equal relish and flair. Taking his bearings from a refined music hall, Tairov was not above learning from Foregger, but carried the dancing lightness to a degree of weightlessness, athleticism to the virtuosity of circus acrobatics.

In 1930 one more bold step was taken in this direction. Tairov, who had seen the Brecht-Weill *Die Dreigroschenoper* in Berlin, became enamoured of it and staged it in his theatre as *The Beggar's Opera*. However, the carefree music-hall motifs which had brought such great success to the production of *Day and Night*, here manifestly constricted the social energy and mordant wit of Brecht's satire. The production was eccentric and light, but it did not last long in the repertoire.

From 'Social Mask' to Theatrical Portrait

Meyerhold, Kurbas and many other directors in the mid 1920s, like Tairov, experienced an ever-increasing pull towards psychological depth in character portrayal. The various means of generalization (and, at the same time, simplification) which had led to good-natured caricature, biting satire or 'social mask', passed out of fashion and interest grew in the individual, in the theatrical portrait presented in close-up. The phantasmagoria of Meyerhold's *The Government Inspector*, completely free from the vulgar, primitive sociology and fairground crudeness of the earlier *The Forest*, eloquently testified to what a sharp turn was being accomplished.

Nevertheless the experience gained in the political revues *The Earth in Turmoil* and *D.E.* became apparent as soon as Meyerhold turned to plays 'on the issue of the day'. Furthermore, the ideological and aesthetic links between the Meyerhold Theatre and LEF still remained strong. The narrow and dogmatic programme put forward by LEF's members was already perceived as a kind of atavism. But Meyerhold, as before, placed great hopes on Mayakovsky whose plays he awaited impatiently. Probably for this reason he also trusted Mayakovsky's colleagues in LEF.

In 1926 at the Meyerhold Theatre the play *Roar China!* by one of LEF's most orthodox members, Sergei Tretyakov, was staged. It was at once evident that the production by no means possessed the former consistency but, on the contrary, revealed symptomatic contradictions. The until recently complete and integrated system of 'the theatre of social masks' had begun to show signs of cracking.

This was partially explained by the fact that the young Vasily Fedorov directed rather than Meyerhold. The master only corrected the gifted pupil's first independent work. Meyerhold made radical changes, but all the same he did not manage to overcome the stylistic rift in the production.

Tretyakov took the play's subject from a newspaper article about a certain English businessman accidentally drowned in China in the Yangtse River. When the captain of the English gunboat could not find the perpetrators of the Englishman's death, he ordered the execution of two Chinese boatmen selected by lot. 'That is the fact. I hardly had to change it,' declared Tretyakov proudly in the foreword to the play. Nonetheless the play presented not only 'the fact' but also a completely professional organization of the action and an unequivocal appraisal of the characters' deeds as well.

The director's composition proffered the simplest division of the space: the downstage area belonged to the poor, oppressed Chinese, 'us', and the upstage area to the European colonizers, 'them'. A boundary ran between 'us' and 'them' in the form of a wide band of real water (in order to see the water it was necessary to go up to the dress circle, for it was not visible from the stalls). Chinese junks glided along the water. A little way off in the distance towered the frightening bulk of the gunboat. The muzzles of its guns, directed at the Chinese coolies, looked out at the audience, into the auditorium.

The play prompted this division of the stage into two parts, for it contained two antagonistic groups of characters – the Europeans and the Chinese. The director decided to intensify the contrast further by portraying the Chinese with photographic authenticity and the Europeans in caricature. Accordingly the Chinese 'sections' were formulated with maximum lifelikeness, and the European ones were exaggerated, presented in the clichéd style of 'foxtrotting Europe'. The arrogant officers in gleaming uniforms, the free-and-easy tourists with their ladies, the saccharine missionaries and lascivious nurses were not in fact any different from the characters of *D.E.* The Chinese were another matter. Here the Meyerhold Theatre suddenly revealed a taste for ethnographic accuracy in the reproduction of costumes, daily life and customs. A whole collection of musical instruments was gathered together especially for the production. A great variety of genuine objects was brought from China. Chinese students in Moscow were invited to rehearsals and asked to check that there were no blunders in the details of everyday life and behaviour. Apart from boatmen and porters, there appeared on stage rickshaws, confectionery traders, vendors of fans, a barber, a corn surgeon, a knife grinder, and so on.

The performance began with an excessively long episode during which (for a good ten minutes!) Chinese coolies loaded hundreds of bales of tea into the holds.

Despite such excesses, the aim was achieved: instead of exotic 'chinoiserie' the audience saw unusually lifelike tableaux. The crowd scenes recalled those of the early MAT and in the reviews the word 'naturalism' cropped up accompanied by the epithets 'ethnographic', 'dismal', 'earth-bound', and so on. The scene of the execution of the two Chinese, 'shown in all its repugnant details', shocked the critics.[49] Markov wrote ironically that this episode certainly arouses indignation against the colonizers, but simultaneously 'a certain feeling of protest towards the director as well'.[50] The Chinese 'sections' created a more striking impression than the sharply caricatured European episodes. 'The bourgeoisie rotting in the inevitable foxtrot,' miserably confessed Sergei Radlov, 'induces not wrath but depression.'[51]

The delicate figure of the Chinese boy played by Babanova occupied a special position in the production's entire dual system of imagery. The Chinese boy who served the Europeans was situated on their side of the border separating the whites from the yellows. Babanova, performing *en travesti* for the first time, underlined the tragic quality of the boy's life amidst the foreign masters alien to him, nervously and precisely playing on the contrasts between the disciplined evenness of an obedient servant and the sudden surges of fierce hatred for the oppressors. Toward the end of the play the boy came out alone onto the ship's empty deck. Babanova sang a melancholy song under her breath, fell to her knees clasping her hands in prayer-like manner, then quickly jumped up and hurriedly began to clamber up the mast. The boy skilfully tied a knot in the rope, then – a noose. He was rushing, afraid he would be prevented. An instant more, and the little figure, with one last shudder, hung from the cross beam.

This was the tragic culmination of the performance, beautifully composed by the director and exquisitely rendered by the actress.

The production as a whole remained within the confines of the opposition between oppressors and oppressed, typical of the agit-plays from the early 1920s. Yet Meyerhold succeeded in concluding the action very effectively: the construction began to move, and the gunboat sailed menacingly toward the shore, that is, toward the forestage where the crowd of mutinous Chinese were clustered. In formation on deck the English sailors readied their rifles. A little lower, between them and the audience, the coolies and boatmen stood in a straight line, immobile in the face of death.

The final point of the production brought forth stormy applause from the audience. But the applause was not for the production, it was for this one set-piece and for one actress, Babanova.

In 1927 Sergei Tretyakov reluctantly admitted that the production 'constructed as an ethnographic study on the one hand, and as a newspaper article on the other, was only perceived by the majority as an exotic and touching show'.[52]

All the same for quite some time yet Meyerhold and Tretyakov believed that they could find a common language. In 1928 at the Meyerhold Theatre rehearsals were in full swing for Tretyakov's play I Want A Child, in which the then fashionable idea of eugenics was debated. This science called for the creation of 'a breed of new people' through the calculated selection of healthy, strong parents, of men and women who mated with each other according to medical recommendations rather than the caprice of love. Maintaining that

it is criminal 'to waste sexual energy', Tretyakov added 'his own' social criteria to eugenics: he believed that not only physical health was important, but also the parents' proletarian origin. The heroine of his play, the young Communist Milda, duly ordered her personal life in accordance with this set programme.

As this was patently controversial stuff, the graphic artist El Lissitzky to whom Meyerhold had entrusted the design of the play was given the task of turning the theatre into a kind of forum for public discussion of the issues. The action was supposed to unfold in a stage-arena surrounded on all sides by a ring of spectators and be interrupted by their debates at every turning point in the plot. 'Then,' said Meyerhold, 'we shall have a guarantee that not a single one of the questions wrongly posed or wrongly answered by the author will be resolved incorrectly. We shall put people on whom we can rely in the place of the orators.' Rather than writing 'first show', 'second', 'third' on the poster, he proposed to write 'first discussion', 'second', 'third'.[53]

Ostensibly the performance debate was to be open (any of the spectators could take the floor) but in fact it was directed by orators 'who could be relied on' and whose discussion would be definitely 'correct'. As the close of the 1920s drew near this entire attempt to return to the mass meeting form of The Dawn already seemed archaic as did both the play's primitive structure and its characters, not so much living people as walking statements. Furthermore, contrary to the expectations of the author and director, the play provoked strong objections long before the planned first-night. The excessively intimate theme of the proposed debate was embarrassing, the 'coarse expressions' used in the text were shocking. Perhaps Meyerhold could have defended the play but he himself had also cooled toward it. And so the performance-debate did not even take place. The form in which the director was preparing to present I Want A Child – the stage-arena surrounded on all sides by the audience – was subsequently appropriated without ceremony by Meyerhold's student Nikolai Okhlopkov in his Realistic Theatre.

Meanwhile at the Berezil Theatre in Kharkov, Les Kurbas was defending a no less sharp and no less debatable but far more talented play by Mikola Kulish, The People's Malakhy. In March 1928 he succeeded in bringing this work to its première. Unquestionably the most talented of the Ukrainian dramatists, it was not the first time that Kulish had been connected with the Berezil Theatre: his drama The Commune on the Steppes had already successfully run on this stage. The hero of Kulish's new work, the old postman Malakhy Stakanchik, was preoccupied by the idea of the immediate and radical transformation of all 'weary mankind'. If in Tretyakov's play a dubious social Utopia had been advanced by the author himself, relying on the authority of science, then in Kulish's tragi-comedy the vague notion of reforming the human race obsessed a strange fantasizer who aroused in the author mixed feelings of sympathy and pity, irony and trust.

The whole play is set in motion by the strange personality of Malakhy, a personality rooted in an everyday milieu who breaks away from his background. A small and timid man, he suddenly seems to defy the laws of gravity, seeing himself as all but the Messiah, imagining he is empowered to regulate the people, to organize life reasonably and beautifully. Arrogating to himself the title of 'the people's Malakhy' and laying claim to great deeds, the hero, however, obviously possesses neither greatness nor even sound judgment. On the contrary, his enthusiasm is often completely reckless, divorced from reality. Malakhy's theatrical portrait therefore required particular poignancy and acute psychological analysis. The success or failure of the production depended entirely on how this single role would be performed.

Les Kurbas saw two sides to the character of Malakhy, although the gap between them was greater in the production than in the play: it swung from overt sarcasm to unconcealed affection for the hero. The director was at one with Malakhy in all those instances when he clashed with the 'non-class solidarity of the malicious', with the cruelty, greed, cynicism and 'proprietorial swinishness' of the petit bourgeois. The director viewed Malakhy with cold contempt when alone he naively, like some unctuous priest, tried to preach good and teach those around him. In Malakhy as played by Maryan Krushelnitsky there was an air of 'pathetic submissiveness, the gentleness of a person accustomed to giving way to everyone'. But 'in his inflamed eyes gleamed the obstinacy of a maniac, the resolution of a fanatic.'[54] Krushelnitsky acted the role on the border between a Quixotic fanaticism and madness, a heartfelt pathos and the frightening sense of being possessed.

Malakhy's fate in the play is fantastical, carrying this quiet enthusiast who has deserted his family 'for the sake of an idea' first to a clandestine brothel where he is quite out of place, then to a psychiatric clinic where he immediately finds soul-mates. In all the settings, except for the asylum, the hero who has seemingly veered off the co-ordinates of the real, everyday world is met by completely real, sensible people.

In designing *The People's Malakhy* Vadim Meller was concerned that the details of everyday life should seem to refute Malakhy's illusions and fantasies with their cruel, irresistible authenticity, and Kurbas brought him into contact with rough, earthy, full-blooded people, first of all Kum, a Ukrainian Sancho Panza played by Iozef Girnyak, and Malakhy's daughter Liubunia, played by Valentina Chistyakova.

The veracity achieved was unprecedented. 'The staging was done superbly,' said the film director Alexander Dovzhenko. 'Krushelnitsky and Girnyak performed brilliantly. At times it even seemed that working in this way was dangerous to the actors' psyche.'[55] Of course Dovzhenko exaggerated this 'danger': he felt this way because the authenticity of character that Kurbas achieved in his production had almost no precedents on the Ukrainian stage. Buchma had recently played Jimmy Higgins with equal poignancy and veracity but then there had been no living figures around the hero, only placard-style 'social masks'. Now all the acting ensemble was regulated according to one tuning fork, thus greatly intensifying the effect.

The centre of attention in the overwhelming majority of productions in the second half of the 1920s definitely shifted toward the actor, focusing on his performance. For a time the overall staging plan lost its dominating significance. The use of space and the visual impact of productions became less important than the actor, served him, for it was the actor who, in the final analysis, brought the full emotional impact to the performance. The complex, multi-character arrangement of the Meyerholdian production *Roar China!* had reason for giving prominence to Babanova alone in the small part of the boy. It became clearer with each passing year that it was the fate of the individual character that interested audiences.

In some loudly acclaimed productions of this period it was the fate of the intellectual in particular that attracted the most attention. The evolution of the theme of the intellectual on the Soviet stage in the 1920s reflected the distinctive changes in the social climate. And in this sphere too the movement from biting, crudely tendentious theatrical satire and biased caricature to an objective, psychologically rich theatrical portrait occurred steadily, although at times inconsistently with capricious zigzags.

One must not forget that not so long before, in the early 1920s, the figure of the intellectual, the person engaged in mental work, aroused great suspicion amongst Soviet writers. In Bill-Belotserkovsky's *Storm* 'specialists' (who were then called *spetsy* for short) are portrayed as hidden counter-Revolutionaries. In the novel *The Rout* by Alexander Fadeev the sole intellectual, Mechik, turned out to be a traitor. At other times, though, intellectuals were granted a more favourable view: in *Liubov Yarovaya* by Konstantin Trenev the Professor Gornostaev is depicted as wholly sympathetic and honourable; in *The Days of the Turbins* by Bulgakov the Russian intelligentsia is perceived as the bearer of noble traditions of high morality and humanism. But these exceptions (which at times, as with *The Days of the Turbins*, provoked angry protests) only confirmed the general rule: the intellectual, placed in an ambiguous position by history – neither the proletariat nor the exploiter, neither 'one of us' nor 'one of them', today a Red and perhaps tomorrow a White – seemed a dubious, unreliable fellow-traveller to the Revolution. He seemed 'petit-bourgeois'. And this led to the presumption that sooner or later he would turn away from the Revolution, would betray it.

In 1928 Alexei Faiko wrote a melodrama, *The Man With the Briefcase*, the central character of which, the professor and linguist Granatov, embodied precisely this idea of the intellectual as potential villain. The play was written with Faiko's characteristic theatrical craftsmanship: spiritedly convoluted plot and unexpected turns of action, all of which guaranteed it sure success. Alexei Diky, based at the Moscow Theatre of the Revolution after his split with Mikhail Chekhov, was the first to stage Faiko's melodrama. Nikolai Akimov designed the production, sharply magnifying some of the props. One was immediately struck by the enormous, monumental ashtray, huge cigarette ends and a 'giganticized' galosh. The action took place on a stage slightly tilted toward the hall, and the play's nine scenes were broken into thirty-three episodes which succeeded one another with cinematographic speed. Devices of this sort were intended to give the melodrama dynamism and to attract publicity, to augment Faiko's mastery of theatrical plot construction with the wrathful intonation of Granatov's exposure, with the sarcasm and bitter mockery of the props.

Maria Babanova played a central role as the professor's son, the adolescent Goga who has returned with his mother from emigration. She played the delicate thirteen-year-old boy, half Russian, half French, tormented by loneliness, but grown-up beyond his years, who is entering timidly and mistrustfully into an unfamiliar life. Instinctively he senses danger in Granatov and, with touching, almost masculine solicitude, he protects his mother, Xenia Trevern (played by Olga Pyzhova).

In Mikhail Lishin's performance Professor Granatov, the villain without a dagger but with an ordinary briefcase, a demagogue and hypocrite, seemed not so much a life-like character of contemporary social reality as a stylized theatrical product of the melodramatic genre. The contrast between the sincere truthfulness in the manner of Babanova and Pyzhova on the one hand, and the out-moded, almost provincial style of Lishin's acting on the other, underlined all the play's artificiality.

A year later at the Kamerny Theatre Tairov staged an adaptation of a 1920s Soviet bestseller which caused a sensation (and is now completely forgotten), Sergei Semenov's novel *Natalia Tarpova*. This novel paints a vivid picture of the story of the champion worker Natalia Tarpova's passion for the solid, impressive engineer Gabrukh, their intimacy and then her realization that he is socially alien to her.

In Semenov's novel Gabrukh appeared as an interesting, attractive person, honest in his own way, and Tairov, who awarded the role of Gabrukh to the charming actor Nikolai Chaplygin, strove to deepen and extend the image of the intellectual.

But the critics, inclined to apply straightforward sociological standards to all characters, with deliberate preconception saw in Gabrukh an ideological adversary. Vladimir Blyum accused Tairov of 'disgraceful truckling' expressed in the 'abstract humanist' approach to the heroes instead of a 'class approach'.[56] Blyum's article was ironically entitled 'Natalie de Tarpoff', thus hinting that the 'abstract humanist' Tairov had 'Frenchified' the play and torn it away from Soviet reality.

This attack was right on target. The 'room temperature' of the conversational drama did not suit the tragic actress Alisa Koonen and she searched in vain for a way to apply herself to this role. Furthermore the heroine's sharp swing from love to hatred as prescribed by the play occurred without foundation, too hurriedly. And this is why both Koonen and Chaplygin fell into an affected tone, evoking unpleasant associations with vulgar Parisian theatre.

Tairov's attempts to give the melodrama a publicist intent and therefore to bring the heroes forward onto a rostrum constructed in the centre of the stage (both Tarpova and Gabrukh delivered their monologues from here, addressing them directly into the auditorium and crossing the Kamerny Theatre's 'sacred' line of footlights for the first time), changed nothing. The 'device of the rostrum' which Tairov considered a 'lucky find'[57] did not compensate for the production's emotional poverty.

In contrast, the outwardly extremely modest production of a play by the young Alexander Afinogenov, *The Eccentric*, at the Second MAT in the same year, 1929, testified that a different, more optimistic view of the intelligentsia's social prospects changed matters at once.

The Eccentric was performed in a staging by Ivan Bersenev and Alexander Cheban soon after Mikhail Chekhov left the Soviet Union. Superficially the production appeared entirely traditional: standard office interiors with 'typical' desks, shelves for papers, electric lights hanging from flexes and the customary slogans on the walls. But the people did not prove to be standard. The convinced careerist, the cold and handsome Igor Gorsky (Bersenev) seemed a strong, grand person in his own way. All the more poignant, in contrast to his importance, was the modest, shy and delicate sincerity of the 'eccentric' Boris Volgin, played by Azary Azarin. No barrier whatsoever could be sensed between this intellectual and the factory workers surrounding him. A dreamer who fought head on with the stagnant daily routine, with stupid authorities and philistinism, with the unruly hooligans who maliciously pursued a Jewish worker, in the finale Volgin seemed to have suffered defeat. The persecuted Sima has thrown herself into the lake, the good people, including Volgin, have been driven out of the factory. But the

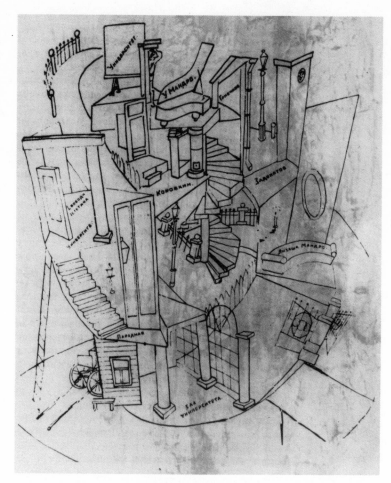

Stage plan for Bely's *Moscow!*, which Meyerhold was considering producing at the Meyerhold Theatre in 1926.

workers rushed after him 'to find him, to make him return!'. *The Eccentric* played more than 500 times, so the public clearly shared this sympathy for the intelligentsia.

That same question of the intelligentsia undoubtedly preoccupied Meyerhold when he was considering producing the drama *Moscow*, written by Andrei Bely in 1926 after his novel of the same name. Negotiations and correspondence between the author and theatre dragged on for several years, but Meyerhold never started rehearsals. However, as a result of the preliminary explorations at Meyerhold's theatre, an original plan was created, most probably by Vladimir Dmitriev (we do not have precise information) for a spiral construction containing seventeen acting areas spilling into one another thus enabling the director to organize 'permanent action'. As is evident from the single surviving sketch, the distinctive feature of the construction consisted of its being simultaneously both concretely representational (a labyrinth of acting areas spiralling upwards consisted of rooms furnished in various styles; each room had its 'own identity', and taken together they gave a wholly convincing picture of the life of Moscow's intelligentsia) and capable of changing instantly. 'A dynamic crescendo, presented in static form,' wrote Bely, rightly assuming that Meyerhold here again was inspired by 'the principles of the cinema' and that 'if he succeeds in staging it, this will represent a new achievement not only for the stage but also for dramatic art; dramatists will be able to write differently.'[58]

What is interesting, however, is not only this project's expression of Meyerhold's long-standing and persistent effort to create a mobile stage form essential for immediate changes of scene in a multi-episodic drama. No less serious is another problem also resolved by the use of this 'spiral': it enabled Meyerhold to show from the stage contemporary, everyday life 'in permanent action' and to characterize specific people through the use of specific objects, in far greater detail than a few years before in Erdman's *The Warrant*.

Recently objects on Meyerhold's stage had been trying to emancipate themselves from people. Every object, like an instrument in an orchestra, had its own musical part predetermined by the directorial score. An object could be at odds with one character, on friendly terms with another, remain neutrally indifferent to a third. Now objects received a more modest and more traditional function, entering once more into the service of man whose spiritual world and psychology the director wanted to discover.

Terentiev's Reply

Independently of their rigging, theatrical ships embarked one after another on the course to social and psychological authenticity and sailed toward the shore of realism. 'A period is beginning in theatrical life,' wrote Sergei Tretyakov, 'when the innovative force of Meyerhold, Eisenstein and Foregger emanating from Theatrical October has spread in a calm, stabilizing film over the entire face of theatrical activity.' Directors felt that the social climate had changed, that audiences required more substantial spiritual nourishment. 'Now,' continued Tretyakov, 'the nucleus of the production is not in the design but in the subject matter.'[59] The name of the dramatist now meant more than the name of the director.

At this moment the director Igor Terentiev, a lawyer by training and previously a rather undistinguished Futurist poet, suddenly audaciously directed his little theatrical tub against the current. His productions at the small theatre of the Leningrad Journalists' Club stunned everyone and incensed many.

· Terentiev's theatrical experience was not great. In the past he had only produced one noteworthy work, *John Reed* after the book *Ten Days That Shook the World* at the Leningrad Red Theatre (1924). No one would have called the undisputed success of *John Reed* sensational: in this production Terentiev exploited, with only slight renewal and modification, a well-worn form of the light political revue. It stood somewhere mid-way between the experiments of Radlov and Foregger and Meyerhold's larger-scale political revues. Sandro Moissi, who had been to this production, spoke of it in strong terms: he 'saw how John Reed's noble drama was played and rejoiced in the *joie de vivre* of the young performers and the enthusiastic attention of the simple and wise audience of workers.'[60] Hardened theatre-goers, however, were restrained in their reception of *John Reed*.

The excitement and commotion around Terentiev broke out two years later when he organized his theatre at the Journalists' Club and staged four productions one after another – *Foxtrot* by Vasily Andreev, his own play *The Tangled Web*, Gogol's *The Government Inspector* and *Natalia Tarpova*, which we have come across previously, after the novel by Sergei Semenov.

A group of young artists who were students of Pavel Filonov invaded the Journalists' Club together with Terentiev. They not only

designed Terentiev's productions but also took over the entire premises of the former Shuvalov palace on the Fontanka Embankment. In the vestibule, in the foyer and along the walls of the small (200-seat) auditorium, the painters hung their pictures executed according to the rules of 'Analytic Art' as dictated by Filonov. 'On the canvases, in delicate, transparent colours were portrayed lilac- and rose-coloured cows, and people from whom,' recalled an imperturbable eyewitness, 'the layers of skin had seemingly been removed by a wonderful surgeon. Veins, arteries and internal organs were distinctly visible. The bright green shoots of trees and grasses sprouted through the figures.'[61] These surrealistic paintings created a kind of visual prelude to Terentiev's productions. The sinister panel 'Chubarov Lane' also thematically anticipated the brutal naturalism of the production *Foxtrot*.

In the chronicle of Leningrad crime Chubarov Lane was notorious for the gang-rape of a young female worker unparalleled for its brutality. Fifteen offenders appeared in court in 1926 and ever since the word *chubarovets* has had a pejorative meaning. Andreev's *Foxtrot* was a series of fleeting sketches of the lives of those same *chubarovtsy*, gangsters, muggers, murderers, and also of their girlfriends, professional prostitutes. The prose of that time had already touched on such themes, Veniamin Kaverin's story *The End of a Den* being read avidly, but it was the first time that characters from the 'bottom' of the modern city had appeared on stage. They aroused great interest, and with this in mind Terentiev had deliberately intensified his characters, depicting them without any romantic aura, firmly and finely accentuating the baseness of their motives, their cynicism, greed and cowardice. The play, however, was very primitive and all the director's efforts were undermined by its flaccidity and dullness.

The failure did not trouble Terentiev who intended anyway to work by 'trial and error' and was pleased as it was that the hall invariably overflowed at performances of *Foxtrot*. *The Tangled Web*, which he wrote, was also an undoubted mistake and this time not even the relevance of the theme saved him. Terentiev's play dealt with the widespread embezzling in those years of poverty. Having acquired State money, the embezzlers would set off on a binge, then after two or three weeks of the 'high life' with restaurant orgies and prostitutes, they invariably ended up in the dock. Terentiev was not, however, a pioneer of this theme, for plays about embezzlers (usually comedies) were staged frequently, and little distinguished *The Tangled Web* from its predecessors. But a number of directorial inventions did attract notice. Terentiev ingeniously used the play of 'shadow puppets' against lighted screens, and attempted devices of 'sound montage' when the dialogue on stage joined a cacophony of city sounds, demonstrating an ability to stage action very wittily and expressively on the small stage of the Journalists' Club. The critic Adrian Piotrovsky thought the principal merit of the production of *The Tangled Web* was that 'it strengthened the position of pointed and controversial art.'[62]

It was, however, Terentiev's *The Government Inspector* that turned out to be controversial in a real sense, arousing the stormiest disputes and bringing the most undisputed success to the theatre of the Journalists' Club. Terentiev staged his Gogolian production as an open challenge to Meyerhold's. Where Meyerhold had given to the small provincial town the opulence and gloss of the capital city, Terentiev restored a remote provincialism to the play; where Meyerhold 'held course for tragedy', Terentiev reduced comedy to the level of slapstick. Meyerhold's production was gloomily fatalistic; Terentiev's was unrestrainedly merry. The enigmatic Khlestakov (Garin) stood at the centre of the Meyerholdian work, but with Terentiev the central position was occupied by the Mayor – stupid, lustful and greedy.

The artists from Filonov's studio worked with great diligence and thoroughness to create 'speaking costumes' for the Gogolian characters, that is, attire which in itself would give sufficiently detailed information about each one's occupation. For example, the Postmaster's costume consisted of envelopes and stamps with sealing wax imprints; doctor Gibner's was decorated with an emblem of death – the skull and crossbones – as well as a large thermometer. And in addition he was given a chamber pot. Shackles were portrayed on the police uniforms, and so forth. This device had an unforeseen effect: the audience examined the costumes intently for a long time without paying any attention whatsoever to the actor's words and actions. This is why the 'speaking costumes' were soon relinquished and replaced by more banal ones.

Terentiev's principal innovations, which shocked public and critics alike, bore a Rabelaisian character. Terentiev devised and sharply accentuated base, crude physical details. While the Mayor imagined with horror the possible consequences of the impending inspection, 'Montezuma's revenge' struck him. Crumpling a little piece of paper in his hand, he hurriedly hid in the WC from where his chaotic instructions were delivered to the officials. But of course the WC was a highly stylized one. The entire set of *The Government Inspector* consisted of five tall black parallelepipeds which were moved about within the stage area. These 'cupboards' or 'crates' were enclosed on three sides, open on one, and by manipulating them in various ways, moving them from place to place, now turning the solid black surface to the audience, now the open side, Terentiev was able to impart flexibility and fluidity to the production's spatial form. The unexpected application of Craig's 'tragic geometry' to comic ends proved to have great potential: the action at times shrank into the narrow stage area compressed by the 'crates' that had been moved together, at others took over the entire stage floor, moved obliquely along the diagonal or spread out frontally. Furthermore, every one of the 'crates' could itself serve as a place of action – a WC, for example.

The scenes with Khlestakov and the Mayor's wife and daughter exceeded all expectations in their unambiguous frivolity, and even more so after the hastily unceremonial prelude when Anna Andreevna and Maria Antonovna in turn hurriedly threw off their skirts and blouses, Khlestakov withdrew with each of them to one of the black 'cupboards', and the sound effects eloquently communicated the nature of their activities there.   As if this was not enough, Terentiev introduced Ukrainian, French, Polish and German monologues into the text, and had the sergeant's widow sing a Gypsy romance while one of the merchants performed the popular aria of the Indian guest from the opera *Sadko*. At the very beginning of the play when the Mayor reports that he has dreamed about two rats ('they came in, sniffed about and left'), trained white mice ran along a wire above the stage.

While challenging Meyerhold on all points, however, Terentiev also showed signs of being influenced by him, particularly in the famous 'lies scene' where he employed the Meyerholdian effect of slowed-down speech. He had Khlestakov telling lies 'without enthusiasm', telling lies like a man 'who has been telling lies from

the theatrical boards for eighty years, and he is bored by these lies, bored beyond tears.'[63] But this episode was also parodically comic.

Like a true Futurist, Terentiev wanted scandal and scandal he got. Boris Lavreniev published an indignant article in the Leningrad *Krasnaya gazeta* where he accused the director of sinking to 'the most obscene bedroom farce', and at the same time, 'obscurantist mysticism'.[64] Another newspaper review stated that the production 'plays into the hands of theatrical reactionaries'.[65] In a third, a comparatively restrained article by Mikhail Bleiman, it was noted that individual episodes were done 'conscientiously and clearly' and some actors performed 'with considerable mastery', but nonetheless on the whole 'this is eccentricism without foundation.'[66] And even Adrian Piotrovsky who had recently encouraged 'debate' of Terentiev's works angrily declared it time 'to question the directions and limitations of formal experimentation'.[67]

Hardly anyone noticed the marvellously witty ending that Terentiev had devised: in the finale instead of the real Government Inspector, the same Khlestakov appeared, to the menacing sounds of a march, under the red beam of the searchlights. He went up to each character frozen immobile in 'The Mute Scene' in turn, and as a final verdict pronounced Gogol's character-sketch of the type in question.

This conclusion, like the 'leap-frog of kings' in Kurbas's finale to *Macbeth*, suddenly extended the play's limits and placed a sombre ellipsis at the end of the mischievous Terentiev vaudeville.

While the production received a hostile reception from Leningrad critics, it was greeted much more sympathetically on tour in Moscow. In particular, one of the Moscow reviews pointed out that 'many parts of the Gogol text, lost in both the Academic and Meyerhold renderings, had sounded fresh, cogent and convincing in the Terentiev *The Government Inspector*.'[68]

Six months later Terentiev presented the Leningrad public with one more surprise: he staged *Natalia Tarpova*, the play which Tairov had tried in vain to master in Moscow. Terentiev subsequently explained the secret of his success very simply: he 'presented an ironic interpretation of Semenov's novel', while Tairov had been defeated because he tried to interpret the novel 'heroically'.[69] At the theatre of the Journalists' Club the melodramatic conflicts presented in earnest significance in Semenov's novel were indeed almost parodied. The ironic reading of the text prompted a corresponding style of acting: in *Natalia Tarpova* a gentle psychological shading of the characters was employed with a light, but persistent, exaggerated tone, a certain excess of emotion and a barely perceptible bombast. But the principal deployment of irony, where parody acquired complete freedom, had hitherto been unknown in the serious theatre. Terentiev had the actors speak all the author's stage directions as well as large, unaltered chunks of Semenov's narrative text. For example, before delivering Tarpova's lines to Gabrukh, the actress spoke at length – in the third person – about what Tarpova was thinking, what she was feeling, what she wanted and had resolved not to say and so forth. This device, previously only employed in specifically parodic performances, 'nine times out of ten produces an irresistibly comic effect,' noted a reviewer.[70]

Subsequently, in the 1960s and 1970s in the Moscow Taganka Theatre, Terentiev's method of merging the narrative with direct speech was revived (or re-invented) and used frequently but in a different key, and now it did not by any means provoke laughter.

Yet another of Tairov's interesting innovations in the production of *Natalia Tarpova* was a large, tilted mirror with which the inventive

Emilia Ink as Sappho in Semenov's *Natalia Tarpova*, directed by Terentiev in the Journalists' Club, 1929.

director sought to imitate a cinema frame that could expressively augment the action on stage. In the mirror were reflected whole episodes, performed behind the scenery, behind a screen outside the audience's field of vision and nonetheless visible to them. The train compartment where the engineer was riding and conversing with his fellow traveller suddenly appeared in the mirror above a room in Gabrukh's flat; the audience saw both the compartment and Gabrukh's flat, and his wife patiently waiting for her husband to return.

The action progressed synchronously and simultaneously on two planes – Terentiev made his parody stereoscopically capacious. 'The carriage and the flat,' recalled the writer Gennady Gor, 'were two poles, two different dimensions. Reflected in the mirror, the interior of the sleeping car came into relief, like a detail in Olesha's prose. The everyday trivialities of life were shown as if through a magnifying glass. On stage Semenov's novel suddenly became polyphonic.' Terentiev was able 'to show life in full swing, moving, in cross-section, in all its aspects, life as it always is on the street and at home, yet hardly ever on the stage.'[71]

There were talented actors at the theatre of the Journalists' Club. Some of them, in particular the star of the company, Emilia Ink, followed Terentiev when he left Leningrad to organize a travelling theatre in the Ukraine. But this new enterprise did not catch on. Terentiev's experimental work was not popular with the audiences of Dnepropetrovsk, Zhitomir, Vinnitsa, and so he decided to try his hand at cinema. His theatrical career came to an unexpectedly abrupt end.

Mikhail Sokolovsky and the 'TRAM Movement'

Igor Terentiev's fame was sensational but brief. Another Leningrader, Mikhail Sokolovsky, commanded attention for a much longer period and turned many young heads. He had enthusiastic imitators in nearly every city, genuinely convinced that they were fulfilling great tasks.

Everything developed from small beginnings. Sokolovsky led one of the utterly unremarkable factory drama groups, in which young workers performed short dramatizations on current local issues in the factory club. The recitation of verse alternated with choral songs, dances, athletic mimes. Sometimes the amateurs organized theatrical street processions corresponding to the forms of the 'living newspaper' of the time. But the 'living newspaper' had died out by the mid 1920s. Sokolovsky then conceived the idea of turning the amateur group into a larger-scale amateur theatre. In 1925 he organized the Leningrad Theatre of Young Workers (TRAM).

The theatre's programme presupposed that only productions dedicated to the lives of young workers would be produced on its stage, and that only the young workers themselves would collectively create these productions, writing the plays and performing them as well. TRAM's stage categorically renounced the desire to have anything in common with 'real' theatres: the plays of professional dramatists and the skills of professional actors were both rejected. The members of TRAM had no intention either of learning from them or imitating them. They intended to create a different art, the principal distinguishing feature of which would be the indissoluble link between the young people's stage and the contemporary, real lives of young people working in factories.

This link was to be guaranteed by the simple circumstance that the TRAM actors did not give up their production work. During the day they stood by the machines, and in the evenings prepared or performed their productions, plays composed by them in which they were both the characters and the performers.

Sokolovsky wanted the theatrical action to be a picture drawn directly from life, so that it would actively intervene in the work and everyday life of the young workers, express their vital interests, prompt the resolution of the questions disturbing those same young people who were participating in the action. In other words, the theatre was conceived above all as an instrument capable of introducing correctives into reality, amending and improving it. Sokolovsky therefore declared that TRAM was not art at all but something more important: 'the means of organization of young people's everyday lives.' Sokolovsky stipulated that there must be no histrionics whatsoever on the TRAM stage: 'the working lad plays himself', does not perform as an actor but as an 'excited public speaker'.[72]

The Leningrad TRAM gained popularity surprisingly quickly. The young authors of the plays, who had rallied round Sokolovsky – Arkady Gorbenko, Nikolai Lvov, Pavel Marinchik and others – all came from a workers' milieu and were completely inexperienced, so their works tended to be undemanding comedies or primitive melodramas. But these naive compositions in actual fact broached pointed and at times even painful questions which disturbed the young people. The authors of TRAM's plays introduced into theatrical usage a profusion of slang used by youth at that time, and some expressions even figured in the titles of productions, which of course appealed to the youthful audience. Sokolovsky, ardently preaching TRAM's independence from professional theatres and proclaiming far and wide the spontaneity and freshness in the acting of the 'working lads', completely untrained in acting technique, revealed in his productions the great inventiveness, resourcefulness and imagination of a born director. He himself had a superb command of the tricks of the theatrical trade but did not wish to admit this, preferring to create the impression that he worked by intuition and guess-work, and was guided only by the burning relevance of the chosen theme. Nonetheless he drilled the 'working lads' persistently enough, teaching them to sing and dance, achieving athletic dexterity and sculptural control of movement.

Sokolovsky's first productions – *Crazy Sashka* by Gorbenko, *The Bourgeois Woman* by Marinchik and *The Days are Melting* by Lvov – were captivating in their freshness and immediately won the heart of the Leningrad youth who filled TRAM's little hall every evening and stormily applauded 'their own' actors. The press ardently supported the success of Leningrad TRAM. Sokolovsky's experiment therefore stimulated a great host of imitations. Theatres of young workers sprang up everywhere, in Moscow, Vladivostok, Kharkov, Rostov-on-Don, Sverdlovsk, Baku, Minsk, Samara, copying Sokolovsky's methods and often the Leningrad TRAM's repertoire too. In 1928 the number of TRAMs in the country was eleven; in 1930 there were already seventy. The term 'the TRAM Movement' began to appear on the pages of newspapers and journals and attempts at the theoretical interpretation of this phenomenon were undertaken. Lunacharsky was inclined to the idea that TRAM 'is an agitational propagandistic institute', 'an instrument of youth's self-awareness', but he advised that it should not be afraid of the experience of the professional theatre; on the contrary, it could learn quite a bit from both Stanislavsky and Meyerhold: 'there's nothing wrong with that.'[72] Adrian Piotrovsky held another opinion: he supposed that the TRAM movement inevitably heralded 'a thorough and fundamental reconstruction of theatre both as a whole and in its parts,' that TRAM opened previously unprecedented prospects to the art of the stage and 'must itself initiate a new system of theatrical spectacles radically opposed to traditional theatre'.[74]

In other words in the second half of the 1920s some critics and theoreticians placed the same hopes on the 'TRAM movement' that had been placed on 'mass pageants' during the years of 'war Communism'. Both then and now the theoreticians were particularly inspired by the participation in productions of workers who had not left the factory. The principle 'at the machine by day, on stage by night' was attractive not only because it ensured art's ostensibly stable link with life, but further because it seemed to herald the reverse link also – the immediate and direct influence of art on life. The great temptation to turn the stage into a powerful means of life-construction, the reformation of social reality, which in their time had allured Vyacheslav Ivanov and, later, the agents of Proletkult, again troubled the theoreticians.

However, theatre professionals regarded the 'TRAM movement' with great calm, either with indifference or benevolence. Unlike other avant-gardist experiments, Sokolovsky's productions shocked no one. For all the apparent radical nature of his programme, it was not perceived as a threat by professional directors and actors and did not alarm them in the least. There was even sympathy towards TRAM within the academic theatres. And when the company of the Leningrad TRAM in full strength, supported by its admirers and proponents, organized something like a protest demonstration on the square in front of the Academic Theatre's building (an eye-witness recalled that 'an enormous iron fist towered upwards on a lorry accompanying the demonstration') to the great disappointment of the 'insurgents', the chief director of the Academic Drama Theatre, Nikolai Petrov, 'came out onto the square' to meet them, glanced with a smile at the 'iron fist' and 'said something sympathetic'.[75]

Such condescending sympathy was explained by the fact that the avant-gardism of the TRAM movement was extremely moderate, if not spurious, and its 'leftism' was not new. The productions usually had no scenery or just simple wooden constructions, they were accompanied by light music and dialogues alternated with songs, dances and sometimes athletic mimes. Light and sound effects were employed in relatively moderate doses. The general tone was invariably cheerful, the general atmosphere more or less carefree. The familiar, tried and tested devices of 'leftist theatre' were used again on TRAM stages, although in a simplified, toned-down form adapted to the naive youthful comedy, or even to crude melodrama invariably crowned by a 'happy ending'. An almost obligatory attribute of the TRAM productions were the slogans written in large letters on red banners: the idea behind the work was declared through such elementary means. The short scenes in which the 'working lads played themselves' or appeared as 'excited public speakers' illustrated and commented upon this idea.

The lack of pretension, simplicity and unambiguous clarity of the theatrical form furthered the popularity of the TRAM productions. Time and again their characters turned to the auditorium, inviting the audience to judge who was right, who was wrong, to support the progressive and hiss at the recalcitrant. The young audience responded eagerly and happily to these invitations. They did not notice the TRAM actors' somewhat artificially animated acting style, accepted at face value the highly wrought liveliness of the crowd scenes. Furthermore, the spectators were undoubtedly excited by the subject matter, so near to their own experience: the play *Crazy Sashka* dealt with the struggle against hooliganism; *The Bourgeois Woman* with the question of which is preferable – 'free love' or marriage; *The Days are Melting* with the everyday problems encountered by a young family, and so forth. After performances there were often passionate debates devoted to these burning issues.

But the experienced professionals knew very well that the art of TRAM was indelibly stamped with amateurism, dilettantism and that it did not bring anything fundamentally new. Mikhail Sokolovsky apparently understood this as well. In any case, in 1928 he suddenly took a decisive step which surprised and puzzled all the disciples of the TRAM movement and greatly confounded its theoreticians. On Sokolovsky's initiative the Leningrad TRAM became a professional theatre. The 'working lads' and 'factory lasses' left their shop floors. Henceforward they received their wages as actors. Moreover, Sokolovsky no longer insisted on absolute rejection of the experience of the professional theatre; on the contrary, he and his closest assistants, the directors Firs Shishigin and Rafail Suslovich, now expressed a willingness to learn a little from such professionals as Meyerhold. But, as before, they considered it their duty to wage war against 'theatrical academicism' and as before declared that classical plays could not be tolerated in TRAM's repertoire 'because their content could not correspond in any way to the content of the Komsomol's work.'[76]

The transfer on to the professional rails enabled Sokolovsky to develop and enrich his work. Two productions were given in succession – in 1928 the operetta *Friendly Hillock* and in 1929 the drama *The Pensive Dandy* – which noticeably surpassed all previous TRAM productions in their gracefulness of form and mastery of acting.

The operetta *Friendly Hillock*, by the composers Vladimir Deshevov and Nikolai Dvorikov, was performed over 500 times; its success was not explained by anything fundamentally innovative in this work but, on the contrary, by the attempt to adapt old, proven devices to the subject matter of contemporary youth. 'The most notable thing about this operetta,' wrote the music critic M. Yankovsky, 'is that *Friendly Hillock* does not retreat an inch from the formula established by the recipes of the Viennese cuisine.' Each of the banal characters in the Viennese operetta is simply presented 'in a new wrapping'. This is 'one of the reasons why the production is attractive'.[77] Another reason lay in the light, spontaneous and humorous style of performance which Sokolovsky this time attained. The acting was conducted merrily, jauntily, with verve.

Nikolai Lvov's play *The Pensive Dandy*, on the contrary, aspired to seriousness. The author defined it as 'a dialectical performance in three rings', thereby clearly displaying his willingness to follow the 'dialectical method' which the influential RAPP theoreticians were earnestly propounding. However, the deliberately 'intellectual' tone of Lvov's composition did not prevent Sokolovsky from presenting for the first time a genuinely new form of production. Igor Vuskovich, the designer, built two rotating semi-circular cylinders on the stage. 'By turning first the convex side then the concave side toward the auditorium,' explained A. Piotrovsky, 'these cylinders distinguish indoor and outdoor episodes.' An enormous mirror, like Terentiev's in *Natalia Tarpova*, was suspended above the cylinders. It did not, however, serve to show events occurring at the same time in another place, but the shift of action to another time: in the gigantic mirror pictures of the past, recollections, suddenly intruded. The 'intrusions' gave Sokolovsky's production a distinctive stereoscopic clarity of visual spectacle and polyphonic quality of sound.

Just after the première of *The Pensive Dandy* in 1929, for the first time Sokolovsky staged at the Leningrad TRAM a play by a professional dramatist from the repertoire of a professional theatre – Alexander Bezymensky's satirical comedy *The Shot*. Sokolovsky's production was just as successful as Meyerhold's production of the same play in Moscow. But this success meant that the Leningrad TRAM had finally rejected the pretension to the special position of being specifically a youth theatre, totally isolated from the rest of theatrical life.

Following the Leningrad TRAM, others turned professional one after another. Their members wanted to study acting technique from the professionals. In Moscow the Zamoskvoretsky TRAM invited two Vakhtangov men, Boris Zakhava and Iosif Tolchanov, to be their leaders. Members of MAT, Ilya Sudakov, Nikolai Khmelev, Nikolai Batalov and Nikolai Gorchakov, headed the Moscow Central TRAM. Directors from the Academic Theatre of Drama, Vladimir Kozhich and Natalia Rashevskaya, came to assist Sokolovsky at the Leningrad TRAM. They were going to teach the TRAM members according to Stanislavsky's 'System' but soon became convinced that the former 'working lads' who believed they had become actors were not ready for such lessons – they had no knowledge of the rudiments of theatrical grammar. It was decided to send almost the whole company of the Leningrad TRAM to a theatrical school.

Such was the finale of the TRAM movement. It was summed up sorrowfully by Adrian Piotrovsky, who had so recently believed that the theatres of working youth were destined completely to transform the theatrical art. Now he wrote that the success of TRAM's best productions 'achieved despite the actors' want of skill, thanks to the talent, energy and optimism of the theatre and the youth that had created it, were fraught with very great dangers.

'To TRAM's old weaknesses, to lack of culture and "leftist excess", new weaknesses were added: an intolerant conviction that theirs was the exclusively correct path, that TRAM had a kind of "providential" role to play in all Revolutionary art. The next stage was a blindness to the growth of the surrounding theatre and to criticism of its own mistakes. This led to self-absorption and isolation, a kind of "sectarianism". This in turn led to a self-opinionated refusal to learn from the art of the past and the present.'[78]

Subsequently, on the basis of the TRAM collectives, the Lenin Komsomol Theatres in Moscow and Leningrad were created. They exist to this day.

The 'Magnifying Glass' of Comedy

In the comic repertoire of the mid 1920s, satire was ousted by humour. Sharp, lashing, wrathful notes were seldom to be heard and the dominant tone was one of relative benevolence.

The Satire Theatre, which opened in Moscow in 1924, did not justify its name: the jokes were funny but toothless. The company of the newly formed theatre established itself in the basement of the former Nirenzee house in one of the lanes off Tverskaya (now Gorky) Street, the location that had housed Nikita Baliev's famous cabaret theatre The Bat, and seemed to have inherited its frivolity. The actors who united to form the company at the Satire Theatre had previously worked in various cabarets and theatres of miniatures (The Crooked Jimmy, The Grotesque, Don't Sob, Bi-Ba-Bo and others). Even the most talented among them, Rina Zelenaya, Fedor Kurikhin, Pavel Pol, Dmitri Kara-Dmitriev, Rafail Korf – and these were marvellous comics – had become accustomed to the brevity of the light entertainment 'number', the sketch, the humoresque. They could not perform full-length plays. But on the other hand they had splendid success with quick, sharply caricaturized 'sketches from life', and the audience burst out laughing as soon as an actor appeared on stage. The theatre's chief director, David Gutman, realized that his company was not suited to whole, multi-act plays, but to divertissements consisting of individual short scenes, stories, brief comic sketches. But Gutman tried to impart unity, if only thematic, to every new programme. Thus there developed the genre of the 'revue' which, however, possessed neither the large scale nor passion of Meyerhold's 'political revues', but on the whole inclined toward gibes at NEP-men (traders, speculators), embezzlers, petty swindlers, negligent housing managers and so on. Such 'revues' at the Satire Theatre as *A View of Moscow, Keep Still – I'm Taking a Picture, Concerning Love, Current Affairs, Contest for the Best Family* and others displayed Gutman's orientation towards entertaining or, as he liked to say, 'smiling' art.

At first the public displayed great interest in these productions and soon the theatre even opened a subsidiary, performing on two stages every evening. Gutman also attempted to stage 'real', full-length plays. The best of these were composed by Viktor Ardov in collaboration with Lev Nikulin. Their comedies *Clause 114, The Squabble* and *Cockroachism* were witty and humorous but nonetheless superficial.

The experience of the Moscow Art Theatre provided convincing evidence that audiences apparently liked 'smiling' superficiality. In 1928 the MAT produced in succession *Untilovsk* by Leonid Leonov, a rather darkly ironic drama inclined toward hyperbole and the grotesque; *The Embezzlers* by Valentin Kataev, a satirical comedy; and, finally, *Squaring the Circle*, also by Kataev, a carefree and feckless vaudeville. And although the most famous MAT actors – Moskvin, Luzhsky, Tarkhanov and Lilina – performed in the first two plays, *Untilovsk* ran only twenty times, *The Embezzlers* eighteen, while *Squaring the Circle*, as staged by Nikolai Gorchakov and performed by young actors, lasted for nearly ten seasons and enjoyed 650 performances.

The Studio of the Maly Theatre in Moscow directed by Fedor Kaverin became yet one more comic oasis at that time. Although he had graduated from the school attached to the Maly Theatre and from his youth had regarded the traditions of the House of Ostrovsky with respect and admiration, it was Vakhtangov's art that attracted Kaverin and the artistic youth grouped around him, and so he sought to 'theatricalize' the traditions of the Maly Theatre in the spirit of Vakhtangov.

Kaverin was the first to discover and appreciate the great talent of the comic writer Vasily Shkvarkin. Shkvarkin's plays *The Harmful Element* and *The Cheat*, staged by Kaverin, derisively portrayed smooth operators and tricksters trying to adapt to the new social conditions, to swindle everywhere, twist everyone round their little finger, grow rich without working. The satirical purpose of Shkvarkin's comedies, though, was weakened to a certain extent by the mischievous play of hyperboles by which Kaverin was seduced. In the production of *The Cheat*, for instance, the characters spinning round on a carousel, appeared to double and treble (three identically dressed actors played one part). Kaverin was fascinated not so much by the typical or even socially precise as by everything surprising, unusual, effective. And this is why the 'tragi-comedy of the petit-bourgeoisie' offered by Shkvarkin with his customary accuracy of observation and aphoristic, hard-hitting dialogue slipped in Kaverin's production into a chimerical grotesque inspired by Vakhtangov's production of Chekhov's *The Wedding*.

In the meantime, the Vakhtangov company itself had lost its former taste for the grotesque. Mikhail Bulgakov's comedy *Zoika's Apartment*, staged at the Vakhtangov Theatre by the director Alexei Popov, was brilliant and stylish in its execution. The main roles were played by Tsetsilia Mansurova as Zoika and Ruben Simonov as Ametistov, and in addition the performance employed Boris Shchukin, Elizaveta Alexeeva, Anna Orochko, Anatoly Goryunov, Viktor Koltsov – almost all of the company's best actors. But the unrestrained playfulness of their acting betrayed a naively idealistic certainty that the social vices depicted by Bulgakov were easily eradicable. If the innocent front of a dressmaker's salon covered a high-class brothel where well-to-do Moscow ladies sold their bodies, respected public figures indulged in debauchery and former aristocrats abandoned themselves to drug addiction, then all this was temporary, short-lived even, all this was the 'intoxicating fumes of NEP' which would soon disperse. Light-winged humour fluttered over the Vakhtangov stage.

Satire, however, did make its presence felt at the very end of the 1920s, when Meyerhold produced Mayakovsky's comedies *The Bed-bug* (1929) and *The Bath-house* (1930). If these plays are compared with even Romashov's *Soufflé* and Erdman's *Warrant*, then it immediately becomes obvious where their fundamental newness lies. The satire of Romashov and Erdman fell upon 'yesterday's men', scourged the 'remnants of the past', mocked the attempts to adapt by those who had either been destroyed by the Revolution or thrown by

it on to the scrap-heap of history. But Mayakovsky dared to direct the 'magnifying glass' of his satire at those for whom the Revolution had cleared the way and to whom it had given power.

Prisypkin, the hero of the 'magical comedy' *The Bed-bug* is characterized in the cast list as follows: 'former worker, former party member, now a bridegroom.' Prisypkin is of 'impeccable proletarian origin' and in the new Soviet State he feels the complete master. Those bourgeoisie whom Erdman portrayed in *The Warrant* sought to hide from the new life in any crevice. Prisypkin however is aggressive and stops at nothing, believing that the Revolution occurred so that he can satisfy his 'major requirements' unimpeded. Consciousness of his own strength and supposedly 'conquered' right to the 'good life', gives Prisypkin a boldness the like of which Pavel Gulyachkin from *The Warrant* or even Semyon Rak from *The Soufflé* could never even contemplate.

Pobedonosikov in the *Bath-house*, similarly, is not a figure from the 'accursed past' of the pre-Revolutionary period. He is, at least on the surface, a completely new Soviet man, proudly acting on behalf of 'government personnel' and boasting that he is establishing 'socialism in the brilliant foot-steps of Karl Marx and as prescribed by the Centre'. The words are new, the essence is old. The bureaucrat formed under the new social conditions is hardly distinguished from any head of a civil service department in Gogol, Sukhovo-Kobylin or Shchedrin. As if to complete the similarity, alongside Pobedonosikov Mayakovsky places his secretary Optimistenko, a fat pen-pusher. Both these bureaucrats are capable of burying any matter in a mountain of words, papers, resolutions. Through all this both of them, in complete accordance with the surnames given to them by the poet (Pobedonosikov is Victorman; Optimistenko, McOptimist) constantly deliver optimistic and triumphant tirades at the drop of a hat.

In his staging of Mayakovsky's play Meyerhold treated the text lovingly and carefully and did not change a single line, or make any rearrangements or abbreviations. To the astonishment of many critics, he compared Mayakovsky to Molière, Pushkin and Gogol. The director enthused particularly over Mayakovsky's great and sweeping parody of contemporary theatre in the third act of *The Bath-house*. Along with the Bolshoi Theatre, where 'they always make it beautiful for us', Mayakovsky ridiculed the MAT: 'Yes, yes, yes! Have you seen *Squaring the Cherry*? And I was at *Uncle of the Turbins*. Amazingly interesting.' The poet ironically placed *The Cherry Orchard* on a par with Valentin Kataev's *Squaring the Circle*; *Uncle Vanya* on a par with Mikhail Bulgakov's *Days of the Turbins*. He believed that time was passing but the Moscow Art Theatre was not changing at all, was aging, remaining a theatre of Chekhovian intonations. He was wrong on this point, for it would have been more accurate to say – and many were saying so loudly – that the forms of expression of 'leftist' theatre had quickly become obsolete.

But the agit-play also became a target of parody in *The Bath-house*. The director (a character in the play) commanded: 'Free male cast – onto the stage! Stand on one knee and bend over with an enslaved look. Swing an invisible pickaxe at invisible coal. Faces, faces more gloomy. . . The dark forces are savagely oppressing you. . . . Stand over here, Comrade Capital. Dance above everyone with an air of class supremacy.'

If the Moscow Art, the Bolshoi, Kamerny and all theatres generally where 'things were made beautiful', if the 'psycholatry' of individuals living in 'apartment cages' were not necessary to anyone, and the 'mass pageant' and agit-play had degenerated, been vulgarized, then where, in what direction was the theatre of Mayakovsky and Meyerhold intending to go?

Mayakovsky's new comedies were an attempt to provide the answer to this question. In place of the social masks of *Mystery-Bouffe* with its allegories and theatrically stylized characters, monumental types appeared – Prisypkin, Bayan, Pobedonosikov, Optimistenko and others, captured with all their specific life-like qualities, but, as one of the poet's most active opponents of the day, the critic Vladimir Yermilov, expressed it, 'giganticized'.

The fact that in both *The Bed-bug* and *The Bath-house* the liberation from the Prisypkins and Pobedonosikovs is linked with a hope in the people of the distant future, with the theme of a future social Utopia, is highly significant. The technique of shifting the action into the future permitted an optimistic prognosis to be made 'beyond the parameters' of modern times.

The Bed-bug opened successfully in 1929. Meyerhold's directorial plan divided the show into two distinct parts: the first part, contemporary, was designed by the still very young but subsequently widely known artists who called themselves the Kukryniksy (Mikhail *Kupriyanov*, Porfiry *Krylov*, Nikolai *Sokolov*). They created a photographically precise section of Petrovka Street, familiar to every Muscovite, near the entrance to the department store, and here Meyerhold brought together in a picturesque crush dozens of oddly dressed street traders with their diverse wares. Prisypkin, Bayan and Madame Renaissance appeared for the first time in this crowd. Later in the crowded scene of the 'Red wedding' Meyerhold created a genuine bourgeois bacchanalia. The director's imagination ran wild and each of Mayakovsky's lines became a pretext for witty mime. First one, then another character in the crowd scene acquired a solo part in this most complex score of an unbridled orgy, seizing the attention of the audience. The binge quickly turned into a fracas, the fracas into a brawl. The fight took over the entire stage and suddenly a great tongue of flame leaped out from behind the piano. A fire blazed up.

A stormy, grotesque musical interlude by Dmitri Shostakovich concluded the first part of the performance, then the action was transferred fifty years ahead into the future.

Alexander Rodchenko designed the pictures of the future, creating a humorously fantastic image of the sterile, silvery-white gleaming shine of gadgets, dials and lights of signal lamps, a completely mechanized life. Against this background the slovenly, fat figure of the 'resurrected' Prisypkin (Igor Ilinsky) produced a particularly strong comic effect.

However, many critics thought that in *The Bed-bug* Mayakovsky and Meyerhold were mistakenly 'inflating' the danger of the petit-bourgeoisie. Especially hostile to the play's satire were the activists of the Russian Association of Proletarian Writers (RAPP). RAPP stood against satire in principle. Mayakovsky and Meyerhold were accused of the 'artificial magnification' of the phenomena they portrayed and of unjustified intent to portray an 'individual case' as something typical. Furthermore the means of expression employed by the director and poet appeared in the view of some critics crude and primitive, in the style of the placard.

Almost thirty years later one of the leaders of RAPP, the writer Yury Libedinsky recalled, 'Mayakovsky criticized us for "psychologism" and we criticized him for reducing the task of art to the agit-play and placard. . . . It seemed to us then that Mayakovsky was

exaggerating when he stressed in *The Bed-bug* the "problem of the exposure of today's petit-bourgeoisie", and that the petit-bourgeoisie was finished forever. Now it is evident that we were wrong on this question, and Mayakovsky was right.'[79]

However, the question of the interrelationship between the 'agit-play' and the 'placard' on the one hand and the art of psychological theatre on the other, at the very end of the 1920s was not at all such a simple one.

As has already been mentioned, in *The Bath-house* the Moscow Art Theatre was ridiculed along with the bureaucrats. And the audiences, who, like Mayakovsky, also hated bureaucrats, unlike him, loved the MAT very much, and this devotion grew stronger with every year. While far from all the productions played to a full house at the State Meyerhold Theatre in the late 1920s, tickets at the MAT sold out immediately and in advance. People queued all night in any kind of weather at the box office in the passage of the Art Theatre. The numerous attacks against the MAT in both the text of *The Bath-house* and on the posters hung during the performance evoked no sympathy whatsoever among audiences.

In the decade that had passed since the première of *Mystery-Bouffe*, the situation had changed. If the audiences of *Mystery-Bouffe* had been prepared to believe that all old theatres were 'hostile', 'bourgeois' and that a war must be waged against them, then the audiences of *The Bath-house* perceived the Maly and the Moscow Art Theatre as their own theatres. The call to replace 'the MATs' with the 'mass pageant' did not inspire them in the least.

Moreover, Meyerhold's staging of *The Bath-house* was much less successful than that of *The Bed-bug*. Rehearsals were difficult, with all kinds of complications. Mayakovsky wanted Ilinsky to play Pobedonosikov, but Ilinsky did not like the play and refused the part, which was given to another actor, Maxim Shtraukh. The staging was simple but not particularly expressive. The heavy comfort of Pobedonosikov's office with its enormous leather chair and numerous telephones was sharply contrasted to the light staircase with three flights of steps which the heroes ascended into the future; the entirely contemporary costumes of the bureaucratic officials were contrasted to the *prozodezhda* of the inventors and the tightly fitting jumpsuit and aviator helmet of the Phosphorescent Woman played by Zinaida Raikh; the bureaucratic prose of the present was contrasted with the fantasy and poetry of the future.

But Sergei Vakhtangov's hastily arranged 'construction' creaked, and the noise of the moving pavement and the overly loud music drowned the text. In terms of acting the production was less successful than *The Bed-bug*. The première dragged. 'As usual Mayakovsky imperiously and sweepingly roamed around the semi-circular foyer of the bleak, cold theatre. This time he tried in vain to conceal his agitation. The show finished in confusion. . . . Backstage,' recalled Markov, 'I didn't see the usual excitement of a première. Zinaida Raikh was gloomily removing her make-up in the dressing room, Meyerhold was pacing about, not in the least inclined to accept the customary congratulations.'[80]

According to the actress Maria Sukhanova, Mayakovsky himself 'said that the show was a flop; he was unsettled, gloomy.'[81]

The failure of *The Bath-house* meant that 'leftist art' was losing influence. This greatly delighted RAPP activists who perceived the failure of Mayakovsky's comedy as proving the truth of RAPP's theory that 'satire was dying out'.

Their triumph was, however, short-lived.

RAPP and Theatre. The 'Indoor' and 'Outdoor' Debate

The numerous literary groups which sprang up during the 1920s as a rule displayed no interest in theatre, but RAPP was the exception. Perhaps because its leaders included the dramatists Alexander Afinogenov and Vladimir Kirshon alongside the prose writers Dmitri Furmanov and Alexander Fadeev, perhaps simply because RAPP had pretensions to a monopoly in all cultural spheres, this mighty organization did not let theatre escape its attention.

The members of RAPP proposed to introduce the method of 'dialectical materialism' as the foundation of 'proletarian' theatre, insisting that the representation of the struggle between the hero's 'conscious' and 'subconscious' was essential to any work of art. Afinogenov devoted a special booklet, published in 1931, to the basis of these ideas – *The Theatre's Creative Method: The Dialectic of the Creative Process*. The book was academic and obscure. It meant nothing to theatre people. Mechanically transferring philosophical categories to the field of artistic creativity, RAPP theoreticians appealed to actors 'to perform dialectically'.[82] But actors did not understand what this meant.

In the so-called RAPP 'theatrical document' – a verbose declaration of 'RAPP's tasks on the theatrical front' published in 1931 – the Moscow Art Theatre was denounced as 'conservative', 'idealistic', 'metaphysical'. Stanislavsky's System was rejected since it supposedly entailed the justification 'of the class enemy from the position of people's biological equality'. In Meyerhold's work RAPP saw 'a fascination for technology and machinery', 'the substitution of technology for ideology' and 'reactionary restoration-like tendencies'. They charged Tairov with 'petit-bourgeois subjectivism', found a 'mystical, idealistic root' in Vakhtangov and so forth.[83] The RAPP 'theatrical document' in fact negated all the successes of Soviet drama of the 1920s without putting forward anything resembling a realistic programme of action in their place.

Confused theoreticians, the leaders of RAPP were careful politicians capable of employing the old 'divide and rule' tactic. They designated certain writers, artists and theatre workers 'proletarian' and recognized them unconditionally; they graciously agreed to regard others as the proletariat's 'fellow travellers' and criticized them in a relatively moderate tone; and they declared a third group 'enemies' for whom there was no mercy. Bulgakov, Trenev, Lavrenev, Romashov, Faiko and others were vilified in the press. They all learned the meaning of the 'RAPP bludgeon'. After he had been attacked, Mayakovsky announced that he was moving from LEF to RAPP. In November 1928 the artist Viktor Shestakov wrote to Meyerhold: 'Yesterday in the Polytechnical Museum, a month after Mayakovsky, the Briks, Aseevs and Kirsanovs organized a public repentance at which they surrendered their LEF weapons and left the group.' Shestakov believed that 'the majority were completely confused,'[84] and it has to be said that he was not far from the truth. Almost everyone realized that 'leftist art' had exhausted its potential, that a shift in a new direction was inevitable, but almost no one believed that it could be rescued by the method of 'dialectical materialism' zealously recommended and even imposed by RAPP.

In 1929 in the Leningrad Academic Theatre of Drama the directors Nikolai Petrov and Leonid Vivien staged a play called *The Heights* by one of the leaders of RAPP, Yury Libedinsky. It proved an embarrassment. Libedinsky attempted to show how people, individually far from perfect, individually torn by conflicts between the 'conscious' (sound) and the 'subconscious' (dubious), together become unified in the collective, become 'a united will' striving for a beautiful future. It was a complete fiasco. Libedinsky declared he was against 'vulgar oversimplification', against 'ultra-radicalism' and 'shrill leftist' theatre; and the directors promised to seek subtleties 'in the contemporary rendering of the psychological scenes'. But all this mountain of declarations produced an utterly boring production. And although reviews were deferentially servile (critics were obviously afraid to undermine the authority of Libedinsky, one of the RAPP 'generals'), *The Heights* did not last in the repertoire.

Gorky, who returned to the Soviet Union in 1928, immediately waged an urgent campaign against RAPP. To a significant degree it is due to his efforts that this organization was disbanded in 1932.

The dramatists Vladimir Kirshon and Alexander Afinogenov, even after RAPP's inglorious end, continued passionately to defend the necessity for a turn to intimate, psychological drama. However, the method of 'dialectical materialism' was given up and forgotten, and the issue of the permanent struggle of the 'conscious' with the 'subconscious' was discarded. In the disputes that flared up at the start of the 1930s, another question was being debated: what kind of play does the Soviet stage need – one set 'indoors' or one set 'out of doors'? Vishnevsky and Pogodin declared themselves opponents on principle of Afinogenov and Kirshon. Arguing against the 'old forms' and asserting that 'new material requires new forms of expression,'[85] Nikolai Pogodin and Vsevolod Vishnevsky fought for the outdoor play in which the masses, large collectives, participate, and where the action is conducted not in rooms, 'indoors', but in the open air, on the battlefields, on the decks of warships, on the scaffolding of building sites, and is split up into short dynamic episodes. (In Vishnevsky's *The First Cavalry Army* there are thirty-nine episodes, in Pogodin's *Aristocrats*, twenty-five.)

Family issues and domestic troubles did not, in the opinion of Pogodin and Vishnevsky, merit the attention of the theatre. 'It is in the highest degree immaterial,' declared Pogodin, 'whether Ivan Petrovich is getting married, while it is very important whether this Communist is keeping up the struggle.'[86] Later he recalled: 'We maintained that you wouldn't find our hero at home. He's on the building site, he's in the factories.'[87]

Afinogenov and Kirshon believed, on the contrary, that the hero could and must be found 'at home', in the family circle, that the old form of family drama was not exhausted in the least. 'If the family is a part of society,' wrote Afinogenov, 'and in the family, too, as in a drop of water, social shifts and changes are reflected, then surely it is possible to resolve general questions with the family, and to show general issues through the family?'[88] Revealing an attraction for the traditions of Ibsen and Gorky, Afinogenov and Kirshon stood for drama which concentrated on the interior, was attentive to the everyday life, customs and characters of people, outwardly extremely ordinary, inwardly highly significant. Their concept was of a psychological drama, penetrating into man's soul, intimate in form, divided not into short episodes but into capacious acts and scenes (the fewer the better).

The 'indoor' question acquired the significance of a world-view. Debates were conducted not only on the pages of newspapers and magazines but also on theatrical stages, where productions were advanced as arguments. Gradually, however, it emerged that conflicting and seemingly incompatible tendencies were coming together, that these extremes too were converging, mutually enriching one another.

Storm

Until the 1925 production of Bill-Belotserkovsky's *Storm* the Moscow Trades' Union Theatre, led by Evsei Liubimov-Lansky, had dragged out a fairly miserable existence somewhere on the fringes of Moscow's theatrical life. With this play the modest collective became the centre of attention. Liubimov-Lansky's production had the precision of a documentary and the dry spareness of an official report. It presented pictures of the harshness of life during the Civil War without any romantic exaltation or lofty pathos but with a cruel veracity previously unknown on the stage. Suddenly it became clear that the very recent past, common to all and completely unembellished, could be movingly dramatic. The production was performed in simple and easily identifiable sets by Boris Volkov and the main role of the lame sailor, 'Swabbie', was played with rough humour by Vasily Vanin.

Three scenes from *Storm*.

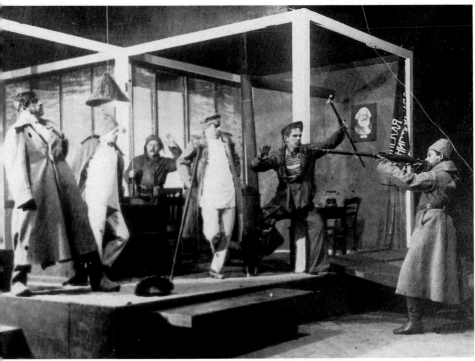

Virineya

Lidia Seifullina's story *Virineya*, popular in the 1920s, depicted the changes that took place deep in the Russian countryside after the Revolution. The story was dramatized and staged at the Vakhtangov Theatre in 1925 by the director Alexei Popov. Popov managed, with captivating humour and rare naturalness, to recreate on a metropolitan stage the village way of life, an environment in the midst of disturbing changes, the peasants greeting the social upheaval first with suspicion and then gradually, and not without difficulty, realizing the advantages that the Revolution was bringing to the poor folk of the village.

Two scenes from *Virineya*.

Opposite: A scene from *Virineya*, with E. Alexeeva as Virineya (*see also inset*) and Boris Shchukin as Pavel.

A model of the set by Nikolai Menshutin for *Liubov Yarovaya*. *Below*: The final scene.

Liubov Yarovaya

Konstantin Trenev's play *Liubov Yarovaya* (1926) was a major event in the history of the ancient Maly Theatre not only because it brought figures from the Civil War on to the traditional academic stage, but also because the conservative art of the 'House of Ostrovsky' was immediately transformed, coming into closer contact both with the contemporary audience and the newest theatrical experiments. The very fact that Nikolai Menshutin had built on a revolving stage a set that resembled a construction was in itself an innovation, completely unprecedented within the walls of the Maly Theatre. And although the pathos with which Vera Pashennaya played the title role was rather old-fashionedly romantic and the heroine's rival Panova as played by Elene Gogoleva was slightly reminiscent of a banal 'vamp', nonetheless the large crowd that seethed around the dashing and cheerful sailor Shvandya (Stepan Kuznetsov) delighted the audience with its genuine vitality.

Top: A scene from *Liubov Yarovaya*.

Left: Vera Pashennaya as Liubov Yarovaya.

Right: E. Gogoleva as Panova.

Sketch of a set by Nikolai Ulyanov for
The Days of the Turbins.

Scene from *The Days of the Turbins.*

The production of Mikhail Bulgakov's *The Days of the Turbins* (1926) at the Moscow Art Theatre provoked a storm of the most furious protests. Reviewers were indignant that the theatre should have shown interest in the inner world of people who were either hostile to the Revolution or, at best, indifferent to it – apolitical. The fact that White officers were treated with unconcealed sympathy, that their inevitable defeat was unaccompanied by the usual gloating, that the production showed anxiety over the fate of the Russian intelligentsia – all this was made grounds for accusation and criticism. However, in this particular case the opinion of the critics did not coincide with that of the public. The production by the young Ilya Sudakov with the Moscow Art Theatre's young actors – Nikolai Khmelev, Mikhail Yanshin, Vera Sokolova, Boris Dobronravov, Mikhail Prudkin and others – was a triumphant success. Khmelev, playing Alexei Turbin, gave a particularly memorable performance in the scene on the stairs of the school where he dismisses his soldiers and then dies. The play, which only the MAT was allowed to perform, remained in the repertoire until 1941 when Nikolai Ulyanov's sets were destroyed in a bombardment while on tour in Minsk.

The Days of the Turbins

Two scenes from *The Days of the Turbins*.

Sketch of a set by Nikolai Ulyanov for
The Days of the Turbins.

Opposite: Two scenes from *The Days of
the Turbins*.

Sketch by Ulyanov of Alexei Turbin's
costume.

Civil War plays

Right: Scene from the Leningrad production of *Armoured Train No. 14-69.*

Below: Scene from the Moscow production of *Armoured Train No. 14-69.*

Civil War themes, such as the behaviour of people of different classes in extreme circumstances, continued to interest the theatres for a long time. In the Moscow Art Theatre *The Days of the Turbins* was followed by two plays by Vsevolod Ivanov, *Armoured Train No. 14-69* (1927) and *Blockade* (1929); in the Vakhtangov Theatre Alexei Popov followed *Virineya* with a drama by Boris Lavrenev, *The Break* (1927).

A scene from *Blockade*.

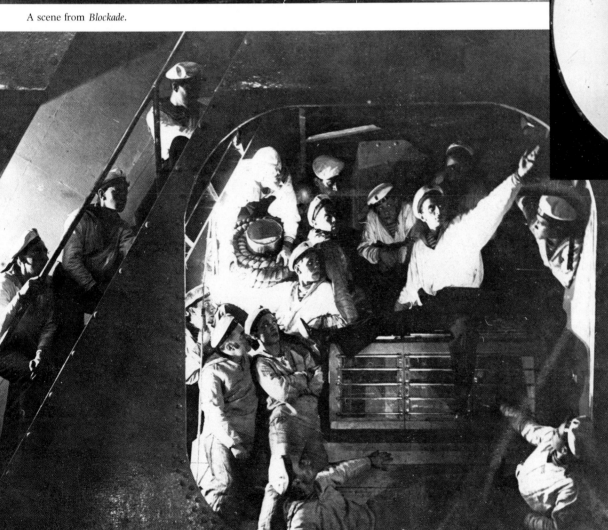

Two scenes from *The Break*.

These plays ran simultaneously in Leningrad theatres. The production of *Armoured Train No. 14-69* in the Leningrad Academic Theatre of Drama, directed by Nikolai Petrov, was more imposing in its appearance than that of Ilya Sudakov in the Moscow Art Theatre. In all the above-named productions the central problem as perceived by their directors was the relationship between the individual and the mass, the hero and the crowd. More and more often the spiritually rich personality of the thinking hero came to the fore, while the crowd merely provided a colourful background.

Le Mariage de Figaro

Beaumarchais' *Le Mariage de Figaro* was staged by Stanislavsky in 1927 with sets by Alexander Golovin. Golovin had previously worked with Meyerhold for many years and was renowned as the creator of such ravishingly beautiful productions as Molière's *Don Juan* (1910), Ostrovsky's *The Storm* (1924) and Lermontov's *Masquerade* (1917). The alliance of Stanislavsky and Golovin worked very well: Stanislavsky's infectiously amusing production of Beaumarchais' comedy acquired in Golovin's supremely elegant sets and festive costumes a satirical edge and a triumphant *joie de vivre*. Figaro (Nikolai Batalov), Suzanne (Olga Androvskaya), Count Almaviva (Yury Zavadsky), Chérubin (Alexander Komissarov), Bazile (Nikolai Podgorny) and Antonio (Mikhail Yanshin) became the favourites of the Moscow public immediately after the première. It is generally recognized as one of Stanislavsky's masterpieces.

Opposite: A scene from *Le Mariage de Figaro*. *Inset*: Yury Zavadsky as Count Almaviva.

Olga Androvskaya as Suzanne.

Nikolai Batalov as Figaro.

Nikolai Podgorny as Bazile.

A scene from *Le Mariage de Figaro*.

Mikhail Yanshin as Antonio.

222

The Government Inspector

Almost at the same time as Stanislavsky's *Le Mariage de Figaro* Meyerhold created one of his directorial masterpieces: his 1926 production of Gogol's *The Government Inspector* has entered the history of the Soviet stage as an event of enormous importance. Many of Meyerhold's decisions in his work on Gogol's play seem paradoxical. He transferred the action from the provincial backwoods to the capital city, played the comedy with tragic gloom, and placed all the characters on cramped little stage 'trucks' which moved out from the back to the very front of the stage. The figure of Khlestakov, played by Erast Garin, was demoniacally sinister. The Mayor's wife (Zinaida Raikh) and daughter (Maria Babanova) acted their roles in a frankly erotic manner which embarrassed some of the shyer critics. In addition, the critics' astonishment and wrath were provoked by Meyerhold's tampering with the Gogol text and, in particular, by the appearance on stage of some characters not invented by Gogol. The debate around the production raged for nearly two years; it was the subject of hundreds of articles and three whole books which appeared from 1927 to 1928. But finally even the most convinced opponents of this Meyerhold work were forced to admit that it initiated a completely new method for the interpretation of the classics and that the director was fully justified in taking on the mission of 'author of the production'.

Two scenes from *The Government Inspector*. *Inset above*: Erast Garin as Khlestakov.

224

Woe for Wit

Meyerhold was also called 'author of the production' on the poster announcing the première of Griboedov's *Woe from Wit* in 1928. (Meyerhold's production was called *Woe for Wit*.) Griboedov's satirical play was read as a romantic drama and Chatsky (Erast Garin), a solitary dreamer, alienated from the self-satisfied people who surrounded him, looked like a man too far ahead of his soulless time. A similar atmosphere of oppressive spiritlessness was also felt in the 1925 production of *Petersburg*, after Andrei Bely's novel of the same name, which was staged in the Second Moscow Art Theatre. Bely himself took an active part in the preparation of this production. The sets were by Mikhail Libakov, and the main role of Senator Ableukhov was played by Mikhail Chekhov with gloomy sarcasm, anger and bile.

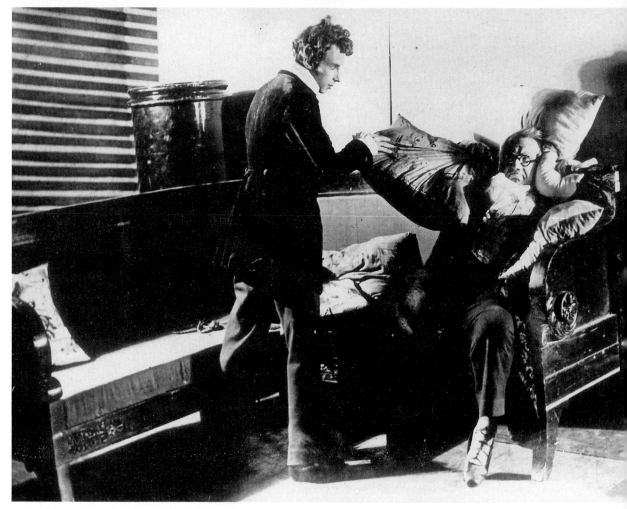

Opposite, above left: Erast Garin as Chatsky. *Above right*: A scene from *Woe for Wit*. *Below*: Erast Garin as Chatsky and Igor Ilinsky as Famusov.

Mikhail Chekhov as Ableukhov.

Costume sketches by Mikhail Libakov for *Petersburg*.

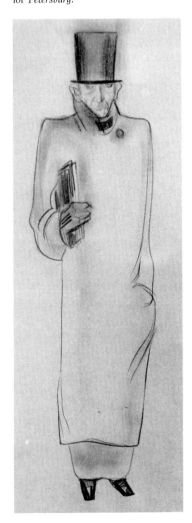

227

Evgraf

As leader of the Second Moscow Art Theatre Mikhail Chekhov was mainly orientated towards a classical repertoire. Plays based on contemporary life did not as a rule interest him. Among the few exceptions to this rule was Alexei Faiko's tragicomedy *Evgraf, Seeker of Adventures* which was produced by Boris Sushkevich in 1926. Faiko's play was in some ways reminiscent of Nikolai Erdman's *The Warrant*. His hero, the hairdresser Evgraf, a 'Soviet Figaro', recalled *The Warrant*'s hero Gulyachkin with only one significant difference: Erdman had laughed at the petit-bourgeois Gulyachkin but Faiko treated Evgraf with sympathy and compassion. The sets and costumes by Nikolai Akimov (published here for the first time) introduced a stinging irony into Sushkevich's production besides conveying the stifling atmosphere of Moscow during the NEP period.

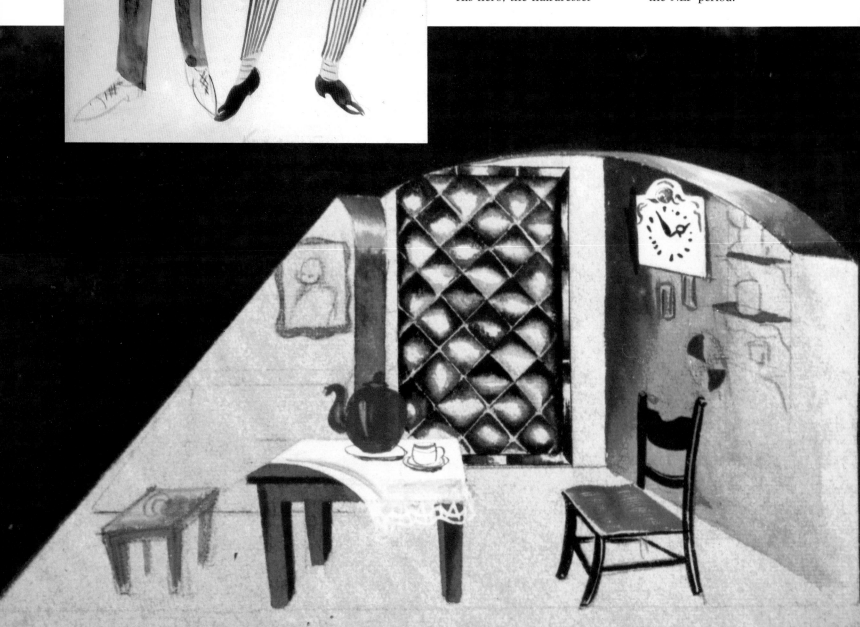

Costume designs (*opposite, above*) and set designs by Nikolai Akimov for *Evgraf, Seeker of Adventures*.

A scene from *The Man with the Briefcase*.

M. Lishin as Granatov and O. Pizhova as Xenia.

In many plays of the 1920s the authors turned their attention to what was then a burning social issue – the problem of the intelligentsia. Not infrequently dramatists were inclined to think that the intellectual must inevitably come into conflict with the new life. Professor Granatov in Faiko's play *The Man with the Briefcase*, staged by Alexei Diky at the Theatre of Revolution in 1928, is just such a secret enemy of the new social structure. In the Kamerny Theatre in 1929 Alexander Tairov tried to adapt for the stage Sergei Semenov's novel *Natalia Tarpova*, a work now totally forgotten but avidly read then. The passionate love of the factory worker Natalia Tarpova for the non-Party engineer Gabrukh (played by Alisa Koonen and Nikolai Chaplygin) is regarded as a sinful feeling which the heroine long tries to overcome. Her success in this is represented in the play as a moral victory. But audiences failed to share the joy of this triumph, the production was poorly attended and was soon taken off.

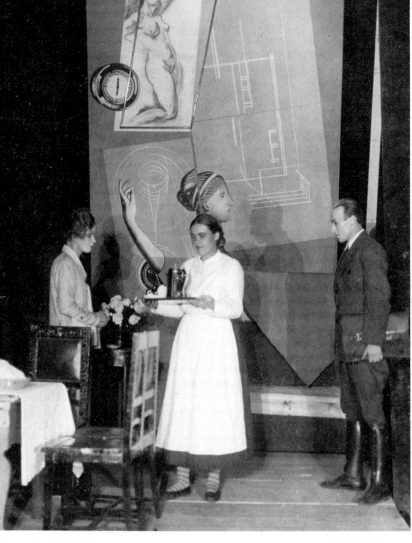

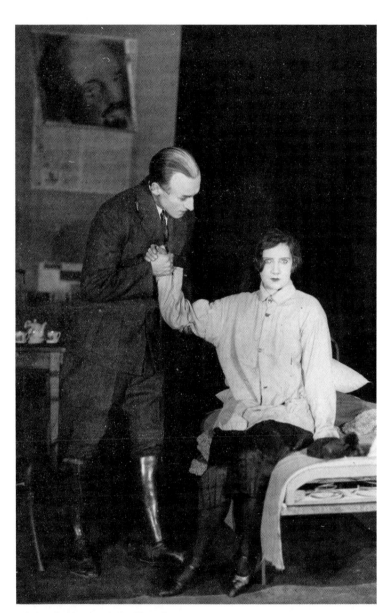

Nikolai Chaplygin as Gabrukh and
Alisa Koonen as Tarpova.

Left: Two scenes from *Natalia Tarpova*.

The Flea

Azary Azarin as 'Lefty' and Serafima Birman as Mashka.

V. Popov as the Tsar.

Against the minor-key background of the generally rather sombre repertoire of the Second Moscow Art Theatre, the adaptation of Nikolai Leskov's *The Left-Hander* exploded with unexpected laughter and anarchic mischief. The story had been turned into a play, *The Flea*, by the writer Evgeny Zamyatin and produced in 1925 by the promising young director Alexander Diky with sets by Boris Kustodiev that were stylized imitations of old Russian popular prints. The comedy in *The Flea* was deliberately crude, almost farcical, but parallel to the comic line ran the poignant theme of the mutual love between 'Lefty' (Azary Azarin) and Mashka (Serafima Birman).

A group of women who sing *chastushki* (folk songs).

Opposite: Two designs by Boris Kustodiev for *The Flea*.

Opposite: A scene from *Roar China!* (*above*) and a scene from *The Eccentric* (*below*).

In Meyerhold's 1926 production *Roar China!*, based on the play by Sergei Tretyakov, the influence of the propaganda theatre and the political placard was still very strong. Meanwhile, the public was already showing an increasing interest in the fate of the individual, his personal drama and his interaction with his social milieu. Many theatres developed to meet this interest. In particular the Second Moscow Art Theatre, in Alexander Afinogenev's play *The Eccentric* (1929), successfully depicted a modern young man who has dared to oppose the stagnant bureaucracy of local leaders. This type of conflict was exposed even more sharply and boldly by the Ukrainian writer Mikola Kulish in his tragicomedy *The People's Malakhy* produced by Les Kurbas in 1928 in his Berezil Theatre. Malakhy, played by Maryan Krushelnitsky, is a fantasist, an other-worldly preacher of love for all men, who ends up in a lunatic asylum as a result of his vain attempts to change the world. The production, designed by Vadim Meller, did not remain on the stage for long: Kulish's play was soon banned.

Two scenes from *The People's Malakhy.*

The Fate of the Individual

Eugene O'Neill at the Kamerny Theatre

In the 1920s Alexander Tairov's Kamerny Theatre staged three plays by Eugene O'Neill one after the other: *The Hairy Ape* (1926), *Desire Under the Elms* (1926) and *All God's Chillun Got Wings* (1927) (which was produced by Tairov under the title *The Negro*). These productions not only introduced O'Neill to Soviet audiences for the first time but were also the first demonstrations of his drama on the major professional stage: in Moscow, on the Tverskoi Boulevard, O'Neill was fully appreciated earlier than he was on Broadway.

All three productions were designed by the Stenberg brothers. They indicated the place of action sparely but precisely, geometrically outlining the functions of the construction which thereby acquired a concrete representational character. The deck and hold of the ocean-liner in *The Hairy Ape*, the isolated farm in *Desire Under the Elms*, a New York street in *All God's Chillun Got Wings* – all were easily recognizable. Tairov's 'structural realism' had a clearly defined tension of social motifs and the theatre's

leading actress, Alisa Koonen, performing the main roles in *Desire Under the Elms* and *All God's Chillun Got Wings*, gave these social motifs a tragic power.

Opposite: Design by the Stenberg brothers of a set for *The Hairy Ape* and a scene from the production.

Above: Design by the Stenberg brothers of a set for *Desire Under the Elms* and (*right*) a scene from the production.

Day and Night

In the repertoire of the Kamerny Theatre, according to Tairov's programme, the tragic was always accompanied by the comic, social drama co-existed side by side with playful and sunny operetta. One of Tairov's most conspicuous successes in this genre was the production in 1926 of Charles Lecocq's *Day and Night*. This time Tairov, together with the Stenberg brothers as designers, gave the musical comedy the lightness and freshness of an athletic-dance spectacle. The dance numbers, choreographed by the ballet-master Natalia Glan, were particularly fine.

Three scenes from *Day and Night*.

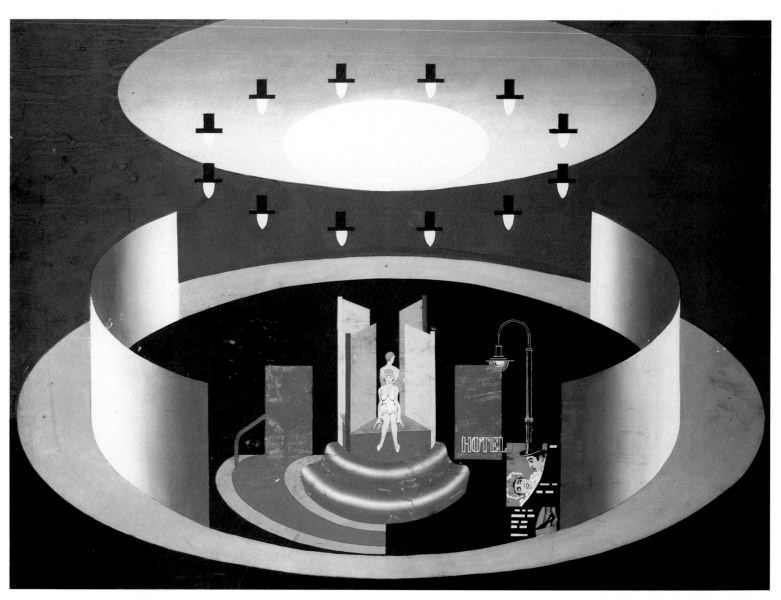

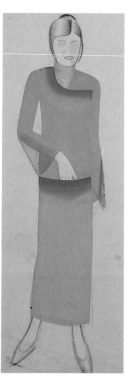

The Stenberg brothers

In their designs for Tairov's *Day and Night*, the Stenberg brothers were inspired by music hall and the latest Western fashions.

The most significant of the musical productions staged by the Kamerny Theatre at this time was the Russian première in 1930 of the Brecht-Weill *Die Dreigroschenoper*. But in Tairov's production, elegantly designed by the Stenbergs, the work's satirical fire was a little dampened by Yuly Khmelnitsky's engaging performance of Macheath as a charming and insouciant adventurer.

Two scenes from *Die Dreigroschenoper*.

Opposite, above: Design by the Stenberg brothers for the set of *Die Dreigroschenoper*.

Opposite, below: Three costume designs by the Stenbergs for *Day and Night*.

TRAM

It was in Leningrad that the first Theatre of Working Youth (TRAM) sprang up, led by the director Mikhail Sokolovsky. The initial idea was that TRAM should not use professional actors. The productions were performed by young workers, theatrical amateurs, who followed the dictate 'at the machine by day, on stage by night'. It was assumed that the young workers would compose the plays and make the sets themselves, that they had no need of help from specialists, whether dramatists, artists or composers. At first all these principles were strictly observed, TRAM's early productions enjoying great success with young people, and the 'TRAM movement' rapidly spread throughout the country.

A scene from the Leningrad TRAM's production of *The Days are Melting* by N. Lvov.

Opposite: A scene from *Friendly Hillock* by Vladimir Deshevov and Nikolai Dvorikov, staged by the Leningrad TRAM (*above*) and a scene from *Call Factory Committee!* by Ershov and Korovkin, staged by the Moscow TRAM (*below*).

242

243

Two scenes from the Leningrad
TRAM's production of *The Shot*.

Fairly soon it became clear that professionals were needed. By 1929, when the Leningrad TRAM staged *The Shot*, a play by the well-known poet Alexander Bezymensky which had already been produced at the Meyerhold Theatre, all the company had left their factories and workshops, and the actors were now being paid for their work in the theatre. So the idea of an amateur theatre was abandoned, and TRAM simply turned into yet another new theatre.

At this time new Satire Theatres opened in both Leningrad and Moscow. To begin with their repertoire consisted of revues comprising short sketches. Then more and more frequently these theatres began to perform comedies in several acts.

Poster for a revue at the Moscow Satire Theatre, entitled *'Turn round, Mishka!'*

Two scenes from *The Cheat*.

Comedy and satire

Interest in the light-hearted genres grew and the most diverse experiments were conducted in search of a form for the comic production. In the Studio of the Maly Theatre the director Fedor Kaverin staged Vasily Shkvarkin's satirical vaudevilles *A Harmful Element* (1927) and *The Cheat* (1929) in a free-and-easy, cheerful manner. In the Moscow Art Theatre in 1928 Stanislavsky and Vasily Sakhnovsky put on Leonid Leonov's strange play *Untilovsk*. The action took place in a remote northern province, in a distant 'back of beyond', and was accompanied by painstaking but funny conversations on philosophical themes; but from time to time a shift occurred towards biting and angry satire of the petit-bourgeois mentality.

Two scenes from *Untilovsk*, with Vera
Sokolova as Raisa and Ivan Moskvin
as Chervakov.

Mikhail Bulgakov's *Zoika's Apartment* enjoyed a short but hugely successful run at the Vakhtangov Theatre in 1926 in a production by Alexei Popov. All the actors – in particular Ruben Simonov, Tsetsilia Mansurova and Anatoly Goryunov – performed with energy and flair. The play's fundamental setting – an innocent dressmaker's atelier which is in reality a well-disguised brothel – was absolutely normal for Moscow during the NEP but fairly risqué for the stage. This risqué quality was beautifully captured by the designer, Sergei Isakov.

Three scenes from *Zoika's Apartment*, with A. Kozlovsky as Obolyanov and E. Alexeeva as Madame Ivanova (*below left*).

Three characters from *Squaring the Circle*. *Left*: V. Bendina as Ludmilla. *Below left*: M. Yanshin as Vasya. *Below*: B. Livanov as Emelyan Chernozemny.

If *Zoika's Apartment* touched on several dark and hidden sides of the contemporary milieu, Valentin Kataev's vaudeville *The Squaring of the Circle*, staged by Nikolai Gorchakov at the Moscow Art Theatre in 1928, was on the contrary cloudless and carefree in its optimism. Here everyone smiled at everyone else, everyone was cheerful and everyone was full of faith in the glorious future.

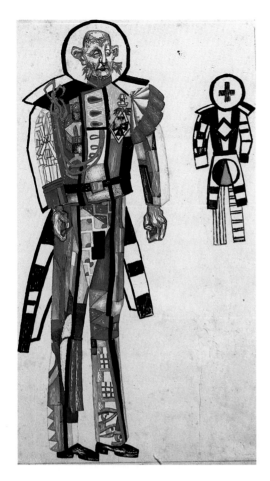

Costume designs by pupils of Pavel Filonov for *The Government Inspector*.

The director Igor Terentiev mounted several extravagant productions on the small stage of the Journalists' Club which caused an unexpected stir in Leningrad theatrical life of the late 1920s. The most interesting of these was a production of Gogol's *The Government Inspector* (1927) designed with the co-operation of a group of young artists, pupils of Pavel Filonov. Filonov himself watched their enthusiastic search for 'the speaking costume': the idea was that a character's costume should immediately convey to the audience his occupation, nature and even thoughts. Several dozen sketches were prepared. (Of the sketches reproduced here and overleaf nearly all are being published for the first time.) Terentiev's productions, with their buffoonery and farce, were on the edge of parody and although the critical response was extremely hostile, *The Government Inspector* enjoyed a resounding success not only in Leningrad but also on tour in Moscow.

A set design by pupils of Pavel Filonov for *The Government Inspector*.

Terentiev and the Filonov school

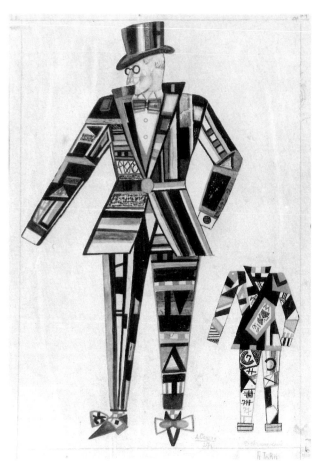

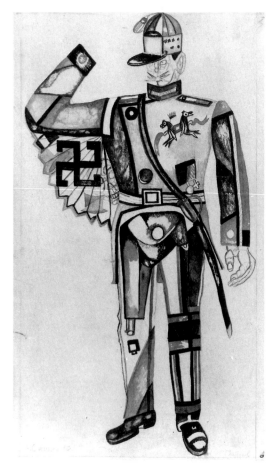

Costume designs by pupils of Pavel
Filonov for *The Government Inspector*.

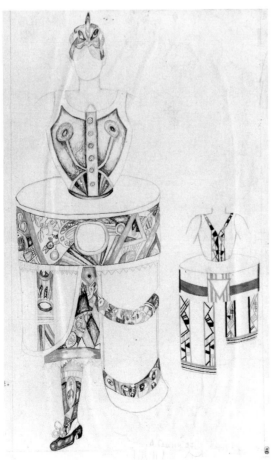

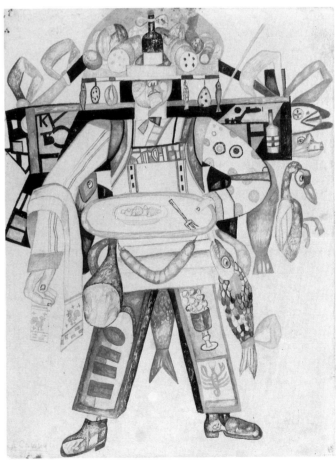

The Embezzlers

A stage adaptation of Valentin Kataev's story *The Embezzlers* was produced at the Moscow Art Theatre in 1928 by the director Ilya Sudakov, with costumes and sets by Isaak Rabinovich. It is interesting to compare the designer's sketches with photographs of the production: what immediately catches the eye is that the directorial plan consciously brought the artist's hyperbolic, expressive ideas 'down to earth' and instead of grotesque images the stage carried photographically exact reproductions of the contemporary milieu and contemporary types. The artist had striven for generalized, capacious, metaphorical forms; the theatre insisted on a precise reproduction of the social clashes of the day.

Costume designs by Isaak Rabinovich for *The Embezzlers*.

A scene from *The Embezzlers*.

A set design by Isaak Rabinovich for
The Embezzlers.

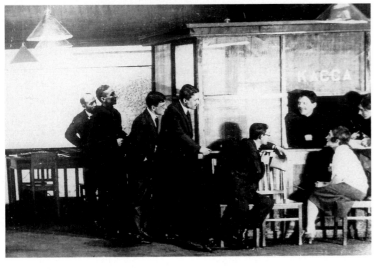

A scene from *The Embezzlers.*

The Bed-bug, Mayakovsky's angry, militantly energetic satire, loudly announced its presence in Meyerhold's production on the stage of the Meyerhold Theatre in 1929. The first part was designed by the then still very young but subsequently famous group of artists, the Kukriniksy. (Their sketches, hitherto unpublished, are shown here.) The music for Mayakovsky's comedy was written by Dmitri Shostakovich, then at the very start of his career. The main role of Prisypkin was played by Igor Ilinsky.

Left: A scene from the first part of The Bed-bug. Below left: Sketch of Prisypkin by the Kukriniksy. Below: Igor Ilinsky as Prisypkin.

Design by the Kukriniksy for the first
part of *The Bed-bug*.

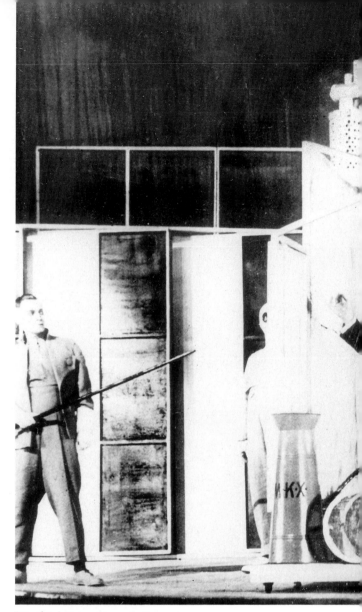

The professor in the second part of
The Bed-bug.

Prisypkin being unfrozen, in the
second part of *The Bed-bug*.

**The Bed-bug,
Part 2**

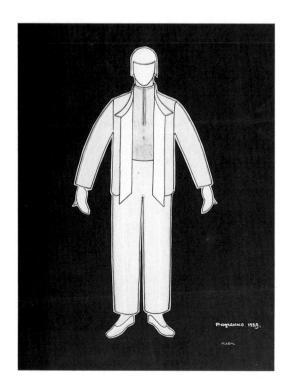

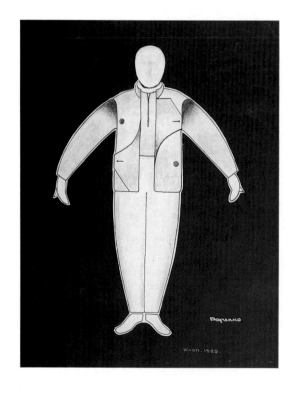

258

A character in the second part of *The Bed-bug*.

The second, fantastic part of *The Bed-bug*, where the action is transferred fifty years into the future, was designed by Alexander Rodchenko. It is interesting to compare his costumes with those of Kazimir Malevich for *Victory Over the Sun*. Although there is a clear similarity, one difference stands out, that Rodchenko tends to idealize – and hence aestheticize – the militarized aspect of his figures, half-people, half-robots.

Bottom row: Costume designs by Rodchenko for *The Bed-bug*.

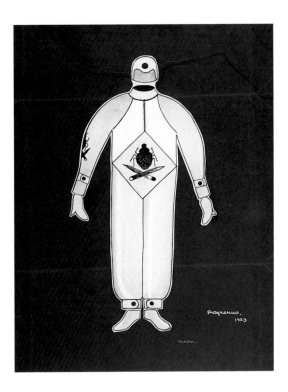

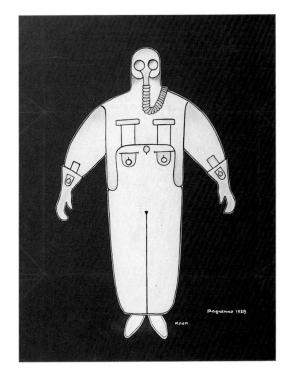

The Bath-house

Zinaida Raikh as the Phosphorescent Woman and Maxim Shtraukh as Pobedonosikov.
Zinaida Raikh as the Phosphorescent Woman.

Opposite: The final scene of *The Bath-house*.

Mayakovsky's second satirical comedy, *The Bath-house*, staged in the Meyerhold Theatre in 1930 not long before the poet's suicide, was incomparably less successful than *The Bed-bug*. Zinaida Raikh played the unearthly Phosphorescent Woman and Maxim Shtraukh appeared in the role of the all-too-earthly bureaucrat Pobedonosikov. To a great extent the indifference of audiences to *The Bath-house* can be explained by the fact that the crude placard-style satirical devices employed by Mayakovsky and Meyerhold had by then lost their power. The public had cooled towards all forms of propaganda theatre and wanted something more subtle and refined.

Set designs by Ivan Leistikov for *The Suicide*.

The Suicide

In 1930 Nikolai Erdman wrote his splendid tragicomedy *The Suicide*, which immediately attracted both Stanislavsky and Meyerhold. They started rehearsals without delay, the main role of Podsekalnikov in the Moscow Art Theatre being given to Vasily Toporkov, in the Meyerhold Theatre to Igor Ilinsky. Because the play had been banned by the Glavrepertkom (the organ of theatrical censorship), Stanislavsky addressed an appeal to Stalin to pass *The Suicide*. Stalin's response to the play was hostile, but in his letter to Stanislavsky he said that he would not object to the theatre 'testing its strength', after which a final decision would be taken by the experts: 'I am a dilettante in these matters.' And the rehearsals set off at full speed. Meyerhold, of course, overtook Stanislavsky and showed his production much earlier. The 'expert' entrusted with pronouncing a final judgment on the play was Lazar Kaganovich, the People's Commissar for Transport. He banned the play finally and irrevocably and Erdman's *Suicide* appeared on the Soviet stage only in 1981 in a production by a pupil of Meyerhold's, Valentin Pluchek. The sketches by Ivan Leistikov for Meyerhold's production have been preserved and are published here for the first time.

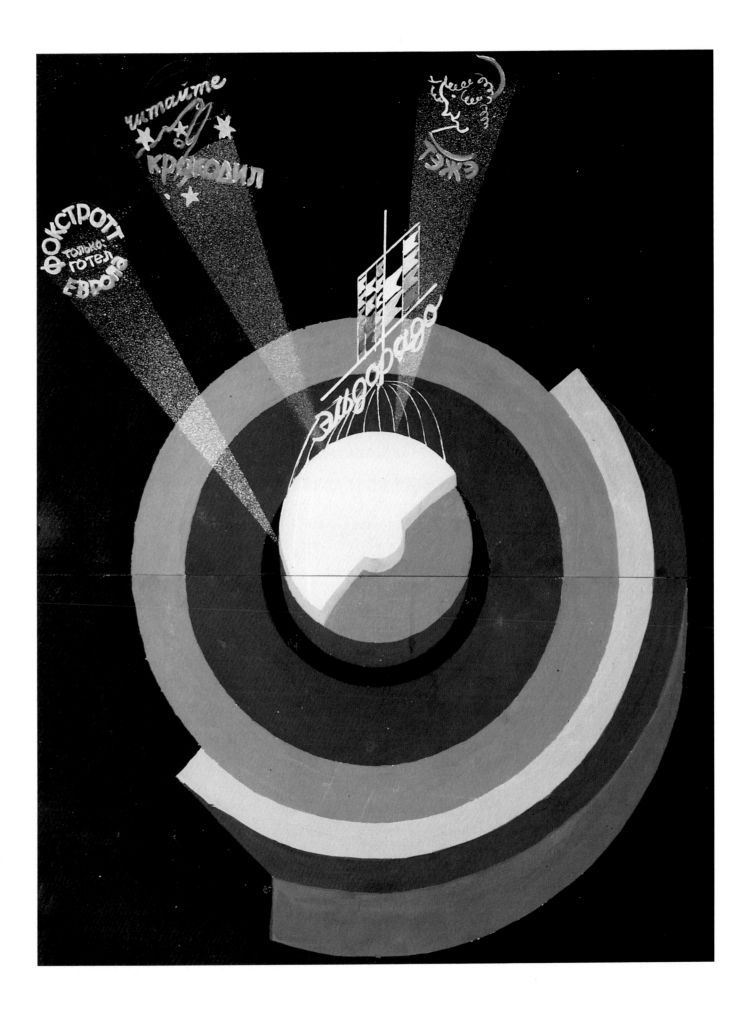

Set designs by Ivan Leistikov for *The Suicide*.

5 Some Outcomes

Afinogenov and Kirshon

The attempts by Afinogenov and Kirshon to revive the traditions of psychological drama naturally pleased the directors of the Moscow Art Theatre, and in the very early 1930s *Bread* by Kirshon and *Fear* by Afinogenov appeared on the MAT stage.

Although Afinogenov and Kirshon were ardent supporters of each other, their actual positions by no means always coincided. Kirshon's plays invariably manifested a rational, schematic structure and his heroes embodied specific theses, almost completely lacking the lyricism characteristic of Afinogenov. But on the other hand the issue which concerned Kirshon was indicated distinctly, specifically and, as a rule, it possessed topical relevance.

All these attributes were revealed in Kirshon's drama *Bread*, staged by Ilya Sudakov in 1931. The play is based on the contrast between two types of managers, Mikhailov and Raevsky. Raevsky epitomizes the romantic type, inclined to aim headlong for his objective, who has retained from the times of war Communism a fervour, a love of loud words and effective actions. Mikhailov, on the contrary, is reserved, markedly prosaic, he understands that the era of eloquent phrases and gestures has long since gone and that it is necessary to act judiciously, tactfully. Raevsky represents an emotionalism that has become obsolete, Mikhailov rationalistic efficiency. Kirshon ennobled Mikhailov and dethroned Raevsky, showed a decided preference for tactful 'prose' and rejected highflown yet impractical 'poetry'. In the MAT production there were attempts to conceal the rigidity of the dramaturgical outline, subjecting the parts of Mikhailov and Raevsky to a gentle and authentic shading. This was accomplished largely through the acting of Boris Dobronravov and Nikolai Khmelev.

Dobronravov did not want to play Mikhailov as a man who 'thinks in resolutions' and appears as 'a walking regulation'. On the contrary, he invested the laconic hero with an incontestable charm. In his turn Khmelev stripped Raevsky of excessively bright plumage, verbosity and pose, insisting that the character was deeply sincere in his urge to work honourably and selflessly, although orientating himself in the rural life with less confidence than Mikhailov. The production's heroes were much closer to each other than the heroes of the play.

The pictures of the country on the eve of collectivization, on the threshold of the abrupt break from the thousand-year-old style of peasant life were painted very approximately by Kirshon. In Sudakov's production the mass scenes acquired the distinct flavour of a strained, deliberately picturesque dynamism.

At the Moscow Art Theatre they regarded Kirshon's play, not without reason, as somewhat alien to them. There was much greater enthusiasm in MAT for the rehearsals of Afinogenov's *Fear*, a drama which touched on issues concerning the life of the contemporary intelligentsia with which the theatre had an affinity.

Sudakov staged *Fear* (1931) in the theatre's customary psychological manner. At the centre of the production there loomed the prominent figure of a tragically mistaken scientist, forcefully and profoundly acted by Leonid Leonidov. 'Thick-set, loud, with his tie askew, wearing a flat cap carelessly pulled over his forehead, Leonidov's Borodin,' wrote Knebel, 'seemed like a labourer.'[1] There was nothing especially 'professorial' about him. Leonidov, according to Markov, played 'not so much a professor as a thinker and philosopher. . . . When he appeared he seemed to fill the stage with his massive figure. He himself was conscious of his authority and inspired it in those around him; his judgments were definite and absolute, and his humour was devastating, pure "Leonidov". Such a Borodin could be feared.'[2]

Borodin's most spirited protagonist in the MAT production was his young student Makarova. Alla Tarasova played a bold, strong-willed woman, uncompromising in the struggle for her convictions, someone for whom the atmosphere of the laboratory or scientific debates seemed to be her native element. There was nothing of the 'blue stocking' about her; on the contrary, Makarova grew distinctly more attractive, blossomed in the heat of disputes, and Borodin, with whom she argued fiercely, was open in his admiration of her.

In Leningrad, *Fear* was staged by Nikolai Petrov at the Academic Theatre of Drama. The interesting set design for the production was by Akimov, with whom Petrov worked inseparably at that time. The director wanted the scenery 'to give the idea of a room' while at the same time evoking the sensation of 'a theatrical space of enormous proportions'[3] and monumental form.

In accordance with this demand Akimov simply and boldly 'giganticized' Afinogenov's interiors, removed the ceilings, opened up the entire stage area and steeply inclined the stage. The broad, slanted strip of floor leading from the front to the back of the stage became the design's principal motif. Human figures could be 'read' on this strip as though they were in city squares rather than in rooms. Gigantic walls, very tall doors – everything was magnified in scale and the drama really acquired a monumental ring. The duel between the scientist Borodin, enclosed in the world of his abstract science, and the old Bolshevik Klara Spasova, who had been through tsarist prisons and hard labour, formed the production's nerve-centre. All the play's remaining characters moved into the background.

Borodin (Illarion Pevtsov), a bookworm accustomed to the quiet of his study and the green light of a desk lamp, peered short-sightedly and perplexedly, through the thick lenses of his pince-nez at an incomprehensible and hostile world. The scientist felt confident that 'man's existence is not determined by the class struggle but by the eternal incentives of fear, love, hatred and hunger.' And mounting the rostrum which was moved forward into the auditorium, he said calmly, hardly glancing at the audience, that 'Soviet power is only maintained by fear.' After this an old woman, in a dark suit buttoned up the front and a severe masculine tie, with glasses sliding down her nose and straight grey hair held back by a comb, climbed up onto the rostrum. Klara (Ekaterina Korchagina-Alexandrovskaya) began her speech against Borodin quietly, holding her indignation in check, but gradually she became incensed. A dead silence fell over the auditorium when the old woman, taking out a yellowed piece of paper, read out the executioner's bill for the cost of her son's execution. The actress delivered the concluding words of Klara's speech forcefully: 'In this way terror gave birth to the fearlessness of the oppressed, who had nothing to lose!'

The Leningrad production of *Fear* brought significant success to the psychological drama. But the fact that Petrov and Akimov staged an 'indoor' play on a wide-open stage space rather than in modest interiors was nevertheless highly symptomatic. All the more so because the 'outdoor' plays of Pogodin and Vishnevsky were at this time making an even stronger impact.

Nikolai Pogodin's Industrial Poems

Nikolai Pogodin came to drama from journalism; his reports about the construction of the great factories – the Stalingrad Tractor Plant, the Magnitogorsk Metallurgical Works and the Gorky Automobile Factory – were published on the pages of *Pravda*. A first-hand knowledge of new facts, events and people, the very atmosphere of the building site could be felt in his plays *Tempo*, *The Poem of the Axe* and *My Friend*. They were all written outside the customary dramatic canons. The action developed along a chain of fleeting, apparently fortuitous episodes, accurate, pointed and vivid sketches from life. The people inhabiting the plays, labourers, seasonal workers, works clerks and engineers, spoke in a rough language, at times uncouth and coarse, but through all this apparently randomly caught, unpolished exterior, there emerged the deep-running processes of time.

The director Alexei Popov, the first to appreciate Pogodin's talent, decided to stage *Tempo* at the Vakhtangov Theatre. But as real scaffolding rose up on stage in place of scenery and the production's highly unusual appearance became evident, the Vakhtangov actors became more and more doubtful about the play. They felt it seemed too 'rough' and 'raw' and, moreover, were distressed by the smallness of the parts and cursory outline of the characters. Such a serious conflict arose between Popov, who supported the playwright on all points, and the actors, who presented Pogodin with numerous demands, that the director moved from the Vakhtangov Theatre to the Theatre of the Revolution without completing work on the production.

The members of the Vakhtangov company opened *Tempo* without Popov, who proceeded to stage the next two plays by Pogodin (*The Poem of the Axe* and *My Friend*) at the Theatre of the Revolution.

In his Pogodin productions Popov further perfected the art of organizing crowd scenes, staging them sweepingly, broadly. Ilya Shlepyanov, an artist who had previously worked with Meyerhold, designed the productions. At Popov's insistence he strove to combine the mobile stage construction with the concrete aspects of contemporary existence to the extent that the construction would seem like a photographic reproduction of an industrial still-life. *The Poem of the Axe* was set in a Urals steel mill and Shlepyanov's radiant metallic set reproduced the shape of an open-hearth furnace, opened up wide and deep, within which darted workers in protective clothing. At the back of the stage the mouth of the smelting furnace with its blazing fire could be seen. Popov entrusted the two principal roles, the steel founder and the young worker Anka, to Meyerhold's students Dmitri Orlov and Maria Babanova.

The Poem of the Axe was filled with humour and lyricism. But if this play with all its triumphant cheerfulness nonetheless remained a fleeting theatrical sketch of factory life, then in the drama *My Friend* all threads converged in the centre, in the figure of Grigory Gai, who was played by Mikhail Astangov. Gai, the manager of the construction of one of the giant factories during the first Five Year Plan, appeared exceptional, outstanding. Gai's romantic enthusiasm was based on far-sighted, sober calculation: he was both a man of dreams and a man of action. A seething, impatient energy came through in all of his gestures, confidence was heard in every word.

The culmination of the performance was the scene where Gai approached the Man in Charge. A most difficult ordeal awaited him. Maxim Shtraukh played the Man in Charge and although he did not use make-up to create a likeness, the character was clearly intended to represent the Narkom for Heavy Industry, Sergo Ordzhonikidze. A weary, bearded man who spoke softly in an even voice, he sat at a desk in a large office by the doors of which waited dozens of those factory bosses just like Gai, industrial 'kings', 'Soviet Fords', the leaders of the urgent construction undertaken during the Five Year Plan. They all needed money and metal. Each one came before the Man in Charge when their enterprise got into trouble, and to win his support was a major victory.

In the production of *My Friend*, Shlepyanov successfully employed enormous photo-posters. The action was set against a background of large screens which extended across the entire stage and portrayed a panoramic bird's-eye view of a building site. The silhouette of Lenin, his arm pointing ahead, was projected as a faint shadow on to this panorama. Trolleys dashed about the clear, empty stage; on these trolleys scaffolding, tables, chairs and telephones appeared as needed then disappeared again.

Documentary and Legend

At the turn of the 1930s, theatres were looking back to the past, enthusiastically giving performances dedicated to the heroics of the Civil War. Sometimes these new works were stylistically attuned to previous successes. For instance, Lev Prozorovsky, rehearsing *The Bridge of Fire* by Boris Romashov at the Maly Theatre, was clearly inspired by the experience and example of Trenev's *Liubov Yarovaya* produced several years earlier on the same stage. The contours of the production as well as the acting style of Vera Pashennaya, Stepan Kuznetsov and Nikolai Rybnikov, all recalled *Liubov Yarovaya* but now the same excitement was not aroused. The public's restrained response could easily have been explained by the sketchiness and even stereotyped character of Romashov's play, but this was not the only reason. Shaped in the mid 1920s, the standard model of the popular heroic spectacle was becoming obsolete not with each day but with each hour. A short time later, when Mikhail Narokov produced an adaptation of Alexander Fadeev's novel *The Rout* at the Maly Theatre, it became perfectly clear that this form was no longer viable. *The Bridge of Fire* in 1929 could still have been considered a success, though not a great or a sensational one. But the 1932 production of *The Rout* at the Maly Theatre was universally considered to be a disappointing failure.

Directors and playwrights together were obstinately searching for untrodden paths, striving to give freshness and purity to the theatrical picture of the country's militant youth. In their explorations two completely opposite tendencies clearly emerged.

One of them, using the aesthetic aspect of Bill-Belotserkovsky's *Storm* as a basis, gravitated toward reportage, towards the appearance of the maximally authentic stage documentary and very often found expression in the specific form of the 'drama without a hero'. There seemed to be something indelibly theatrical in the idea of the hero. Vsevolod Vishnevsky proclaimed: 'Away with the psychology of heroes, the prominent, significant figures who talk and act a lot. Let the masses flow. . . . Let the individual drown in the stream of socially significant events.'[4] Vishnevsky's play *The First Cavalry Army* was written according to this principle. It was staged in 1930 at the Theatre of the Revolution by Alexei Diky. The story of the transformation of the mass of ignorant, down-trodden soldiers from the former tsar's army into the conscious and able fighting men of the Red Army became the plot line on which the play's episodes were strung together. The action of the noisy and turbulent crowd scenes was organized on stairs and acting platforms of different heights, stylized evocations of soldiers' barracks, dug-outs and trenches. The numerous episodes flashed by quickly like cinema frames. They alternated with excerpts from newsreels recording a soldier's life in the days of the First World War, the February Revolution, October Revolution and Civil War. Nevertheless some highly distinctive characters did stand out from the seething crowd. Of particular note was Ivan Sysoev, a soldier in the tsar's army whose fate Vishnevsky intended to be seen as unremarkable, ordinary, common. However in its stage embodiment Sysoev's role became major: the most typical figure proved to be the most significant.

The idea of the heroic spectacle which focused on a mass rather than an individual remained attractive and particularly lured Nikolai Okhlopkov who at the beginning of the 1930s headed the small Realistic Theatre in Moscow. The Realistic Theatre's company was composed of pupils from the ill-starred, dull Fourth MAT Studio, and the Meyerholdite Okhlopkov at once began to teach them all over again.

The Iron Flood, adapted from the well-known novel by Alexander Serafimovich, was the production that declared his programme. In many respects Okhlopkov's work was impressive. An avalanche of people moved incessantly throughout the auditorium and across the stage, making noise, bawling songs, being tormented by hunger and the burning sun, carrying wounded and children in their arms, lugging cannons and machine guns, dragging their pathetic belongings on creaking carts and waggons. Now and then the flood stopped for a little while: the soldiers pulled off their faded shirts soaked in sweat and wearily collapsed on the spot, near the waggons. The thin women breastfed the infants. The dead were buried.

Okhlopkov squeezed this series of short episodes into the theatre's tiny premises, scattering the individual bits of action along a few acting platforms that projected into the auditorium, and trying to achieve the merging of audience and actors. For example, an actor in exiting often firmly shook hands with someone in the audience or slapped his shoulder in a friendly way. Tragic moments of deaths and murders alternated with lyrical moments, comic, crudely farcical and eccentric numbers. The genres were mixed up and whisked into a kind of picturesque mass, just like the people in the production's continuously moving flow. Sometimes the hall was darkened, and the beam of the searchlight quickly picked out an individual figure or group of people from the darkness.

In Okhlopov's flashing spectacle it was difficult to distinguish individual faces, never mind characters.

Such authenticity, almost importunate, and such imagery, rather more cinematographic than theatrical, were also exploited by Okhlopkov in the production of *The Mother* after Gorky and in the production of *The Run* after Vladimir Stavsky's rural essays. Okhlopkov was all the time totally aware that his works were experimental. The posters for *The Iron Flood* described it as 'directorial sketches towards a staging'.

Meyerhold and Tairov meanwhile chose another route. In their productions action that took place in comparatively recent times was moved back into a legendary past, shedding the skin of familiar details, of well-remembered trivialities. The distance of a decade and a half was intentionally extended and became indeterminately great. The heroics avoided earth-bound and polluting specificity. They gravitated towards the purity of the absolute and the austerity of paradigm. Yesterday's opponents and rivals, Meyerhold and Tairov were now endeavouring with astonishing unanimity to achieve a majestic beauty of spectacle, a passionate sublimity of tone. They had no desire to recall the smell of blood and stench of leg bindings, soldiers' shirts in rags, lice-ridden trench life. Their will towards a generalized, crystallized, severe form inevitably involved the will to concentrate subject matter in a living personification – in the figure of the hero.

In 1929 when Meyerhold staged Ilya Selvinsky's tragedy in verse, *The Second Army Commander*, the critic Boris Alpers pointed out with some amazement: 'The heroic past appears on Meyerhold's stage as legend. It becomes myth.' It seemed as though, of the warriors who appeared on stage, 'not a single man would have survived to our day'. 'They are,' continued Alpers, 'the legendary heroes of a legendary time. That is why they stand so still holding their long lances. That is why their movements are so slow and solemn and the imprint of some strange reverie lies over their whole aspect. . . . The heroic epoch retreats into the distant past, acquires prominent, majestic contours in counterpoise to the fleeting sketches of everyday life of the documentary drama.'[5]

Meyerhold recruited the painter Kuzma Petrov-Vodkin to work on *The Second Army Commander*. The artist not only styled the great-coats, pea-jackets, fur hats and sheepskin coats as in ancient times, but also gave long Scythian spears to the cavalrymen, silver sabres to the heroes, silver trumpets to the crowd. The remoteness and even aloofness from recent reality was the form of its poeticization.

In Nikolai Bogolyubov's performance, the hero of the tragedy, Chub, appeared significant, strong ('superb make-up, an energetic face, sparkling eyes and severe, rather hollow voice,' wrote Alpers). Alexei Gvozdev even noted that Bogolyubov 'unexpectedly came before the audience as a major tragic actor'.[6] But Chub's part was fragmentary, patchy, so Bogolyubov could only truly move the audience in a few episodes. On the whole Meyerhold's monumental and simple plan was undermined by the verbose rhetoric of Selvinsky's text. In this sense Tairov proved luckier, for he took on an immeasurably stronger play, Vishnevsky's *An Optimistic Tragedy*.

It could be said that in *An Optimistic Tragedy* Vishnevsky was challenging his own *First Cavalry Army*. In any case the majestic figure of the heroine, the Commissar, was now elevated to the focal point of his drama and while retaining its importance, the crowd of sailors nonetheless moved to a secondary position. Tairov at once understood what great potential such a structure presented for Alisa Koonen. The sailors' regiment came onto the Kamerny Theatre's stage in a dashing and energetic manner, radiant in the whiteness of their brand new sailor shirts, just as energetically replacing them later with the traditional black pea-jackets. All the sailors wore caps and the names of ships sparkled in gold on their cap-bands. The military formation ritually wheeled round marching then stood rigidly to attention, the synchronization and statuesque precision of these evolutions representing a graphic alternative to the teeming, swarming, seething jumble of Okhlopkov's crowd scenes.

Tairov defined the formula for the production concisely: 'Sky. Earth. Man.' A work of epic scale was contemplated and the tragedy was seen in broad, global proportions. The regiment's progression 'from chaos to harmony' defined the entire style of the scenic composition. The artist Vadim Ryndin provided a laconic, capacious and expressive visual formulation of this movement: in the centre there was a round, hollow crater, above which a three-tiered road spiralled away towards the horizon beneath a vast sky where clouds floated.

The set constructed by Ryndin represented nothing in itself, but the slightly angled revolving stage was easily transformed and could become either a ship's deck or a battlefield. 'The generalized image of reality,' wrote Konstantin Derzhavin, 'possessed an impressive epic actuality, that realism and pathos of the legendary epos which needs no petty detailing.'[7]

The construction, outwardly very simple and ascetic, promptly came to life when the actors appeared on its bright planes. 'All the emotional, visual and rhythmical lines of the staging,' stated Tairov, 'must be built along a distinctive curve leading from negation to affirmation, from death to life, from chaos to harmony, from anarchy to conscious discipline.'[8]

Alisa Koonen as the Commissar was the embodiment of volition, fortitude, order. She appeared severe, with straight hair and a white face on which were clearly drawn straight eye-brows, elongated eyes and bright lips, as though on her face the tragic mask had already emerged. Her black leather jacket was buttoned up to the neck. Her boots made her step firm. Her eyes were calmly attentive and cold, her voice usually quiet. 'But,' recalled the critic Boris Medvedev, 'Koonen tightly interwove the heroine's femininity with sternness, lyricism with an unbending will.'[9]

The action developed swiftly. In the intersection of differently directed surges of will – the blind anger of some, the doubts of others, the inert apathy of others still – the Commissar had unerringly to find the correct line of behaviour in order to unite the crowd of sailors and lead them. Among the sailors Alexei (Mikhail Zharov) was particularly noticeable; his role seemed gradually to become enlarged, and if in the beginning of the performance he was an episodic figure, one of the many minions of the Leader (Sergei Tsenin), then later he came to the fore, standing firmly next to the Commissar.

Tairov boldly resorted to an expressive play of contrasts. The farewell ball on the ship and the sharp, ruthless signal of the bugle-call to battle, the death of the Commissar and the victory of the regiment – such sudden abrupt changes of mood gave the action an emotional intensity.

An Optimistic Tragedy was one of Tairov's best productions. After its première even the most vicious opponents of the Kamerny Theatre had to bite their tongues. Criticism that the theatre seemed to be in a state of permanent discord with the audience ceased – and for a long time.

The taste for the generalized and extended theatrical form characteristic of the productions of Meyerhold and Tairov also appeared at this time in the work of the director Sandro Akhmeteli, then head of the Georgian Rustaveli Theatre. Akhmeteli took over the leadership of the strongest Georgian company in 1926 after a fierce and stormy conflict with his teacher and predecessor in this post, Kote Mardzhanishvili. Their disagreements are a special subject which there is no need to examine in detail here; I shall observe only that Akhmeteli rebelled against Mardzhanishvili's implantation of general European theatrical principles on to Georgian soil. He felt that by initiating the Georgian stage into the experiments of European innovators, Mardzhanishvili was neglecting the distinctive features of 'national Georgian rhythms' and was propagandizing Stanislavsky's 'subjective theory' too zealously.[10] But the root of the conflict was not in these subtleties, but simply in the rivalry between two brilliantly gifted directors. The younger, purposeful Akhmeteli pushed the carefree Mardzhanishvili out relatively easily. The company split over this, and Mardzhanishvili's supporters left with him for Kutaisi, while Akhmeteli's proponents remained in Tbilisi.

Akhmeteli quickly proved that he had a rich imagination, a sharp eye and firm hand. His first triumph was a staging of Boris Lavrenev's *The Break*, the second a staging of the play *Anzor* by Sandro Shanshiashvili, a Georgian version of Vsevolod Ivanov's *Armoured Train No. 14–69*. Shanshiashvili transferred the action from the Far East to the Northern Caucasus and turned Siberians into Lezghins and Georgians.

Both productions ran in laconic and austerely contoured constructed stage sets designed by Irakly Gamrekeli. In *Anzor*, for example, Gamrekeli turned the rural scenery into a sort of 'formula for a Caucasian mountain village'. Peasant mountain huts, closely adjoining one another, formed a system of flat roof-platforms which ascended upwards by means of terraces and were all linked by narrow stairway-crossings. The result was a combination of acting platforms of varying heights which was very convenient for organizing the crowd scenes.

Akhmeteli sought to impart a sculptural expressiveness to the crowd's movement. He was among the first to employ a device in theatre similar to the 'freeze frame' of cinema: the turbulent dynamics of the mass scene suddenly stood still for an instant. All voices ceased. In the total silence of the pause the monolithic, multi-figured composition stood motionless. Akhmeteli was not lured by the colour of genre sketches. He wanted no 'naturalism' whatsoever. The director sought monumentality, an epic tone, at times even an archaic feeling, particularly clear in *Anzor*. The central figure in the

Rustaveli Theatre's ensemble under Akhmeteli was Akaky Khorava, an imposing, powerful and slow-paced actor. A stormy temperament seethed and rumbled in the baritone intonations of his voice, but Khorava's speech as Bersenev (in *The Break*) and Anzor came across firmly and imperiously; his gestures were invariably majestic, proud. His heroes did not act, they performed deeds.

There were other great actors in Akhmeteli's company, notably Tamara Chavchavadze and Akaky Vasadze. But Ushangi Chkheidze and Veriko Andzhaparidze, actors of another, lyrical mould, of a more open temperament, could not work harmoniously with Akhmeteli and they left the Republic's capital to follow Mardzhanishvili to Kutaisi.

Avant-garde or Arrière-garde?

After the premières of *The Break* and *Anzor*, Sandro Akhmeteli turned to the classics. The staging of Schiller's *Die Räuber*, with Akaky Khorava as Karl Moor and Akaky Vasadze as Franz Moor, was Akhmeteli's highest achievement and the most distinctive example of his monumental theatrical form, which permitted both enormous expression and exaggeration but invariably elevated the heroes, removed them from the everyday milieu and endowed them with romantic grandeur. Irakly Gamrekeli, the designer, surpassed himself in *Die Räuber*. The scenery for the Bohemian forest was bold and simple: in the middle of the stage towered the immense trunk of an ancient oak tree, much larger than life, with exposed roots. All the action was conducted amidst the network of these mighty roots. The rebels in flapping cloaks of various colours jumped out of an opening in the hollow trunk, a scene which always precipitated stormy applause from the audience. Khorava performed the part of Karl Moor marvellously, and Akhmeteli, who had presented *Die Räuber* in both Moscow and Leningrad with enormous success, had every reason to celebrate a triumph. All the more so because his former teacher and current rival Kote Mardzhanishvili had just presented *Othello* without particular success; the title role was played by Shalva Gambashidze, and Ushangi Chkheidze, a recent Hamlet, appeared as Iago.

Work on *Othello* also proved distressing for Stanislavsky. The agonizing question as to whether the Moscow Art Theatre was capable of performing Shakespeare's tragedies once again was unresolved. To some extent the failure was probably explained by the fact that the production was prepared in an unusual way: Stanislavsky, who was in Nice after an illness, wrote the directorial plan for the production there, far from his theatre, and Ilya Sudakov ran the rehearsals in Moscow according to this plan. Leonidov's psychological instability complicated matters still further; at rehearsals he gave a powerful performance as Othello, but before the full auditorium it was dull and apathetic. Vladimir Sinitsyn, who had previously occupied a rather modest place in the MAT company, unexpectedly found himself in the centre of attention in the role of Iago, which he played with both originality and passion. His Iago was a golden-curled and solitary demon of evil, exhausted by hatred. Sinitsyn eclipsed Leonidov as well as both Alla Tarasova as Desdemona and Boris Livanov as Cassio. The production, opulently and beautifully designed by Alexander Golovin, lasted for only ten performances.

Stanislavsky's directorial plan for *Othello* was, however, interesting in many respects. It testified to his passionate desire to

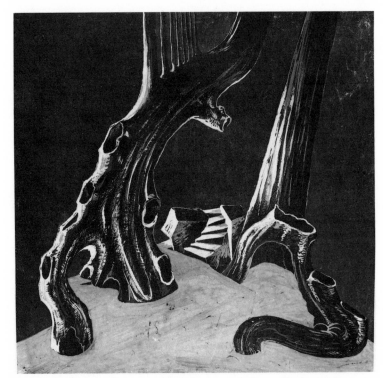

Sketch of the set by Irakly Gamrekeli for Schiller's *Die Räuber*, directed by Akhmeteli at the Rustaveli Theatre, 1933.

saturate the tragedy with a multitude of vivid details, to create the intoxicatingly beautiful atmosphere of Venice, to contrast its poetry with the dry scorched earth of prosaic Cyprus and, moreover, to oppose the Venetian wealth and grandeur with the harsh, strong scenes of the Cypriots' uprising. Of course all these details bore very little relation to Shakespeare's plot, although they did manifest Stanislavsky's characteristic imaginative thrust towards the lifelike, that thirst for realism which constantly overcame him.

Meanwhile attempts 'to modernize' the classics by persistently emphasizing the social motifs and vigorously pulling out all the satirical stops, were still sufficiently widespread. In 1929 at the Leningrad Academic Theatre of Drama Molière's *Tartuffe* was produced on a grand scale by the directorial triumvirate of Nikolai Akimov (who was also the production's designer), Nikolai Petrov and Vladimir Soloviev.

The classical play in this case served as a pretext for the expansion of 'leftism' on to the territory of the academic stage. The directors, without altering Molière's text, inserted a number of satirical mime interludes into the comedy in order to expose the 'hypocrisy', or 'Tartuffism', in religion, politics and everyday life. Taking part in the interludes were figures caricaturing contemporary politicians, Briand, Chiang Kai-shek, Léon Blum and others, with enormous heads made of papier mâché according to Akimov's drawings. Two colossal gold cornucopia were suddenly turned into sewer pipes from whose openings the 'foulness' (that is, the comedy's characters) poured out onto the stage. Pert chorus girls were supposed to symbolize the meretricious 'yellow press', which is why they performed an energetic cancan. In the finale streams of water washed away all the characters from the stage, which then became a screen onto which were projected documentary frames from newsreels, pictures of building sites, tractors, aeroplanes. . . .

Nikolai Petrov asserted that this production was influenced by Vakhtangov's *Princess Turandot*. But the means of expression employed by the directors more closely resembled those in Meyerhold's political revues *The Earth in Turmoil* and *D.E.*, and in collision with Molière's text they appeared too crude, too primitive and, most important of all, terribly out-dated. Although Ilarion Pevtsov performed Tartuffe effectively (in red wig, with a thin 'sinuous' mouth and ravenous eyes), this clumsy production nonetheless seemed both over-simplified and naive, if only compared to Petrov's stagings of Soviet plays on that same stage.

At the turn of the 1930s it became apparent that the decisive modification of the classics, their adaptation to the demands of 'current events', which the avant-gardists proclaimed and carried through, had lost its novelty value.

However there was one later example of this approach – the *Hamlet* staged by Nikolai Akimov at the Vakhtangov Theatre in 1932. It could be said that if this production had not been, it would have had to be invented; such was the extent to which it revealed clearly, directly and uncompromisingly all the distinctive traits of the vulgar sociological perception of the classics. Proposing that the actors look at the tragedy 'with the fresh eyes of modern times', the director asserted that the problems tormenting Hamlet had long since been resolved and were of no interest for people of today. What is interesting, however, is something quite different which Akimov's predecessors had not thought to pick up on: Hamlet actively carries out a 'power struggle' for the throne and crown. Only one thing is important to him: to overthrow Claudius and occupy the throne. Such a reading of the play enables the entire baseness of motive underlying any monarchy to be shown and exposes the outmoded feudal order, looking at the past from on high, from the position of 'social optimism'. But in Akimov's production as soon as Hamlet became a cunning schemer leading the 'power struggle', the tragedy promptly turned into a comedy, and this comedy, stripped of romanticism but burdened by the Shakespearian tragic text, did not turn out at all funny. Akimov's production more than anything else resembled a parody of *Hamlet*.

Anatoly Goryunov played Hamlet as an obese glutton who in outward appearance was nearly Falstaff. Dreaming of seizing the throne, this picture of health intrigued against his uncle, the King Claudius, a timorous neurasthenic (played by Ruben Simonov in a sharply grotesque manner). All Hamlet's philosophical soliloquies were deleted or else transferred to a flat, mercenary plane. For instance, Hamlet asked himself the question 'To be or not to be?' while trying on his uncle's crown, and this question signified only one thing: would he get the crown? The voice of Hamlet's father, the Ghost, was heard from a clay pot, and it was Hamlet himself who was shouting into it so as to frighten Claudius's retainers and by means of this practical joke justify his claims to the throne. Ophelia looked like a dissolute wench, and in her madness scene she seemed frankly tipsy.

Akimov himself designed the production and its individual episodes were indubitably picturesque in quality. Markov noted in particular the expressive scene after 'The Mousetrap' when the frightened Claudius ran down a steep staircase and his long scarlet cloak swirled behind like a stream of blood or tongue of flame. But the critic could not resist the sarcastic remark: 'You only see, skimming down the stairway, an enormous red cloak with the actor Simonov stuck on to it.'[11]

Sketch of costumes by Nikolai Akimov for his production of *Hamlet* at the Vakhtangov Theatre in 1932.

In principle all the other actors were also 'stuck' in exactly the same way to the conception of the director and artist. Soon after the première Boris Shchukin, who played Polonius, admitted that he had 'pushed' his portrayal 'into the shape sketched out' by Akimov.

Of course Akimov was less radical than Sir Barry Jackson or Terence Gray in England. But nonetheless he expected his adaptation of *Hamlet* at least to evoke animated discussion and heated debate. These expectations were not fulfilled. There were no debates over Akimov's *Hamlet*; he did not find any defenders. Members of the Vakhtangov company tried to reply to the critics, but unconvincingly. The Vakhtangov Theatre very quickly acknowledged that Akimov's *Hamlet* was a fiasco. The aggressiveness of the directorial approach to the play did not in itself excite anyone now. Many years later the film director Grigory Kozintsev rightly observed: 'Akimov's *Hamlet* would have been fine in 1919 and 1920. In the 1930s such a staging was already an unholy anachronism.'[12] The view of Shakespeare 'from on high' was now perceived as frivolous and to their great amazement the avant-garde suddenly found themselves in the *arrière-garde* of theatrical explorations. The time of aggressive but ill-founded experimentation had passed.

The Turn to Realism

In the early 1930s the Moscow Art Theatre enjoyed much greater popularity than the Meyerhold Theatre. Such MAT productions as *The Days of the Turbins*, *A Passionate Heart* and *Le Mariage de Figaro*, first staged in 1926 and 1927, had secured a firm place in the repertoire and invariably played to full houses. In 1929 and 1930 to these titles were added two more selected by the Moscow public: *Uncle's Dream* after Dostoevsky and *Resurrection* after Lev Tolstoy. Both productions were staged by Nemirovich-Danchenko.

In directing *Uncle's Dream* he interpreted the old chronicle of Russian provincial life with caustic cutting irony. The acting duo of Olga Knipper-Chekhova and Nikolai Khmelev stood at the centre of the performance. Alongside Knipper-Chekhova's haughty schemer and district dictator who has decided to marry the distinguished visiting guest to her daughter, the prince, whom Khmelev portrayed as a totally helpless milksop, 'made up' (as the actor explained) 'of uncoordinated parts of the body, arms and legs which operated separately and independently of each other,'[13] looked like a pitiful marionette, doomed to submit to the onslaught of this imperious individual. Amidst the provincial ladies, with all their everyday bustle, mutual petty rivalry, lies, backbiting and hypocrisy, the barely living prince who moved as though he was on hinges, frequently picking up his own legs with his hands and moving them in the right direction, time and again gracefully inserting his false teeth into his mouth, seemed like some kind of monstrous puppet – a mannequin rather than a man.

Khmelev had few equals in the art of transformation, and watching his prince the audience could not believe they had seen this very actor as Alexei Turbin, Peklevanov in *Armoured Train No. 14–69* and Silan in *A Passionate Heart*. The sharp, sarcastic picture of the prince drawn by Khmelev changed unexpectedly at the end of the performance. For an instant something human, living, suddenly awakened in the mannequin. The prince cried real tears upon hearing the tune of a familiar romance from his youth, and with trembling hands he bashfully tried to cover his bare head from which the insolent ladies had snatched his wig. Then, stumbling, he fell to the floor and died – life left the puppet. This final moment, which brought all the intricate scheming to nought, concluded the satirical performance on a tragic note.

In another of his works, *Resurrection*, Nemirovich-Danchenko developed the idea which he had realized as early as 1910, in *The Brothers Karamazov*: the form of the 'performance-novel' was held together here also by the role of the author. But if in *The Brothers Karamazov* the narrator accompanied the show's action, then in *Resurrection* the 'Character on the Author's Behalf' led the performance, sometimes suspending its course then starting it up again and linking the stage area with the auditorium, the characters of Tolstoy's novel with the audience of the 1930s.

Wearing a dark blue jacket buttoned all the way up the front and holding a small notebook and pencil, Vasily Kachalov opened the performance, standing down below in the stalls with the audience; then he ascended to the stage and stopped before the drawn curtain; when the curtain opened, he strolled about the stage among the novel's characters, listening to their speeches, now mockingly, now sympathetically, now compassionately, now angrily, sometimes mingling with them cordially, sometimes turning away in disgust. The plan for the part as Nemirovich-Danchenko proposed it to Kachalov turned the 'Character on the Author's Behalf' into the true master of the show. Freely moving from scene to scene, Kachalov, whom the other characters did not see, of whose presence they were unaware, not only saw and heard them but could also read their thoughts. Again and again he went down to the stalls, walked along the aisle silently and softly and related what Katyusha Maslova was thinking, what Nekhlyudov wanted, what he feared, what was disturbing the Chairman of the trial, what was causing the Prosecutor to fidget and fret. The 'Character on the Author's Behalf' possessed the wisdom and omniscience of the author, Lev Tolstoy,

and Kachalov's rich, deep, expressive voice was perceived as that of Tolstoy himself.

Nemirovich-Danchenko wanted Tolstoy's prose to pour onto the stage in a free, broad flow, uninhibited by theatrical conventions, so that the novel's epic course should not disintegrate into individual dramatic episodes.

The accent – and it was a strong one – fell upon the fate of Katyusha Maslova; the fate of Prince Nekhlyudov, a motif which is extremely important to Tolstoy, was of little interest to Nemirovich-Danchenko. Nekhlyudov was portrayed as the bearer of social ills, as the perpetrator of all Katyusha Maslova's misfortunes, and only in this capacity did he attract the audience's attention. They did not believe in the sincerity of his repentance and placed no hopes whatsoever on his spiritual revival. Katyusha Maslova, the former peasant now turned prostitute, was dressed in grey prison gown with a white shawl thrown carelessly over her shoulders, dishevelled, at times half drunk, weeping, bawling, at other times as if paralysed, withdrawn into herself. As performed by Xenia Elanskaya the character occupied a prominent place in the production: in her could be sensed a recalcitrant, rebellious nature.

The figure of Katyusha Maslova appeared against a broad social panorama where the cynical comedy of the trial, the soulless ritual of high society, the destitution of the countryside, the gloomy crowd of prisoners shuffling along in transit and their rapacious and cruel pack of escorts were depicted with genuinely Tolstoyan vigour and angry, denunciatory passion. The Chairman of the trial, officers of the court, jailers, Petersburg aristocrats and prison inmates – this motley throng of people that formed the scenic composition – breathed a genuine truthfulness to life.

For an illustration of MAT's position at that time and of the whole theatrical conflict of the 1930s there is a very indicative moment – the sharp change of course that occurred when Stanislavsky joined the rehearsals of Gogol's *Dead Souls*. In the initial work on *Dead Souls*, the director Vasily Sakhnovsky and the author of the stage version, Mikhail Bulgakov, directed their collaborative efforts along lines prompted by Meyerhold's *Government Inspector*. They wanted to preserve the polyphony of Gogol's poem, and the unusual form of the play conceived by Bulgakov had the advantage that it provided an opportunity to introduce into the action Gogol's striking lyrical digressions – on Russia, her melancholy and mysterious song, the 'bird-troika', travel, the institution of provincial balls, his own vocation as a writer. The work proceeded, as Sakhnovsky explained, 'with a measure of the grotesque in view.'[14] Individual excerpts from the play were linked together by a narrator, who was called the 'First Person in the Play' and in whom Gogol himself could easily be detected. Kachalov rehearsed the part, before this entire plan was rejected and destroyed by none other than Stanislavsky.

Stanislavsky's position in the work on *Dead Souls* declared itself above all in his desire to give the comic element free reign. Gogol's lyricism, so powerfully expressed in the great poem-novel, was simply removed.

In 1926 when Meyerhold staged *The Government Inspector*, his Gogol sounded gloomy. In 1932 when Stanislavsky presented *Dead Souls*, Gogol was humorous.

Stanislavsky wanted the set to create a feeling of the epoch, the provinces in the time of Nicholas I and, he maintained, it should not 'strike the eye'. The artist Viktor Simov succeeded in fulfilling these requirements. The two-hander scenes were set simply and sparingly, with a minimum of indispensable objects. It was not merely coincidental that subsequently the two-handers from *Dead Souls* were so frequently and eagerly used by MAT actors at all kinds of performances. Of course the duets between Chichikov and Manilov, Chichikov and Sobakevich, Chichikov and Nozdrev, Chichikov and Plyushkin, Chichikov and Korobochka, inevitably form the structural element of any stage version of *Dead Souls*. But in Stanislavsky's composition Gogol's characters were to express themselves on their own, without the aid of a narrator: the 'First Person in the Play' stood in the way of comedy so Stanislavsky removed him. Lyricism, sadness and lofty pathos also had to make way for comedy. The comic comes across most distinctly and vigorously in the duets, which is why Stanislavsky's production was on the whole made up of them. But Chichikov takes part in each of these duets. Consequently, Stanislavsky reasoned, it was Chichikov who would unite all the show's episodes; Chichikov, not the 'First Person in the Play', would lead the action and raise the comedy up to the height of Gogol's satire.

Stanislavsky perceived all the figures of *Dead Souls* as entirely real from beginning to end and attractive only in this undisputable reality. He saw them as living, believed in them as living, and on his own account endowed them with the logic of the most natural behaviour even in those cases when they acted absurdly or in an improbably fantastic way.

And although at first Stanislavsky's *Dead Souls* was greeted by the critics with coolness, even hostility (one of the most disappointed articles came from the pen of Andrei Bely), gradually it became clear that Stanislavsky had divined the requirements of the time much more surely than the critics. The production grew more successful from season to season. Chichikov (Vasily Toporkov), Sobakevich (Mikhail Tarkhanov), Nozdrev (Ivan Moskvin), Plyushkin (Leonid Leonidov) and Korobochka (Anastasia Zueva) became not merely favourites of the Moscow public but Moscow tourist attractions – as did all the characters from MAT's best productions. Arriving in the capital, any provincial intellectual set as his first task an attempt to get into the MAT, to make communion with its art, to go to *Days of the Turbins* or *A Passionate Heart*, to see *Le Mariage de Figaro*, *Uncle's Dream*, *Resurrection* and *Dead Souls*. By no means everyone managed this: in the 1930s crowds of people besieged the Moscow Art Theatre every evening hoping for the miracle – a spare ticket.

The Vakhtangov Theatre also enjoyed great popularity. In 1932 when the 'outsider' Nikolai Akimov suffered a fiasco with *Hamlet*, the native Vakhtangovite Boris Zakhava staged a new drama by Maxim Gorky, *Egor Bulychov and Others*. In this production the distinct class descriptions were based on specific historical detail, broad generalizations were condensed and concentrated on the psychologically subtle aspect of the characters, and the personal, the unrepeatedly individual, even the unique, was filled with social meaning.

Above all the fate and nature of Egor Bulychov as played by Boris Shchukin were unique in their own way. As distinct from Gorky's earlier plays such as *The Philistines*, *The Lower Depths*, *Enemies*, *The Barbarians* and others, which have a centrifugal structure, the new play was centripetal and everything was drawn together round Bulychov. Shchukin understood the theme of illness and Bulychov's approaching death as a social tragedy. The actor said that he 'could not accept the image of a gloomy, corpulent, frowning, slightly hunched, sick man. My Bulychov fought death because he loved the joys of life. . . . This new strong taste for life in Bulychov defined much in the image.'[15] The acting was in the major key. 'He can not sit still,' wrote the critic Yuzovsky about Shchukin's Bulychov, 'he has to leap up, pace across the room, and this release of energy reveals the feverish rhythm of his thinking which induces him to action. In his eyes there flashes a spark that fires his interlocutor, a spark behind which is sensed his mind, sharp, restless, mocking. His head thrown back and his half-closed, challenging, mischievous glance – these were the main features of Shchukin's outward appearance.'[16]

Every one of Bulychov's encounters with 'others' was turned into a theatrical metaphor. They were crowned by the final scene with the trumpeter Gabriel who tries to cure all illnesses with a fireman's trumpet. The emaciated, feeble trumpeter (Viktor Koltsov) wearing an old fireman's uniform, glanced slyly at Bulychov. The peals of the trumpet shook the entire house, and their threatening sound brought great delight to Bulychov. With broad sweeps of his hand, he directed the frenzied roar of the brass instruments like a conductor.

The production was designed by Vladimir Dmitriev. He portrayed Bulychov's two-storey home in cross-section. All the rooms, studies, attics, closets furnished in ornate Art Nouveau style, but also with old steel-bound trunks and an old-fashioned stove-bench, conveyed the inertia of the ceaseless course of firmly established life. But its imminent end could also be felt. The play of light and shadows created a disturbing mobility throughout the entire space which was partitioned into a chequered pattern.

The play's polyphonic structure pre-determined Zakhava's entire directorial composition. Alongside Shchukin's Bulychov there lived distinctive, individual people and each one had his own rights, each one asserted his own truth. The intricate multi-voiced acting ensemble was interrupted only during the intervals between scenes when the characters of the play came out onto the forestage and read communiqués from newspapers of 1916 and 1917, as though immersing all the drama's events in the political context of the immediate pre-Revolutionary epoch.

But neither these overtly publicist interpolations nor the free flow of events from one interior to another, from the first floor to the second and back again, nor the provocative metaphor embodied in some of the episodes, conflicted with the production's principal tendency: it was dominated by realistic means of expression.

Historical detail, social and psychological truth, emotional saturation of the acting – this is what had become firmly established in the Soviet theatre at the beginning of the 1930s. Polemical extremes and the antagonism of aesthetic positions hostile to one another receded into the past. The division of theatres into 'leftists' and 'rightists', avant-garde and traditional, finally lost all meaning. Life had introduced decisive correctives into the former correlation between artistic movements and all this terminology now no longer corresponded to the real course of the theatrical process. The boundary that had formerly separated the old and new theatres disappeared.

This does not mean they were 'stripped of individuality'. On the contrary, the theatre of the 1930s was distinguished by a diversity of directorial and scenographic renderings, a wealth of acting individuality and intensity of creative explorations.

But the very nature of the explorations became different, the panorama of theatrical life had been transformed. And its story is the theme of another book.

Bread

Vladimir Kirshon's *Bread*, a play set in the countryside on the eve of collectivization, was staged at the Moscow Art Theatre in 1931, directed by Ilya Sudakov. Kirshon's contrasting types of manager – one a romantic idealist, the other a down-to-earth rationalist – are very rigid, one-sided characters, but in this production they were softened and rounded by the acting skills of Boris Dobronravov and Nikolai Khmelev.

Two scenes from *Bread*.

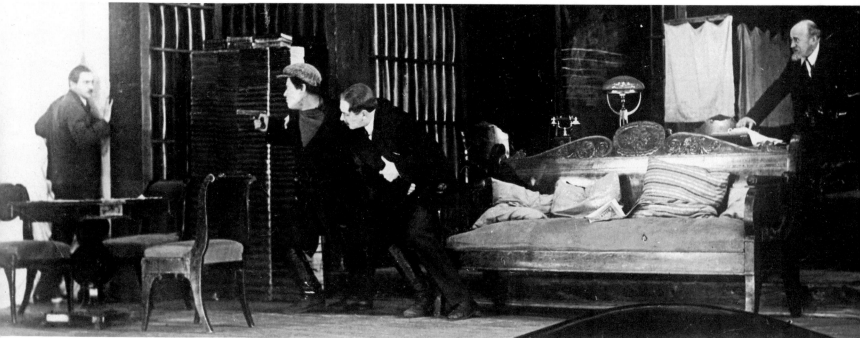

Opposite: Two scenes from *Fear*.
Inset: I. Pevtsov as Borodin.

Topical drama

At the turn of the 1930s there was a marked increase of interest in plays devoted to topical problems, to 'the burning issues' of the day. Alexander Afinogenev's drama *Fear* (1931) once again debated how far intellectuals of pre-Revolutionary formation could be trusted. This play, staged in the Moscow Art Theatre by Ilya Sudakov and in the Leningrad Academic Theatre of Drama by Nikolai Petrov, provoked a lively debate. But around 1929, rightly called 'the year of the great turning point', Soviet Russia had set course for industrialization.

Throughout the country huge factories, power stations and railways were being urgently constructed. And therefore public attention was focused on theatrical productions in which the action took place not in flats, studies or scientific laboratories, but in factories and on building sites. The journalist Nikolai Pogodin offered the theatre a whole series of plays which he called 'theatrical sketches': they captured swiftly but vividly both the enthusiasm of the builders and the difficulties that they were overcoming. The first of these plays, *Tempo*, was staged at the Vakhtangov Theatre in 1930.

Two scenes from *Tempo*.

The Poem
of the Axe

Left and opposite, above and below:
Three scenes from *The Poem of the Axe*. *Below left*: Dmitri Orlov as Stepan. *Below right*: Maria Babanova as Anka.

In the Theatre of the Revolution work on Pogodin's plays created an enthusiastic triumvirate: the dramatist Pogodin, the director Alexei Popov and the designer Ilya Shlepyanov were moving very firmly towards the same goal – the poeticization of a world apparently quite remote from poetry, the practical world of economic productivity. In *The Poem of the Axe* (1931) there were some obvious echoes of the theatrical Constructivism of the early 1920s, but Shlepyanov's constructions were light and delicate. The action was full of humour and the main characters – the young worker Anka and the steel-founder Stepan (played by Maria Babanova and Dmitri Orlov) – were irresistibly authentic and totally captivating.

The production *My Friend* (1932) was emotionally and thematically close to *The Poem of the Axe*, but Shlepyanov for the first time replaced scenery with enormous photo-placards which filled the whole width of the stage and formed the background to the acting.

Alexei Popov's mobile production plan focused on the figure of Grigory Gai, manager of a large construction project, a role played with great energy by Mikhail Astangov. Popov's productions of Pogodin's plays established for the Theatre of the Revolution a leading position in Moscow's theatrical life for quite some time to come.

Left and opposite, above and below:
Three scenes from *My Friend*.

Mikhail Astangov as Grigory Gai.

My Friend

278

Documentary drama

At the beginning of the 1930s, several plays looked back to the heroics of the Civil War for their subject matter. The 1932 production of *The Rout*, based on Alexander Fadeev's novel and staged at the Maly Theatre by Mikhail Narokov, bore eloquent witness to the fact that the old devices which had been used for Civil War plays in the early 1920s did not possess their former emotional force. The fairly clichéd, externally dynamic crowd scenes were internally static, inert – as can be seen from photographs. The production disappointed both the critics and the public.

Boris Romashov's play *The Bridge of Fire* was staged at the Maly Theatre in 1929 by Lev Prozorovsky. The director was perhaps trying to resurrect the methods of theatrical expression that had brought the Maly Theatre a resounding success in the early-1920s production of *Liubov Yarovaya*. But

repetitions in the theatre do not usually come off, and the audience response was decidedly cool.

Alexander Diky's production of Vsevolod Vishnevsky's play *The First Cavalry Army* (1930) at the Theatre of the Revolution staked its success on a completely new form of 'drama without a hero'. Both Vishnevsky and Diky wanted the action to consist entirely of crowd scenes. The hero of the production was to be the soldier masses and their movements over the stage floor were complemented and strengthened by frames from documentary films of the Civil War period. This device initially brought Diky recognition and success, but the success was not long-lived.

Opposite, above: A scene from *The Rout*.
Opposite, below: A scene from *The First Cavalry Army*.

Above: A scene from *The Bridge of Fire* and (*left*) a model of the set by A. Arapov.

The Iron Flood

Two scenes from *The Iron Flood*.

Original experiments were undertaken during the early 1930s by Nikolai Okhlopkov in the tiny premises of the Realistic Theatre. Okhlopkov, more boldly and more vigorously than other

directors, tried to destroy the boundary between actors and audience, between stage and auditorium. The action took place in a small arena surrounded on all sides by spectators and, in addition, many episodes of the 1934 production *The Iron Flood* (based on the novel by Alexander Serafimovich) were performed on small stages that protruded into the stalls. A powerful accompaniment of light and sound effects intensified the illusion that the audience were co-participants in the ceaseless movement of the soldier masses directed by Okhlopkov.

The action of *The Iron Flood* (1934) took place during the Civil War, that of *The Mother* (a 1933 production adapted from Gorky's novel) on the eve of the 1905 Revolution and the events of *The Run* (1932), based on Vladimir Stavsky's documentary essays, in the contemporary countryside. Okhlopkov's 'directorial sketches' and variations were usually based on prose writings, and sometimes he managed to give true expressive force to separate, striking episodes. But still more often the dynamics of his productions became confused, the pathos shrill. Okhlopkov always lacked a sense of judgment and strict taste.

Two scenes from *The Mother*.

Two scenes from *The Run*.

An Optimistic Tragedy

Alisa Koonen as the Commissar.
Above and right, centre and bottom:
Three scenes from *An Optimistic
Tragedy. Top right:* Sketch of the set by
V. Ryndin.

Alexander Tairov's production
of Vsevolod Vishnevsky's *An
Optimistic Tragedy*, in 1933 in
the Kamerny Theatre,
demonstrated a fundamentally
new approach to the heroics
of the Civil War and therefore
became a key event in the
history of Soviet theatre.

Tairov categorically
renounced the reproduction of
minute detail in this
representation of life from the
recent past. With the help of
the designer Vadim Ryndin he
strove for austerity and purity
of form, abstraction from the
concrete and earth-bound. His

centripetal circular composition focused on the heroine, the Commissar, played firmly and masterfully by Alisa Koonen. The crowd scenes completely lost the spontaneity that the directors of heroic productions were usually concerned to achieve.

Tairov's production plan prescribed a strict, spare, controlled form for the crowd scenes. The movements of the regiment of sailors on the Kamerny Theatre's stage had a military precision and the geometrically pure beauty of a blueprint.

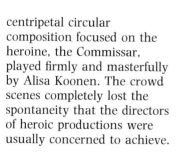

Model of the set by Irakly Gamrekeli for *Anzor*.

Below and right: Two scenes from *Anzor*.

Anzor

A characteristic tendency towards formal and monumental structure was displayed by the Georgian director Sandro Akhmeteli in a whole series of productions at the Rustaveli Theatre in Tbilisi. His partnership with the artist Irakly Gamrekeli proved a very fruitful one. Sandro Shanshiashvili's play *Anzor* (a Georgian variant of Vsevolod Ivanov's play *Armoured Train No. 14-69*) was performed in 1928 on stage-steps of varying heights, the whole set representing a kind of schematic image of a mountain village in the stormy years of the Civil War.

Akhmeteli, like Tairov (although completely independently from him), also sought solemn purity in his crowd scenes, lovingly recording the sculptural expressiveness of Georgian movement and gesture.

Die Raüber

Schiller's *Die Räuber* was
produced by Akhmeteli in
1933 under the title *In
tirannos!*, and he was
successful in his aim of
conveying the angry, anti-
tyrannical pathos of Schiller's
work. But this time too it was
the powerful, integrated form
of the production, devised in
collaboration with Irakly
Gamrekeli, that created the
strongest impression. The
image of a huge, centennial

oak tree, amongst whose
gnarled roots Akhmeteli
deployed his actors on
platforms of varying heights,
served as a metaphor for an
ancient but doomed authority.
Akhmeteli's actors, in
particular Akaky Khorava,
performed splendidly, and the
production, shown not only in
Tbilisi but also in Moscow and
Leningrad, enjoyed enormous
success in all three cities.

Above: Two sketches of the set by
Irakly Gamrekeli for *Die Räuber*.
Right: A scene from *Die Räuber*.

Othello

Right: V. Andzhaparidze as Desdemona, S. Gambashidze as Othello and S. Gomelauri as Iago in the Tbilisi production by Mardzhanishvili.
Below: A. Tarasova as Desdemona and V. Sinitsin as Iago in the Moscow Art Theatre production.

The Moscow Art Theatre's 1930 production of *Othello* took a long time to prepare. Stanislavsky, who was abroad at the time for medical treatment, sent from Badenweiler and Nice his detailed, scene-by-scene production plans for Shakespeare's tragedy. These plans provided the basis for the rehearsals, conducted by Ilya Sudakov in Moscow. The sets and costumes were designed by Alexander Golovin. But Leonid Leonidov as Othello was defeated by the role and this predetermined the failure of the production. In Tbilisi *Othello* was staged in 1932 by Kote Mardzhanishvili (Mardzhanov). The gifted artist Petr Otskheli offered him a very unusual design for the staging (two of the sketches are reproduced here). But the director declined Otskheli's sketches, preferring a more traditional form, and in the end his productions turned out to be very run-of-the-mill.

Two designs by Petr Otskheli of the set (*above*) and Desdemona's costume (*below*) for the Tbilisi production. They were not used.

Tartuffe

Molière's *Tartuffe* (1929) in the Leningrad
Academic Theatre of Drama was the
combined production of three directors –
Nikolai Petrov, Vladimir Soloviev and Nikolai
Akimov (who was also the designer). This
was one of the last attempts to create a
contemporary political revue out of a
classical play. The directors did not tamper
with the Molière text, but they interpolated a
whole series of satirical interludes and mimes
which were intended to transfer the action
into the twentieth century and to ridicule
bourgeois customs. There was a high-kicking
chorus line whose cancan was supposed to
symbolize the licentiousness of the 'yellow
press', and some of the characters wore
masks of contemporary politicians –
Chamberlain, Chiang Kai-shek, Léon Blum
and others, who appeared out of a sewage pipe.

Opppsite and above: Three scenes from
Tartuffe.
Right: Two costume sketches by
Nikolai Akimov.

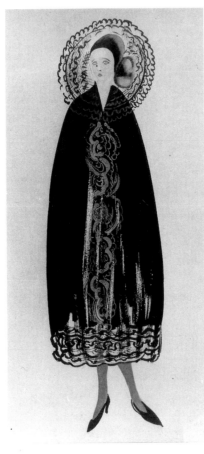

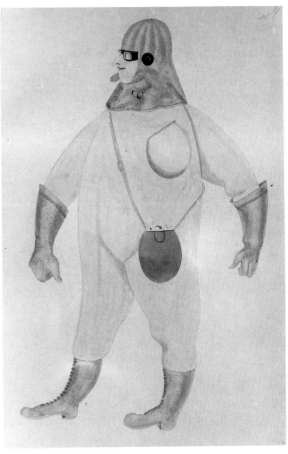

Uncle's Dream

The times dictated a more serious and thoughtful approach to the classics. One of the first to sense this was the most senior of Soviet directors, Nemirovich-Danchenko, who in 1929 staged an adaptation of Dostoevsky's *Uncle's Dream*. Against a background of realistically authentic scenes from Russian nineteenth-century provincial life, he wrested a grotesquely sarcastic performance from the actors, notably Nikolai Khmelev as the prince, Olga Knipper-Chekhova as the parochial schemer and Maria Lilina as the local scandalmonger. A return to concrete realism, it would seem, by no means inhibited eccentricism in the actors' performances.

Three characters in *Uncle's Dream*. *Above*: Olga Knipper-Chekhova as Moskaleva. *Above right*: Nikolai Khmelev as the prince. *Below right*: Maria Lilina as Karpukhina.

Opposite: Two scenes from *Uncle's Dream*.

A scene from *Resurrection. Inset*: Vasily Kachalov as 'the author'.

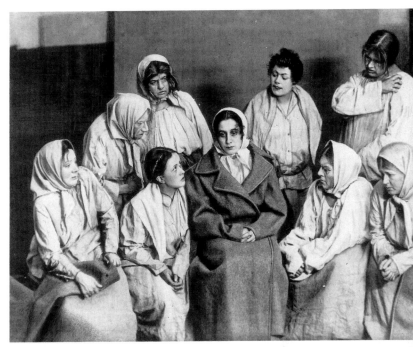

Two scenes from *Resurrection*.

In Nemirovich-Danchenko's adaptation of Tolstoy's *Resurrection* (1930), one of the Moscow Art Theatre's most talented actors, Vasily Kachalov, was given the role of 'the author'. Kachalov, reciting Lev Tolstoy's text, strode about the stage explaining and commenting on the speeches and actions of the novel's characters; he descended into the auditorium and, standing in the stalls, shared with the audience the author's angry and passionate cogitations.

The tone of the production was ironic and sarcastic: the director seized on the satirical pathos of Tolstoy but remained indifferent to his religious and ethical preaching. This predetermined the whole structure of the play, in which the theme of Prince Nekhlyudov (played by Vladimir Ershov) was far less prominent than it is in Tolstoy's novel.

The new play *Egor Bulychov and Others*, written by Gorky at the beginning of the 1930s, served as the basis for a magnificent production by the Vakhtangov Theatre in 1932. It seemed as though the director Boris Zakhava and the designer Vladimir Dmitriev were summing up, in terms both of meaning and style, the many varied theatrical experiments of the period between 1917 and 1932. Particularly in Boris Shchukin's performance of the title role as a man approaching death yet still fighting for life, their production demonstrated the political tendentiousness characteristic of the Soviet stage in the 1920s but it also indicated the thirst for social truthfulness and a firm basis in everyday life; most important of all, it projected the need for a deeper awareness and a philosophical grasp of the social clashes touched upon by the stage.

Two scenes from *Egor Bulychov and Others*.

300

Egor Bulychov and Others

Four characters from *Egor Bulychov and Others*. *Left*: Boris Shchukin as Bulychov, T. Mansurova as Shurka. *Below left*: N. Rusinova as Melania. *Below*: Boris Shchukin as Bulychov and N. Rusinova as Melania.

V. Toporkov as Chichikov.

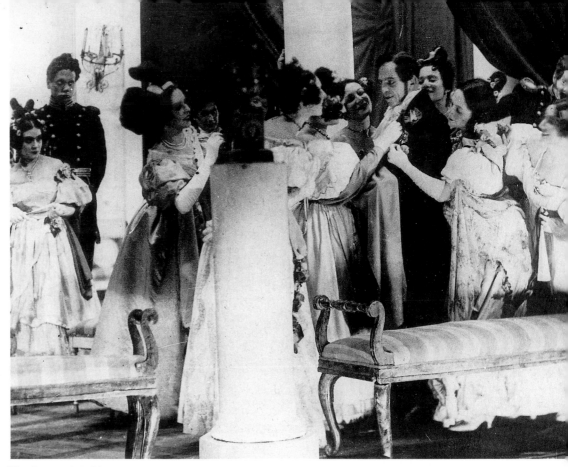

'The Governor's Ball.'

Dead Souls

Gogol's *Dead Souls* was adapted for the Moscow Art Theatre by Mikhail Bulgakov, who strove to retain the unique fusion of satire and lyricism that is the characteristic feature of Gogol's epic poem. But Stanislavsky decisively turned his back on Bulgakov's ideas and directed all his energies to one end – the creation of a comic sequence of the most vivid Gogolian types.

V. Toporkov as Chichikov and M. Tarkhanov as Sobakevich.

M. Tarkhanov as Sobakevich.

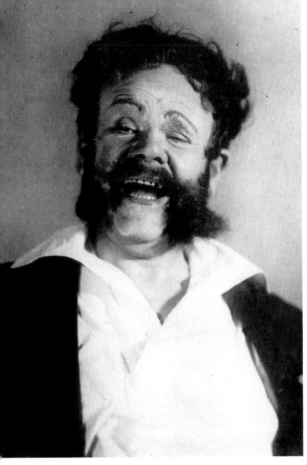

I. Moskvin as Nozdrev.

V. Toporkov as Chichikov and I. Moskvin as Nozdrev.

Although this 1932 production met with a very hostile critical reception, after a few years *Dead Souls* became one of the Moscow Art Theatre productions most loved by the public. Set in the provinces in the time of Nicholas I, various digressions examined the provincial balls of the era, travel and the character of Russia herself. The acting duets in *Dead Souls* were hilariously funny and very entertaining, linked by the figure of Chichikov in each, and Stanislavsky's scrupulous, persistent work with the actors was eventually crowned with irrefutable success.

V. Toporkov as Chichikov and A. Zueva as Korobochka.

Maria Lilina as Korobochka.

'The Governor's Ball' in *Dead Souls*.

Notes on the Text

Chapter 1

1 Ivanov, Vyach., *Borozdy i mezhi* (Moscow, 1916), pp. 276, 280–81.

2 Averintsev, S. S., 'Vyacheslav Ivanov', introduction to the book *Vyacheslav Ivanov. Stikhotvoreniya i poemy* (Leningrad, 1976), p. 17.

3 Bely, Andrei, 'Teatr i sovremennaya drama', *Teatr. Kniga o novom teatre* (St Petersburg, 1908), pp. 271–273.

4 Averintsev, op.cit., p. 16.

5 Mayakovsky, V. V., *Teatr i kino*, 2 vols. (Moscow, 1954), vol. 1, pp. 379–381.

6 *Ezhegodnik rukopisnogo otdela Pushkinskogo doma na 1974 god* (Leningrad, 1976), pp. 177–179.

7 Livshits, Benedikt, *Polutoraglazyi strelets* (Leningrad, 1933), p. 187.

8 Matyushin, M. V., 'Tvorcheskii put' khudozhnika', IRLI, fond 656, p. 79.

9 Ibid.

10 *Den*, 4 December 1913.

11 *Teatr i iskusstvo*, 1913, no. 49.

12 Cited in N. Khardzhiev 'Iz materialov o Mayakovskom', *Zhurnal 30 dnei*, 1939, no. 7, p. 39.

13 Yartsev, P., 'Teatr futuristov', *Rech'*, 7 December 1913.

14 *Russkoe slovo*, 4 December 1913. Kuzma Prutkov was the humorous invention of Count Alexei Tolstoy and several other literati of the mid nineteenth century. Prutkov, a clerk in the Ministry of Finance, wrote a great deal, his naive and complacent arrogance expressing itself in pompous platitudes. He was an ideal vehicle for parodies of various literary styles then in vogue. His 'dates' were 1803 to 1863, most of his 'works' appearing late in his 'career', from the 1850s until his much lamented 'death'. Everything about him is fictitious – except the bibliography of his published works.

15 Livshits, B. op. cit., p. 185.

16 Mgebrov, A., *Zhizn' v teatre* (1939), vol. 2, p. 274.

17 Yartsev, P., op. cit.

18 Livshits, B., op. cit., pp. 184–5.

19 *Den*, 31 November 1913.

20 Tomashevsky, K., 'Vladimir Mayakovskii', *Teatr*, 1938, no. 4, p. 140.

21 Pasternak, Boris, *Okhrannaya gramota* (Leningrad, 1931), p. 100.

22 Cited in S. Bushueva, *Polveka ital yanskogo teatra* (Leningrad, 1978), p. 141.

23 Until 1918 Russia used the Julian calendar, whereas the rest of Europe used the Gregorian calendar. By the twentieth century the dates of the Julian calendar were thirteen days behind those of the Gregorian.

24 *Teatr*, 7–8 April 1918.

25 *Maski*, 1913, no. 3, p. 87.

26 *Maski*, 1913–1914, no. 2, p. 53.

27 Geronsky, G., *Alisa Koonen* (Moscow-Leningrad, 1927), p. 10.

28 Efros, A. M., Introduction to *Kamernyi teatr i ego khudozhniki* (Moscow, 1934), p. ix.

29 Tairov, A. Ya., *O teatre* (Moscow, 1970), pp. 113–114.

30 Meyerhold, V. E., *Stati, pisma, rechi, besedy*, 2 vols. (Moscow, 1968), vol. 2, p. 37.

31 *Teatralnaya gazeta*, 14 February 1916.

32 Koonen, A., *Stranitsy zhizni* (Moscow, 1975), p. 207.

33 Tairov, A. Ya., op. cit., p. 100.

34 Koonen, A., op. cit., p. 207.

35 Tairov, A. Ya., op. cit., pp. 100, 102, 104.

36 *Teatr*, 1916, no. 2952, p. 10.

37 Efros, A., op. cit., p. xxii.

38 Ibid., p. xxiv.

39 Tairov, A. Ya., op. cit., p. 167.

40 *Apollon*, 1917, no. 1, p. 74.

41 Koonen, A., op. cit., p. 231.

42 *Sovetskii teatr. Dokumenty i materialy. 1917–1921* (Leningrad, 1968), p. 164.

43 Efros, A., op. cit., p. xxv.

44 *Teatr i musyka*, 1923, no. 10, p. 176.

45 Bachelis, Tatyana, 'Rezhisser Stanislavskii,' *Novyi mir*, 1963, no. 1, p. 207.

46 Stanislavsky, K. S., *Sobranie sochinenii*, 8 vols (Moscow, 1954–61), vol. 7, p. 539.

47 Ibid., vol. 1, p. 346.

48 *Rech*, 31 March 1915.

49 Markov, P., *V Khudozhestvennom teatre* (Moscow, 1976), pp. 125, 126.

50 *Rech*, 7 April 1915.

51 Stanislavsky, K. S., op. cit., vol. 1, p. 365.

52 Markov, P., *O teatre*, 4 vols. (Moscow 1974–77), vol. 1, p. 367.

53 Vinogradskaya, I. N., *Zhizn i tvorchestvo K. S. Stanislavskogo, Letopis*, 4 vols, (Moscow 1971–76), vol. 2, pp. 412, 413.

54 Stanislavsky, K. S., op. cit., vol. 1, p. 354.

55 Markov, P., op. cit., vol. 1, p. 371.

56 Ibid., p. 364.

57 Popov, A. D. *Vospominaniya i razmyshleniya o teatre* (Moscow, 1963), p. 126.

58 Nemirovich-Danchenko, V.I., *Izbrannye pisma*, vol. 2 (Moscow, 1979), pp. 204–206.

59 *Rech*, 11 January 1916.

60 *Birzhevye vedomosti*, 21 February 1916.

61 *Teatr i iskusstvo*, 1916, no. 3, p. 60.

62 Expression of the theatre historian Alexander Matskin. *See* Matskin, A. P., *Portrety i nablyudeniya* (Moscow, 1973), p. 259.

63 *Teatr i iskusstvo*, 1917, no. 10–11, p. 192.

64 Sergei Bondi recounted to Rudnitsky.

65 Alexei Gripich in a letter to Rudnitsky.

66 Cited in K. Rudnitsky *Rezhisser Meierkhold* (Moscow, 1969), pp. 172–173.

67 *Pravda*, 4 (17) February 1918.

Chapter 2

1 *Khodozhestvennaya zhizn*, 1919, no. 4–5, p. 26.

2 *Zhizn iskusstva*, 4 April 1920.

3 *Pechat i revolyutsiya*, 1921, no. 3, p. 117.

4 Lunacharsky, A. V., *Stati o teatre i dramaturgii* (Moscow-Leningrad, 1938), p. 87.

5 Lenin V. I., *Polnoe sobranie sochinenii*, 55 vols (Moscow, 1958–65), vol. 26, p. 127.

6 *Teatr i iskusstvo*, 1918, No. 3, p. 43.

7 Mayakovsky, V. V. *Teatr i kino* (Moscow, 1954), vol. 1, p. 322.

8 *Zhizn iskusstva*, 11 November 1918.

9 Lunacharsky, A. V. *Taatr segodnya* (Moscow-Leningrad, 1927), p. 101.

10 *Russkoe iskusstvo*, 1923, No. 1, p. 11.

11 Blok, A., *Zapisnye knizhki* (Moscow, 1965), p. 435.

12 *Teatralnyi kurer*, 9 October 1918.

13 *Teatralnyi kurer*, 14 November 1918.

14 *Vestnik teatra*, 7 November 1919.

15 *Kultura teatra*, 1921, no. 4, p. 2.

16 Cited in *Istoriya sovetskogo teatra*, vol. 1 (Leningrad, 1933), p. 279.

17 *Vestnik rabotnikov iskusstv*, 1920, no. 2–3, p. 6.

18 Kerzhentsev, P. M., *Tvorcheskii teatr* (Petrograd, 1923), pp. 67, 78, 89.

19 *Vestnik rabotnikov iskusstv*, 1920, no. 2–3, p. 7.

20 Lunacharsky, A. V., *Chemu sluzhit teatr* (Moscow, 1925), pp. 43–46.

21 *V.I. Lenin o literature i iskusstve* (Moscow, 1969), p. 665.

22 *Gorn*, 1919, no. 1, pp. 2, 6.

23 *Izvestiya*, 27 October 1918.

24 Kerzhentsev, P., *Revolyutsiya i teatr* (Moscow, 1919), pp. 9, 10, 28.

25 *V. I. Lenin o literature i iskusstve*, p. 443.

26 Ibid., p. 455.

27 *Sovremennyi teatr*, 1927, no. 10, p. 148.

28 *Vestnik teatra*, 1919, no. 14, p. 3

29 *Sovetskii teatr. Dokumenty, materialy 1917–1921* (Leningrad, 1968), pp. 317–318.

30 Yuriev, Yu. M., *Zapiski* (Moscow-Leningrad, 1948), p. 565.

31 Prozorovsky, L., *Iz proshlykh let* (Moscow, 1958), pp. 121–122.

32 Nemirovich-Danchenko, V. I., *Teatralnoe nasledie*, vol. 1 (Moscow, 1952), p. 147.

33 *Moskovskii Khudozhestvennyi teatr v sovetskuyu epokhu. Materialy i dokumenty* (Moscow, 1974), p. 44.

34 Lunacharsky, A. V., *Sobranie sochinenii*, 8 vols (Moscow, 1963–67), vol. 8, p. 50.

35 Stanislavsky, K. S., *Sobranie sochinenii* (Moscow, 1954–61), vol. 5, pp. 249–50.

36 Nemirovich-Danchenko, V. I., *Teatralnoe nasledie*, vol. 1 (Moscow, 1952), pp. 151–152.

37 Cited in A. Yufit, *Revolyutsiya i teatr* (Leningrad, 1977), p. 98.

38 *Khudozhniki teatra o svoem tvorchestve* (Moscow, 1973), pp. 211–212.

39 Yureneva, Vera, *Zapiski aktrisy* (Moscow-Leningrad, 1946), p. 169.

40 Stepnaya, E., *V velikie gody* (Saratov, 1925), p. 22.

41 Sobolev, Yury, *Za kulisami provintsial'nogo teatra*, p. 63.

42 Blok, Alexander, *Sobranie sochinenii*, vol. 6 (Moscow-Leningrad, 1962), pp. 282, 299.

43 *A. V. Lunacharsky o teatre i dramaturgii*, 2 vols. (Moscow, 1958), vol. 1, p. 163.

44 *Rabochii i teatr*, 1936, no. 13, p. 17.

45 *A. V. Lunacharsky o teatre i dramaturgii*, vol. 1, p. 165.

46 Michurina-Samoilova, V. A., *Shestdesyat let v iskusstve* (Leningrad-Moscow, 1946), p. 95.

47 Cited in D. Zolotnitsky, *Zori teatralnogo Oktyabrya* (Leningrad, 1976), pp. 27–28.

48 *Zhizn iskusstva*, 7–9 June 1919, p. 5.

49 Yuzhin-Sumbatov, A. I., *Zapiski, stati, pisma* (Moscow, 1941), p. 170.

50 Ibid., p. 187.

51 *Izvestiya*, 23 October 1918.

52 Cited in *Istoriya sovetskogo dramaticheskogo teatra*, vol. 1 (Moscow, 1966), p. 115.

53 Stanislavsky, op. cit., vol. 1, p. 325.

54 *Sovetskii teatr. Dokumenty*, p. 126.

55 Vinogradskaya, I. N., *Zhizn i tvorchestvo K. S. Stanislavskogo, Letopis*, vol. 3 (Moscow, 1973), p. 32.

56 Markov, P. A. *V Khudozhestvennom teatre* (Moscow, 1976), p. 146.

57 *Teatr*, 1922, No. 2, p. 39.

58 Vakhtangov, E., *Materialy i stati* (Moscow, 1959), pp. 166–168.

59 Zograf, N. G. *Vakhtangov* (Moscow-Leningrad, 1939), p. 94.

60 Markov, P., *O teatre*, vol. 1 (Moscow, 1974), p. 391.

61 *Teatr i muzyka*, 1923, No. 5, p. 17.

62 Zograf, N., *Vakhtangov* (Moscow-Leningrad, 1939), p. 121.

63 *Muzyka i teatr*, 25 June 1923.

64 Volkov, Nikolai, *Vakhtangov* (Moscow, 1922), pp. 17, 20.

65 Vakhtangov, op. cit., p. 209.

66 Volkov, op. cit., pp. 18–19.

67 Simonov, R., *S Vakhtangovym* (Moscow, 1959), p. 139.

68 Markov, P., *O teatre*, vol. 3 (Moscow, 1976), pp. 81–83.

69 *See* Vakhtangov, *Materialy i stati*, pp. 217–219.

70 Tairov, Alexander *Proklamatsii khudozhnika* (Moscow, 1917), pp. 21–22.

71 *Sovetskii teatr. Dokumenty*, p. 161.

72 *Teatralnyi kurer*, 1918, no. 2, p. 4.

73 Efros, A. M., Introduction to *Kamerny teatr i ego khudozhnimki* (Moscow, 1934), p. xxx.

74 *Izvestiya*, 27 November 1919.

75 Markov, P. A., *O teatre*, vol. 2 (Moscow, 1974), p. 292.
76 Grossman, Leonid, *Alisa Koonen* (Moscow-Leningrad, 1930), p. 54.
77 *Vremennik TEO Narkomprosa*, vyp. 1, 1918, p. 30.
78 *Zhizn iskusstva*, 15 January 1920.
79 Ibid., 27–29 March 1920.
80 Ibid., 11 May 1921.
81 Radlov, Sergei, *Desyat let v teatre* (Leningrad, 1929), p. 179.
82 *Dom Iskusstv*, 1921, No. 2, p. 65.
83 *Zhizn' iskusstva*, 19–20 June 1920.
84 *Novyi mir*, 1968, No. 3, p. 24.
85 *Zhizn iskusstva*, 12 November 1920.
86 Lunacharsky, A. V., *Sobranie sochinenii*, 8 vols, (Moscow, 1963–67), vol. 3, p. 127.
87 *Vestnik teatra*, 20 November 1920.
88 *Zhizn iskusstva*, 10–12 December 1920.
89 Alpers, B., *Teatr sotsialnoi maski* (Moscow, 1931), p. 23.
90 *Vestnik teatra*, 7 November 1920.
91 Collection, *O teatre* (Tver, 1922). p. 73.
92 Lunacharsky, A. V., *Teatr i revolyutsiya* (Moscow, 1924), pp. 106–107.
93 Mayakovsky, V., *Polnoe sobranie sochinenii*, 13 vols (Moscow, 1955–61), vol. 12, p. 246.
94 *N. K. Krupskaya ob iskysstve i literature* (Leningrad-Moscow, 1963), p. 141.
95 TsGALI, fond 963, op. 1, no. 10, 1. 16–25.
96 *Vestnik teatra*, 30 November 1920.
97 Mayakovsky, op. cit., vol. 12, p. 246.
98 Cited in K. Rudnitsky, *Rezhisser Meierkhol'd*, p. 244.
99 Collection, *Mayakovsky v vospominaniyakh sovremennikov* (Moscow, 1963), p. 308.
100 Ibid., pp. 284, 285.
101 *Vestnik rabotnikov iskusstv*, 1921, no. 10–11, p. 122.
102 Ibid., no. 7–9, p. 31.
103 Furmanov, D., *Sobranie sochinenii*, vol. 4 (Moscow, 1961), p. 254.
104 Lunacharsky, A. V., *Teatr segodnya* (Moscow-Leningrad, 1928), p. 106.
105 *Pechat i revolyutsiya*, 1921, no. 2, p. 226.
106 Lunacharsky, A. V., *Teatr segodnya* (Moscow-Leningrad, 1928), pp. 101–102.

Chapter 3

1 *Zhizn*, 1922, no. 1, pp. 150–151.
2 Collection *O teatre* (Tver, 1922), pp. 2–3.
3 *Pechat i revolyutsiya*, 1922, no. 1, p. 307.
4 *Zhizn*, 1922, no. 1, p. 155.
5 Ibid., p. 149.
6 *Chitatel i pisatel*, 11 February 1928.
7 Bulgakov, Mikhail, *Black Snow* (written 1936–37).
8 *Chitatel i pisatel*, 1 February 1928.
9 *Literaturnye manifesty* (Moscow, 1924), pp. 257–258.
10 *Ermitazh*, 1922, no. 11, p. 3.
11 *Iskusstvo trudyashchimsya* vyp. 1 (Moscow, 1921), p. 8.
12 Arvatov, B., *Iskusstvo i klassy* (Moscow-Petrograd, 1923), p. 85.
13 Collection *Teatralnyi Oktyabr* (Leningrad-Moscow, 1926), p. 34.
14 *Zhizn iskusstva*, 1923, no. 20, p. 3.
15 GVYRM – Gosudarstvennaya vysshaya rezhisserskaya masterskaya (State Higher Directors' Workshop); GVYTM – the same, but re-named 'Theatrical'; GEKTEMAS, the same but 'Experimental Theatrical'; GITIS – Gosudarstvennyi institut teatralnogo iskusstva (State Institute of Theatrical Art).
16 Alpers, B., *Teatralnye ocherki* (Moscow, 1977), vol. 2, p. 463.
17 Meyerhold, V. E., *Stati, pisma, rechi, besedy*, vol. 2 (Moscow, 1968), pp. 21–22, 30–34.
18 *Pravda*, 19 January 1924.
19 Eisenstein, S., *Izbrannye proizvedeniya*, 6 vols, (Moscow, 1964–67), vol. 1, pp. 309–310.
20 *Izvestiya*, 20 April 1922.
21 Gvozdev, A. A., *Teatr imeni Vs. Meierkholda* (Leningrad, 1927), p. 28.
22 Collection *Teatralnyi Oktyabr* (Leningrad-Moscow, 1926), p. 34.
23 Ilinsky, Igor, *Sam o sebe* (Moscow, 1961), p. 148.
24 *Ermitazh*, 1922, no. 6, p. 9.
25 Ibid., 1922, no. 6, p. 10.
26 TsGALI, fond 998, op. 1, no. 786, p. 12.
27 *Zhizn iskusstva*, 1927, no. 27, pp. 8–9.
28 *Teatr i muzyka*, 1922, no. 1–7, p. 24.
29 Kozintsev, Grigory, *Sobranie sochinenii*, 5 vols (Leningrad, 1982–86), vol. 3, pp. 73–74.
30 Ibid., vol. 1, pp. 55–56.
31 *Vremennik RTO* (Moscow, 1925), p. 239.
32 *Iskusstvo kino* (1968), no. 1, p. 102.
33 Meyerhold, op. cit., vol. 2, pp. 451, 470.
35 *Zrelischa*, 1924, no. 69, p. 12.
36 Eisenstein, op. cit., vol. 5, p. 62.
37 *Zhizn iskusstva*, 1927, no. 46, p. 7.
38 *Vechernyaya Moskva*, 21 March 1924.
39 *Ermitazh*, 1922, no. 6, pp. 5–6.
40 *Sovetskaya estrada i tsirk*, 1963, no. 1, p. 9.
41 Yutkevich, Sergei, *Kontrapunkt rezhissera* (Moscow, 1960), p. 232.
42 *Teatralnaya Moskva*, 1925, no. 25, p. 5.
43 Ibid., 1922, no. 23, pp. 9–10.
44 Uvarova, E., *Estradnyi teatr: miniatyury, obozreniya, myuzik-kholly* (Moscow, 1983), p. 58.
45 Ibid., p. 62.
46 *Zrelishcha*, 1923, no. 68, p. 15.
47 Ibid., no. 25, p. 3.
48 Markov, P., *O teatre*, vol. 3, p. 165.
49 Ibid., p. 60.
50 Collection *Ritm i kultura tantsa* (Leningrad, 1926), p. 45.
51 *Rabochii i teatr*, 1931, no. 24, pp. 8–9.
52 *Zhizn iskusstva*, 1927, no. 21, p. 15.
53 Alpers, B. V., *Teatr Revolyutsii* (Moscow, 1928), pp. 49–50.
54 Piotrovsky, Adrian, *Teatr. Kino. Zhizn.* (Leningrad, 1969), p. 115.
55 *Zhizn iskusstva*, 1923, no. 35, p. 5.
56 Ibid., 1924, no. 17, p. 3.
57 *Khudozhestvennyi trud*, 1923, no. 4, p. 5.
58 *Izvestiya*, 11 November 1924.
59 *Zhizn iskusstva*, 1927, no. 46, p. 7.
60 Collection *U istokov* (Moscow, 1960), p. 214.
61 *Zhizn iskusstva*, 1924, no. 23, pp. 12–13.

62 Ilinsky, Igor, *Sam o sebye*, p. 182.

63 Mayakovsky, V. V., *Polnoe sobranie sochinenii*, 13 vols (Moscow, 1955–61), vol. 12, p. 472.

64 *Izvestiya*, 16 July 1921.

65 Mayakovsky, V. V., op. cit., vol. 12, p. 472.

66 Ilinksy, Igor, op. cit., p. 196.

67 Collection *V. E. Meierkhold* (Tver, 1923), pp. 5, 6, 28.

68 *Zrelishcha*, 1923, no. 30, pp. 15–16.

69 *Zhizn iskusstva*, 1923, no. 32, p. 18.

70 Freidkina, L. M., *Dni i gody V. I. Nemirovich-Danchenko. Letopis.* (Moscow, 1962), p. 364.

71 *Ermitazh*, 1922, no. 8, p. 6.

72 *Ezhenedelnik akademicheskikh teatrov* (Leningrad, 1924), no. 12, p. 6.

73 Koonen, Alisa, *Stranitsy zhizni* (Moscow, 1975), p. 857.

74 Efros, A. M., Introduction to *Khudozhniki Kamernogo teatra*, (Moscow, 1934), p. xxxi.

75 *Kultura teatra*, 1921, no. 3, p. 44.

76 Tairov, A. Ya., *O teatre* (Moscow, 1970), p. 293.

77 Markov, P., *O teatre*, vol. 2, p. 92.

78 *Teatr i muzyka*, 1923, no. 55, p. 111.

79 *Pravda*, 11 October 1922.

80 TsGALI, fond 2328, op. 1, ed. khr. 12, 1. 6.

81 *Dni*, 15 April 1923.

82 Markov, P., *O teatre*, vol. 2, p. 293.

83 *Izvestiya*, 11 February 1922.

84 *Zveno*, 26 March 1923.

85 Grossman, Leonid, *Alisa Koonen* (Moscow, 1927), p. 60.

86 *Izvestiya*, 11 February 1922.

87 Derzhavin, K., *Kniga o Kamernom teatre* (Leningrad, 1934), p. 109.

88 Tairov, A. Ya., *O teatre*, p. 207.

89 *Teatr i muzyka*, 1923, No. 35, p. 1107.

90 Zhan Kokto (Jean Cocteau), *Portrety i vospominaniya* (Moscow, 1985), p. 119.

91 *Ogonek*, 1924, no. 2, p. 17.

92 *Izvestiya*, 14 December 1923.

93 *Zrelishcha*, 1923, no. 68, p. 12.

94 *Teatr i muzyka*, 1922, no. 9, p. 110.

95 Ibid., p. 111.

96 *Mikhoels. Stati, besedy, rechi. Stati i vospominaniya o Mikhoelse* (Moscow, 1981), pp. 342, 344.

97 *Sovetskoe iskusstvo*, 5 April 1935.

98 Lenin, V. I., *Polnoe sobranie sochinenii*, 55 vols, (Moscow, 1958–65), vol. 44, p. 146.

99 *Iskusstvo*, Kiev, 1919, no. 1, p. 18.

100 Kuzyakina, N. B. *Stanovleine ukrainskoi sovetskoi rezhissury* (Leningrad, 1984), pp. 23–24.

101 *Siluety*, (Odessa, 1924), no. 31, p. 11.

102 *Internatsional'nyi teatr*, 1933, no. 4, p. 45.

103 *Voprosy literatury*, 1983, no. 9, p. 161.

104 *Krasnaya gazeta* (Leningrad), 17 June 1926.

105 Kuzyakina, op. cit., p. 39.

106 Ibid., p. 40.

107 *Kultura teatra*, 1921, no. 6, pp. 18–20.

108 *Vestnik rabotnikov iskusstv* (Moscow, 1921), no. 7–9, p. 34.

109 Koonen, Alisa, *Stranitsy zhizni* (Moscow, 1975), p. 268.

110 *Teatr*, 1966, no. 5, p. 107.

111 Alpers, B., *Teatralnye ocherki*, vol. 2 (Moscow, 1977), p. 67.

112 *Zhizn iskusstva*, 1924, no. 49, p. 7.

113 Markov, P., *O teatre*, vol. 1, pp. 406–407.

114 Mardzhanishvili, Kote, *Tvorcheskoe nasledie*, vol. 1 (Tbilisi, 1958), p. 279.

115 Cited in the book: Dzhafarov, Dzhafar, *Azerbaidzhanskii dramaticheskii teatr (1873–1941)* (Baku, 1962), pp. 178–179.

116 Ibid., p. 181.

117 Ibid., p. 182.

118 *A. V. Lunacharsky o teatre i dramaturgii*, vol. 1 (Moscow, 1958), p. 247.

119 *Rabochii teatr*, 1935, no. 19, p. 16.

120 Collection *O teatre* (Leningrad, 1926), p. 59.

121 *Zhizn iskusstva*, 1924, no. 21.

122 Derzhavin, Konstantin, *Kniga o Kamernom teatre*, pp. 137–138.

123 *A. V. Lunacharsky o teatre i dramaturgii*, vol. 1, p. 414.

124 *Zhizn iskusstva*, 1924, no. 21.

125 Cited in Grossman, Leonid, *Alisa Koonen* (Moscow-Leningrad, 1930), p. 71.

126 Cited in Grossman, Leonid, *Alisa Koonen* (Moscow-Leningrad, 1930), p. 71.

126 Markov, P., *V Khudozhestvennom teatre*, p. 158.

127 Stroeva, M., *Rezhisserskie iskaniya Stanislavskogo, 1917–1938* (Moscow, 1977), pp. 104–105.

128 *Krasnaya niva*, 1926, no. 8, p. 18.

129 Ibid.

130 *A. V. Lunacharsky o teatre dramaturgii*, vol. 1, p. 247.

131 *Rabochii i teatr*, 1925, no. 39, p. 11.

132 *Pravda*, 24 February 1925.

133 *Novyi zritel*, 1925, no. 6, p. 11.

134 Collection *Dmitry Nikolaevich Orlov. Kniga o tvorchestve* (Moscow, 1962), p. 207.

135 *Vechernyaya Moskva*, 6 April 1925.

136 Ibid.

137 *A. V. Lunacharsky o teatre i dramaturgii*, vol. 1, pp. 282–283.

Chapter 4

1 Collection *Teatr Moskovskogo proletariata* (Moscow, 1934), p. 147.

2 See *Vasilii Vasilievich Vanin* (Moscow, 1955), pp. 110, 131.

3 *Literaturnaya gazeta*, 8 January 1955.

4 *Krasnaya gazeta* (evening edition), 20 January 1928.

5 Trenev, K., *Izbrannye proizvedeniya* (Moscow, 1959), p. 800.

6 *A. V. Lunacharsky o teatre i dramaturgii*, vol. 1, p. 345.

7 *Vechernyaya Moskva*, 7 January 1926.

8 *Novyi zritel*, 26 October 1926, p. 2.

9 Popov, Alexei, *Vospominaniya i razmyshleniya o teatre* (Moscow, 1963), p. 78.

10 *Teatr i dramaturgiya*, 1934, No. 3, p. 28.

11 *Sovremennyi teatr*, 1929, No. 7, p. 111.

12 *Vechernyaya Moskva*, 25 February 1929.

13 *Literaturnaya gazeta*, 22 February 1947.

14 Popov, op. cit., p. 192.

15 Stanislavsky, K. S., *Sobranie Sochinenii* (Moscow, 1954–61), vol. 6, p. 250.

16 Vinogradskaya, I. N., *Zhizn i tvorchestvo K. S. Stanislavskogo, Letopis*, 4 vols, (Moscow 1971–76), vol. 3, p. 492.

17   Ibid., p. 512.
18   *Voprosy literatury*, 1977, No. 3, p. 187.
19   *A. V. Lunacharsky o teatre i dramaturgii*, vol. 1, p. 497.
20   Markov, P., *O teatre*, vol. 3, pp. 169–170.
21   Collection *Gogol i Meierkhold* (Moscow, 1927), p. 79.
22   *Krasnaya gazeta* (evening edition), 22 December 1926.
23   *Vechernyaya Moskva*, 27 November 1926.
24   *A. V. Lunacharsky o teatre i dramaturgii*, vol. 1, p. 406.
25   *Izvestiya*, 10 December 1926.
26   *A. V. Lunacharsky o teatre i dramaturgii*, vol. 1, pp. 393–407.
27   *Chitatel i pisatel*, 24 March 1928.
28   Ibid.
29   *Izvestiya*, 12 October 1935.
30   *Novyi zritel*, 1925, no. 7, p. 7.
31   Diky, Alexei, *Povest o teatralnoi yunosti* (Moscow, 1957), pp. 342, 349.
32   Cited in Andrei Bely, *Peterburg* (Moscow, 1981), p. 521–522.
33   Markov, P., *O teatre*, vol. 3, pp. 303, 311–312.
34   *Vechernyaya Moskva*, 13 January 1928.
35   *Programmy Gos. Ak. teatrov* (Moscow, 1927), no. 7, pp. 2–3.
36   *Izvestiya*, 16 March 1924.
37   *Krasnaya panorama*, 1927, No. 17, p. 13.
38   *Zhizn iskusstva*, 1927, No. 21, p. 15.
39   Collection *Kamernyi teatr. Stati, zametki, vospominaniya* (Moscow, 1934), pp. 38–39.
40   Grossman, Leonid, *Alisa Koonen* (Moscow-Leningrad, 1930), pp. 76–78.
41   *Teatr i dramaturgiya*, 1935, No. 1, p. 27.
42   Berkovsky, N. Ya., *Literatura i teatr* (Moscow, 1969), p. 380.
43   Koonen, Alisa, *Stranitsy zhizni* (Moscow, 1975), p. 317.
44   Markov, P., *O teatre*, vol. 3, pp. 377–378.
45   *Programmy gos. akademicheskikh teatrov*, 1926, no. 61, p. 9.
46   *Sovremennyi teatr*, 1927, no. 6, p. 85.
47   *Zhizn iskusstva*, 1927, no. 20, p. 7.
48   Ibid., no. 19, p. 11.
49   *Zhizn iskusstva*, 1926, no. 6, p. 12.
50   Markov, P., *O teatre*, vol. 3, p. 829.
51   Radlov, Sergei, *Desyat let v teatre* (Leningrad, 1929), p. 146.
52   *Zhizn iskusstva*, 1927, no. 46, p. 7.
53   Meyerhold, V. E., *Stati, pisma, besedy, rechi*, vol. 2, (Moscow, 1968), p. 495.
54   *Vsesvit* (Kharkov, 1928), no. 16, pp. 14–15.
55   *Vechernii Kiev*, 31 May 1929.
56   *Novyi zritel*, 1929, no. 42, p. 3.
57   Tairov, Alexander, *O teatre*, p. 484.
58   *Teatr*, 1984, No. 2, pp. 125–126.
59   *Chitatel i pisatel*, 26 May 1928.
60   *Vospominaniya o Zabolotskom* (Moscow, 1977), pp. 86–87.
61   *Rabochii i teatr*, 1924, no. 15, p. 7.
62   *Krasnaya gazeta*, 12 June 1926.
63   *Novyi Lef*, 1928, no. 5, p. 33.
64   *Krasnaya gazeta*, 14 April 1927.
65   *Smena*, 16 April 1927.
66   *Leningradskaya pravda*, 12 April 1927.
67   *Krasnaya gazeta*, (evening edition), 11 April 1927.
68   *Chitatel i pisatel*, 26 May 1928.
69   Entry of 1936 in Terentiev's album, from the archive of his daughter, T. I. Terentieva.
70   *Zhizn iskusstva*, 1928, no. 8, p. 8.
71   *Zvezda*, 1968, no. 4, p. 185.
72   *Sovremennyi teatr*, 1929, no. 28–29, pp. 396–397.
73   *Iskusstvo*, 1929, no. 5–6, pp. 16–18.
74   *Zhizn iskusstva*, 1929, no. 22, p. 11.
75   Cited in A. Piotrovsky, *Teatr. Kino. Zhizn* (Leningrad, 1969), p. 363.
76   *Sovremennyi teatr*, 1929, no. 28–29, pp. 396–397.
77   *Smena*, 18 November 1928.
78   *Leningradskii teatr rabochei molodezhi* (Leningrad, 1935), pp. 19–20.
79   Libedinsky, Yu., *Sovremenniki* (Moscow, 1958), p. 172.
80   Markov, P., *V Khudozhestvennom teatre* (Moscow, 1976), pp. 267–268.
81   *Mayakovsky v vospominaniyakh sovremennikov* (Moscow, 1963), p. 314.
82   *Literaturnaya gazeta*, 9 February 1931.
83   *Sovetskii teatr*, 1931, no. 10–11, pp. 4–16.
84   TsGALI, fond 998, No. 2314.
85   *Sovetskii teatr*, 1933, no. 2–3, p. 17.
86   *Teatr i dramaturgiya*, 1933, no. 4, p. 28.
87   *Literaturnaya gazeta*, 5 September 1957.
88   *Teatr i dramaturgiya*, 1935, no. 3, p. 7.

Chapter 5

1   Collection *Leonid Mironovich Leonidov* (Moscow, 1960), p. 595.
2   Markov, P., *V Khudozhestvennom teatre* (Moscow, 1976), pp. 367–68.
3   Petrov, Nikolai, *50 i 500* (Moscow, 1960), p. 313.
4   *Teatr i dramaturgiya* (Leningrad, 1959), p. 410.
5   *Novyi zritel*, 1929, no. 40, pp. 7–8.
6   *Zhizn iskusstva*, 1929, no. 42, p. 5.
7   Derzhavin, K., *Kniga o Kamernom teatre* (Leningrad, 1934), pp. 207–208.
8   Tairov, A., *O teatre* (Moscow, 1970), p. 331.
9   Collection *Spektakli i gody* (Moscow, 1969), p. 167.
10   *Sovremennyi teatr*, 1928, no. 24–25, pp. 469–470.
11   *Sovetskii teatr*, 1932, no. 7–8, p. 17.
12   *Iskusstvo kino*, 1977, no. 7, p. 139.
13   *Ezhegodnik MKhAT, 1945*, vol. 2 (Moscow, Leningrad, 1948), p. 381.
14   Sakhnovsky, V. G., *Rabota rezhissera* (Moscow, Leningrad, 1937), p. 212.
15   Collection *Boris Vasilievich Shchukin* (Moscow, 1965), p. 284.
16   Collection *Spektakli i gody* (Iskusstvo, Moscow, 1969), p. 150.

Further Reading

General Background

BOWLT, J. E., (ed.) *Russian Art of the Avant-Garde. Theory and Criticism 1902–34*, New York 1976.

BROWN, EDWARD J., *Russian Literature sincè the Revolution*, 2nd edn, New York, 1968.

MARKOV, VLADIMIR, *Russian Futurism – A History*, London, 1969.

MIRSKY, D. S., *A History of Russian Literature*, ed. by F. J. Whitfield, New York 1949.

NETTL, J. P., *The Soviet Achievement*, London 1967.

Paris – Moscou, 1900–30, Exhibition catalogue, Centre Nationale d'Art et de Culture, Georges Pompidou, Paris, 1979 (2nd rev. edn).

RUDENSTINE, A., *Russian Avant-Garde Art: The George Costakis Collection*, London and New York 1981.

STRUVE, GLEB, *Russian Literature under Lenin and Stalin 1917–1953*, London 1972.

Theatrical Background

AMIARD-CHEVREL, C., *Le Théâtre Artistique de Moscou 1898–1917*, Paris 1979.

BABLET, DENIS, *Revolutions in Stage Design of the XXth Century*, Paris and New York 1977.

BABLET, DENIS (ed.), *Les Voies de la Création Théâtrale. Mises en scène années 20 et 30*, Paris 1979.

BAKSHY, ALEXANDER, *The Path of the Modern Russian Stage*, London 1916.

BOWLT, JOHN E., *Russian Stage Design: Scenic Innovation 1900–30 from the collection of Mr and Mrs Nikita D. Lobanov-Rostovsky*, Exhibition catalogue, Jackson, Mississippi Museum of Art, and other cities, 1982.

BURGESS, M. A. S., *The Nineteenth and Early Twentieth Century Theatre* in R. Auty and D. Obolensky (eds.) *An Introduction to Russian Language and Literature*, Companion to Russian Studies, vol. 2, Cambridge 1977.

CARTER, HUNTLY, *The New Theatre and Cinema of Soviet Russia*, London 1924.

—— *The New Spirit in the Russian Theatre*, London 1929.

CHAMOT, M., *Goncharova: Stage Designs and Paintings*, London 1979.

COHEN, R., *Alexandra Exter's Designs for the Theatre*, Art-Forum, Summer 1981, pp. 46–49.

The Drama Review: Russian issue, New York 1973 (vol. 17, No. 1, T57).

EVREINOV, NICHOLAS, *The Theatre in Life*, ed. and trans. Alexander Nazaroff, London 1927.

—— *Le Théâtre en Russie Soviétique*, Paris 1946.

—— *Histoire du Théâtre Russe*, Paris 1947.

FÜLÖP-MILLER, R., and J. GREGOR, *The Russian Theatre*, tr. from German by Paul England, London 1930.

GLENNY, MICHAEL, *The Soviet Theatre* in Robert Auty and Dmitri Obolensky (eds.) *An Introduction to Russian Language and Literature*, Companion to Russian Studies, vol. 2, Cambridge 1977.

GORCHAKOV, NIKOLAI A., *The Theatre in Soviet Russia*, tr. Edgar Lehrman, New York and London 1957.

GRAY, C., *The Great Experiment, Russian Art 1863–1922*, London 1962. Rev. edn under the title *The Russian Experiment in Art 1863–1922*, London 1986.

HOFFMAN, L./WARDETSKY, D. (Hrsg), *Meyerhold, Tairow, Wachtangow*: Theateroktober, Leipzig 1972.

HOUGHTON, NORRIS, *Moscow Rehearsals*, London 1938.

—— *Return Engagement*, London 1962.

KLEBERG, LARS and NILS AKE NILSSON (eds.), *Theater and Literature in Russia 1900–1930*, Stockholm 1984.

KOMMISSARZHEVSKY, V., *Moscow Theatres*, Moscow 1959.

LAW, A., *'Le Cocu Magnifique' de Crommelynck. Les Voies de la Création Théâtrale*, vol. 7, Paris 1979, pp. 13–40.

LOZOWICK, L., *Moscow Theatre, 1920's*, Russian History, vol. 8, pts 1–2 1981, pp. 140–4.

MACLEOD, JOSEPH, *The New Soviet Theatre*, London 1943.

—— *Actors Cross the Volga*, London 1946.

—— *A Soviet Theatre Sketch Book*, London 1951.

MARSHALL, HERBERT, *The Pictorial History of the Russian Theatre*, New York 1977.

SLONIM, MARC, *Russian Theatre from the Empire to the Soviets*, London 1963.

VAN GYSEGHEM, ANDRÉ, *Theatre in Soviet Russia*, London 1943.

VARNEKE, B. V., *History of the Russian Theatre, Seventeenth through Nineteenth Century*, trans. B. Brasol and ed. B. Martin, New York 1951.

Individual directors

Eisenstein

SETON, MARIE, *Sergei M. Eisenstein. A biography*, London 1952.

Meyerhold

Meyerhold on Theatre, tr. and ed. with a commentary by Edward Braun, London 1969.

Meyerhold at Work, ed. Paul Schmidt, Austin 1980.

BRAUN, EDWARD, *The Theatre of Meyerhold: Revolution on the Modern Stage*, London 1979.

EATON, KATHERINE BLISS, *The Theatre of Meyerhold and Brecht*, London 1985.

GORDON, M., 'Meyerhold's Biomechanics', *Drama Review*, vol. 18, no. 3, Sept. 1974.

HOOVER, MARJORIE L., *Meyerhold: the Art of Conscious Theater*, Amherst, Mass., 1974.

RUDNITSKY, K., *Meyerhold the Director*, ed. S. Schultze, Ann Arbor, Mich., 1981.

SYMONS, JAMES M., *Meyerhold's Theatre of the Grotesque: the Post-Revolutionary Productions 1920–1932*, Coral Gables, Fla., 1971.

TURKELTAUB, I., 'The Bedbug at the Meyerhold Theatre', *Zhizn Iskusstva* no. 12, Petrograd 1929.

Nemirovich-Danchenko

NEMIROVICH-DANCHENKO, V., *My Life in the Russian Theatre*, New York 1968.

Stanislavsky

STANISLAVSKY, KONSTANTIN, *Selected Works*, comp. Oksana Korneva, Wellingborough 1984.

STANISLAVSKI, CONSTANTIN, *An Actor Prepares*, London 1937, rep. 1980.

—— *Building a Character*, London 1950, rep. 1979.

—— *Stanislavsky on the Art of the Stage*, tr. D. Magarshack, London 1950, New York 1986.

—— *Stanislavski's Legacy*, ed. Elizabeth Reynolds Hapgood, London 1959, rep. 1981.

—— *Creating a Role*, London 1963, rep. 1981.

—— *My Life in Art*, Harmondsworth 1967, rep. London 1980.

BENEDETTI, JEAN, *Stanislavski: an Introduction*, New York 1982.

EDWARDS, CHRISTINE, *The Stanislavsky Heritage*, London 1966.

GORCHAKOV, NIKOLAI MIKHAILOVICH, *Stanislavsky Directs*, tr. Miriam Goldina, New York 1954.

MAGARSHACK, DAVID, *Stanislavsky. A Life*, London 1950, rep. 1985.

MOORE, S., *The Stanislavsky System: the Professional Training of an Actor*, London 1966, rep. Harmondsworth 1984.

POLIAKOVA, ELENA, *Stanislavsky*, tr. L. Tudge, Moscow 1982.

TOPORKOV, V. O., *Stanislavski in Rehearsal. The Final Years*, New York 1979.

Vakhtangov

Evgeny Vakhtangov, comp. Lyubov Vendrovskaya and Galina Kaptera, tr. Doris Bradbury, Moscow 1982.

GORCHAKOV, NIKOLAI MIKHAILOVICH, *The Vakhtangov School of Stage Art*, tr. G. Ivanov-Mumjiev, ed. Phyl Griffith, Moscow 1960.

SIMONOV, RUBEN, *Stanislavsky's Protégé: Eugene Vakhtangov*, tr. M. Goldina, New York 1969.

Tairov

TAIROV, ALEKSANDR YAKOVLEVICH, *Notes of a Director*, Coral Gables, Fla., 1969.

Contemporary Memoirs

BENJAMIN, WALTER, *Moscow Diary*, Cambridge, Mass., and London 1986.

LIVSHITS, BENEDIKT, *The One and a Half-Eyed Archer*, tr., intro., and annotated by John E. Bowlt, Newtonville, Mass., 1977.

PASTERNAK, BORIS, *Safe Conduct* in Boris Pasternak, *The Voice of Prose*, vol. 1, ed. Christopher Barnes, Edinburgh 1986.

Index

Page numbers in *italic* refer to illustrations.